# AN AFRICAN CLASSICAL AGE

# An African Classical Age

## Eastern and Southern Africa in World History, 1000 B.C. to A.D. 400

## CHRISTOPHER EHRET

University Press of Virginia
*Charlottesville*

James Currey
*Oxford*

The University Press of Virginia
©1998 by the Rector and visitors of the University of Virginia
All rights reserved
Printed in the United States of America

*First published 1998*

∞ The paper used in this publication meets the minimum
requirements of the American National Standard for Information
Sciences--Permanence of Paper for Printed Library Materials,
ANSI Z39.48-1984

Library of Congress Cataloging-in-Publication Data

Ehret, Christopher.
An African classical age : eastern and southern Africa in world
history, 1000.B.C. to A. D. 400 / Christopher Ehret.
p.  cm.
Includes bibliographical references (p.   ) and index.
ISBN 0-8139-1814-6 (alk. paper)
1. Africa, Eastern—History. 2. Africa, southern—History—To
1899. I. Title.
DT365.65.E37  1998
967.6—dc21                  97-44239
CIP

British Library Cataloging in Publication Data
A catalogue record for this book is available from the British Library
ISBN 0-85255-7590-0 (cloth)

To Bethwell Alan Ogot, mentor and friend

# Contents

# Illustrations

## Tables
*Denotes table with adjunct table in Appendix A*

*Illustrations*

## Appendix B

# Maps

# Figures

# Acknowledgments

I am indebted to more people than I can ever name for their help and for sharing with me, over thirty years, the various bits of knowledge and experience that have gone into the writing of this book.

Among the foundations for this work were the field collections of language evidence that I have made in Eastern Africa at various times over the past thirty years. Many, many Africans from all walks of life have assisted me in that effort, giving of their time to acquaint me with their languages and their words for the things, ideas, and activities of their cultural worlds. Among my most important consultants over the years have been Aloisi Pius Kidara, James Lugonzo, Naiman of Samonge, Matayo Gidageney, Stanley Ole Mukishae, John Ole Sailenyi, Petre Mutui, Welang'uria of Katabok, Henry Mwambu, Henry Bikeri, Faustine Luzangi, Petro Muhina, Mary Masibai, John Mjungu, Hamisi Mohamedi, Dulubanta of Ntarasaa, Edward Kaaya, Laali Omari, Lepeitan Ole Lolseli, Njokilae Ole Supuko, and Soda of Bankolo.

To many of my fellow scholars of history and of linguistics, I also owe a great debt for their critical comments and their sharing of ideas. For what they had to say directly about the manuscript of this book, I must especially thank: to Derek Nurse, Randall Pouwels, Thomas Spear, Joseph Miller, Nicolas David, and Patrick Manning. Many others have contributed indirectly over the years by bringing me up short with telling comments, or by helping me to see other directions of thought or argument, or by sharing their invaluable original work with me. Thanks in this respect go to (alphabetically) Edward Alpers, Stanley Ambrose, David Appleyard, Lionel Bender, Patrick Bennett, Cynthia Brantley, Terry Child, Norbert Cyffer, James Denbow, Edward Elderkin, Randi Haaland, Richard Hayward, Bernd Heine, Thomas Huffman, Baluda Itandala, Angelika Jakobi, Isaria Kimambo, David Lewis-Williams, Henry Mutoro, Sheikh Ahmed Nabhany, Gerard Philippson, Merrick Posnansky, Mechthild Reh, Franz Rottland, Tilo Schadeberg, Peter Schmidt, Paul Sinclair, J.E.G. Sutton, Serge Torney, and Rainer Vossen, I know I have forgotten still others who equally deserve mention here, and I proffer my apologies to them. Needless to say, these scholars are not responsible for any errors or omissions that I might have made here.

I have learned, I think, even more that is important to this book from working with several of my former Ph.D. students—in particular (again alphabetically), Christine Ahmed, Mohamed Nuuh Ali, John

Distefano, Alice Gold, Douglas Johnson, Kairn Klieman, Mary McMaster, Carolan Ownby, Robert Papstein, and David Schoenbrun. I learned from their careful work and their discoveries and through the interchange of ideas that went on in the course of teaching them. Many of the ideas presented here are theirs or are theirs and mine together. I have tried to give credit to them whenever it is due, although I surely must have failed on a number of occasions to do so.

Finally, several scholars were crucial mentors for me in the early stages of my work on some of the topics that eventually contributed to what I have written here. My thanks go especially to Professor Oswald Werner and to the late Professor Jack Berry, both of Northwestern University; to Professor Jan Vansina at the University of Wisconsin; and, above all, to Professor B. A. Ogot, who encouraged and supported my work and who inspired me by his example as a pioneer in the professional study of Eastern African history.

Funding from a variety of granting agencies at different times supported fieldwork that has contributed to ideas and data used in this book. I owe thanks to the Social Science Research Council for supporting my earliest research in Africa with twenty months of fellowship assistance in 1966–68; to the Ford Foundation for supporting other periods of extended fieldwork in the early 1970s; to a Fulbright grant for still another period of work in Africa in 1982; and to a variety of smaller grants over the years from the Faculty Senate of the University of California at Los Angeles and the UCLA African Studies Center, each funding various smaller portions of the work that has found its way into this book.

Additional special thanks are due the British Institute in Eastern Africa, its director J.E.G. Sutton, and authors Kurt Odner, John Barthelme, Peter Robertshaw, and Randi Haaland for allowing me to reproduce their pot drawings, and to Hamo Sassoon for his picture of an East African rock painting, all of which were published in *Azania*; to Marie-Claude van Grunderbeek for permission to use pottery drawings and her reconstruction of the earliest known African iron furnace; to J. Desmond Clark for allowing use of pot drawings from *Kalambo Falls Prehistoric Site*, Vol. 2; to J. D. Lewis-Williams and the Rock Art Research Unit, University of the Witswatersrand, for permission to reproduce a picture of one of the rock paintings of South Africa; to Paul Sinclair for permission to use several pot drawings of his and similarly to Tim Maggs and to T. N. Huffman for permission to reproduce their pot drawings; and to the *South African Archaeological Bulletin* and Judith Sealy for permission to make use drawings of several other pots and a stone bowl from articles in that journal. To

## Acknowledgments

the South African Museum I offer my sincere gratitude for their graciously allowing me to reproduce their pictures of one of the Lydenburg heads. The conclusions reached in this work are, of course, not necessarily those of the British Institute, the South African Museum, or any of the scholars who permitted the use of their materials here.

# PREFACE

This book, *An African Classical Age: Eastern and Southern Africa in World History, 1000 B.C. to A.D. 400*, brings to light 1,400 years of social and economic history across Greater Eastern Africa. Its geographical scope, the eastern side of the continent of Africa from Uganda and Kenya on the north to the Cape of Good Hope at the far south, forms a complex of regions larger than the whole of mainland Europe, excluding only the Russian Republic. Its telling reveals a history driven by the clash of strikingly different economies and cultures and invigorated by the opportunities and the challenges of technological change. The major currents in that history link its events, both indirectly and directly, to the wider developments of world history in those times.

These are ideas that would hardly surprise if the book were about, say, European history. But here we speak of African history. And so these points need emphasizing right from the outset. They need emphasis especially for European and American readers, whose traditional educational curricula tend to mistake a lack of knowledge about Africa for a lack of salience, and proceed on that basis to dismiss the very real significance of the African past for the world we all live in today.

That very lack of knowledge is what this book seeks to be a partial antidote for. It essays a deeper and more detailed exploration of early cultural, social, economic, and technological history than has yet been attempted, not only for Greater Eastern Africa, but for almost any other comparable-sized part of the African continent. It is designed to be the possible precursor of a second volume, which would deal with the developments of the "Middle Age" of Greater Eastern Africa, from the fourth to the fifteenth centuries. Another historian, Jan Vansina, not long ago performed the similar task for the equatorial rainforest zones of west-central Africa in his book, *Paths in the Rainforests*. What is now needed are more such historical works, with the same kind of depth, detail, and geographical comprehensiveness, dealing with still other parts of the continent, such as West Africa in the last millennium B.C. and the early first millennium A.D., or the Sudan, Ethiopia, and the Horn of Africa over the same period.

But there is more than this to restoring Africa to its proper place in human history. If and when these books are written, they must effectively engage the wider world-historical context of developments within Africa. Cultures and livelihoods changed greatly among Africans over the long run of history just as they did among other humans; and the developments of sweeping consequence for the long term of African history, such as the several separate African inventions of agriculture, tended roughly to parallel in time similar developments outside the continent. Africans were *not* isolated actors on their own historical stage. And, more important even than that, Africans have been the innovators of things and ideas that spread to other parts of the world every bit as often as they have been the receivers of innovations made elsewhere. Because *An African Classical Age* does actively engage these issues, it has much to say that is of far wider implication than for just the history of Eastern Africa alone.

With very few exceptions, we do not know the names that early Eastern African peoples gave to their own societies. In general, the names applied to the numerous early societies dealt with here are thus ones of geographical implication, indicative of where the people speaking a particular earlier language most probably resided. The majority of these names are already established in the African linguistic or archeological literature; but a number of new terms had to be coined for societies not previously recognized. One spelling convention followed here needs particular mention: to distinguish societal names from geographical descriptions, societal appelations that consist of two words have generally been hyphenated. For instance, "East-Nyanza" designates a particular Bantu society of about 2,000 years ago that inhabited a part of the eastern Nyanza Basin.

On a more personal level, this work weaves together a variety of lines of research the writer has pursued at different times over the past thirty years. It is a fabric of many threads. The loom of language relationships that give texture and design to the fabric has two sets of components. Part of its structure is provided by the historical comparative work on the Bantu languages undertaken by a variety of scholars over the past century. The finishing pieces, which made it possible to bring the whole structure together, were the writer's own detailed historical reconstructions of the Nilo-Saharan language family, now in press, and of the Afroasiatic language family, published in 1995.

Necessarily, the writer of a history with such a long gestation as this one must often find himself in disagreement with ideas or conclusions he proposed years earlier. As the years pass, new information appears, and new critical perspectives can be brought to bear; and a scholar must be ready to grow and change in response to the availability of new information and new ways of processing that information.

*Preface*

Along with a variety of lesser revisions in this book, there has been, in particular, one set of materials on which I have had very sharply to correct my earlier claims. Historians need specifically to be warned about this instance, simply because the work in question is still often cited by scholars. In an article published over twenty years ago (Ehret 1973b), I identified a set of old Mashariki ("Eastern Bantu") root words as probable loans from Central Sudanic. Having since then put together a detailed phonological reconstruction of the Nilo-Saharan family, I can now demonstrate that a majority of my individual postulations in that article were simply wrong. A not insignificant minority of the root words still turn out truly to be Central Sudanic loanwords. Several others, it is now apparent, belong to a previously unsuspected set of loanwords coming into early Mashariki from an Eastern Sahelian language of the Nilo-Saharan family. But the majority cannot as yet be shown to be loanwords at all. (Of course, only the materials that still remain valid are included in the relevant tables of data of this book.)

*An African Classical Age* is, in any case, a different kind of work. It is above all a history of people and their livelihoods and cultures and how those changed and evolved over a particular period of 1,400 years—a period in which crucial transitions took place in economy and technology all across the Eastern Hemisphere, including Eastern Africa. Language evidence is a key resource for uncovering that past, but it has been relegated as much as possible to the background here, so as not to detract from the narrative flow. What people knew, believed, saw, and did in their daily cultural and economic lives constitute the central themes in this story. It is a story well worth telling.

# AN AFRICAN CLASSICAL AGE

# 1. Setting the Historical Stage

In the wide skein of lands that stretch down the eastern side of Africa, the centuries from 1000 B.C. to A.D. 400 constitute a Classical Age. For in those times were laid the cultural and economic foundations on which the societies of Greater Eastern Africa, from Uganda to Natal, were to build their institutions and livelihood for the following fifteen hundred years. Not until the nineteenth and twentieth centuries was another era of such transformative consequence to begin.

Like the roughly contemporary classical age of Mediterranean history, from which the Europeans of later centuries drew inspiration, the Classical Age of Greater Eastern Africa brought into being new forms of belief, culture, and technology. And like the Mediterranean classical era, although distinct from it in inspiration and content, this African Classical Age was marked by the full establishment of iron technology, the emergence of important new agricultural processes and technologies, and the spread of new religious and social ideals.

As also in the classical Mediterranean world, the seminal societies of the Eastern African Classical Age eventually extended their influences far beyond the initial areas of cultural transformation. In the Mediterranean region, it was Roman conquest in the latter half of classical times that directly imposed a transformative social and cultural presence across southern, central, and western Europe. In Greater Eastern Africa, in contrast, a very different kind of expansion carried forward the new cultural and economic dispensation, spreading it outward from the African Great Lakes region and implanting it as far east as the Indian Ocean seaboard and as far south as modern-day Natal and the eastern Cape province of South Africa. Roughly contemporaneous with the centuries of early Roman expansion and then empire, but not at all conquest driven, the spread of the mature Classical Age of eastern and southern Africa came instead through a vast scattering out of small, independent agricultural communities, Bantu in language and having as yet neither the institutions nor the inclinations of empire building.

1

The innovations and inventions of the Classical Age diffused widely beyond the regions directly bound up in that history. Much as the ideas and practices of the Mediterranean classical world spread during and after Roman times to northern and eastern Europe, so did many of the contributions of Classical Eastern Africa pass westward to the peoples of the equatorial rainforest and the southern savannas of Africa. The most notable exemplars of these processes appear in material culture and include the spread of iron technology and new crops and animals from east to west.

What is especially significant is the degree to which the developments of the Classical Age of Greater Eastern Africa reveal the peoples of those regions as vibrant participants in the trends of world history, even as they marched to the drummers of their own particular historical pasts. Like the peoples of those times who lived in Middle America or in Europe or in East Asia, they engaged in the creation of more complex and more adaptive forms of agriculture. Some East Africans, it now appears, were early contributors as well to an independent African invention of ironworking, separate from but roughly contemporary with that of the eastern Mediterranean world. And eastern and southern Africans of the Classical Age were not immune either to a particularly momentous set of developments of the last millennium B.C., developments that began for the first time truly to link together the distant regional theaters of world history—the rise, namely, in the eastern Mediterranean of long-distance, merchant-driven commerce.

For the peoples of Greater Eastern Africa, the span of centuries stretching from the early last millennium B.C. till the fourth century A.D.—the Classical Age—was therefore a time of immense reshaping of belief, custom, and livelihood. Too easily historians have condensed the panorama of technological and social change that took form in those eras into a single unfolding pageant of the spread of Bantu-speaking peoples across the historical landscape. It is an understandable misprision of history. The demographic predominance of Bantu speakers in recent centuries, from Uganda and Kenya in the north to South Africa in the south, seems an overwhelming fact.

But it misdirects our attention. A myriad of complex histories of interethnic interaction and economic and social change, as well as wide regional developments tied to no particular ethnicity, lie behind the social formations and economies that had come into being by the fourth century A.D. Many of the Bantu-speaking societies drew a major portion of their human ancestry from earlier African peoples of quite different languages and cultural backgrounds—from Southern

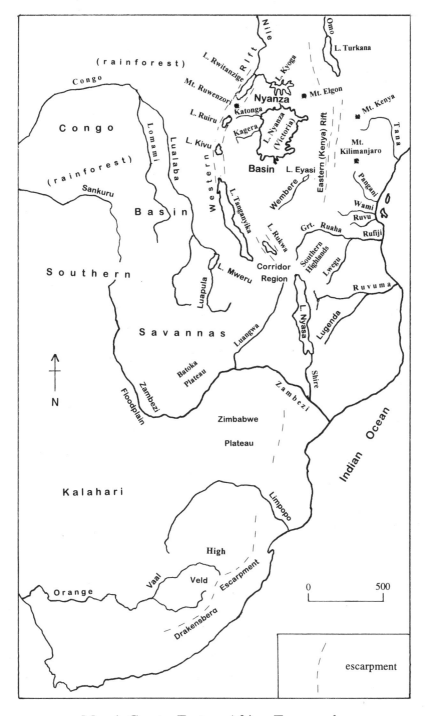

Map 1. Greater Eastern Africa: Topography

3

Cushites and Southern Nilotes in Kenya and northern Tanzania; from Central Sudanic and other Nilo-Saharan-speaking groups in the Great Lakes region; and from Khoisan peoples in southeastern Africa. All along, wide-ranging new developments in technology and in custom and belief further shaped and reshaped the varied practices of life and livelihood that emerged by A.D. 400. This study commences the unveiling of that complex history.

In so doing it sets in motion an even more important, long-term effort—the presenting of a truly new construction of the *longue durée* of African history as a whole. The full and sweeping reappraisal of the continent's past embodied in that construction belongs to another book. But the Classical Age of eastern and southern Africa lies at a key juncture of the defining and integrating themes of continental history. The major developments of the age were fundamentally shaped by such factors, and necessarily those themes emerge in the telling of the eastern and southern African story.

## Themes of Change, 1000 B.C. to A.D. 400

So the drama of Greater Eastern African history was not played out on a closed historical set. Eastern and southern Africa in the last millennium B.C. and the early first millennium A.D. formed, as it were, one of several regional stages of world history, each adjacent to other such stages where different historical plots unfolded and different historical actors strutted their stuff. From time to time, bits of the action on one stage would spill over onto another stage, disarranging the subplots playing in the wings and pushing the actors there toward improvisations that might in time ripple across the whole stage, sometimes altering in perceptible ways even the central storyline of the drama.

Three great, long-term historical themes integrate Greater Eastern Africa into the multiple dramas of world history during those thirteen or fourteen centuries. One theme, with contemporary parallels in North America, northern Europe, and north Asia, is the increasing establishment of more fully agricultural ways of life in regions that before then had successfully maintained either low-complexity food-producing livelihoods or less labor-demanding gathering-and-hunting economies. A second theme, of wide impact through much of the Eastern Hemisphere during the last millennium B.C., concerns the spread of iron technology. The third theme is the Commercial Revolution, a set of developments that produced consequences as sweeping in their reach over the *longue durée* as those of the Industrial Revolution have been in very recent history.

## Classical Eastern Africa and the History of Agriculture

From the aspect of world history, agricultural invention was a recurrent phenomenon of the early Holocene era. The ancient Middle East, to which Western scholars have traditionally accorded the seminal position in world history, was in fact nothing special in those times. It was merely one of as many as eight or nine distinct, far-separated regions of the globe in which agriculture independently emerged from the tenth to the sixth millennium B.C. Southeast Asia, Mexico, highland South America, at least three and possibly four different regions of Africa, and possibly also North China and lowland northern South America, were equally seminal centers in the creation of agriculture as we know it in the world today. In East Africa over the last millennium B.C., the expansion of agricultural economies and the growth in agricultural complexity built on the heritages of three separate ancient food-producing traditions of African inspiration and origin.

Two of these traditions were present already among the eastern African peoples of the fourth to second millennia B.C. One of those two, associated historically with Nilo-Saharan peoples, such as the Eastern Sahelians and the Central Sudanians, can be described as the Sudanese agripastoral tradition. Its cultural roots lay in the Saharo-Sudanese Neolithic, an archeological tradition of the early Holocene in the eastern parts of the southern Sahara.[1] The other early agriculture, associated with Cushitic-speaking peoples, can be characterized as the Erythraean agripastoral tradition.[2] Its cultural roots trace to an as yet archeologically undefined "Erythraean Neolithic," the beginnings of which can be expected to be discovered eventually, once serious archeological study becomes possible there, in the Red Sea hills region and probably in parts also of the far northern Horn of Africa, and to be datable, like the Saharo-Sudanese Neolithic, to the very early Holocene.

A third kind of agriculture, with West African origins, spread into eastern Africa only during the last millennium B.C., with the arrival on the scene of the early Mashariki peoples. To this third form of food production can be given the name the West-African planting tradition.

The Sudanese Agripastoral Tradition

The Saharo-Sudanese Neolithic economy took shape initially around the activities of wild-grain-collecting communities, who in about the tenth millennium B.C. inhabited the southern Sahara, today an extreme desert, but in those days, in the aftermath of the glacial retreats of the northern climes, a dry steppeland. Speaking a language or languages of the Northern Sudanic branch of the Nilo-Saharan family, these peoples added the raising of cattle to their previously non-food-producing livelihood and so initiated the first stage of the agricultural transformation of their part of the world. During the eighth millennium B.C.—as the African climatic optimum of the early Holocene reached its peak in rainfall, and many parts of the Sahara became a still more hospitable steppe—the Saharo-Sudanese Neolithic peoples of the farther eastern Sahara entered into a second stage of this historical process: they began to cultivate grains that they had previously collected wild, notably sorghum, and to build larger, more permanent settlements.[3] Already by the later eighth millennium, or so the evidence of their reconstructible vocabulary tells us, they had begun to construct the thorn-fenced kind of combined cattle pen and homestead that long remained such an effective style of residence among their distant Eastern Sahelian cultural heirs of later eastern African history. Within that homestead they built even then, as both language and archeology reveal, an early variety of the round, Sudanic style of house.[4]

For over a thousand years longer, an alternative, highly successful economic approach continued to thrive among other peoples, who lived nearby, their territories often interspersed within those of the Sudanese agripastoralists. Based around the utilization of riverine and lakeside resources, this Aquatic tradition eschewed cattle-raising and cultivation and emphasized in its day-to-day livelihood the hunting of hippos along with extensive and varied kinds of fishing. Its makers resided along the Nile and other northward-flowing streams and also farther south in the then relatively well-watered lands of the southern Sahara and the modern Sahel zones. Not until the sixth millennium B.C., with the first retreat from the high rainfall levels of the African climatic optimum, did an agricultural way of life begin to take hold widely across the more southerly regions. The lakes and streams on which the Aquatic peoples depended began then to shrink, and numerous streams that had been perennial became seasonal. Many a community must literally have found itself high and dry and its people facing a food crisis.

6

Differently equipped to deal with this changing environment, the peoples of the early Sudanese agripastoral background, especially those whose languages belonged to the Eastern Sahelian subgroup of Northern Sudanian, quickly emerged as the most prominent actors in a newly apparent spread of agripastoral pursuits.   For them the shrinking back of water-covered areas provided opportunity rather than crisis.   Over the sixth and fifth millennia, their descendants expanded progressively southward all across the central parts of the modern-day nation of Sudan, absorbing and assimilating formerly Aquatic peoples into their societies.[5] Their farthest south outliers, by the fourth and third millennia, had reached the northernmost edges of East Africa, giving rise there to the ancestral societies of the Sog and Rub communities, which were to be so important in the developments of the Classical Age.

At the same time several hundred kilometers farther north, in eastern Middle Nile Basin south of the Abbai River, there resided another grouping of Eastern Sahelian peoples of recurrent importance to later East African history, the Nilotes. Only around the second millennium B.C., however, did particular Nilotic communities begin to move southward into the far southern Sudan; and except for the Southern Nilotes, who pressed on into western Kenya between 1000 and 500 B.C., these communities remained on the peripheries of the developments of the Classical Age of Eastern Africa.

During the same overall span of time, from the seventh to the fourth millennium, the range of crops and animals raised in the Sudanese agriculture grew.   Gourds and calabashes, sesame, black-eyed peas, cotton, and Voandzeia groundnuts—all these indigenous cultigens were added over the course of time to supplement the early Sudanese dietary staples, sorghum and pearl millet.   As early as the seventh millennium, goats and sheep, domesticated in the separate Middle Eastern center of agricultural invention, had probably diffused southward to the Saharo-Sudanese food producers, to be joined to their existing herds of cows.[6]

In several regions food-collecting societies lay far enough away from the main lines of the initial advance of the Eastern Sahelian agripastoralist settlement that they could long avoid being absorbed into these expanding communities. They were able to adopt the ways and means of food-production in a less direct manner, through diffusion from the Eastern Sahelian communities. Readapting in this way to the new historical circumstances of the age, such societies began themselves to be able to grow in numbers and expand their territories and

7

to withstand eventual competition from Eastern Sahelians for the resources of the land.

Most notable among such peoples for the course of later Eastern African history were the proto-Central Sudanians, whose lands in the fifth millennium B.C. lay to the immediate south of the Bahr-al-Ghazal flood basin in the modern far southern Sudan Republic. The vocabulary evidence strongly intimates that proto-Central Sudanians descended from practitioners of the Aquatic food-collecting tradition. Their root word *we for "harpoon" (table 12), the typical instrument of the Aquatic economy, is an especially telling indicator of this kind of subsistence emphasis. Perhaps sheltered from direct early Eastern Sahelian agricultural impact by the then perennial wetlands of the Bahr-al-Ghazal and by tsetse-fly–infested areas, the proto-Central Sudanians made the ideas and practices of grain cultivation into major elements of their own heritage (table 11), although remaining strongly committed to fishing and perhaps only gradually, under later Eastern Sahelian influences, taking up the raising of goats and cows. Expanding from the Bahr-al-Ghazal region, one group of their descendants, the early East Central Sudanian communities, moved south into the lands immediately along the great Western Rift. There their settlement laid the basis for the Central Sudanian role in the Classical Age and—if the palynological evidence from Kigezi region proves out[7]— may have spread the Saharo-Sudanese grain-cultivating, seed-agricultural tradition as far as southwestern Uganda by 3000 B.C.

## The Erythraean Agripastoral Tradition

The conjectured Erythraean Neolithic, to which the deep Cushitic historical background can be imputed, remains to be explored archeologically. But the language evidence gives us a good idea of what we might expect to find as prominent features of this neolithic and where we should expect to find them. The Erythraean tradition, it can be argued, would best be looked for in the Red Sea hills region that extends from the northern edge of the Ethiopian highlands northward to the eastern side of Egypt. This tradition can be expected to have emerged among peoples whose languages belonged to the Afroasiatic language family. Among those early affected by this development would have been the peoples who spoke the languages ancestral to the Cushitic, Chadic, and ancient Egyptian branches of the Afroasiatic family.[8] The early archeological artifacts of their proposed Erythraean Neolithic culture should date to around the tenth or ninth millennium B.C.

Like the Saharo-Sudanese Neolithic, the Erythraean Neolithic would have begun with the development of cattle raising by people who had previously relied principally on wild-grain collecting,[9] and in fact the rise of cattle raising most probably constituted a single historical development linking the two traditions. The projected Erythraean lands lay immediately east of the southern Saharan territories that were inhabited by the early Northern Sudanians, themselves the makers of the Saharo-Sudanese Neolithic.[10] The environments of these earliest known Saharo-Sudanese cattle keepers could have supported cattle only with human assistance.[11] But the Red Sea hills to the east, because of their elevation and their access to moisture-laden winds rising from the Red Sea, would have abounded during the climatic optimum in springs and small streams capable of sustaining a wild cattle population. The earliest domestication of cattle, known archeologically as yet only for certain Saharo-Sudanese Neolithic peoples, was thus surely a wider development of the far eastern Sahara in the ninth millennium B.C., common to both the Nilo-Saharan and the Afroasiatic communities of that region. And one day that history should be visible in the archeology of the Red Sea hills just as it already is for the desert plains west of the Nile.

The domestication of cattle should have set off, as it did for the Saharo-Sudanese Neolithic—and as the development of food production has commonly entailed elsewhere in the world—a period of population movements and expansions among the newly food-producing peoples. Just such a set of consequences do seem apparent in the developments of the next few thousand years in several adjoining regions.

Across the northern half of the Sahara, the neolithic Capsian tradition, emerging in the ninth and eighth millennia B.C., stands off as a set of developments parallel in its effects to the contemporaneous spread of the cattle-keeping version of the Saharo-Sudanese tradition across the southern half of the Sahara.[12] First adding the keeping of sheep and/or goats to wild-grain collection, Capsian people by perhaps 7000–6000 B.C. began also here and there to raise cattle.[13] The timing and locations of Capsian sites make this archeological complex a highly probable offshoot of the projected Erythraean Neolithic. Its makers may have spoken the particular Erythraic language that was ancestral to modern Chadic tongues or, alternatively, a different Erythraic language, of the Boreafrasian subgroup (to which belonged later Egyptian, Berber, and Semitic).[14]

The period of roughly 7000 to 5000 B.C. marked also the spread, attested linguistically but not as yet known archeologically, of another descendant grouping of the Erythraic peoples, the Cushites, southward into the northern edges of the Ethiopian highlands. From there, various subdivisions of the Cushites pressed farther southward in about the sixth and fifth millennia, into north-central and eastern parts of the highlands.[15] By the fourth millennium two major long-term developments had overtaken the participants in this history.

One was the Cushitic contribution of a separate, independent African cultivating tradition. By as early as the sixth millennium, the Cushites who had moved into highland grasslands in Eritrea may have begun a switchover from supplementing their diet with wild-grain collection to the deliberate cultivation of two indigenous highland grains, t'ef and finger millet. There is no reason to attribute the emergence of this core cultivating feature of the Erythraean agripastoral tradition to stimulous diffusion from either the Middle Eastern or the Sudanese center of domestication.[16] Its vocabulary is entirely Cushitic; and the sixth millennium, as a period of rainfall decline, would have been characterized by a natural shrinking back of montane forest, an environmental change that would only have increased the attractiveness of grain cultivation for the growing and expanding Cushitic populations, with their long previous history of wild-grain collection.

The second long-term development was the spread, by stages before 3500 B.C., of Cushitic societies and cultures into all but the southwestern quadrant of the Ethiopian highlands, with one branch of these peoples, the Southern Cushites, emerging as a distinctive society at the dry far south of the highlands, where the highlands verged on lowland northern Kenya.[17] The long Holocene climatic optimum, though well past its peak, had not yet come wholly to an end in the fourth millennium B.C.; and lands eminently suited by climate and vegetation to both grazing and the cultivation of grain crops, but still occupied wholly by food collectors, lay open to the south of these particular Cushitic communities. In the second half of the fourth millennium, the Southern Cushites began to respond to that opportunity. They settled first in northern Kenya west of Lake Turkana. Then, by sometime in the second millennium—by which time the climatic optimum had ended and the modern climatic regimes of tropical Africa had largely come into being—they began to establish themselves through the rich grasslands of southern Kenya and northern Tanzania, from whence their descendants would enter into the opening acts of our early Classical Age.

10

## Independence and Interconnection in Agricultural Invention

Although separate and distinctive in their inventions of cultivation, the Sudanian and Cushitic worlds did not lack for elements of historical interconnection. To misquote John Donne, no regional stage of world history has been for long an island entire unto itself. At its very onset, possibly over ten thousand years ago, the keeping of cattle in northeastern Africa probably was a development shared between the two traditions, even if contributory in separate fashions to the rise and expansion of each. The domestication of cattle, moreover, may have taken place there first in all the world.[18] From outside of northeastern Africa, goats and sheep arrived later, probably by sometime in the seventh millennium, and were added thus onto Saharo-Sudanese and Erythraean Neolithic economies that had already in differing degrees crossed over to food-production—the Saharo-Sudanese already cultivating grains as well as raising cattle, and the Cushites in northern Ethiopia perhaps soon to turn to domestication of their own wild grains. At about the same period the raising of donkeys, domesticated probably by Cushites in the southern Red Sea hills, may have started diffusing northward toward the Middle East.

Not only agricultural influences may have passed between these then neighboring sets of societies. The adoption by Cushites of the Sudanic belief in a single Divinity, associated with rain, lightning, and the heavens, very possibly belongs, too, to this early era of interconnections in the eastern Sahara regions.

Despite the occasional early spread of particular domestic animals from one regional stage of world history to another, still it was not until the last four millennia B.C. that the theme of the elaboration and growth in human reliance on agricultural production came into its own as a recurrent feature in world history. The expansion of agricultural peoples across the tropical and subtropical parts of our globe had reached so widely by the fourth millennium B.C. that different, originally independent agricultural traditions began increasingly to encounter each other directly; and with increasing frequency crops and animals began to diffuse from one tradition to another, yielding a growing complexity in the crop repertoires of many societies. In Africa wheat, barley, and chickpeas from the Middle East passed to the suitably cool highlands of Eritrea and Ethiopia, probably via the Red Sea hills in about the fifth or fourth millennium.[19] The Sudanese crops sorghum, pearl millet, cotton, and sesame spread equally early in a counterdirection, reaching India well before 2000 B.C.; and both sor-

11

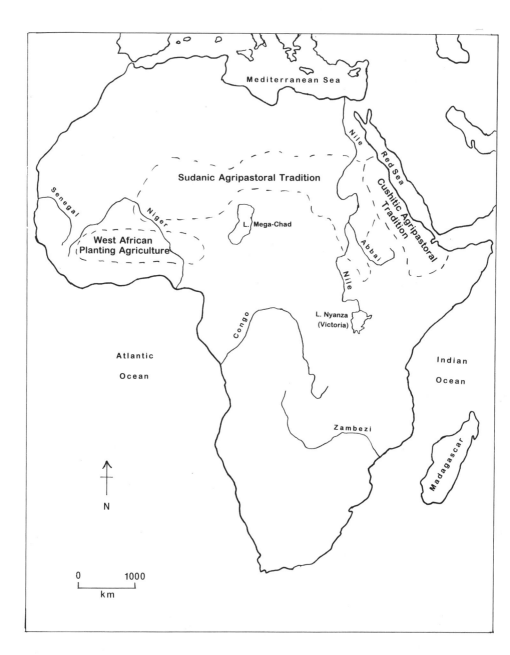

Map 2. African agricultural traditions, c. 5000 B.C.

ghum and sesame early diffused still farther eastward, to become major crops in northern China. Accompanying these long-term trends, a gradually growing portion of the daily diet among the food-producing peoples of those eras came from their tilling and pastoral pursuits.

Within the continent of Africa, too, this theme emerged in the agricultural developments of the fourth to last millennium B.C. Sorghum, Voandzeia groundnuts, and black-eyed peas, for example, were Sudanese food crops raised apparently already, or at least well known through interethnic contact, by Southern Cushites of the later fourth millennium. Similarly, finger millet, a crop of Ethiopian provenience, became familiar somewhat later to Central Sudanians at the far northwest of East Africa, perhaps not that long before 1000 B.C. (as argued in chapter 3). Even before 1000 B.C. and the opening of the Classical Age, then, the trend seen elsewhere in the world toward reliance on more elaborate kinds of food production had become a feature of the eastern African historical drama.

## The Mashariki Bantu and the West African Planting Tradition

The arrival of a new population, the Mashariki Bantu, at the western margins of East Africa around 1000 B.C. accelerated and expanded the working out of this theme in eastern Africa. The early Mashariki and their descendants became the instigators and in the end the spreaders of the culminating consequences of early agricultural innovation across the wide expanse of Greater Eastern Africa. Their early settlements in western East Africa were the incubators in which a new agricultural synthesis was nurtured.

The West African planting agricultural tradition, brought into East Africa by the Mashariki, originated among peoples who spoke languages of the Niger-Congo language family, and the initial stages of its development fell well before the fifth millennium B.C. The key ancient staples of this independent West African tradition were indigenous African yams. We speak of the food-production system itself as a planting agriculture because its basic crop, the yam, had to be reproduced through the planting of a piece of it back into the ground.

The environmental requirements of the yam locate the inventors of this agriculture in the woodland savanna zone of West Africa, in areas where natural clearings would have provided suitable sites for yams to thrive. Because of the perishability of plant evidence for yam cultivation, its early development may always remain difficult to date and situate directly from the archeology. But eventually a variety of

13

indirect material indicators of the invention and spread of the West African planting tradition will probably come to be accepted as diagnostic by archeologists.

One such set of material changes connected to Niger-Congo yam cultivation can be given probable identification even now. The linguistic evidence consistently places the initial settlement of the rainforest zone of West Africa by the Benue-Kwa peoples—so named because their languages belong to the Kwa and Benue-Congo sub-branches of the Niger-Congo family—at around about the fifth millennium B.C.[20] At just that period of time and across just the particular regions of early Benue-Kwa settlement—from southern Cote d'Ivoire in the west to western Cameroun in the east—archeology records the settlement of peoples with a new kind of tool tradition, the most notable implements of which were polished stone axes.[21] The close geographical correlation of these two bodies of evidence surely reveals the spread of an already established yam-based agriculture into a new kind of environment. In that rainforest environment, the stone axes provided the means by which the incoming farmers could reshape that environment, specifically by cutting the sunlit clearings required for the growing of yams.

The spread of the West African planting tradition farther east and south came toward the close of the African climatic optimum, in the very early third millennium B.C. The particular peoples who carried it southeastward from Cameroun into the equatorial rainforest of the Congo Basin were the Bantu, an easterly offshoot of the Benue-Kwa communities who had settled the West African rainforest two thousand years earlier. By the close of the second millennium B.C. a wide array of Bantu communities had emerged among those who had moved into the equatorial rainforest regions—most notably for our history of the Classical Age of eastern Africa, the early Mashariki people who had begun at that point to establish themselves at the far western edge of the African Great Lakes region.

# Africa and the Invention of Iron Technology

As for ironworking, this new approach to tool making was an integral element in the genesis of the Classical Age of Eastern African history. It took hold across the eastern side of the continent during the last millennium B.C., broadly parallel in time to the establishment of iron technology elsewhere in the Old World. This loose contemporaneity of events used to fit in with a scholarly assumption, unexamined till recently, that Eastern Africa, like western Europe, owed its knowledge of iron to the diffusion of that expertise from a Middle Eastern locus of origin, to be found in early second-millennium Anatolia.

But as the archeology of African ironworking has become better understood, this assumption has begun to look increasingly shaky. Iron was already smelted and forged before 500 B.C. by peoples in northern Nigeria in West Africa and as early as 900 B.C. by Bantu-speaking communities in the Great Lakes region of East Africa (see fig. 4). For ironworking to have reached from Anatolia to Nigeria or to the Great Lakes by that period, it had to have spread far more rapidly in Africa than in Europe, over a greater distance and across a much severer geographical obstacle, the Sahara desert, than any in Europe. Iron had, as well, to have become a common material south of the Sahara when it was still not common in Egypt, a country that was far nearer to Anatolia and lay on the most direct route between Anatolia and sub-Saharan Africa.

Moreover, the actual chronological discordance is probably still greater than the available archeology allows. The vocabulary evidence indicates that, for the Great Lakes peoples at least, the knowledge of iron and ironworking traces back before the Bantu acquaintance attested in the presently known archeology, to earlier peoples of Central Sudanic and Eastern Sahelian background, who lived to the immediate north and northwest of the Great Lakes in regions as yet almost unknown archeologically (see chapters 2 and 4).[22] The beginnings of ironworking in those regions surely dates to before 1000 B.C.

Eastern Africans thus contributed integrally to the diffusion of a major technological breakthrough that took hold through most of the Eastern Hemisphere in the last millennium B.C. Yet the contemporaneity of their contribution to this major world historical development may well have been a chronological coincidence. While European ironworking clearly was derivative, stemming from an invention that took place in the second millennium B.C. in Anatolia, iron technology in much of sub-Saharan Africa may have had an independent, purely African origin. The most likely region where we might search archeologically for that proposed separate origin would be in the woodland savannas that are located to the north of the equatorial rainforest and that lie between the known archeological outposts of early African ironworking in Nigeria and in the western Great Lakes. The dating of this invention would most probably fall in the range of about 1000 B.C. or somewhat earlier. Such a location in time and place would economically allow for an early spread of the use of iron several hundred miles westward toward Nigeria, and several hundred miles eastward toward the Lakes region, by 900 B.C., and would also account for the indications of the eastern African vocabulary evidence, that ironworking reached the Great Lakes from the northwest.

An interesting additional possibility is that ironworking may have arisen independently in still a third portion of the Old World, in southeastern Asia. The archeology does not as yet support that hypothesis, but serious linguistic arguments for that conclusion have been offered.[23] For world historians and for archeologists, the possibility of multiple inventions of ironworking in the Eastern Hemisphere—but not in the Americas—during the last 2,000 years B.C. raises intriguing questions. What were the material and social preconditions that might have favored roughly contemporary, parallel technological developments in worlds that were so far apart geographically and so different culturally? What practical conjunctions of material cultural activities and resource availability might have been involved in triggering off invention in the first place?

## Africans and the Commercial Revolution

### Defining the Commercial Revolution

The third major development of world history in the last millennium B.C., the Commercial Revolution, had both direct and indirect consequences for eastern and southern Africa's Classical Age. It began as no more than a subplot running through the drama of Middle Eastern and Mediterannean history in the early last millennium B.C. But by the time of the mature Classical Age of Eastern Africa, from about the third century B.C. to the early first millennium A.D., its effects were beginning to be felt all around the northern shores of the Indian Ocean and down the east coast of Africa.

The Commercial Revolution emerged slowly, from somewhere around or a bit before 1000 B.C., as a new approach to carrying out long-distance trade. Earlier, in the third millennium B.C., such trade had generally been controlled by rulers and, in Mesopotamia, perhaps also by corporate religious groups. In Egypt it was carried out by agents of the king and took the form of expeditions capitalized by the court. This sort of long-distance trade predominated probably through most of the second millennium.

By the start of the last millennium B.C., however, there are increasing indications of a long-distance trade carried out at a less than expeditionary complexity. The newly prominent trading factors were the Phoenician city-states; and from around the eleventh century B.C. onward, they spread their trading connections especially westward through the Mediterranean Sea by settling colonies along the shores of that sea, including most notably, among others, the city of Carthage in Tunisia. In the eighth century the Greek city-states began to imitate the Phoenician example, establishing colonies of their own and rapidly becoming an equally powerful commercial element in the Mediterranean, soon spreading their settlements and influences to the Black Sea as well. Along with the growth of sea-borne commerce, a second new, major direction of expanding long-distance trade in the early last millennium B.C. passed overland from Phoenicia and Israel to southern Arabia. After the fourth century, the regular sea routes of commerce spread farther afield, reaching India via the Persian Gulf and the Red Sea, and before the turn of the era extending down the East Africa coast as far as Tanzania and expanding east from India to encompass western Indonesia.

The key to the long-range historical importance of these commercial developments was the fundamental shift they occasioned in the social economy of trade. Increasingly a new class emerged in societies of the eastern Mediterranean region, composed of people who specialized in carrying on commerce; for the first time in history a class of merchants came into being. The emergence of this class was probably gradual and slow. For a long time the major capitalization of commercial ventures must still have come from kings and people wealthy in land. Merchants initially were people who carried on trade for others. Even as late as the Roman Empire, this kind of economic relationship of trade to wealthy landowners surely predominated in the West. But in the Levant, real merchant capitalist enterprise increasingly took shape. Wealthy merchants able to outfit ships emerged in time; and less wealthy merchants, in the manner of Sinbad in the later *Arabian Nights* stories, could band together to hire a captain and ship to carry them to their destinations.

Now a merchant has a different relation to trade than do agents of a king who seeks luxury goods for ostentatious display, expressive of his exalted position in society, and for redistribution to his loyal clients and lords. Merchants serve a more eclectic clientele, and they must compete for markets and for products. They do not have a single, powerful consumer to satisfy. If they are to continue over the long run to profit and to be able to maintain or expand their economic position, they will from time to time be forced to seek out new goods to buy and new places to sell the products they bring with them. The natural long-term tendency of merchant-run trade is thus a recurrently expanding trading network and a progressive growth in the variety and quantity of goods traded.

Because of the Commercial Revolution, a wide range of other processes and developments new to human history first appeared in the last millennium B.C.

For the first time the planting of colonies in distant lands became possible. The Phoenician settlements in the central and western Mediterannean, such as at Carthage, and the slightly later establishments of Greek colonies are early examples, while the settlement of South Arabians in Eritrea around the middle of the last millennium marks the subsequent spread of this sort of commercial consequence to the Horn of Africa. In the third and second millennia B.C., a state such as Egypt might colonize areas outside its heartland, as in Nubia. But this colonization comprised military outposts and ethnic settlements that were planted to hold the contiguous territories of a land empire, not distant localities far separated from the home country.

The Commercial Revolution constructed the economic basis as well for a new kind of town or city, an urban center that above all serviced trade and was home to the crafts and occupational specializations that went along with commercial development. The urban locations of earlier times commonly drew trade simply because their populations included a privileged elite of potential consumers. But such towns had arisen in the first place as political and religious centers of the society; they attracted population because power and influence resided there and access to position and wealth could be gained through service to the royal or hieratic leadership.

The natural political manifestation of the Commercial Revolution was the city-state. Empires and large kingdoms still rose and fell in the regions affected by the transformation in exchange relations, and they often had the power to rule over the nearby city-states. But that power still rested in the last analysis on the mastery of extensive areas of land and people. Empires could control the city-states because they could muster a much larger military force out of their much larger populaton.

Wherever the effects of the commercial transformation penetrated over the last millennium B.C., kings and emperors increasingly lost their ability to treat trade as a royally capitalized and instigated activity, intended to preserve the commodities of trade as the perquisites of immemorial power and position. Instead their policies shifted

18

toward controlling geographical accessibility to the products of commerce and to ensuring security and other conditions that attracted and enhanced the movement of goods. No longer could kings rely on agriculturally supported and religiously based claims to an ability to protect their lands and people; now they had also overtly to support the material prosperity of their people vis-à-vis other societies. And rather than exerting monopoly over prestige commodities, as had Egyptian kings of the third and second millennia, and redistributing such commodities in ways designed to reinforce the allegiance of their subjects and enhance the awesomeness of their position, rulers turned to the taxation of trade and to the creation and control of currency, more and more relying on duties and other revenues to support the apparatus of the state. It was no historical accident that the first metal coinage in the world began to be made in the eighth-century Anatolia and that the use of coins rapidly spread with the expanding Commercial Revolution. The material bases and the legitimizations of state authority as we know them today had begun to take shape.

The Commercial Revolution tended also to spread a particular pattern of exchange. The early commercial centers of the Mediterranean most characteristically offered manufactured goods—purple dye, metal goods, wine, olive oil, and so forth—for the raw materials or the partially processed natural products of other regions, such as the tortoise shell and the frankincense and myrrh of the northern Horn of Africa, or the wheat of the Black Sea ports. As the Commercial Revolution spread, this kind of exchange tended to spread with it, with the more recently added areas of commerce providing new kinds of raw materials or new sources for familiar products of the natural world, and the longer established commercial centers—which might themselves formerly have lain at the margins of this transformation—producing, or acting as the middlemen in the transmission of, manufactured commodities. India, for instance, had developed by the turn of the era into a major exporter of its own cotton textiles as well as naturally occurring materials, such as gems of various kinds, and at the same time its merchants were the middlemen of the silk trade. But African markets continued mostly to provide raw materials. Already in the last millennium B.C., in other words, one thread in the fashioning of modern Africa's patterns of exchange with the other regions and of its less competitive position in the world economy was being spun—long before the eras to which modern scholarly theory has credited Africa's "underdevelopment."

Finally because of the Commercial Revolution, long-distance lanes of the diffusion of ideas, practices, and things emerged. No

19

longer did innovation and influence spread only from community to neighboring community or through the expansions of ethnic and language frontiers. Crops, technology, and religion, as well as the valued commodities of the trade, might spread in a short span of time to new and distant areas. The establishment of Christianity in Aksum in the fourth century A.D., for instance, owed a great deal to the major commercial connections of the Aksum kingdom with the largely Christianized Levant of that period. Two and three centuries before that, at the period of the Han dynasty in China and the early empire in Rome, a few goods, notably silk cloth, had begun to move through various hands, all the way from China to the Mediterranean. Thus did the events of even distant regional dramas of world history begin for the first time, in small ways, here and there, to connect up.

The socioeconomic consequences of the Commercial Revolution, then, opened a new era for all of human history, an era still with us today. Its spreading and evolving consequences formed the world we know. Slowly, exceedingly unevenly, the developments it set in motion built up a common stage for the playing out of human history—bit by bit over the centuries between then and now more intricately linking the multiple regional dramas of earlier eras, eventually replacing them with the inextricably tied-together world of the twentieth century.

European expansion of last six centuries did not by itself alone create the modern world economy that underpins our now interdependent world. Rather it extended a set of developments that were begun in the Levant by the Commercial Revolution of the last millennium B.C. and perpetuated and gradually expanded by other peoples, especially Arabs and Indians, across the intervening centuries. European expansion was possible in the first place only because the commercial framework for creating a truly worldwide movement of goods and people was already in place by the fourteenth century A.D. The western and southwestern Europeans had the good fortune in the fifteenth and sixteenth centuries to have had the perceived material needs, the requisitely presumptuous outlook on the world, and the kinds of seaward locations that allowed them to take full advantage of the times. But they built on what other commercially minded peoples had already constructed over the previous 2,000-plus years, and they directly tapped the knowledge and expertise of such peoples in their early commercial expansions.

## The Commercial Revolution and the Eastern African Coast

The spread of long-distance sea-borne commerce to the East African coast in the late last millennium B.C. introduced the new pattern of economic activity—the commercial exchange of imported manufactured goods for local raw materials—directly to only a very limited number of East Africans. One notable trading emporium, Rhapta, had come into being at the coast before the first century A.D. and continued to be an important port town as late as the third or fourth century.

But the rise of the wider Indian Ocean networks of commercial interchange had far-reaching, indirect consequences for Eastern African participation in two of the broad trends of world history in those times, technological change and agricultural expansion and elaboration. At Rhapta, in particular, iron and iron goods were in high demand. The seagoing trade provided local people with an alternative access to the products of metalworking, separate from the African ironworking technology contemporaneously spreading outward from the Great Lakes region. The arrival of the Commercial Revolution, in other words, helped to link up the technological inventiveness of interior Africa with the parallel trends of metallurgical development outside of the continent.

On the agricultural side, the most important intermediaries in the spread of Indian Ocean influences seem to have been an immigrant group, the forebears of the Malagasy, who followed the Indian Ocean routes to the Eastern Africa coast sometime in the first three centuries A.D. These colonists, of Indonesian origin, constitute an example of the long-distance resettlement of people made possible by the Commercial Revolution. They did not apparently come, however, like the South Arabians merchants who traded at Rhapta, or like the Phoenicians at Carthage or the Greeks at Syracuse, for the purpose of setting up a commercial colony, but more probably to establish new homes for themselves. They were peripheral actors in Eastern African history. But because their earlier lands in the East Indies were areas of high rainfall, they brought with them several new crops and one new animal, the chicken, that adapted well to several African climates and so began sooner or later to spread widely inland across the continent. In this way the effects of the Commercial Revolution begin to reach indirectly far into the African interior during the closing centuries of the Classical Age of Eastern and Southern Africa.

# Telling the Story of the Classical Age

Our tale of Greater Eastern Africa's Classical Age opens in chapter 2 with a laying out of the patterns and stages of establishment of Mashariki Bantu communities in the western Great Lakes region during the early and middle last millennium B.C.—the very places and times in which the formative developments of the Classical Age took shape. Chapter 3 fills out the historical geography of this formative era by surveying the variety of other cultures and peoples that contributed to the emerging trends of the Early Classical Age. Both these chapters look in some detail at the testimony of word histories from which the patterning of human settlement can be inferred. Chapters 4 and 5, in contrast, provide integrative overviews, exploring the long-term regional developments and the cross-cultural courses of change that characterized, respectively, material culture (chapter 4) and society and custom (chapter 5) in the Early Classical period.

Chapters 6–8 shift our attention to the succeeding Later Classical Age, extending from around the fourth or third century B.C. through the third century A.D. Chapters 6 and 7 lay out the particular course of events of Later Classical times by which the new cultural and economic developments spread, along with Bantu populations, across the breadth of Greater Eastern Africa. East Africa proper is the focus of chapter 6; the more southerly regions, from Mozambique, Malawi, and Zambia to the southern edge of the continent, draw attention in chapter 7. Chapter 8 rounds out the coverage of Later Classical times by evoking key integrative themes of the age—the form and content of societal and economic transformations in those centuries all across East and southeastern Africa; the encounter of Eastern Africans with the commerce of the Indian Ocean and the varied consequences of that encounter; and the diffusion of the Classical Age's technological and agricultural innovations westward, far beyond Greater Eastern Africa itself.

Finally, chapter 9 looks back at what we have learned, both about developments across the eastern side of Africa and about the fit of the Classical Age of Greater Eastern Africa within the context of developments elsewhere in the continent and in the world.

Needless to say, the key directions of change in the Classical Age were not necessarily those of the past 1,000 or even 1,500 years. Numerous cultural elements fundamental to the developments of later centuries did indeed make their first appearance during the Classical Age of Greater Eastern Africa. Still, the overall cultural world of Eastern Africa in that far-off time was very different from the world of the recent past. Some of the notable historical topics that the reader may have come to expect in a book of East African history make no appearance here because they emerged only in the eras since the fourth century. Significant elements of Classical Mashariki Bantu custom, for instance, were woven into the ideologies and institutions of much later states. But states as we know them from the past nine centuries in Greater Eastern Africa did not yet exist. Bananas, to take another example, had arrived at the coast of East Africa by some point in the first three centuries A.D. But the importance of that crop in several interior highlands areas of East Africa, as well as much farther to the west, in the equatorial rainforest of west-central Africa, first began to take shape only in the several centuries after A.D. 400. Such later developments, as interesting and salient as they are in their own right, properly belong to another book, still to be written, about the middle periods of Greater Eastern African history.

## Getting Comfortable with Language Evidence

The most powerful sources from which to write this history are not the usual ones of the historian. Language evidence forms the most comprehensive and dense documentation available to us. Archeology offers a fundamental interpretive resource, but is still uneven and often very thin in its coverage of Greater Eastern Africa. Oral tradition rarely, and written sources only slightly less rarely, provide episodic glimpses into particular moments in this history.

Languages, by their nature as vehicles of social communication, contain immense vocabulary resources that express and name the full range of cultural, economic, and environmental information available to their speakers. With care and perseverance, the scholar trained in historical-comparative linguistics can use the data available in a set of related modern languages to reconstruct their relationships and their earlier histories. The reconstruction of language relationships in turn allows us to periodize the societal divergences and the ethnic expansions and contractions engaged in by the human communities who spoke those languages in the past. And from the innumerable individual histories of the words used in the languages we can piece together all manner of information on social, cultural, and economic change in those earlier communities.

23

Language Relationships as a Historical Timeline

To say that two or more languages are related has a very specific meaning in linguistics. It does not imply that in some vague way the languages resemble each other, and it does not mean that they have simply influenced each other or have some features in common. It means nothing more and nothing less than that they each have evolved, by their own lines of historical development, out of a single ancestral language spoken in earlier times, called a proto-language.

The biological parallel to language relationship is found in the mitotic generation of new cells. As the mother cell undergoes mitotic division, it first develops two nuclei and then splits into two separate daughter cells, each daughter cell forming around one of the nuclei. Similarly, a language begins to diverge with its development into two or more dialects, different but still interintelligible forms of the one language. After several centuries have passed and these dialects grow increasingly different from each other, they come eventually to form distinct languages, by which we mean forms of speech no longer mutually intelligible to the speakers of each. By this process the mother language, or proto-language, diverges over time into its daughter languages, just as the mother cell in mitotic division breaks up into its daughter cells. And just as each daughter cell can itself further split into two daughter cells, the daughter languages, in their historical turn, can become mother languages, undergoing divergence over a period of centuries into further daughter languages. Apart from the fact that a proto-language can divide into not just two, but sometimes into several daughter languages, the analogy is a remarkably close one.

Now a living, spoken language is always changing. In every generation some of its words, and often one or more of its grammatical rules, will change, and every so often a sound shift will come along as well. As long as the people of a society retain a feeling of belonging to a common cultural and social world, their language, though successively changing in one way or another, will remain still one language. If the society dies out, the speaking of the language will of course die out also. But if, alternatively, a people's sense of belonging to a single cultural world begins to weaken, and they come increasingly to identify themselves as members of two or more distinct communities within the wider society, then language divergence begins. Societal continuity persists, but it begins to follow two or more diverging paths of historical change. This reshaping of social self-identification has, as its consequence, the divergence of the ancestral society's language initially into as many dialects, and eventually—as

24

the dialect differences grow greater and greater—into as many languages, as there are new societies that emerge out of the old.

The sequence of language divergences that take place in the
history of any group of related languages translates directly into a
natural time line of the societal divergences that drove those successive
splits. It provides, in other words, a linguistic stratigraphy of societal
divergences.

Broadly speaking, two categories of cause are most often at work
in the diverging of mother languages into daughter languages. On
one hand, intrasocietal conflict of one kind or another can bring to an
end the sense of the speakers that they belong to a common social or
cultural world. On the other hand, the geographical contiguity of the
language's speech area can break down for either of two reasons.
One is that the people speaking the language spread across far-flung
or new and geographically varied lands. As they spread more widely,
it becomes increasingly difficult for the language changes that develop in any one locale to spread to other parts of the speech area, and
thus dialect and, eventually, language differences progressively evolve.
Or, second, a different people may expand across the speech area of
the existing society, splitting it in two and relegating the speakers of
the language to geographically separated territories. In this way a
fairly abrupt breakup of the society is brought about, and language
divergence follows.


## Regular Sound Change in Language History

The establishment of language relationships and the fitting of
individual word histories into a linguistic stratigraphy depends on one
and the same key characteristic of language history, the regularity of
sound change. As a part of the normal course of history in any language, there arise from time to time changes in how particular sounds
are pronounced. When such a *sound shift*, as it is called, takes hold, it
tends to affect all cases of the sound in question. For instance, if a *b*
became a *p* at the end of one word in a language, it normally does so
because of the operation of a sound shift rule that changes all cases of
former word-final *b* into *p*. In other words, sound change in any language proceeds on the whole according to regularly formulatable
rules.

Because of this characteristic, history always creates a regular
correspondence of sounds between related languages. For example, a
proto-Bantu sound represented by linguists as *b regularly became a

*w* in the daughter language Swahili and dropped out of pronunciation entirely in another daughter language, Gikuyu of Kenya. By still other sound shifts, the proto-Bantu consonant sequence *nt changed into simple *t* in Swahili, while becoming *nd* in Gikuyu. And by two further sound change histories, original Bantu *a remained *a* in both languages, and original *u stayed *u* in Swahili while producing a sound spelled *ũ* (but pronounced like *o*) in Gikuyu. Thus we say that Swahili *w* regularly corresponds to Gikuyu Ø (zero); that those particular Swahili *t* which derive from proto-Bantu *nt correspond regularly to Gikuyu *nd*; and that Swahili *a* and Gikuyu *a* and also Swahili *u* and Gikuyu *ũ* show regular sound correspondences. Reflecting these regularities, the proto-Bantu root word *bantu "persons, people" became modern-day *watu* in Swahili and *andũ* in Gikuyu.

Word Histories as Historical Documents

Regular sound change allows us to do more than certify the relatedness of languages. It allows us, even more importantly, to identify the words in the related languages that have been preserved in a direct line of descent from the vocabulary of the common mother, or proto-language. It enables us, consequently, to distinguish from such inherited items the words that a particular language has adopted or, as linguists say, "borrowed," from other languages over the course of its history. If the sound correspondences are regular *throughout* in the words being compared—as they are in the instance of Swahili *watu* and Gikuyu *andũ* just cited—then the probabilities are usually exceedingly high that the words are directly inherited in each language from their distant, ancestral proto-language—each is, in linguistic terminology, a reflex of the proto-word. We also say that the words are cognates. If sound correspondences fail even in any one of the sounds in the two items being compared, then some other kind of history, usually involving the borrowing of the word into one or both languages, may have to be invoked instead.

Each kind of word history in some manner reveals a portion of the human history of the speakers of the language. For instance, the widespread use in Eastern Africa Bantu languages of an old, inherited word for "goat," *-búlì, reconstructible back to the proto-Mashariki language (and back earlier than that, to proto-Bantu), shows that the proto-Mashariki communities without a doubt knew of goats and that the knowledge was maintained from the proto-Mashariki period down to the present among each of the peoples who use the word today.

Borrowed words reflect a different range of histories. Individual borrowings often reveal the adoption of a new item of knowledge or a new practice by a society. But a whole set of loanwords borrowed from one language into another needs a more delicate interpretative hand. The differing kinds, quantity, and rapidity of borrowing in such instances can reflect a variety of different histories of interethnic contact.[24]

Interpreting the loanword data also requires understanding what happens over time to vocabulary in a language. Words adopted during a particular era become, *from then on*, individually subject to the normal processes of vocabulary change—deletion, retention, semantic modification, and, of course, regular sound change—that operate in any spoken language. Because of these processes, most words borrowed as much as 2,000 to 3,000 years ago, as were, for example, the Central Sudanic loans in early Mashariki, will in the interim have been replaced here and there in different descendant languages by newer words for the same meanings. That is, the early loanwords will no longer be retained in all the descendant, or daughter, languages of the borrowing mother language. Even where it is retained, a particular word may have undergone semantic shifts. For example, a word adopted originally to mean "ram" might apply to "sheep (in general)" in some daughter languages, while retaining the narrower connotation of "ram" in a number of other such languages and dropping out of use entirely in still others.

A few of the root words borrowed into a proto-language will by now have dropped from use nearly everywhere, appearing today in only a few, sometimes far separated daughter languages. Such words have what we call a *relict* distribution. This term, as it does in geology and biology, describes a scattered and residual occurrence of something, left over from an earlier time when the item in question could still be found all across the intervening areas. At the other extreme, a few borrowed words will have been retained almost universally among the descendants of the earlier proto-language.

And if words were adopted during an era when dialect differences were strongly emerging in the adopting language, such borrowings will often tend to become established, not everywhere, but rather across differing contiguous portions of the language's speech area. In later eras they will thus be retained only in the daughter languages that evolved out of the particular incipient dialects that were spoken in one or another part of the mother language's speech area. This kind of distribution is especially important for mapping out the

27

early Mashariki Bantu dialect communities in Greater Eastern Africa (in chapter 2).

## From Language Evidence to Human History

In the chapters that follow, language evidence has been woven into the history that derives from it. Word histories play a prominent role in limning that past, but are presented in forms meant to be revelatory and enlightening to the reader who is interested in history and its sources. Most of the actual vocabulary data that unveil past cultural knowledge and practices have been set off from the narrative by placing them in tables. Short, easily readable forms of the tables have been interspersed within the text, near to the history they illustrate. Full versions of the tables, containing distributional and other relevant linguistic data, have been placed, however, in the appendix to the book, so as not to detract from the flow of the history that is based on them.

For the general reader, the important items to view in the short tables are the word meanings; these directly attest to objects, ideas, and practices known to the different societies at different past times. The titles and section headings of those tables provide the reader with the second essential kind of information: when and by whom the words in question were used. The remainder of the data, placed in the appendix in the fuller versions of the tables, provide information on the sources and derivations of the historically salient words and their meanings, so that the more technically inclined reader can review the bases for the historical arguments. In many cases, the detailed phonological reconstructions that validate the language evidence appear in other works, and the reader who wishes to assess such data firsthand should turn to those materials.

With the interpretative background now in place, and the main actors in the first stage of this history identified—the Eastern Sahelian peoples, the Rub, Sog, and Southern Nilotes; the Central Sudanians; the Southern Cushites; and the Mashariki—we are ready to proceed to constructing a historical understanding of life and livelihood in the long Classical Age of Greater Eastern Africa. We begin our story in chapter 2 with the arrival of the proto-Mashariki Bantu at the western edges of the Great Lakes region.

# Notes

[1] Ehret 1993.

[2] To accord with the standard rules for the creation of Latin and Greek-based words in English, the term "agripastoral" has been chosen here in replacement of the oft-used term, "agro-pastoral." The former properly combines two Latin elements, whereas the latter word less acceptably bonds a Greek combining form to a Latin base.

[3] Wendorf, Schild, and Close 1984; Wasylikowa et al. 1993.

[4] Ehret 1993. One key point needs to be noted about the dating followed in this section: the times given here in approximate millenniums are suggested, estimated calendrical dates. The actual radiometric dating of the relevant archeological sites for each stage of the proposed development of Sudanic agripastoral pursuits is about 1,000 years more recent. An estimated calendrical date of the eighth millennium B.C. would thus represent a radiometric (radiocarbon) date of the seventh millennium. The correlation of archeology with peoples depends in these instances on the correlative mapping plus historical linguistic reconstruction of culture of the successive stages in the history of the divergence of the Nilo-Saharan language family. Glottochronology was *not* used in this exercise.

[5] Wendorf, Schild, and Close 1984; Ehret 1993.

[6] Ehret 1993.

[7] Hamilton, Taylor, and Vogel 1986. But this interpretation has been strongly challenged by Taylor 1990.

[8] Ehret 1979; Ehret 1995b.

[9] Ehret 1979.

[10] Ehret 1993.

[11] Wendorf, Schild, and Close 1984.

[12] Ehret 1993

[13] See Close 1988 for a survey of recent archeological finds.

[14] The subgrouping of the Afroasiatic (Afrasian) language family followed here is taken from Ehret 1995b.

[15] Ehret 1976b.

[16] de Wet 1977.

[17] Ehret 1976b.

[18] Wendorf et al. 1984.

[19] Ehret 1979.

[20] Armstrong 1964; Wilson 1980.

[21] A summary view of this evidence appears in Shaw 1978/79.

[22] See also Ehret 1995/96.

[23] Blust 1976.

[24] Ehret 1981a.

# 2. The Formative Eras
## of Classical Mashariki Society


## The Inception of the Classical Age, c. 1000–300 B.C.

The seminal developments of the Classical Age of Greater Eastern African history had their setting in the African Great Lakes region in the early and middle centuries of the last millennium B.C. (map 3). At around 1000 B.C., at the threshhold of the Classical Age, the peoples of this region, as we have already seen, viewed their world from a variety of cultural and economic perspectives. Cultivation and some raising of livestock predominated among the various Central Sudanian and Eastern Sahelian communities scattered along the far west, the north, and the northeast of the region. Southern Cushites, predominantly but not solely pastoral in economy, occupied areas to the east of the Great Lakes, in central Kenya and in northern Tanzania. All around and among these various peoples lived numerous other, smaller communities who still centered their livelihoods on the hunting and gathering of wild food resources.

Into that mix of economies and cultures, a major new ethnic element, the Mashariki Bantu, began to intrude from the west at a date around or not long after 1000 B.C. Their arrival at the western edge of the Great Lakes region initiated a long period of economic and cultural change and ethnic shift that occupied the early and middle centuries of the last millennium B.C. Out of that history came the new mix of cultural ideas and practices, above all agricultural, that were to enable the later Mashariki societies, of the last few centuries B.C., to embark on a series of expansions all across the eastern and southeastern parts of the continent of Africa.

The last millennium B.C. saw also the establishment of iron technology throughout the Great Lakes. But it was the agricultural innovations brought about by the cultural interactions of Mashariki Bantu with Central Sudanians and Eastern Suhelians, and the demographic developments associated with these interactions, that seem to have been the essential motor of that later Mashariki history. Iron-working itself, the language evidence indicates, came first from these

31

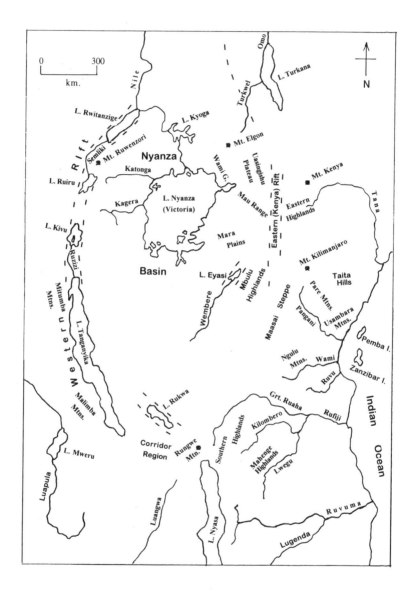

Map 3. The geographical setting of the Early Classical Age

Nilo-Saharan-speaking peoples to the early Mashariki Bantu in western East Africa; and in many cases iron technology seems to have been only weakly established among the more southerly Bantu communities even as late as the turn of the era,[1] when the wider Mashariki expansions of the later Classical Age were already underway.

In other words, the early Mashariki Bantu, with their resoundingly different approaches to livelihood and cultural expression, gradually became the prime movers in a radical realignment of society, economy, and ethnicity—primary actors in the very developments that define the Classical Age of Greater Eastern African history. In the end, that realignment spread its effects all across eastern and southeastern Africa, from Uganda to Natal.

But throughout the first half and middle centuries of the last millennium B.C., the Mashariki communities, although gradually growing in population and in social and economic importance, continued to occupy a more restricted historical landscape. The heartland of the founding era of Mashariki settlement lay in areas adjoining the great Western Rift, that long run of mountains and rift valleys that extend north and south along the western edge of the Great Lakes region. The language evidence reveals three successive stages of shifting population alignment and cultural change within that formative era.

## Early Mashariki Times (to c. Eighth Century B.C.?)

In the Early Mashariki stage, the initial penetration of Mashariki communities into the region took place, probably along a broad front to the immediate west of the Western Rift. A variety of cultural interactions of Mashariki Bantu with Central Sudanic and Eastern Sahelian societies were set in motion by this settlement, and two areal groupings of Mashariki communities, the Kaskazi and Kusi, began to take shape. Even at this early stage, incipient dialect differences were present among the speakers of proto-Mashariki. The Kaskazi and Kusi from the beginning formed, not single communities with single dialects, but clusters of communities who spoke several slightly differing versions of a single proto-Mashariki language. The dating of this period is imprecisely known, but most probably belongs to the very beginning of the last millennium B.C.

## Middle Mashariki Times (Eighth to Fifth Century B.C.?)

At the second stage, in Middle Mashariki times, the Kaskazi cluster of communities expanded somewhat farther eastward, probably principally into areas that would have included parts of modern-day Rwanda and Burundi. The pottery of the Chifumbaze tradition found in Rwanda and dating as early as the eighth and seventh centuries B.C.[2] most probably belongs to this Middle Mashariki period. These new movements considerably rearranged the cultural and social geography of the Kaskazi communities. In northerly areas, somewhere near the Western Rift zones that adjoin the Semliki Basin, the Lakes and Upland communities emerged as geographically separate groups among the Kaskazi; in more southerly areas, possibly in western areas of Burundi and southern Rwanda, a Southern-Kaskazi areal clustering of communities continued to persist. Interactions with Central Sudanic and Eastern Sahelian societies again characterized the course of culture history among the Kaskazi communities of this era. The Kusi cluster of communities of the Middle Mashariki period, located in more southerly parts of the Western Rift region, probably similarly grew in population and territory. They remained in contact with the developments affecting the Kaskazi peoples, but no longer in so direct a fashion.

## Late Mashariki Times (Fifth to Third Century B.C.?)

The third stage in these developments, the Late Mashariki period, belongs to the centuries immediately following the middle of the last millennium B.C. In this period a new regional configuration of peoples took shape once again among the Kaskazi. The Southern Kaskazi cluster of communities came to an end, and the Lakes society expanded farther east. The most notable new development was the settlement of one Southern Kaskazi community, two Lakes Bantu communities, and the Upland and pre-Langi peoples in several adjacent areas southwest of Lake Nyanza (Lake Victoria).[3] There they soon came to form a new areal cluster, the Southern-Nyanza grouping. Their period of common history, extending from perhaps the fourth through the second century B.C., was characterized by additional cross-cultural interactions, especially with Southern Cushitic peoples. We know little as yet about the contemporaneous developments among the southerly Kusi cluster of Mashariki communities beyond the clear evidence that, by this time, Kusi peoples formed a grouping of increasing internal divergence.

To the array of cultural interactions and demographic developments that define these three successive periods we now turn our attention.

# History and Environment in the Early Mashariki Period

## Early Regional Groupings among the Mashariki

As the Mashariki people pressed eastward into the Western Rift region in the early last millennium B.C., two primary areal clusterings of communities, the Kaskazi and the Kusi, soon began to take shape among them. The names Kaskazi and Kusi are taken from the Swahili words for, respectively, "northwind" and "southwind" and reflect the historical geography of the early Mashariki settlement. The Kaskazi grouping of communities comprised those Mashariki people from whose dialects derive the modern-day Bantu languages spoken *north* of far northern Mozambique and far northern Malawi.[4] The Kusi cluster of communities gave rise to the remainder of the Mashariki tongues—roughly those spoken today to the *south* of far northern Mozambique and far northern Malawi.[5] The original lands of the Kaskazi most probably lay along and to the immediate west of the Western Rift, roughly between the latitude of the Lake Rweru basin on the north and the northern parts of Lake Tanganyika on the south, while the early Kusi county is probably to be sought to the south, perhaps along the immediate west of Lake Tanganyika (table 1).

In past writings a mistaken nomenclature was followed.[6] The Kusi grouping was called "Pembele," and the Kaskazi group, minus the languages of the Lakes Bantu subgroup spoken west of Lake Nyanza, was given the appelation "Pela." Pembele and Pela were combined in a wider grouping of communities, with the name "Tuli." The reanalysis of the loanword evidence undertaken here requires the redefining of the two groupings into the Kusi and Kaskazi divisions, and the entire elimination of Tuli as a valid cluster.

And, more clearly and strongly than before, the point must be made that the Kusi and Kaskazi were, above all, regionally associated and mutually interacting sets of communities. They formed geographical clusters of people and not necessarily genetic linguistic divisions of the wider Mashariki Bantu group. Each probably from the first was composed of communities speaking already diverging dialects of the proto-Mashariki language.

---

Table 1. Generally recognized subgroupings of modern-day Bantu languages belonging to the Mashariki group

*a. Descendant subgroups of the Kaskazi areal cluster*

1. Lakes (or "Great-Lakes"): a. Western-Lakes (Rwanda, Rundi, Ha, Konjo, Fuliro, etc.); b. West-Nyanza (Rutara [Zinza, Haya, Nyoro, etc.]; Ganda, Soga, etc.); c. East-Nyanza (Gusii, Kuria, Kwaya, Zanaki, etc.); d. Luyia (Gisu, Wanga, Itakho, Samia, Logooli, Suba, etc.). For a full listing, see Schoenbrun 1990
2. Takama (Sukuma, Nyamwezi, Kimbu, Rimi, Ilamba)
3. Njombe (Hehe, Bena, Sangu, Kinga, etc.)
4. Northeast-Coastal (Ruvu: Gogo, Kagulu, Lugulu, Doe, Zalamo, etc.; Seuta: Shambaa, Zigula, Bondei, Ngulu; Asu; Saghala; Sabaki: Mijikenda, Swahili, Pokomu, Elwana)
5. Langi (Langi, Mbugwe)
6. Chaga-Dabida (Chaga, Dabida)
7. Thagiicu (Temi; Gikuyu, Embu, Emberre, Chuka, Tharaka, Meru, Kamba, Daiso)
8. Rufiji-Ruvuma: a. Mbinga (Ruhuhu: Matengo, Ngoni, Mpoto; Ndendeule; Lwegu: Matumbi, Ngindo, Ndengeleko, Ruihi); b. Ruvuma (Yao, Mwera; Makonde, Mabiha)
9. Kilombero (Pogolu, Ndamba, Mbunga)
10. Rungwe (Nyakyusa, Ndali; Safwa, Nyiha, Wanda, etc.)
11. Mwika (Pimbwe, Fipa, Mambwe, Nyamwanga, etc.)

*b. Descendant subgroups of the Kusi areal cluster*

12. Nyasa (Tumbuka; Nyanja, Cewa, Sena, etc.)
13. Makua (Makua, Lomwe, Cuabo)
14. Shona
15. Southeast-Bantu (GiTonga, Chopi, Tsonga, Venda, Sotho, Nguni [Zulu, Xhosa, etc.])

---

## The Natural World of the Early Mashariki: Vegetation

The earliest Mashariki people can thus be viewed as a geo-graphically extended clustering of communities that moved at first into the far western edges of East Africa, coming from previous habitations in the moist savanna woodland that lay along the southeastern fringes of the equatorial rainforest. Initially, it can be proposed, the Mashariki settlements spread out across the areas surrounding the Western Rift zone. At the time, large parts of that region formed essentially an eastern extension of the Congo Basin rainforest and moist savanna woodland, differing in being higher in altitude and often slightly lower in rainfall, but maintaining many of the same genera of plants and a similarly forested aspect. The Mashariki preservation of a proto-Bantu root word, *-súbí, specifically connoting an open grassy area within the forest, reveals that the early Mashariki indeed gravitated to the well-wooded environments adjoining the Western Rift, so like the ones from which their forebears had come.

At the same time, these locales interdigitated with areas of different vegetation. This variety of environments is reflected in the development in proto-Mashariki of a term for "savanna," *-ìkà, and, among both the Mashariki speakers and their other Savanna-Bantu neighbors to the west, of another word, *-to, that probably originally referred to gallery forest along a stream, but has taken a variety of meanings in modern languages (e.g., Swahili "river"; Ndembu "river jungle"; and Luban "thicket").

A third topographical term in proto-Mashariki, *-bándá, may specifically have connoted the environment of the inner Western Rift Valley itself. A feature analysis of its modern meanings in Mashariki languages favors its having originally applied in proto-Mashariki to a terrain that was both a grassland and a valley. Different parts of the Western Rift Valley, such as the bottomlands of the Kivu and Semliki Basins, would have formed just such a feature even 3,000 years ago. Moreover, in one modern-day Mashariki language, Nyiha, spoken in southeastern Tanzania, the word does have exactly that application today, although to a different such rift valley feature—specifically to the plains of the Rukwa Rift, which lie below the highlands the Nyiha people inhabit today.

In sum, for the Mashariki people of three millennia ago, partially wooded savanna (*-ìkà) would have lain probably in the transition zones between the rift valley bottoms and the surrounding highland forests (*-títù), as well as farther to the east in western Uganda. Gallery woodlands along the streambeds (*-to), then as today, would have been prominent features of the grasslands forming the rift valley floor (\*-bándá).

Equally important to these conclusions, no terms for any other kind of vegetation zone can be identified in Mashariki vocabulary until later times. Not till the Middle Mashariki period, after the full emergence of the two far-flung groupings of communities among the early Mashariki, the Kaskazi and Kusi, can words be reconstructed, for instance, for "open savanna," such as might have been found even then in limited parts of central Uganda and much farther east, in central East Africa, but not in the Western Rift zone proper. (Table 2 summarizes these data; for distributional and other evidence see expanded version in table 2A in the appendix.)

---

### Table 2. Natural environment of the early Mashariki society

*a. Terms of very wide Bantu or proto-Bantu distribution*

| | | | |
|---|---|---|---|
| \*-tị̀tù | "forest" | \*-súbí | "flat, grassy area |
| \*-sàká | "secondary forest (?)" | | in forest" |
| \*-kanga | "wilderness (?)" | | |

*b. Terms of Savanna and Mashariki distribution*

\*-to  "gallery forest (?)"

*c. Terms of proto-Mashariki occurrence*

| | | | |
|---|---|---|---|
| \*-ìkà | "savanna" | \*-bándá | "flat grassy plain" |
| \*-bila | "wild area" | | (PB "valley") |

*d. Terms of Kaskazi distribution*

\*-bùgà  "sparsely wooded plain" (open savanna)

*e. Terms of Kusi distribution*

\*-tondo  "thicket"
\*-lala  "grassland" or "sparsely wooded steppe"

---

## The Natural World of the Early Mashariki: The Seasons

The climatic data contained in the proto-Mashariki vocabulary, if anything, even more specifically locate them in the regions of the great Western Rift. Their environment was characterized by a much different seasonal regime from that which must be postulated for their earlier ancestors to the west. For the proto-Bantu only one seasonal name can as yet be reconstructed, *-sìpò. This word recurs through a wide scatter of rainforest languages and in those Western-Savanna and Central-Savanna languages that are spoken in the wetter woodland savanna areas. It consistently denotes a dry period of the year. Apparently rain, as the normative feature of life for rainforest societies, needed no special seasonal identification. Only the brief hiatus in the rains, of one or two months, stood out as something distinctive and worthy of remark. The movement of the Savanna-Bantu out of the rainforest proper, at some point in the second millennium B.C., into the adjoining woodland savanna with its three to five months of dry weather, did, however, lead to the innovation of an additional season name, *-tíkà, found today in both the Central-Savanna and Mashariki languages. Its earliest meaning was surely "wet season."[7]

In the proto-Mashariki language of the early last millennium B.C., a still different distribution of seasons came to be recognized. The word *-sipò dropped entirely from use. The term *-tíkà was retained, but refitted into a yearly cycle of three seasons—in order, *-lìmò, *-tíkà, and *-saano. The first two names of the cycle came to apply to several different kinds of seasons in later Mashariki languages. Their original meanings have thus to be inferred from their linguistic derivations and from their calendrical positions, which have remained remarkably consistent wherever the words are still used. Moreover, the very fact that their placements on the earth's celestial calendar have changed only a little reveals something quite important about intangible culture among the early Mashariki communities: these people must have begun their year at the time of some annual natural event that took place independently of the seasons themselves, whether they rained or shined or were cold or hot. We shall shortly discover just what that event apparently was.

Their year began with *-lìmò. The balance of the calendrical evidence from all across the Mashariki language group places the start of that season in about October and its end no later than January or February. Its derivation from the old Bantu verb *-lìm- "to cultivate" testifies to its having been the season at which cultivation commenced. The calendrical and agricultural inferences are each simultaneously reconfirmed by a bit of celestial terminology: The early Mashariki people gave to the Pleiades, which first appear in the evening sky in about October, the name *-lìmìlà, again a noun transparently deriving from the verb *-lìm- "to cultivate." And here clearly also, we have the natural event from which these Mashariki communities dated the beginning of their cultivating year and their yearly cycle of seasons. The season *-lìmò, it can be inferred as well, was a time of rain; for cultivation in Eastern Africa begins only when the first rains have softened the soil. It was the first season, and the "first-rains" season, of the proto-Mashariki year.

The second season of the year was called by the older Savanna-Bantu term *-tíkà. The balance of the calendrical evidence from Mashariki languages centers this season around the months from about February or March to May or June. It was surely originally a second period of rains, perhaps heavier on the whole than those experienced during *-lìmò.

The closing season of the proto-Mashariki year, *-saano, was dry and possibly also relatively cool, and lasted, the comparative evidence implies, from about June to September. The two relict retentions of this root word, in the Thagiicu languages (of the Kaskazi grouping) and the Nyanja languages (of the Kusi grouping), concur in their indications as to its meaning and timing.

Among all the various climatic regimes of Greater Eastern Africa, this reconstructed cycle of seasons fits most closely with that found in the regions immediately along the Western Rift, exactly where, on other grounds, the earliest Mashariki settlements are best located. There rain falls through a considerable portion of the year, with the one notable break extending from about June or July to September, at just the times reconstructed as composing the dry season *-saano among the early Mashariki. Two rainy periods characterize those areas. One lasts from October to December, coinciding with the beginning of cultivation and corresponding closely in its time of year with the reconstructed proto-Mashariki "first-rains" and first cultivating season, *-lìmò. The second extends from around February or March to May or June, as was inferred for the proto-Mashariki "second-rains," *-tíkà. A notable slackening in the occurrence of rain comes also around about January, but this period is sufficiently brief and transitory in its effects that it could easily have been viewed by the early Mashariki people as simply the transition from one rainy season to the other, rather than a distinctive season of its own.

Overall, these climate data confirm the history implied by both the vegetational evidence above and the faunal evidence considered

40

below. The two-season world of the common ancestors of the Central-Savanna and Mashariki Bantu, characterized by a longer rain season and a shorter dry season, lay in woodland savanna with just that kind of climate, adjacent to the southeastern parts of the equatorial rainforest proper. The speakers of proto-Mashariki, by moving eastward into the higher country along the Western Rift, encountered a different distribution of rainy and dry weather and so reformulated their cognitive system into a three-season cultivating year that began with the rising of the Pleiades in the evening sky.

## The Natural World of the Early Mashariki: Fauna

Developments in the early Mashariki naming of environmentally diagnostic and geographically restricted animals strongly reinforces the implications of the vegetational and climatic terminology both generally and specifically. The distant forebears of the early Mashariki already knew of a variety of animals adapted to the world of the rainforest: the leopard, the elephant, a species of buffalo, and the hippopotamus. They also were acquainted before the beginning of the Early Mashariki period with animals able to survive in woodland savanna environments: the spotted hyena and bushbuck, for instance, among others (table 3a). Only in the proto-Mashariki period itself, however, does the knowledge of animals most at home in grasslands or more open savanna appear: lions, giraffes, warthogs, sable and roan antelopes, and, most tellingly for the presence of drier grassland areas such as existed on the rift valley floor, the black rhinoceros (table 3b). Most interestingly of all, it can be plausibly argued that the proto-Mashariki people initially distinguished white from black rhinoceroses, a datum that, even assuming a formerly wider distribution of the white rhino, requires the placement the proto-Mashariki country somewhere in or near the Western Rift and western Great Lakes region.

Until the Late Mashariki period, most of the Mashariki lands did not apparently include zebras or the wild dog (*Lycaon pictus*) among their wildlife. Only after the full emergence of distinct Kaskazi and Kusi groupings of communities, when Bantu settlement had probably begun to spread much more widely, do several different Kaskazi peoples appear separately to have gained regular acquaintance with either animal. The Kusi may have encountered the wild dog slightly earlier, in the Middle Mashariki period. It should be pointed out that human clearing of forests and woodlands between the middle of the last thou-

## Table 3. Wild animals diagnostic of environment

*a. Terms of Savanna and Mashariki Bantu distribution*

| | | | |
|---|---|---|---|
| *-gùlùbè | "bushpig" | *-gùè | "leopard" |
| *-mbúí | "spotted hyena" | *-sèCú | "eland" |
| *-pítị | "(striped?) hyena" | *-songa | "bushbuck (?)" |
| *-súbị | "serval cat (?)" | *-búlí | "sp. marsh antelope" |

*b. Terms of proto-Mashariki occurrence*

| | | | |
|---|---|---|---|
| *-pembele | "black rhinoceros" | *-pundu(i) | "male eland" |
| | | *-jobe | "situtunga, marshbuck" |
| *-kula (Kaskazi), | | *-kulo | "waterbuck" |
| *-kụla (Kusi: Shona) | "white rhinoceros" | *-kulungu | "bushbuck" |
| | | *-bàbàlá | "(female?) bushbuck" |
| | | *-gulungulu (Kaskazi) | |
| *-tùịgà | "giraffe" | *-gululu (Kusi) | |
| *-gìlì | "warthog" | | "klipspringer" |
| *-sịumba | "lion" | *-sese | "duiker sp. (?)" |
| *-pókụ̀ | "eland" | | |

*c. Terms of wide Kaskazi distribution*

| | | | |
|---|---|---|---|
| *-kondị | "hartebeest" | *-kòlóngò | "roan antelope" |

*d. Terms of Southern-Kaskazi areal distribution*

| | | | |
|---|---|---|---|
| *-tembo | "elephant" | *-punda | "zebra" |
| *-pélà | "rhinoceros" | *-tandala | "greater kudu" |

*e. Terms of more limited areal distributions within Kaskazi*

| | | | |
|---|---|---|---|
| *-jàgí | "zebra" (Upland, East-Nyanza, Langi) | *-bugị | "wild dog" (Kati) |
| | | *-suuji | "wild dog" (Luyia, East-Nyanza groups) |
| *-umbu | "wildebeest" (Kati) | *-juui | "wild dog" (Upland) |

*f. Terms of Kusi distribution*

| | | | |
|---|---|---|---|
| *-bijị | "zebra" | *-pumpi | "wild dog" |
| *-pogu(e/a) | "ostrich" | | |

sand years B.C. and the later first millennium A.D. greatly expanded the environments suitable for zebras and wild dogs in the Nyanza Basin. As late as the end of the last millennium B.C., nearly all of the western parts of the basin would have been too wooded for either animal to thrive.

In the case of the Kusi communities, the evidence of words for the zebra and the wild dog probably requires their subsequent spread south as far as northeastern Zambia, where the two animals occurred natively in those times. Among the Kaskazi peoples the adoption of several different, regionally distributed root words for the zebra confirms the view that Kaskazi groups did not settle close to the nearest semi-open savanna areas naturally suited to the animal—in southern parts of the Nyanza Basin—earlier than the middle Southern-Nyanza period, around perhaps 400–300 B.C. (see below, this chapter). The evidence of names for the wild dog, and also for the wildebeest and greater kudu, indicates that only still later, at the very end of the Southern-Nyanza era—toward the close of the last millennium as the several erstwhile members of the Southern-Nyanza cluster began to go their separate historical ways—did Kaskazi communities begin finally to move near to still more open savannas and grassland, presumably those of the southeastern Nyanza Basin, in which wild dogs could thrive, and kudus and wildebeests might occasionally be found (see table 3 and table 3A in appendix).

# Neighboring Bantu Societies to the West

West of the Western Rift region, in the rainforests and woodland savannas around the lower and middle Lualaba River, the Mashariki communities of the last millennium B.C. would have had as their immediate neighbors several other Bantu-speaking societies.

In the eastern parts of the rainforest proper, a number of such settlements probably date to the second millennium B.C. Their locations suggest that they derived from a first expansion of Bantu speakers that initially followed the course of the middle Congo River eastward into the areas around the confluences of the Lomami and Aruwimi Rivers with the Congo River. The proto-Buans, for one, had settled by no later than the first half of the millennium in the forest lands east of there, in a territory probably roughly demarked by the Lindi and Maiko Rivers. A second Bantu people, the proto-Nyari, likely preceded the Buans into this area.[8] To the west of modern-day Kisangani, a third people, the proto-Enya, had a similar antiquity of settlement.

About three hundred kilometers to the south, a fourth grouping of rainforest communities, the proto-Lega, may have taken shape by

43

the early first millennium B.C. in areas around the Elila and Luama Rivers. The distance of the proto-Lega settlement from those of the Enya, Buan, and Nyari groups suggests their connection to an alternative line of eastward Bantu expansion, following along the Kasai and Sankuru Rivers to the middle Lualaba region.

Mashariki influences contributed to the spread of ironworking to the all four of these early eastern rainforest peoples by possibly as early as 500 B.C.[9] But on the whole, they and their descendant communities played out their histories without significant impact on the major directions of development among the Mashariki Bantu. Some of the Lega and also the later Buan societies of the Amba and Bira did enter into more recent cultural interactions of modest importance with peoples belonging to the Lakes subgroup of Mashariki, and those interactions are reflected in their culture vocabularies.[10] But such episodes belong to eras of history later than those dealt with here.

Three other emerging sets of Bantu-speaking communities of c. 1000 B.C. occupied areas of moist woodland savanna to the south and southwest of the proto-Lega society. All were to have histories of longer-lasting and much closer connection to developments among the Mashariki.

Two of these societies, the Sabi and the Botatwe, resided by the late last millennium B.C. in parts of the woodland savanna zone of southeastern Congo (Zaire). Their specific locations in that era of history remained to be identified. One possibility is that the Sabi originally occupied a somewhat more easterly area, perhaps emerging as a distinct people between the Lukuga River and Lake Mweru, with the Botatwe taking form as their southwesterly neighbors in the modern panhandle of Katanga (Shaba). Both long remained single societies, each giving rise only after A.D. 500 to a series of descendant peoples who expanded southward into Zambia. Latter-day Sabi languages, found variously in Zambia and southeastern Congo (Zaire), include Lamba, Bisa, Bemba, and Malungu (Tabwa). The Botatwe languages are Ila, Tonga, Lenje, and Soli, all now spoken in Zambia.

The Sabi and Botatwe peoples have two sorts of relevance to our story. For one, the early Sabi and Botatwe lands in southeastern Congo (Zaire) were way stations on one of the major routes of diffusion 2,000 years ago of grain agriculture westward across the southern savanna belt. And second, both language groups, in spreading south into Zambia after A.D. 500, incorporated into their societies the Mashariki communities previously resident there during the Eastern African Classical Age. The Sabi and Botatwe peoples, although belonging to post-Classical times as far as Zambian history is concerned, adopted into their vocabularies many words from the languages of their Mashariki predecessors, in this fashion preserving documents relating to the Classical Age that would otherwise be lost to us.

The third of these important societies of the early last millennium B.C., the proto-Central-Savanna people, evolved as a distinctive set of communities in lands located to the west of the proto-Sabi and proto-Botatwe. Their language was ancestral to four major languages of today, Kaonde, Kanyok, Songye, and Luba with its several diverse dialects. The linguistic geography of these languages best place the speakers of their common mother language, proto-Central-Savanna, in the moist woodland savannas and forests which in those days covered the drainage basin of the lower and middle Lubilashi River.[11]

Because the lands of the early Central-Savanna people, like those of the Sabi and Botatwe, lay not far west of the lands of the early Mashariki societies, several of the major economic developments of the Great Lakes region in the last millennium B.C. and very early first millennium A.D. soon spread to them also. An especially notable Mashariki influence is apparent in agricultural and iron technology (see examples later in this chapter in tables 4–7 of the diffusion westward of farming and iron vocabulary from Mashariki languages).[12]

In the same moist savanna zone as the early Central-Savanna society, but still farther to the west—somewhere between the middle Kasai and the upper Kwango Rivers—one other society of some significance to our story here, the proto-Western-Savanna Bantu, took shape before the middle of the last millennium B.C. From the proto-Western-Savanna language derived the later Ovimbundu, Kimbundu, Pende, Lunda-Luvale, and Luyana–Southwest-Bantu language groups. The evidence suggests that the early Western-Savanna society initially expanded widely during the second half of the millennium, its daughter communities spreading in two major directions, southwestward through Angola and also southeastward along the upper Zambezi River.[13] Its farthest southern outliers in the early centuries A.D. would have been the proto-Luyana-Southwest people, whose country by the close of the Classical Age came to center on the Zambezi floodplain of far southwestern Zambia.

There are indications in shared vegetational terms (see *-to "gallery forest (?)" in table 2) and in shared names of several wild animals (see table 3) that the first spread of the Western-Savanna, Central-Savanna, Sabi, Botatwe, and Mashariki peoples across the moist savanna woodlands at south edge of the true rainforest came at a period when their common linguistic forebears formed a continuum of closely associated communities—a period probably corresponding

45

roughly to the second half of the second millennium B.C. The proto-Lega may well have been a northeastern outlier of that Savanna-Bantu continuum of communities, but one that remained tied to fully rainforest environments. The proto-Mashariki society, from that perspective, can be seen as emerging by around 1000 B.C. as the most easterly areal grouping of communities within the wider Savanna-Bantu span, bonded together by their common historical experience of having spread eastward into the edges of a country, the Western Rift region, different in its mixture of climates and environments, and exceedingly different in its topography, from the Congo Basin out of which they had come.

## Interpreting Mashariki Bantu Origins

We need to digress for a moment here to consider just how this understanding of the earliest Mashariki communities and their relations to the rest of the early Bantu contrasts with a hypothesis proposed during the previous decade. In its baldest form, this hypothesis saw the Mashariki as forming one branch of Bantu coordinate with a second branch, "Western Bantu," occupying the Congo Basin.[14] That view is not followed here, for the reason that it is not in keeping with general human historical tendencies and it conflicts with its own supporting evidence.[15]

First, it requires a history of rapid long-distance circumvention of the rainforest by the proto-Mashariki, taking them from Cameroun to the Great Lakes region in a long, strung-out migration wholly improbable on the face of it and unprecedented among the expansions of agricultural frontiers into hunting-and-gathering lands anywhere else in the world. The recurrent, universal pattern elsewhere for the spread of agriculture into previously nonagricultural country is quite different. It features progressive, generation-by-generation extension of the agricultural frontier outward from previously established locales of food production.

Moreover, the Bantu language evidence adduced for the hypothesis has its own fundamental problem: when inspected in detail, it reveals the same patterning as previous scholars have shown to require a different and intrinsically much more plausible Bantu history.[16] Something simply is wrong with the algorithm used in the original formulation of the hypothesis, because a straightforward inspection of the data falsifies the hypothesis.[17] Specifically, the evidence, though blurred in its narrow indications by recurrent histories of word borrowing among nearby Bantu languages, consistently depicts a gradually increasing depth of internal relationship as one travels northwestward across the Bantu-speaking regions.

In other words, Bantu agricultural settlement must be understood as a progressively older historical phenomenon the farther toward the northwest, toward Cameroun, that one turns one's attention. And consequently the Bantu advance can be argued to have unfolded just as the spread of agricultural frontiers has elsewhere in the world, by a progressive expansion—first, in the third millennium B.C., passing from Cameroun along major streams into favorable parts of the western equatorial rainforest; then, in about the second millennium, extending farther south into the northernwestern fringes of the southern woodland savanna belt near the confluence of the Congo and Kwa Rivers; and finally, before 1000 B.C., progressing eastward, very probably via the Kwa and Sankuru Rivers to the Lualaba region, with the leading edge of this last movement, at around 1000, comprising the Mashariki settlement at the western side of the Western Rift region. The second millennium settlements of the proto-Buans, proto-Nyari, and proto-Enya in areas well to the north of the Savanna-Bantu, in the eastern equatorial rainforest, surely constitute a distinct, parallel movement of Bantu communities, following the middle Congo River more directly eastward out of the western rainforest, toward the areas around Kisangani.[18]

# Cross-Cultural Relations in the Early Mashariki Period

## Early Mashariki and the Central Sudanians

To the east of the early Mashariki country lay a very different cultural and economic array of societies, speaking Nilo-Saharan, Southern Cushitic, and even Khoisan languages (map 4). As the Mashariki communities gradually expanded their settlement around the Western Rift zone over the early centuries of the last millennium B.C., their cultural and economic development increasingly incorporated elements of life and livelihood from those neighbors, and the evidence of that history persists in the vocabulary of present-day Bantu languages all across Greater Eastern Africa.

A significant although not large body of verifiable loanwords attests to cultural and social interactions between the proto-Mashariki society as a whole and a Central Sudanic society. A narrow range of

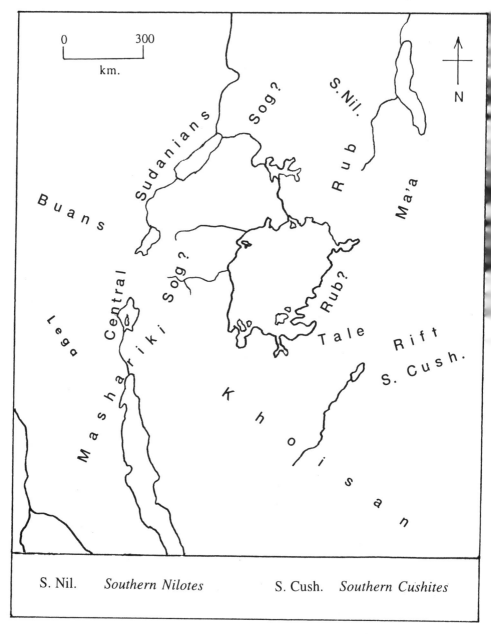

Map 4. Peoples of the Great Lakes Region, c. 900 B.C.

key influences, most notably in cultivation and iron-working, passed via these contacts from the Central Sudanians to the Mashariki people.

Table 4 below, containing this set of word borrowings, is the first of a number of listings presented here of historically significant loanwords in Bantu languages of Eastern Africa. For the general reader whose eyes may begin to glaze over at the mention of linguistic reconstruction, the key items to be looked for in each table are the *word meanings* that follow each main entry. For instance, in the entry *-pú "sorghum" in table 4, the important historical fact is the meaning "sorghum" because it reveals the knowledge of the crop among the earliest Mashariki communities. The old root word that bears the sense "sorghum" happens to have been pronounced in a fashion which is represented by linguists as *-pú, but that is information peripheral to the primary historical fact revealed by this datum.

In addition, of course, the reader will want to know where the loanword comes from, because that information will reveal the direction of the historical influence. Such information, for the benefit of the nonlinguistically inclined reader, is included in the title of each particular table. For instance in table 4, the notation "Central Sudanic loanwords in proto-Mashariki" tells us that the words cited in the table were adopted by the Mashariki communities from a Central Sudanic–speaking people.[19]

In general, the root words considered in table 4 have wide distribution through the Mashariki languages. Normally there are gaps in

---

### Table 4. Central Sudanic loanwords in proto-Mashariki

| (parts of the body) | | (other peripheral basic words) | |
|---|---|---|---|
| *-óngò | "bile" | *-gaga | "crust, hard shell" |
| **(wild animals)** | | **(cultivation)** | |
| *-ŋaaŋa | "ibis" | *-pú | "sorghum" |
| *-tiiti | "sp. warbler" | *-pà, | "gruel" |
| *-kùmbì | "locust" | *-papa | |
| | | *-lùmbù | "Plectranthus sp. (?)" |
| **(other culture)** | | *-sįabe | "edible tuber" |
| | | *-kųlų, | "calabash container" |
| *-òndò, | "hammer | *-kųlu | |
| *-ùndò | (of smith)" | | |

---

49

the distributions of each, as would be expected of old root words, reflecting their replacement here and there in later times by newer, innovated words. As would be expected also, several different members of this word set have evolved new meanings during the centuries of their presence in Mashariki vocabularies. For example, *-gaga "hard covering layer, crust," the root word most affected by semantic shift, bears the meanings "scab" in Swahili, "hoof" in Gogo, and "chaff" in Tumbuka and Nyanja (Nyasa group), and it forms the base of the derived words, Nyoro *nyamagaga* and Gusii *eriagaga*, both meaning "crab" (i.e., animal having a hard covering layer; see table 4A in appendix).

Two root words of the set have distributions that extend outside the Mashariki group of languages. In each instance the wider spread of the words can be laid to processes of technological diffusion at work during the Early Classical Age. The word *-pú "sorghum" has only a single occurrence known as yet outside Mashariki, in Luyana, a Western-Savanna language of the Zambezi River's interior flood plain. But that example forms one element in a cluster of evidence showing that grain cultivation diffused westward from the early Mashariki to the Central-Savanna peoples and to the Western-Savanna Bantu communities. These societies themselves expanded south from the southern fringe of the equatorial rainforest 2,500–2,000 years ago (see chapter 8).[20] The other root word in table 4 that has a significant spread outside Eastern Africa,, *-òndò (alternate shape *-ùndò) "hammer," is explainable as an artifact of the diffusion of iron technology westward through equatorial Africa from the Great Lakes region.[21]

## Eastern Sahelians and the Mashariki

The most widely spread set of Central Sudanic loanwords in Mashariki is paralleled in its distribution by a larger and equally widely occurring set of root words borrowed from a quite different Nilo-Saharan language. The known modern occurrences and phonology of these roots allow us to specify a language of the Eastern Sahelian branch as the source. A wider range of influences passed to the early Mashariki communities from the Eastern Sahelians of this period than from the Central Sudanians, including new information on livestock raising as well as on cultivation and toolmaking.

Three of the root words of proposed Eastern Sahelian origin—*-tùlì "mortar," *-teba, *-tiba "animal pen," and *-lìlì "sleeping place"—can be considered of second-order credibility, rather than first, because they each require postulating a noun derivation not attested in the currently available Eastern Sahelian evidence. But in each instance the noun in question can be given a plausible and straightforward derivation from a well-attested Nilo-Saharan verb (table 5A). The second of these words, *-teba, *-tiba "animal pen," derived from a verb "to stay, dwell," might seem less plausible than the rest until it is realized that the early Eastern Sahelian dwelling lay within the thorn pen—that the pen enclosed animals and people and constituted the homestead as a whole. The early Mashariki residence, in contrast, had no such feature. The item new to Bantu speakers, and thus in need of a name, would have been the pen in its particular function as a place to keep livestock. This kind of adoption of a word—in a more specialized sense than it held in its source language—is, it should be noted, a frequent characteristic in loanwords and in itself can constitute evidence for the direction of borrowing.

---

Table 5.  Eastern Sahelian loanwords in proto-Mashariki

(peripheral basic words)

| | | (cultivation) | |
|---|---|---|---|
| *-tòpè | "mud" | *-bèlé | "grain sp." |
| *-toolo | "bog, muddy place" | *-kímà | "porridge" |
| *-tòb- | "to hit" | *-púpù | "flour (?)" |
| *-bàk- | "to be lit" | *-tùli | "mortar" |
| | | *-tém- | "to cut (vegetation, in clearing for cultivation)" |

(body parts)

*-àyò        "sole (of foot)"

(livestock)

| | | (other culture) | |
|---|---|---|---|
| *-bágá | "livestock pen" | *-tụba | "wooden bowl" |
| (*-bágò | "fence") | *-gèlà | "iron" |
| *-teba (Kaskazi), *-tiba (Kusi) "animal pen" | | *-lìli | "sleeping place" ("bed" in northern Kaskazi) |
| *-golụ | "dewlap" | | |
| *-bolụ | "dewlap" | *-solo | "unmarried male" |
| *-sílè, *-seli (Kaskazi), *-sele (Kusi) "fresh milk" | | | |

51

A primary term for forged iron itself, *-gèlà "iron (point)," shows the importance of Eastern Sahelian example to the development of a knowledge of iron among the early Mashariki communities. Three more roots indicative of the westward spread of grain agriculture from the eastern side of Africa also turn up: *-bèlé "grain (generic)," *-kímà "porridge," and *-tém- "to cut down." The term *-bèlé has since widely come to specify pearl millet (Pennisetum) or, in some southern African languages, sorghum (see table 5 and also table 5A in appendix).

## The Geography of Social and Economic Encounter

Both the Central Sudanic and the Eastern Sahelian loanwords have the kinds of distributions in the Bantu languages that indicate their adoption at a time when the proto-Mashariki language was still spoken over a contiguous territory, with at most the bare beginnings of dialect differentiation. The Eastern Sahelian society involved in these contacts can be proposed to have inhabited drier and perhaps lower lands than the Central Sudanians. The specific reason for this conclusion is that the earliest words for finger millet, a crop requiring moist conditions and native to lower montane environments, came from a Central Sudanic language. As might be expected from this environmental indication, it was the Eastern Sahelians who provided new livestock vocabulary to proto-Mashariki, and not the Central Sudanians. Since the early Mashariki were surely inhabitants of lands near or adjacent to the Western Rift valley, the two loanword sets and their climatic and cultural implications can be most simply accounted for by a placement of the Central Sudanians in highland areas along the Rift, adjoining the earliest Mashariki settlements, and of the Eastern Sahelians in lower areas to the east of the earliest settlements, such as the Karagwe depression or similar terrains in western Uganda.

The Eastern Sahelian influences appear most probably to have kicked in slightly later than the Central Sudanic contacts. The distribution of vowel variations in certain of the borrowed words support this inference. The variant pronunciations most probably reflect alternative choices made by Bantu-speakers in rendering a vowel articulated somewhat differently from any vowel in their own language. In the one Central Sudanic case, *-òndò, *-ùndò "hammer" (see table 4), the two pronunciations intersect throughout the Mashariki region, showing that they go back to a free alternance in a still little differentiated proto-Mashariki language. In contrast, two of the three

52

examples noted from Eastern Sahelian (see table 5) have distinct, geo-graphically separate distributions: *-teba "animal pen" appearing in certain central Kaskazi languages, and *-tiba in Kusi; and *-sile, *-seli "fresh milk" occurring similarly in certain East African lan-guages, and *-sele in Southeast-Bantu. These two cattle-related terms thus appear to have been borrowed long enough after early stages of proto-Mashariki linguistic divergence had begun that their particular alternate pronunciations could end up restricted to different dialect ar-eas. The distributions of each suggest their adoption after the time the proto-Bantu speech community began to devolve into the two wider geographical groupings of local communities, the Kaskazi and Kusi.

## Developments of Middle Mashariki Times (c. Eighth Century to 500 B.C.?)

### The Emergence of the Kaskazi and Kusi Clusters

The full emergence among the early Mashariki of the two re-gionally distinct clusters of communities, the Kaskazi and the Kusi, marks the inception the Middle Mashariki period (map 5). Consider-able lexical evidence additional to the slight indications in the proto-Mashariki word borrowings (see tables 4 and 5) can be adduced for this development in the historical geography of Mashariki settle-ment.[22]

The later locations of the descendant languages of these two groupings, together with the evidence of contacts with non-Bantu peoples, place the Kaskazi to the north of the Kusi, most probably along the west side of the Great Lakes region. The Kusi communities can be understood as those early Mashariki who had spread southward by this second era, away from the area of the first period of contacts. As already proposed above, the likely locations at first for them would have been in or near the middle and southern Lake Tanganyika re-gions. And as the word evidence of faunal knowledge implies (see table 3), by the second half of the last millennium B.C. the southern outliers of the Kusi territories must have been verging on northeastern Zambia. The Kaskazi and Kusi groupings, it should once again be emphasized, need not themselves have represented single dialects of proto-Mashariki. More probably, each was already an incipient dia-lect continuum, but a continuum composed of geographically associ-ated communities sharing in a common set of external influences and relations.

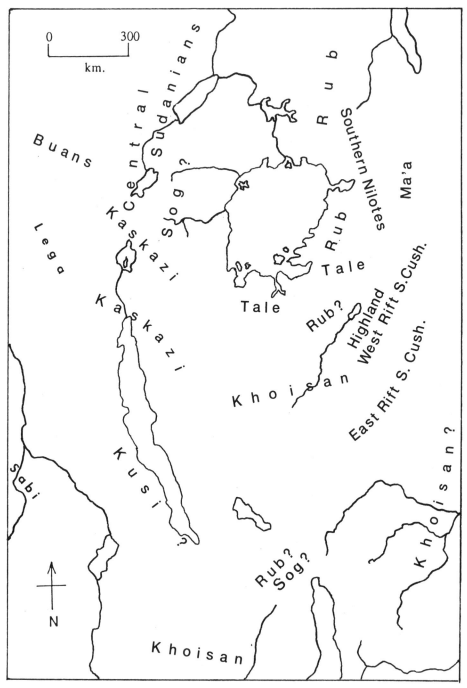

Map 5.  Peoples of the Great Lakes Region, c. 700 B.C.

54

Two additional bodies of evidence further distinguish the Kaskazi grouping of Mashariki communities. These consist of substantial sets of Central Sudanic and Eastern Sahelian loanwords of first-order or near first-order credibility that occur in wide or relict distributions through the Bantu languages of East Africa (tables 6 and 7), but not apparently in those languages forming the Kusi grouping. There is no reason to think that different Central or Eastern Sahelians were involved in the interactions of this second era, and it seems probable therefore that the Kaskazi cluster of communities evolved in areas presumably more extensive but still close to those of the earliest Mashariki settlements. Conversely, the lack of the new Central Sudanic loanwords in Kusi languages conforms to the inferences from other evidence that, by the Late Mashariki period, the Kusi communities had moved southward away from the original areas of settlement.

Differently from the two earlier borrowing sets (see tables 4 and 5), the Central Sudanic and Eastern Sahelian loanwords limited to the Kaskazi languages include subsets of words even further restricted in their occurrence, to just one or two of the subgroupings of Kaskazi communities (see tables 6–8). The subsets of very restricted distribution reveal growing dialect divergences within the Kaskazi cluster over the period of contact. In these differences are reflected the emerging of societal and cultural divergences among the early Mashariki Bantu. the detailed investigation of which has been presented elsewhere. The linguistic subgrouping of the Kaskazi languages shows that a number of separate communities had taken shape by that time. The classification established by D. Nurse, which I have modified in several respects, is followed here (see table 1 above for the present-day member languages of each subgroup): [23]

(1) Lakes (previously "Great Lakes")
(2) Kati (previously "Tanzania Northeast")
(3) Upland (combines proposed Central Highlands and
       Chaga-Dabida groups of D. Nurse) [24]
(4) Langi (single language, with a dialect Mbugwe, included
       previously in the Takama subgroup of Kati)
(5) Rufiji-Ruvuma (formerly "Southern Tanzania" group)
(6) Kilombero (sharply distinguished in Waite and Ehret, un-
       published, from Southern-Tanzania group of D. Nurse) [25]
(7) Rungwe (including Nyiha-Safwa and Nyakyusa-Ndali)
(8) Mwika (including Fipa, Mambwe, Nyamwanga, etc.;
       combined by Nurse with Rungwe in a Corridor group)

These eight subgroups of languages can be understood to have each derived from one of eight incipient dialects that together formed the Kaskazi grouping of the early Mashariki. Their common participation in the contacts of the Middle Mashariki era indicates that each of the eight emerging dialects was spoken by one among a closely associated geographical grouping of communities. But the frequency with which the loanwords are limited in their distributions today to particular subgroups of Mashariki languages, or to pairings of subgroups, demonstrates that the different emerging Kaskazi dialects—and hence the particular communities speaking them—often pursued their own separate courses of contact with the Central Sudanians and Eastern Sahelian peoples.

From a linguistic point of view it is not yet clear whether the close geographical association of the early Kaskazi communities was only that, or if it also involved a closer genetic relationship among the dialects they spoke. There is one unique sound-shift innovation that was once widely shared among all of them, except possibly the Rungwe and Mwika subgroups, and which might therefore support such a closer relationship among at least most of those early Kaskazi dialects. Called Dahl's Law, the original form of this shift added voicing to the first of two voiceless consonants in the same word (voicing means using the vocal cords in the articulation of a sound). Dahl's Law has remained productive down to the present in a minority of the Kaskazi languages. Everywhere else it eventually dropped from use, although often leaving behind scattered relics of its former presence in the form of skewed pronunciations of certain words—cases, for example, where original *k should have gone back to being pronounced *k after the dropping of the rule, but has instead remained *g.[26]

## Kaskazi Communities and Central Sudanians

A continuing major impact of Central Sudanians on the establishment of grain agricultural knowledge and practice among Mashariki communities is apparent in this second, Middle Mashariki period (Table 6). And for the first time a Central Sudanic influence on Bantu livestock raising may just possibly have been manifested, in the form of a *very* tentatively proposed borrowed word for "herd" of animals. The growing importance of savanna environments late in the period, and the Nilo-Saharans' prior mastery of that kind of clime, appears in the restricted adoption from the Central Sudanians of names for key large wild animals (see table 6d). A different sort of influence, interesting because it involved skills already possessed by the early Mashariki people, can be seen in their borrowing of words for baskets and for a wooden vessel of some sort. Presumably styles of woven and wooden containers new to the Bantu communities are indicated in these adoptions of new vocabulary.

---

### Table 6. Central Sudanic loanwords in Kaskazi

*a. Loanwords of broad distribution in Kaskazi languages*

| (basic words) | | (wild animals) | |
|---|---|---|---|
| *-inie | "liver" | *-kebe, *ki-be | "jackal" |
| | | *-gaala | "striped rat" |

| (cultivation) | | (other material culture) | |
|---|---|---|---|
| *-(ì)gì, *-ùgì | "gruel" | *-èlé | "knife" |
| *-(u)nú̧ | "mortar" | *-ibo | "large basket" |
| *-(u)lo | "digging stick" | *-òmbò̧ | "wooden vessel, boat" |
| *-kolo | "small calabash" | *-ábù̧ | "(hunting) net" |

*b. Loanwords in south Kaskazi (Rufiji-Ruvuma, Rungwe)*

(cultivation)

*-ɲa      "uncooked gruel"

*c. Loanwords in central Kaskazi (Kati subroup)*

| (basic and peripheral basic) | (material culture) | |
|---|---|---|
| *-titu    "black" | *-kapu, *-kapo | "basket" |
| | *-ba | "yard of homestead" |

*d. Loanwords in north Kaskazi (Lakes, Upland subgroups)*

| (wild animals) | (cultivation) | |
|---|---|---|
| *-àŋàú    "large spotted carnivore; hyena" | *-kumbi | "hoe" |
| *-lu(i/e) "lion (?)" | | |

*e. Loanwords restricted to Langi subgroup —*

| (cultivation) | (other material culture) | |
|---|---|---|
| ǫdo    "red sorghum" | birǫ | "iron ore" (< *-bu̧lu) |

---

Once again a few of the Central Sudanian words adopted by the Kaskazi peoples show a wider westward spread indicative of the diffusion of certain kinds of technological change from Eastern Africa. The notable instances here are *-(u)nų́ for "mortar" and *-èlé for "knife." Both these root words have relict occurrence in Kaskazi languages, appearing in a few widely separated Kaskazi subgroups, but each then extends in a long block distribution through the languages of the southern savanna belt. Both, in other words, bear the clear marks of being old root words in Kaskazi that only subsequently diffused westward from Eastern Africa, one apparently with the spread of grain cultivation and the other with the coming of iron (chapter 8).

## The Kaskazi and Their Eastern Sahelian Neighbors

While the Central Sudanians resided in locations central to the overall territories inhabited by the Kaskazi communities, the Eastern Sahelians of the Middle Mashariki era apparently comprised at least two distinct societies, one inhabiting areas in or to the immediate north of the Kaskazi lands, and the other in more southerly parts. The reason for this conclusion is a simple one: two separate Eastern Sahelian loanword sets, coming from Eastern Sahelian languages that had notable differences in their subsistence vocabularies, turn up in the Kaskazi languages. One set (see table 7) comprises several subsets of words, some of them of general or wide Kaskazi distribution, but many of them defining a Southern-Kaskazi cluster of communities. The Southern-Kaskazi peoples spoke those proto-Mashariki dialects that were ancestral to the modern Kati, Kilombero, Rufiji-Ruvuma, and Rungwe languages (see the list of these groups above). The other set of Eastern Sahelian loanwords was restricted to the Lakes communities (see table 8). The proto-Upland and pre-Langi communities, as well as the proto-Mwika, seem to have held geographical positions more peripheral to these contacts, less directly and less often partaking of the effects of this period of history.

The two sets of Eastern Sahelian loanwords together reflect a period of historical development, probably dating to shortly before the middle of the last millennium B.C., in which the Lakes people began to develop their own array of contacts with neighboring non-Bantu societies, separate from those of the rest of the Kaskazi grouping of communities. From later language locations it is clear that the Lakes society emerged at the north of the Kaskazi areal clustering, with the proto-Upland society possibly residing in localities close by to them.

The existence in the Middle Mashariki period of a distinct Southern-Kaskazi areal grouping of peoples is revealed in part by the demonstrable Eastern Sahelian word borrowings unique to them (see table 6b), but also by a number of other distinct word innovations (exemplified in Table 7, sections b and f). Some of these latter inno-

---

## Table 7. Eastern Sahelian loanwords in Kaskazi

*a. Loanwords of relict wide Kaskazi distribution*

| (wild animals) | (residence or livestock) |
|---|---|
| *-ŋwali, *-ŋwala "crested crane" | *-saale "thorn fence" |
| (cultivation) | (other culture) |
| *-tele, *-tili "prepared grain" | *-pìlu "thin straight stick" |

*b. Loanwords of Southern-Kaskazi distribution*

| (wild animals) | (cultivation) |
|---|---|
| *-pélà "rhinoceros" | *-gàlì "porridge" |
| (other culture) | |
| *-tapo "iron ore" | |

*c. Loanwords limited to Kati group*

| (wild animal) | (livestock) |
|---|---|
| *-pelele "(tree?) hyrax" | *-kòló "sheep" |

*e. Loanwords in Rufiji-Ruvuma group*

| (wild animals) | (livestock) |
|---|---|
| *-sakata "monitor lizard" | *-belele "sheep" |

*f. Southern-Kaskazi innovations of uncertain or Bantu source*

| (basic and peripheral basic) | | (wild animals) | |
|---|---|---|---|
| *-pùlà | "nose" | *-tomondo | "hippopotamus" |
| *-túmbî | "egg" | *-súbì | "leopard" |
| *-tápik- | "to vomit" | | |
| | | (other culture) | |
| | | *-sábi | "witchcraft" |

Table 8. Notable Eastern Sahelian and Central Sudanic loanwords
in proto-Lakes

a. *Eastern Sahelian loanwords —*

(cultivation)

*-sela, *-sala "porridge"

(other material culture)

*-gono "vessel (wooden?)"
*-tébè "stool"

(livestock)

*-ka "cattle; cow"
*-te "cow, head of cattle"

b. *Central Sudanic loanwords —*

(basic)

*-senyi, *-senyu "sand"

(cultivation)

*-lo "finger millet"
*-le "finger millet"

(wild animals)

*-SuSu(e) "shrew"

(other material culture)

*-pu "hide, skin"
*-ambi "arrow"

vations derive from older Bantu roots of different meaning, and others have phonological shapes that suggest they may possibly be as yet unproven Eastern Sahelian loanwords (see table 7f). The Southern-Kaskazi grouping itself contained several clusters of communities even then starting to follow their own divergent directions of expansion, as the subsets of Eastern Sahelian loanwords limited to particular Kaskazi subgroupings reveal.

The Lakes society's separate history in the Middle Mashariki period is well attested by their own loanword sets from Central Sudanic and Southern Cushitic languages as well as Eastern Sahelian (see tables 7 and 8). As the Lakes people diverged after the fifth century into several descendant societies, these cultural interactions gradually declined in importance, with both the Nilo-Saharan groups and the Cushites beginning in time to be absorbed into the expanding Lakes societies. The working out of this history of social amalgamation reveals itself to us in the smaller sets of words in each table that are limited today to one or another of the modern-day groupings of Lakes societies (for these data, table 8A in appendix). It is a story the main themes of which belong to later times, and a set of topics much more deeply explored in the recent work of David Schoenbrun.

Two of these later historical episodes nevertheless are worthy of mention here because they reconfirm the implications of the early Mashariki evidence—namely, that the Central Sudanic territories lay anciently to the farther west of the Great Lakes region. For one, the proto-Forest people, a Lakes society residing west of the Western Rift in the second half of the first millennium A.D., appears to have had their own separate, important contacts with a Central Sudanic society.[27] Still more recently, in the Nyoro dialect of the Rutara language, spoken at the far northwest of the Great Lakes, a late Central Sudanic loanword set turns up, demonstrably from the Madi language and indicative of the Kitara or early Bunyoro incorporation of Madi populations, between 1000 and 1500 A.D.[28]

In both encounters in the Middle Kaskazi period of Bantu with Eastern Sahelian peoples—those of the Lakes communities and those of Southern-Kaskazi—the loanwords show once again the importance of both livestock raising and grain cultivation for the Sahelians' economy (see tables 7 and 8). Similarly, the evidence on Central Sudanic livelihood seen in the Lakes word borrowings (see table 8) comports with the earlier indications (see tables 4 and 6) that the Central Sudanic communities, although grain cultivators, did not particularly emphasize livestock raising.

Like the Central Sudanic loanwords in Kaskazi as a whole (see table 6), the Eastern Sahelian loans to the Southern-Kaskazi communities, as well as the Central Sudanic and Eastern Sahelian loanwords in proto-Lakes, include several terms that turn up in Bantu languages spoken west of the Mashariki areas and can be understood to mark the diffusion of new technology from the early Mashariki Bantu to their western neighbors. Most notably, *-lùkut- "to blow bellows" (of uncertain derivation) and *-tapo "iron ore" (table 7) confirm in their distributions the indications of *-òndò, *-ùndò "hammer" (see table 4) and *-élé "knife" (see table 6) that early metallurgy diffused directly west from the Great Lakes region into western equatorial Africa and also from East Africa to the central southern savanna zone.[29]

## End of an Era: New Sources of Culture Change (c. 600–400 B.C.)

The winding down of the Middle Mashariki period was marked around mid-millennium by a major reshuffling of the regional groupings of Kaskazi communities. The speakers of the evolving Rufiji-Ruvuma, Kilombero, Mwika, and Rungwe dialects of the Southern-Kaskazi cluster split off to the south, beginning movements that would eventuate in their settlement in far southern Tanzania (see chapter 6).[30] The Kati, another member community of the Southern-Kaskazi cluster, may have moved westward into areas near the southwest of Lake Nyanza. At the same time, major new influences engaged the Lakes society. These came from the Tale Southern Cushites (pronounced *tah-lay*) and commenced as early as mid-millennium. By not long after 500 B.C., the Lakes people themselves began to spread over larger parts of the western Nyanza Basin and diverge into four sets of communities. Of these four, the Western-Lakes grouping emerged at the far west, while the West-Nyanza, pre-Luyia, and East-Nyanza groupings took shape along Lake Nyanza.[31]

These various, roughly contemporary Kaskazi expansions outward from the Western Rift region found expression also in the limited development of new climatic terminology at the southern and eastern margins of the Kaskazi-speaking areas. Certain communities, notably the pre-Langi and the Rufiji-Ruvuma, apparently began to encounter a new distribution of rainy months, to which they gave the name *-tụko. The consistent modern-day application of this term to a single rain season lasting roughly from November to March or April, supports the placement of these communities at the southeastern and southern fringes of the Kaskazi cluster, most probably in western Tanzania or along the immediate west or south of Burundi. Those areas possess just the sort of two-season climate regime that the development of the term *-tụko presupposes, comprised of a wet season from November to March and a dry time from April to October. This seasonal succession, quite different from that of the early Mashariki territories, extends from far western Tanzania southeastward across almost all of southern Tanzania.

The Southern Cushitic contribution newly evident in Nyanza Basin history by around mid-last millennium B.C. strongly focussed on pastoral knowledge. The Eastern Sahelian and Tale Southern Cushitic loanwords, taken together (see tables 8 and 9), suggest that it was during the proto-Lakes period that cattle keeping in particular became an established activity among at least some participants in the local economies of the Lakes communities, and not just something well known among the neighboring non-Bantu societies. The Tale communities, in any case, exerted a strong influence on the proto-Lakes society (see Table 9) and continued to be a major factor in the histories of the Lakes peoples for the next several centuries.

Table 9. Sample Southern Cushitic loanwords
in proto-Lakes

(basic words)

| *-kịa | "nek" | *-sagama | "blood" |
| *-gina | "stone" | | |

| (wild animals) | | (livestock) | |
| *-tale | "lion" | *-kaapụ | "cattle; cow" |
| *-sama, | "waterbuck" | *-masa | "bull or cow that has |
| *-suma | | | not produced young" |
| *-punu | "bushpig" | *-saato | "animal skin" |

## The Late Mashariki Period in the Nyanza Basin
## (c. Fifth to Third Centuries B.C.)

In these encounters of Lakes people with Southern Cushites and with Central Sudanic and Eastern Sahelian societies—which took place at about the fifth century B.C. by the reckoning of Schoenbrun[32]—the Late Mashariki stage of the Classical Age of Greater Eastern African history can be said to have begun. During this period the suites of cultural behavior and economic practice that were to characterize the subsequent establishment of classical Mashariki culture all across eastern and southern Africa came fully into being. To the south, in areas probably adjoining southern Lake Tanganyika, the lands of the Kusi cluster of communities by the fifth and fourth centuries B.C. verged increasingly on drier savanna territory. Their history from this point onward is considered in chapter 7.

In the central Great Lakes region, two main zones of seminal cultural and economic change arose. One lay to the west of Lake Nyanza among the Western-Highlands and West-Nyanza divisions of the Lakes Bantu communities. That history is dealt with in detail in Professor David Schoenbrun's new book.[33] But a second set of crucial areas lay somewhere to the southwest and immediate south of Lake Nyanza. Of extremely wide-ranging importance for the later course of cultural and economic history in the Classical Age all across Kenya and Tanzania, the developments of the southern Nyanza Basin in the Late Mashariki period require our close attention here and now.

## The Emergence of the Southern-Nyanza Cluster of Communities

In the centuries after 500 B.C., a new areal configuration of Mashariki communities took shape probably first to the southwest of the lake, expanding subsequently eastward toward the southeastern side of Lake Nyanza. It arose through the intrusion by speakers of two of the four dialects of proto-Lakes—pre-Luyia and East-Nyanza—into an area already in the process of being settled by the speakers of three other dialects of the Kaskazi group, the Kati, the Upland, and the pre-Langi. Together these several sets of Kaskazi communities, in differing combinations, entered into a series of new interethnic contact situations with Tale Southern Cushites, Southern Nilotes, and Eastern Sahelians. This regional convergence of developments, lasting from the fifth century till late in the millennium, took shape in two stages, to which we may give the names the Early and Late Southern-Nyanza periods.

The first and most powerful economic impact on the lives of the Southern-Nyanza peoples came from the Southern Cushites. Many of the loanwords depicting this multiple encounter were adopted all across the Southern-Nyanza areal grouping of Bantu speakers. Other loans, taking hold in different portions of the grouping, reveal something of the relative positioning of the different Southern-Nyanza dialect communities within the wider zone of contacts. The Central Tale people involved in these contacts probably spoke a somewhat different dialect from that of the Western Tale, whose loanwords (cited in table 9 above) were restricted to Lakes Bantu.[34]

Several Central Tale loanwords—most notably *-saata, *-taasa "barren animal," *-dogowe "donkey," *-tamu "eland," *-salu "dung, mud," *-lílà "umbilical cord," and *-Saija "young man"—appear today in the West-Nyanza branch of the Lakes group as well as in languages deriving from the Southern-Nyanza areal grouping of communities (table 1B). At the earliest stage of the encounter with Tale peoples, it thus seems, the several peoples of the inchoate Southern-Nyanza cluster remained in close contact with the community that gave rise to the West-Nyanza society. The West-Nyanza settlements were situated toward the southern parts of the west side of Lake Nyanza[35] and therefore the early members of the Southern-Nyanza cluster occupied territories nearby, presumably to the southwest of the lake.

A number of the early Central Tale loanwords adopted by the Southern-Nyanza cluster of dialects turn up also in modern-day languages belonging to the Mwika, Rungwe, or Kilombero subgroups of

64

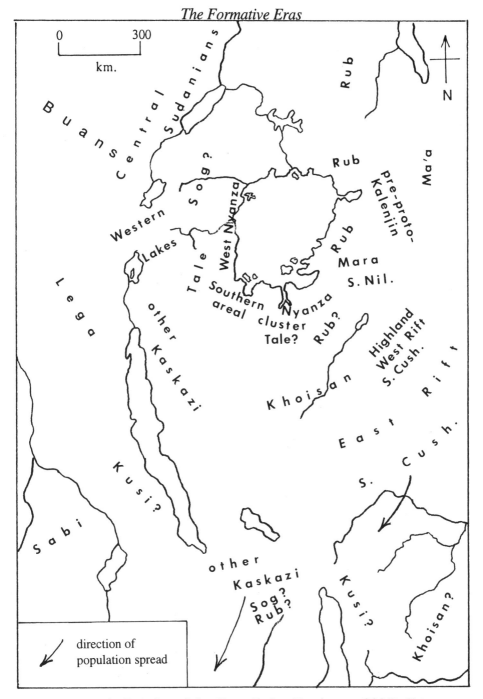

Map 6. Peoples of the Great Lakes Region, c. 300 B.C.

Kaskazi. At least one of those words also occurs in the Nyasa languages of the Kusi grouping, and another two outside Mashariki Bantu entirely, in languages of the Botatwe group and in Nsenga of the Sabi group (see chapter 7 for more on the significance of these particular data).

Most of the instances of such words in the Mwika, Rungwe, and Kilombero tongues are probably secondary word borrowings from languages of the Njombe subgroup of Kati. They represent, in other words, influences stemming from their encounters with the Njombe peoples during more recent centuries. Examples (cited in table 1B of appendix B) include *-lale "soot," *-kasi "beads," *nyànì, *-nànì "greens," *-sale "scarification," *-pụngate, *-pụngati "seven," and *-tupa "rhinoceros." Three such words, however, may be earlier adoptions. One, *-gondị "sheep," which appears in the Rungwe languages, probably is left over from the initial diffusion of sheep raising in the later last millennium B.C. The distribution of another loanword of this set, *-lị̀bà "milk," likely reflects the contemporary spread of the milking of cattle as a newly established feature of subsistence practice among many of the same Kaskazi communities. The southern limits of its spread are marked by the appearance of reflexes of *-lị̀bà in Southern Nyasa dialects in Malawi and in the neighboring Nsenga language of Zambia. A third word, *-dokwe, naming the "donkey" in the Mwika group of languages, may in like fashion date back to a spread by or before the turn of the era of the knowledge of donkeys south to the Mwika from one of the Southern-Nyanza communities.

In contrast, the presence of an isolated term of Southern Cushitic origin, *-Saija "young man," in the Nsenga language of southeastern Zambia probably reflects the fact that Nsenga, a member of the Sabi group, arrived in that region as part of the spread of Sabi languages during the past 1,500 years. That set of developments displaced earlier Kaskazi languages from use in several parts of Zambia, with the consequence that words from the previously spoken Kaskazi languages were often adopted into the Sabi tongues, newly established in the region. Another such example, *-lílà "umbilical cord," appearing in the Botatwe group, can similarly be understood as one of a set of early Kaskazi words, the use of which spread into Botatwe from the language of a former Kaskazi society that inhabited parts of central Zambia prior to the arrival of Botatwe communities there around A.D. 500 (see chapter 7).

## Developments of Late Southern-Nyanza Times

The early period of Southern Cushitic influence on the Southern-Nyanza grouping of Kaskazi communities then gave way to an era of more complex interactions. These developments may have begun around the fourth or third century B.C.

In this Late Southern-Nyanza stage, the pre-Luyia, East-Nyanza, and Upland peoples came under the influence of a Southern Nilotic society, whose loanwords in the Bantu dialects center heavily on livestock terminology. A single word of the set, *-keese "sheep"— known only from North Luyia, in the meaning "sheep" and in Shambaa, of Kati, as "half-grown lamb"—has the kind of rare, scattered occurrence indicative of its having been borrowed at the very beginning of the interaction. Alone it appeared in two disparate dialects of the early Southern-Nyanza areal grouping, and so the beginnings of the Southern Nilotic contacts presumably overlapped with the later Southern Cushitic interactions.

The common participation of the pre-Luyia, East-Nyanza, and Upland communities in these contacts with Southern Nilotes (table 10) show them to have formed for a brief period a separate easterly offshoot of the Southern-Nyanza cluster. Those events also have implications for historical geography—they locate this particular short-lived clustering of Kaskazi communities in areas at the southeast of Lake Nyanza, because it is there that their Southern Nilotic neighbors, on independent archeological and linguistic grounds (see chapter 3), must be placed.

In keeping with their proposed movement into the different climatic environment of the west side of Lake Nyanza, this eastern group

Table 10. Southern Nilotic loanwords common to Luyia,
East-Nyanza, and Upland

| (peripheral basic) | | (livestock) | |
|---|---|---|---|
| *-titiɲo | "heel" | *-mooli̧ | "calf" |
| | | *-keese | "sheep" |
| (other culture) | | *-ti̧gili, *-ti̧gi̧li | "donkey" |
| *muu̧ma | "oath" | *-koolo | "black-and-white" (cow) |

of Southern-Nyanza communities innovated a new season name *-nane, *-nani, for a period of the year that included, inter alia, the months of June through August. Luyia dialects, in which the word denotes the single long western Kenya rainy season, lasting from about March to September, probably preserve its original application. The term has also been retained in some Chaga dialects, but with its application narrowed, in the four-season climatic sequence of the Kilimanjaro region, to a cool, cloudy season centering on July and August.

At about the same time as the the pre-Luyia, East-Nyanza, and Upland communities were coming under a Southern Nilotic influence, the Kati people initiated a new era of relations with West Rift Southern Cushites. The lack of any indication that the Kati people made significant changes in their climatic terminology suggests that they may have continued through this time to inhabit lands to the immediate southwest of Lake Nyanza. Within the overall territories proposed to have been settled by the member communities of the Southern-Nyanza area cluster, these areas had the seasonal distributions nearest resembling those that had been encountered farther to the west by their proto-Mashariki ancestors.

The source of the Southern Cushitic loanwords in early Kati appears to have been a distinct Tale dialect, to which we can give the name Eastern Tale.[36] A focus on cattle-raising practices again dominated the relations between these West Rift Southern Cushites and the Kati society. Not only did major breeding terms for cattle—such as the words for "heifer," "ox," and "herd"—come from the language of the Eastern Tale people, but also the associated terms for "hoof" and "cattle tick." Even more telling was the Kati borrowing from Southern Cushitic of their verb for "to herd," displacing from use the older Mashariki root *-liis- (literally, "to feed," formed from proto-Mashariki and proto-Bantu verb *-li- "to eat"). Some among the Kati communities, it is clear, began at that era, late in the last millennium B.C., to take up cattle raising from the Southern Cushites as a significant economic activity of their own.

At least two words belonging to this Eastern Tale loanword set, *-dama "heifer" and *-diim- "to herd," appear also in languages of the Rungwe and Mwika groups. Like other Southern Cushitic loans in these languages (which see table 1B in appendix B), they can be traced most probably to secondary influences coming from the Njombe peoples during the past 1,000 to 1,500 years.

## Close of the Southern-Nyanza Period (c. 200–1 B.C.?)

The end of the Southern-Nyanza period came about through the breaking down of regional contiguity among the various Southern-Nyanza communities. Already in the developments of the late Southern-Nyanza period, the various communities of the region had expanded more widely, their dialect differences had become more pronounced, and in different parts of the region they had begun to engage in different interethnic contacts. But with the close of the period, entirely new contact histories began, no longer of wide impact but restricted to different of the sets of communities that made up the Southern-Nyanza grouping, and often with non-Bantu peoples quite distinct from those previously encountered. Evidently, the constituent societies of the Southern-Nyanza cluster were each beginning to move off into new areas, some quite far away, where their encounters with different neighboring societies and different historical environments were to shape the future course of events.

# Summing Up

This chapter has sought to identify the groupings of Mashariki Bantu peoples involved in the formative centuries of the Classical Age of Greater Eastern African history and define the key stages in that historical process. The geographical settings of this history lay among the African Great Lakes, and the formative centuries occupied the first two-thirds of the last millennium B.C. Additional trends of change, c. 300–100 B.C., among the Southern-Nyanza cluster of Kaskazi communities, were then considered to more fully round out the picture for the Great Lakes region itself.

The Bantu-speaking proto-Mashariki society entered into the western margins of this region by early in the last millennium B.C. Arriving as settlers from the moist savannas immediately south of the eastern equatorial rainforest, they at first sought out climates much like those they had come from. In the areas along the Western Rift Valley, the early Mashariki communities came into contact with Central Sudanic–speaking peoples, while farther to the east, in Uganda, their neighbors included an Eastern Sahelian people, the Sog, whose language most probably belonged to the Kir sub-branch of the Eastern Sahelian division of the Nilo-Saharan family. The Nilotic, Surmic, and Daju languages are the best-known members of the Kir grouping. The Sog, in contrast to the Mashariki settlers, apparently tended to live in the more open, less wooded environments of the Great Lakes region. The word borrowings from the Central Sudanic and Eastern Sahelian tongues reveal that these Eastern Sahelians were food producers who cultivated grains and raised cows and sheep in addition to goats.

The early Mashariki communities appear progressively to have grown in numbers and expanded their territories in the Great Lakes region over the course of the last millennium B.C. As they expanded, they diverged initially into two broad areal clusterings—the Kaskazi, probably located in or about the central parts of the Western Rift Valley region, and the Kusi, probably emerging in the more southerly zones of the Western Rift, around Lake Tanganyika. As the centuries passed, the Kaskazi peoples expanded still more widely, before mid-millennium diverging for a time into as many as three or four groupings, one comprising the Lakes society, and another, a Southern-Kaskazi cluster, composed of a majority of the rest of the Kaskazi communities.

After mid-millennium the Southern-Kaskazi grouping broke up, with several communities, notably the Rungwe, Rufiji-Ruvuma, and Kilombero, beginning to move off, most probably southward. The Lakes group of Kaskazi communities began about then to spread widely over the lands between the Western Rift and southwestern Lake Nyanza. As these developments progressed, a new areal configuration of Kaskazi communities began to take shape between perhaps roughly 500 and 300 B.C., to the southwest of Lake Nyanza. The participants in this new regional, "Southern-Nyanza" clustering included the Kati, pre-Langi, and Upland peoples and two sets of Lakes communities, the pre-Luyia and the East-Nyanza. Along with these varied shifts in the social geography of Kaskazi settlement, a new set of interethnic cultural interactions took form, drawing Tale Southern Cushites into close relations with both the Southern-Nyanza grouping of communities and those Lakes peoples who remained to the west of Lake Nyanza. The Tale people seem to have been especially prominent cattle raisers.

Finally, toward the close of the last millennium B.C., as the Southern-Nyanza cluster continued to expand eastward, some of its member communities, located by then to the east or southeast of Lake Nyanza, engaged still another non-Bantu food-producing society, Southern Nilotic in language and, like the Tale Southern Cushites, strongly oriented toward livestock raising.

The overall picture of developments in the last millennium B.C. is one, then, in which the Mashariki groups were expanding within the

African Great Lakes region, in ways and for reasons to be explored in subsequent chapters. Other food-producing peoples, of a variety of ethnic and language backgrounds, had major roles at different stages in these developments, but formed, it appears, a declining presence over the long term. Their contributions to this history of cultural reconfiguration, and the mapping out of their encounters with Mashariki societies in the Early Classical Age in Eastern Africa now command our attention as we move on to chapter 3.

# Notes

[1] Ehret 1995/96.

[2] Van Grunderbeek, Roche, and Doutrelepont 1983; Van Grunderbeek 1992.

[3] The name "Lake Nyanza" is admittedly redundant because *Nyanza* means "sea, very large lake." But it is certainly time to replace the colonial name, Victoria, since all the rest of the lakes of East Africa now are given their African names. As almost all the people living around this second largest freshwater lake in the world call it simply "Nyanza," using that name seems amply justified, despite the hidden redundancy of its English rendering as "Lake Nyanza." A second lake of importance in this book, Lake Nyasa, also called Lake Malawi, has in fact the same derivation but is pronounced differently because its name comes from a different African language, Yao.

[4] These languages form the J and E zones of the Tervuren scholars plus Guthrie's (1967–72) F, G, and northern P (groups P.10–P.20) zones and a few languages each from his zones N (group N.10) and M (groups M.10–20).

[5] Guthrie's (1967–72) N (except N.10), S, southern P (group P.30), and far southern M (group M.60) zones.

[6] Ehret 1973b and 1980a.

[7] Contra Guthrie 1967–72, vol. 4, who glossed it as "cold season."

[8] McMaster 1988.

[9] McMaster 1988; Ehret 1995/96.

[10] Ehret, forthcoming

[11] Ahmed 1995.

[12] A much more recent set of strong Sabi influences, dating to the past 1,000 years in Zambia and Malawi, has to some extent obscured the effects of the earlier contacts between the Mashariki and the Sabi. See C. C. Ahmed 1995. The driving force behind these recent influences appears to have been a series of major movements of Sabi-speaking immigrants into those countries (see also chapters 7 and 8). These population movements established the Sabi dialects across large parts of Zambia; and the resulting assimilation of the pre-existing Mashariki populations of those areas into the newly evolving Sabi societies accounts for the presence in the Sabi dialects, such as Lamba and Bemba, of

many words otherwise wholly Mashariki in occurrence (several instances of this kind of word distribution appear in tables 3–7 in this chapter). This history properly belongs to a much later period than those dealt with here; it requires mention only because the evidence for it sometimes obscures the evidence relating to earlier times.

[13] Papstein 1978.

[14] Vansina 1984; Bastin, Coupez, and de Halleux 1983.

[15] See Ehret, forthcoming.

[16] Ehret 1964; Henrici 1973; Heine, Hoff, and Vossen 1977.

[17] Ehret, forthcoming.

[18] Klieman 1997 provides detailed arguments for these conclusions along with a first laying out of proposed archeological correlations for the history involved.

[19] Reconstructed Central Sudanic root words are taken from Ehret 1992, which identifies over 1600 such items.

[20] Ehret 1974a, 1982b.

[21] Ehret, forthcoming.

[22] Two interesting non-loanword examples of this demarcation are the contrasting Kaskazi and Kusi innovations for the meanings: (a) "sorgum": Kaskazi \*-pémbá, \*-pémbé, in contrast to Kusi \*-pila (see also table 38); and (b) "horn": proto-Mashariki \*-pémbè, which was replaced in Kusi by a new root word \*-àngá. That the term \*-pémbè for "horn" was at one time found also in Kusi is attested by the widespread Mashariki word \*-pembele "rhinoceros," found in Kusi languages and also in the Takama subgroup of Kaskazi. This word is composed of the root \*-pémbè plus an old attributive suffix \*-ile "having, characterized by," yielding the form \*-pembe-le "having a horn." The root word \*-àngá is therefore a specifically Kusi innovation.

[23] Nurse 1982; see also Hinnebusch, Nurse, and Mould 1981; Nurse 1988a.

[24] Ehret and Posnansky 1982; Ehret 1984, and 1988.

[25] Davy and Nurse 1982; Bennett 1967.

[26] Davy and Nurse 1982.

[27] See Schoenbrun 1990 for this conclusion.

[28] Ehret, Okihiro, et al. 1974.

[29] As argued in Ehret 1995/96.

[30] Waite and Ehret, unpublished.

[31] For these Lakes communities and the name Tale, see Schoenbrun 1990.

[32] Schoenbrun 1990.

[33] Schoenbrun, forthcoming.

[34] In particular, the Central Tale seem not to have changed proto–Southern Cushitic \*k' to \*g when it was preceded by \*s in the same word, whereas the Western Tale people who influenced the Lakes society did shift \*k' to \*g in such positions (compare the two different forms of the borrowed word for "blood" in table 9 and table 1B in appendix B).

[35] Ehret, Okihiro, et al. 1974; Schoenbrun 1990.

[36] Differently from the word borrowings of the immediately preceding period, the loanwords restricted to Kati tended to preserve Southern Cushitic *d as *[d], adding a new consonant to the Kati phonology. The West Rift language of these contacts also differed in several aspects of its own phonology from the Western and Central Tale dialects of the previous period (see appendix B, table 2B). For instance, the cluster of sounds *(a)C$^w$a did not become *(o)Co (as in table 1B), and Southern Cushitic *k' (Iraqw /q/) always produced *k rather than *g in its borrowed shapes in the Kati language.

# 3. Mapping the Mosaic of Cultural Interaction

## Cross-Cultural Relations in the Formative Eras

The future directions of cultural and ethnic shift across Greater Eastern Africa would by no means have been self-evident to a contemporary observer in the early or middle centuries of the last millennium B.C. The Mashariki communities were gradually expanding their territories. But other peoples over the same period, most notably the Southern Cushites and Southern Nilotes, also grew in numbers and spread their presence and economic activities into new lands. Their long-established economies suited the drier climates that extend across so many parts of East Africa proper and might well have made them seem the peoples best situated to take advantage of what the eastern African environment offered. That the crucial changes setting in motion the Classical Age of Eastern African history were already underway is evident only in retrospect.

To bring balance and perspective to our understanding of the formative centuries of the Classical Age, we must now tackle two intertwined issues. We need first to identify more fully the various non-Bantu societies involved in the early stages of the Classical Age and to locate them within the longer term of Great Lakes and East African history. Second, we need to place their material cultural and economic values and activities in historical context. What can we say, in other words, about the historical geography of interethnic interaction and human settlement and about the variety of eastern African cultural experience during the early and middle centuries of the last millennium B.C.?

## Central Sudanians in the Western Great Lakes Region

### Locating the Central Sudanic Communities

Several periods of interactions between Central Sudanians and Bantu communities in the Great Lakes region have taken place over

75

the centuries since 1000 B.C. The Central Sudanic languages form one major division of the Nilo-Saharan language family; the Eastern Sahelian–speaking peoples to be considered later in this chapter belong to a different, only distantly related branching of the same family. The initial stage of the Central Sudanic interactions with Bantu peoples dates to the Early Mashariki period (see table 4). The second set of interactions, probably a continuation of the previous contacts, appears in the evidence relating to the immediately subsequent Middle Mashariki era, after the early Mashariki people had fully diverged geographically into two clusters of emerging dialects, Kaskazi and Kusi. The Kaskazi communities alone participated in this second era of contacts (see table 6).

Then, as the dialect divergences grew within the Kaskazi cluster and the member communities of the cluster spread out over a wider expanse of territories, those particular communities speaking the emerging Lakes dialect began a third era of close relations with a Central Sudanic society. The language of this society did not apparently differ markedly from that of the first two eras of Central Sudanic contacts (see table 8). All these interactions fit within a period extending roughly from the very early last millennium B.C. into the third quarter of that millennium and probably represent an ongoing history of contacts, differing in its particular Bantu participants because of the successive spreading of Kusi and then Kaskazi communities away from the focal areas of this history.

The overall evidence of the three early Central Sudanic loanword sets (see tables 4, 6, and 8) show the donor language or languages of the loans to have belonged to the East branch of Central Sudanic. Within that branch their closest, although still distant, relationship may have been to the extant Moru-Madi subgroup, but that proposition remains to be adequately demonstrated.

Two other histories of Central Sudanic contacts with Bantu-speaking communities belong to later times. The earlier of the two was limited to the Forest subgroup of the Western branch of the Lakes Bantu group (see appendix: table 8A.f) and thus may date to as recently as the centuries around 1000 A.D.[1] The little evidence available so far does not allow us to pin down the relationships of the particular Central Sudanic language involved; it could have been closest to Moru-Madi or, alternatively, to modern Balendru. The second and most recent encounter of all was of early Nyoro speakers specifically with Madi people and can best be dated to the formative era of a distinct Nyoro dialect, roughly from the thirteenth to the fifteenth centuries A.D. The evidence, not tabled here because it concerns a much

76

later historical era, includes the Nyoro borrowings from Madi of words for such varied items of culture knowledge or practice as donkeys, sugarcane, and bellows, and for at least one wild animal, the ostrich.[2] Apparently during the Bachwezi era, expanding Rutara communities incorporated Madi people living in the Bunyoro region of Uganda. Those former inhabitants themselves probably formed the southern extension of the Madi populations of northern Uganda so amply attested in the Luo oral traditions relating to that era.[3]

All these Central Sudanians had their impact on Bantu communities that can be located at the western side of the Great Lakes region. The first contact period involved the early Mashariki, who are best placed no farther east than the Western Rift itself. The second era of interactions, between the later Mashariki communities and Central Sudanians, may well have included areas extending eastward beyond the Rift proper, presumably into the then forested country between Ruwenzori and southern Burundi. The third period of contacts involved the Lakes offshoot of the early Mashariki, which itself emerged as a distinct group between Ruwenzori and northern Rwanda.[4] Within the Lakes group, the later Forest society resided to the immediate west of the Western Rift, while Nyoro evolved as a distinct dialect of the Rutara language at the northwest of the Great Lakes region. The cumulative picture is of Central Sudanians as the ancient inhabitants of the far west side of the region, but not, as far as present evidence allows, direct participants in the history of the rest of the Nyanza Basin.

## Culture and Economy among the Central Sudanians

The features of Central Sudanic economy and environment revealed in vocabulary reconstruction fit well with such a location for the Central Sudanian communities of the last three millennia B.C. Their kinds of subsistence activities and environmental knowledge (tables 11 and 12) indicate that they had access to both open, relatively dry country, such as would have been found along the floor of the Western Rift Valley, and to better-watered, cooler areas, like those that would have lain on each side of the Rift.

In the food-producing aspects of their economy, the Central Sudanic communities were above all cultivators of grains. A variety of terms demonstrative of such cultivation can be reconstructed back to the proto–Central Sudanic (PCS) and proto-East Central Sudanic (ECS) societies. At least two kinds of grains were grown at the PCS period, most probably sorghum and pearl millet, although the semantic reconstructions of the root words for such crops sometimes remain ambiguous (see *ndo and *kɔyɔ below in table 11a). By the start of

## Table 11. Early Central Sudanic food production

*a. Words used in proto–Central Sudanic*

| | | | |
|---|---|---|---|
| *'a | "to cultivate" | *(kɔ)yɔ | "pearl millet (?)" |
| *ŋga | "cleared ground" (ECS "cultivated field") | | (WCS "pearl millet"; Lugbara "red sorghum"; Balendru "finger millet") |
| *ɔɗo | "to weed" | | |
| *ɲa | "to plant seed, sow" | | |
| *re | "to sow" | *'i | "to crush grain" |
| *re | "seed" | *pai | "flour" (?) |
| *kwi | "seed" | *ku | "relish" (added to porridge) |
| *nɔ | "weed" | | |
| *tsɔ | "hoe" | *θa | "uncooked grain" |
| *gba | "granary (raised hut on four posts?)" | *'yi | "beer" |
| | | *ayɔ | "yam (wild?)" |
| *tru | "sesame" (?) | *kuru | "calabash" |
| *aɲa | "grain (generic)" | *kɔɗɔ | "calabash" |
| *pu | "whole (?) grain" | *Tɛɔ | "gourd" |
| *ndɔ | "sorghum (?)" (Moru-Mangbetu "sorghum"; Kresh "finger millet") | *jɔ | "to milk" |
| | | *co | "animal pen" |
| | | *pa | "to exchange (animal)" |

*b. Words used in proto-East Central Sudanic*

| | | | |
|---|---|---|---|
| *p'u | "to reap" | *ga *or* | |
| *pua | "cleared ground" | *ǵa | "calabash bowl" |
| *ŋga | "cultivated field" | *ti | "cow" |
| *kpa | "seed" | *ṭɛmbe | "sheep" |
| *gi | "sorghum" | *mɛmɛ | "goat" |
| *aɲu | "sesame" | *ndri | "goat" |
| *wa | "beer" | *mɛrɔ | "cream" or "curds" |
| *aǵu | "yam" | *θɛ | "to slaughter (animal)" |
| *biɔ | "round gourd" | | |

*c. Words used in proto-West-Central Sudanic*

| | | | |
|---|---|---|---|
| *nẓɔ | "to cultivate" | *ɔko | "yam" |
| *wa | "red sorghum (?)" | *enɛ | "goat" |
| *ɛnde | "ripe (of grain)" | | |

the last millennium B.C., the raising of finger millet was becoming widespread among Central Sudanians, as the Mashariki Bantu adoptions of Central Sudanic loanwords for the crop makes clear (tables 6 and 8). But the sheer variety of the Central Sudanic terms used for finger millet, and the lack of any reconstructible name for the crop, combine in their implication that finger millet at 1000 B.C. was still a relatively recent acquisition of the Sudanic agricultural system. In addition, it seems that Central Sudanians from an early period made use of at least wild yams (see table 11a), and by the ECS period probably cultivated one species of that plant (see table 11b). They also grew a variety of gourds and calabashes throughout their history. But despite the specific evidence that the proto–Central Sudanic people milked some kind of domestic animal (see the reconstructible verb for "to milk" in table 11), the overall vocabulary indications are that livestock keeping had a secondary importance in the values and practical

## Table 12. Central Sudanic residence and environment

*a. Words used in proto–Central Sudanic*

(environment)

| | | | |
|---|---|---|---|
| *le | "dry season" | *ebi | "lion" |
| *mbou | "valley" | *ngbɔrɔ | "lion" |
| *aʈa | "flat rock surface" | *bi | "buffalo" |
| *mu | "(short?) grass" | *gɔ | "leopard" |
| *tsou | "grass" | *ndo | "big feline" (cheetah?) |
| *mbo | "grass stalk" | *lu | "wild dog" (Lycaon) |
| *mongo | "rhinoceros" (?) | *gbɔɛ | "jackal" |

(food collection)

| | | | |
|---|---|---|---|
| *mba | "to hunt" | *nʑo *or* | |
| *we | "harpoon" | *njo | "(flying?) locust" |
| *ya | "fish-basket" | *ngu | "termite" |
| *ni | "edible seeds" | *nʑui | "kind of termite" |
| *ndre | "cricket" | *mɛnoa | "kind of small termite" |
| *mbi | "locust" | | |

(residence)

| | | | |
|---|---|---|---|
| *ɓa | "homestead" | *ci | "out-structure" |
| *mɔ | "place of residence" | *bu | "to plaster (house)" |
| *dzɔ | "house" | | |

79

12. (continued)  Central Sudanic residence and environment

*b.  Words used in proto-East Central Sudanic*

(environment)

| | | | |
|---|---|---|---|
| *tu | "wooded area" | *ka'wa | "leopard" |
| *Sɛ | "grass" | *ŋa(o) | "spotted hyena" |
| *tsa | "grass stalk" | *gɔ | "bushpig" |
| *yi | "(dry) grass" | *jɔɔ | "bushpig" |
| *kwɔ | "elephant" | *tɔ | "hare" |
| *(l)ewa | "elephant" | *wa | "crested crane" |

(food collection)

| | | | |
|---|---|---|---|
| *na | "to be caught in trap" | *ya | "salt-producing grass" |
| *t'e | "to pick, pluck" (fruit, greens)" | *ɓuo | "canoe" |
| | | *θɛ | "locust" |
| *mbɛti | "fish trap" | *mbɛ | "kind of locust" |
| *nʐɔɛ | "hunting net" | *le | "termite" |

(residence)

| | | | |
|---|---|---|---|
| *ku | "homestead" | *'ye | "locale, neighborhood" |

economic considerations that motivated early Central Sudanic people.[5]

Fishing, gathering, and hunting, especially the first of these, would appear also to have remained very important subsistence activities among the Central Sudanic peoples (table 12). In fishing the Sudanians followed a number of different approaches, including catching fish with fish-baskets, using fish traps, and apparently employing barbed harpoons. An additional notable aspect of their food collection practices was the gathering of termites and different kinds of grasshoppers and locusts for food. This kind of collection has great importance among many of the present-day Central Sudanic peoples, and the considerable variety of reconstructible terms for both termites and orthoptera strongly implies that these practices go far back in Central Sudanian history.

The word evidence indicates as well that the early Central Sudanians resided in lands with wooded areas but where grasses formed a major element of the flora. Besides the variety of terms specifically relating to herbaceous ground cover, proto–Central Sudanic and its daughter language proto–East Central Sudanic preserved two distinct words for the lion, an animal of open savanna and of grassland, as well as words for jackal and wild dog, the latter especially an animal of open country (see table 12).

The Central Sudanic residential pattern would appear to have been one of familial homesteads, grouped into dispersed neighborhoods rather than villages. The scanty word evidence as yet available is consistent with their having built round houses with pole walls plastered over with earth, of the type common among the majority of Central Sudanic peoples who reside today in savanna regions (see the verb *bu "to plaster (house)" in table 12a). The homestead (*ɓa) probably comprised at least one main house (*dzu) and could include a lesser dwelling (*ci), perhaps used by adolescents or old folk; a granary, possibly raised off the ground and having the form of a small hut (*gba, in table 11); and a pen for animals (*co, in table 11). The pen's method of construction is not apparent in the available evidence, and whether or not it might have taken the form of a thornbush cattle pen encompassing the whole homestead, as is found among some other Nilo-Saharan peoples, is not known.

## Eastern Sahelians: The Sog and the Southern Rub

The lands of the Eastern Sahelians, in contrast, should be looked for in the west central Nyanza Basin and through the eastern side of the Great Lakes region. The earliest contacts between them and Bantu communities, broadly contemporaneous with the earliest Central Sudanic relations with the speakers of proto-Mashariki, place an Eastern Sahelian society in areas of more open vegetation, probably in southwestern Uganda and possibly around the edges of forested lands in eastern Rwanda and Burundi, to the east of the Rift Valley, and thus immediately east of the earliest Mashariki settlement areas. These contacts probably continued into the Middle Mashariki period (see table 7) and reemerged in the evolution immediately thereafter of the Lakes society (see table 8).

Still later, toward the end of the last millennium B.C. and in the early first millennium A.D., other Eastern Sahelians left their mark in the linguistic record, influencing, sometimes strongly, the ethnic and economic history of the various Mashariki societies that emerged along the south and east of Lake Nyanza. In two cases, those of the Upland and the pre-Langi, the particular Bantu communities ended up settling well to the east of the Great Lakes, respectively in northeastern and north-central Tanzania. But their interactions with Eastern Sahelians were in each case relatively slight (tables 31 and 32) and may simply have been short eras of contact immediately preceding, or possibly just after, their emigration out of the Great Lakes region. The other interactions of Bantu societies with Eastern Sahelian people all unequivocally must be placed in areas near to Lake Nyanza (tables 33–36).

The Eastern Sahelian populations of the Great Lakes can be divided into two groupings. Those along the eastern side of Lake Nyanza (see tables 33–35), as well probably as those located somewhere to the south or southeast of the lake (see tables 31, 32, and 36), spoke languages whose affiliations, from the preponderance of evidence, were with the extant Rub languages. From their locations we can call them the Southern Rub people.[6] The phonological differences revealed in the Rub loanwords in Bantu show that at least two different languages or dialects were spoken among the Southern Rub peoples.[7]

The Eastern Sahelians west of the lake, to whom the name Sog has been applied, seem most probably to have had quite different affiliations from those of the Southern Rub societies (see tables 5, 7, and 8 for loanword material relating to these peoples). The evidence overall is most consistent with their languages having belonged to the Kir subgroup of Eastern Sahelian rather than to Rub. The Kir subgroup comprises the Nilotic languages, today spoken widely across northern and north-central East Africa; the Surmic languages spoken just north of Uganda in the far southeastern Sudan republic; and the Daju, Nyimang, and Temein languages, spoken at present also to the north of East Africa, in southern central parts of the Republic of Sudan.[8]

Probably at least two Sog languages were spoken in the western Nyanza Basin during the last millennium B.C. Differences appear in some of the specific terms used for particular meanings in the different Sog loanword sets, notably for "porridge" (in tables 6, 7, and 8). One phonological difference has also been noted between the Sog word borrowings in proto-Mashariki (see table 5) and Kusi (table 38) and those appearing in Southern-Kaskazi alone (see table 7): the Eastern Sahelian vowel *i became *e after a preceding *b in the Kaskazi set, but not in the other two (see adjunct versions of these tables in the appendix).

Both the Southern Rub and Sog peoples were cultivators of grains and keepers of livestock, including cattle (tables 13 and 14). Until the entrance of Southern Cushites into Nyanza Basin history around the middle of the last millennium B.C., the Sog society would appear to have been the primary example for Bantu speakers in matters of livestock raising (see tables 5 and 7), and they had perhaps an even greater role than Central Sudanians in transmitting the ideas and practices of grain growing to the Mashariki communities (see tables 5, 7, and 8). A significant scatter of subsidiary livestock terms, such as for fresh milk, dewlaps, and animal pens, appears among the loanword evidence (see tables 5 and 7), although cattle and sheep are the only domestic andimals directly attested as yet for the Sog communities (see tables 7 and 8).

Later, at the end of the millennium and during the early first millennium A.D., the Southern Rub peoples along the east of Lake Nyanza had an impact of their own on herding practices and ideology

---

### Table 13.  Sog (Eastern Sahelian) subsistence terminology

*a.  Words attested in proto-Mashariki borrowings (table 5)*

| (livestock) | | (cultivation) | |
|---|---|---|---|
| *baga | "livestock pen" | *bel | "grain sp." |
| *teba, | | *kima | "porridge" |
| *tiba | "livestock pen" | *pupu | "flour (?)" |
| *bolu | "dewlap" | *turi | "mortar" |
| *godu | "dewlap" | *tem | "to cut (vegetation)" |
| *sil- *or* | | | (in clearing land) |
| *sel- | "fresh milk" | | |

*b.  Words attested in late Kaskazi borrowings (table 7)*

| (livestock) | | (cultivation) | |
|---|---|---|---|
| *kolo | "sheep" | *ter *or* | "prepared grain" |
| *belele | "sheep" | *tir | |

*c.  Words attested in Langi borrowings (table 32)*

| (livestock) | | (cultivation) | |
|---|---|---|---|
| *bolo | "dewlap" | *doŋa | "granary (hut)" |

*d.  Words attested in proto-Lakes borrowings (table 8)*

| (livestock) | | (cultivation) | |
|---|---|---|---|
| *te | "cow" | *seda | "porridge" |
| *ka | "cattle" | | |

## Table 14. Rub subsistence terminology

a. *Proto-Rub*[9]

(cultivation)

| | | | |
|---|---|---|---|
| *ir | "to cultivate" | *rab | "finger millet" |
| *ɗo | "to weed" | *ŋam | "sorghum" |
| *ŋɔ | "to grind grain" | *mosid | "kind of bean" |
| *cayp | "cleared land" | *mɛs | "beer" |

(livestock)

| | | | |
|---|---|---|---|
| *eakw | "to herd" | *ɗodo | "sheep" |
| *ɓore' | "thornbush cattle pen" | *mek | "ram" |
| *sara | "thorn-fence of pen" | *kɔra' | "wether" |
| *asak | "gate of pen" | *wɛras | "ewe lamb, young she-goat" |
| *ɬɔ' | "cow (generic)" | | |
| *kiruk | "bull" | *ɟɛt | "goat" |
| *ɟail | "ox, steer" | *kol | "he-goat" |
| *kɔrɔb | "calf" | *jut | "to milk" |

b. *Southern Rub dialect attested in table 31*

(livestock)

| | | | |
|---|---|---|---|
| *ɓoro | "cattle pen" | *sara | "hedge, thornfence" |

c. *Southern Rub dialect attested in table 33*

(cultivation)

| | |
|---|---|
| *ɓus | "to do second digging in clearing field" |

d. *Southern Rub dialect attested in table 34*

| (cultivation) | | (livestock) | |
|---|---|---|---|
| *jut | "very big calabash" | *mik | "ram" |
| *seed | "half-calabash" | *kole | "he-goat" |
| *oopo | "kind of calabash | *koola | "small hoe" |

e. *Southern Rub dialect(s) attested in table 35*

(livestock)

| | | | |
|---|---|---|---|
| *sarate | "cattle pen" | *korope | "he-goat" |
| *g̊ain | "bull" | *juudu | "ewe-lamb" |
| *taaŋan | "ox" | | |

among the neighboring Bantu communities, in particular those living near the east and southeastern sides of the lake. The loanword record in this case directly testifies to the Southern Rub raising of sheep and goats as well as cows (see tables 33–35), and to their cultivation of a variety of calabashes (see table 34). As yet, however, there are no direct indications that they raised grain crops (see table 13). But the cultivation of grains had certainly long been known to their Rub relatives farther north in northeastern Uganda during the last millennium B.C. (as the proto-Rub root words in table 14 show), and thus seems most probably to have been practiced by the Southern Rub, too.

The Sog and Southern Rub peoples may well have followed the pattern common among other cattle-raising Eastern Sahelians, of residing in neighborhoods of scattered homesteads. This proposition has indirect support in the word evidence of homestead layout, which certainly for the Southern Rub communities, and probably for the Sog people, could include a thornbush cattle pen enclosing the homestead (for Southern Rub words for cattle pens and thorn fences, see table 14; for Sog terms for pens of uncertain construction, see table 13). The Southern Rub communities, in some cases at least, also built the raised hutlike style of granary to store their grain crops (see table 32). From comparative cultural evidence, Eastern Sahelians such as the Sog and Southern Rub peoples might be expected to have constructed round dwellings with conical roofs, but direct lexical testimony of that practice is lacking as yet.

## Southern Cushites in the Southern Nyanza Basin

The Southern Cushites who partook of this history all spoke languages that—along with the existing West Rift tongues, Iraqw, Gorowa, Burunge, and Alagwa—belong in an expanded West Rift subbranch of the Rift branch of Southern Cushitic. This revised West Rift group can be divided into two subgroups: Highland West Rift, composed of the modern languages spoken in Mbulu and Kondoa districts of Tanzania, and Tale,[10] consisting of the extinct languages once spoken in the southern Nyanza Basin. The Tale peoples were probably pressing into the areas south of Lake Nyanza no later than the middle of the last millennium B.C. Their direction of expansion would have been westward out of the Mara and Serengeti regions.

They appear as a major new factor during the emergence of the Lakes society and also shortly thereafter during the period of existence of the Southern-Nyanza cluster of Bantu societies. The words adopted in both contact situations were varied in their implications and in the latter instance fairly numerous. The scale of the impact of the Tale communities on their Bantu neighbors is indicated in the Bantu adoption in both eras of even some basic words. It should be noted, however, that one of the basic words, for "blood," separately borrowed twice (see table 9 and also 1B in appendix), is likely to reflect acquaintance with a new cultural practice, the bleeding of cattle, and, in the case of some of the Southern-Nyanza communities, the actual adoption of the practice. As the Southern-Nyanza grouping broke up toward the close of the last millennium B.C., the Kati continued to be heavily influenced by a Tale people, although not to the extent of adopting any basic vocabulary.

The early Southern Cushites in Kenya certainly had a close acquaintance with cultivation of grains. This conclusion is amply revealed in the reconstructed proto–Southern Cushitic vocabulary of crops and cultivated food (table 27, in chapter 6). But they tended to give livestock raising an at least equally important role in their subsistence practices (Table 15). By the last millennium B.C., many of the Cushites, especially those tending their herds in the Eastern Rift region in central Kenya, emphasized livestock raising almost to the exclusion of cultivation.[11] The Tale Southern Cushites would seem to have been heirs to that way of life, for the outstanding characteristic throughout their interactions with Bantu-speaking groups was the adoption by those Bantu of Tale livestock terminology of all kinds. Even when, as in the proto-Lakes dialect, cultivating terms were being borrowed contemporaneously from Sog, Rub, and Central Sudanians, little or nothing in the way of cultivation vocabulary came from the Southern Cushites (see tables 8–10 and 12). Evidently, the Tale peoples were above all cattle raisers, conceivably growing no grains themselves.

Do the origins of the specialized pastoralists of later western Great Lakes history lie among these particular Southern Cushites? It seems entirely probable that this was so, since none of the other non-Bantu peoples just west of Lake Nyanza show anything at all similar in the way of economic specialization.

In the last stages of the breakup of the Southern-Nyanza group and of the Kati society, several of the different descendant communities moved far eastward across East Africa and began a variety of contacts with other Southern Cushites. These histories will be dealt with in chapter 6.

Table 15.  Southern Cushitic livestock vocabulary

*a. Words used in proto–Southern Cushitic*

| | | | |
|---|---|---|---|
| *ɖeʔ- | "to herd" | *ʔogur- | "he-goat" |
| *raxʷ- | "to bleed cattle" | *ʕaʔa *or* | |
| *ɖe | "herd (of cattle)" | *ʔaʔa | "sheep" |
| *kʷ'atʸ'ara | "cattle transaction" | *rangana | "lamb, kid" |
| *yaakʷ- | "cattle (pl., coll.)" | *legeʔ- | "male kid, male |
| *ɬee | "cow | | lamb, bull-calf (?)" |
| *yawo | "bull" | *dakʷ'- | "donkey" |
| *ⁿkol- | "steer, ox" | *ʔilem- | "to milk" |
| *ɖama | "heifer (?)" | *ʔiliba | "milk" |
| *ʔaf- | "goat" | *fahara | "fresh milk" |
| *ɬaḥ- | "goat (?)" | *ʕat- | "sour milk" |

*b. Words used in early Rift Southern Cushitic*

| | | | |
|---|---|---|---|
| *gʷad- | "calf" (E. Rift) | *daxʷat- | "lamb" (W. Rift) |

# Southern Nilotes of the Eastern Great Lakes Region

A final grouping of peoples of some significance in Great Lakes history were the Southern Nilotes. A fuller look at the historical background, the culture history, and the roles of Southern Nilotes in the Later Classical Age of Eastern Africa will be taken in chapter 6.

The initial contacts between Bantu and Southern Nilotic communities came toward the end of the Southern-Nyanza period, around about the last three centuries B.C. They apparently involved just those Bantu communities who formed the eastern or northeastern outliers of the Southern-Nyanza areal grouping, namely, the pre-Luyia, East-Nyanza, and Upland. The principal territories of the Nilotes who participated in this encounter lay eastward, on the Mara plains, and for that reason we can call them the Mara Southern Nilotes. The Mara Southern Nilotes, like the Tale Southern Cushites, apparently concentrated their energies on livestock raising. In fact, except for two words indicative of more general Southern Nilote influences, the loanword set consists almost entirely of livestock terms (see table 10).

As the last millennium B.C. drew to a close, the era of close interactions between the Mara people and the linguistic forebears of the

Upland, East-Nyanza, and Luyia, too, came to an end. Both the Luyia and some of the East-Nyanza-speaking peoples had later important relations with different Southern Nilotic societies. That history has been covered in other works and will also be touched on in chapter 6. The Upland society had a brief era of relations of their own with a Southern Nilotic people (again, see chapter 6), but these contacts very possibly took place farther east, in northeastern Tanzania, after the Upland people moved out of the Great Lakes region.

# Archeological Expectations, Linguistic Indications

## Before the Classical Age: The Great Lakes to 1000 B.C.

Taken as an interlocking whole, the linguistic-historical picture for the wider Great Lakes region, c. 1000–100 B.C., presents a social and economic panorama of shifting encounter among societies, each period and set of developments overlapping others in both time and place. That history itself rests in part on foundations laid down in the preceding Great Lakes neolithic era, for which as yet only a less dynamic portrait can be sketched out and in which the focal figures were Central Sudanians and Eastern Sahelians.

The initial divergence of the Central Sudanic group into its West and East branches needs to be placed not later than the fifth millennium, and possibly as early as 5000 B.C.[12] The result of that split was the development of two societies: (1) the proto-West-Central Sudanic society, from which derive the later Kreish-Aja and Bongo-Bagirmi subgroups of languages, and (2) the proto-East Central Sudanic society, out of which came four subsequent groupings of peoples, the Moru-Madi, Balendru, Balese-Mamvu, and Mangbetu. The linguistic geography of their dispersals places the proto-West communities in the Bahr-el-Ghazal region, probably around the latitude and longitude of Wau, and the proto-East society to the southeast of there, centering most probably on the modern West Nile area of Uganda and including areas immediately adjoining in northeastern Congo (Zaire) and far southern Sudan.

By about 3000 B.C., the proto-East Central Sudanic society itself was beginning its progressive divergence into several successor societies—a history the details of which lie mostly outside the scope of this book. One direction of expansion in this period, judging from the locations of early Central Sudanic contact with Bantu speakers, would have been southward along the Western Rift. Moving into areas of later key importance to the early Mashariki communities, these East Central Sudanians have direct relevance to the story told here. The evidence for forest retreat in Kigezi by about 3000 B.C. may be an indirect indication that a few East Central Sudanians had moved even that early as far as south as southwestern Uganda.[13]

The settlement of the Sog peoples in the central and eastern Nyanza Basin can be followed with less clarity. Their movements into lands west of Lake Nyanza could conceivably have taken place as early as the first East Central Sudanian spread into the northern edges of the Western Rift zone, c. 3000 B.C., or as late as 1000 B.C., in time to influence the incoming settlement of Mashariki Bantu. The Southern Rub peoples, because of the close affiliation of their languages or dialects to the modern-day Rub group, need not have moved in along the west side of Lake Nyanza before the later second millennium or the early last millennium B.C. The differences among their languages by end of the B.C.'s, as indicated in the early Bantu borrowings of Southern Rub words (see tables 31–36), are enough to suggest, however, that their expansions out of northern Uganda could hardly have begun much later than 1000 B.C. and conceivably they, too, could have established themselves in the Nyanza Basin centuries earlier.

At around 1000 B.C., then, at the threshhold of early Mashariki settlement, the Great Lakes region can be seen already to have been home to several food-producing societies (see map 3).

Parts of the Western Rift region would have been occupied by Central Sudanic communities. Their domestic economy, as revealed in their influences on the early Mashariki society, requires them to have lived in environments where grains, most notably finger millet, could be grown. In other words, the Central Sudanic lands are likely to have lain at the edges of the montane environments on either or both sides of the Rift. Knowledge of cattle and of milking of some kind of livestock is indicated in the reconstructible proto-East Central Sudanic vocabulary, but, as argued above, the loanword evidence from Mashariki does not indicate that these were more than minor or peripheral economic pursuits. The Central Sudanians can be expected, in addition, to have made significant use of fish in their diets.[14] They fashioned pots, which show up well in the archeological record, but they can also be argued from the evidence of their vocabulary histories to have lived in neighborhoods of scattered homesteads, which will have a much lower visibility than villages. The archeology of their presence has still to be sought.

Somewhat farther east lay the country of the Sog people. These communities very possibly occupied parts of the savanna zones of western Uganda and may have extended also south into eastern Rwanda and Burundi. The vocabulary evidence favors this kind of environment for them. In particular, Sog loanwords in early Mashariki show them to have been raisers of grains, principally sorghum and pearl millet, and in some degree keepers of cattle as well as sheep and goats. Other loanword evidence implies that the Sog resided, like the Central Sudanians, in homesteads rather than villages.

Farther afield, another grouping of Eastern Sahelians, the Southern Rub peoples, had already spread out, or were in the process of expanding, into areas just east of Lake Nyanza. Like the Sog, these communities raised cattle and grains. The Southern Rub utilized a variety of calabash containers. The Sog society may well also have utilized calabashes, but what stands out in the available evidence is their making of carved wooden containers (see table 5).

The Southern Rub groups and the Sog communities were surely both makers of pottery. But for neither society is that skill directly attested in the loanwords they have bequeathed to the languages of their Bantu-speaking successors. As would be true for the Central Sudanians, Rub and Sog wares, if they existed, should be found easily enough, but their habitations perhaps less easily.

There is in fact one very strong candidate for the archeology of the Southern Rub society, namely, the Oltome (or Kansyore) tradition.[15] The known distribution of Oltome ware extends over exactly the regions where the several postulated Rub populations can be placed—on the eastern side of Lake Nyanza and in locations to the south and southeast of the lake, along with a northerly facies, known from a site just north of the northeastern Uganda border, close to the lands where the proto-Rub would have lived.[16] It just might be time to start accepting that the association of Oltome pottery and cattle bones in several Oltome archeological sites is real.

Oltome ware has also been reported from the immediate west of Lake Nyanza and from islands in the lake. There it might be associated, if those finds do validly relate to the Oltome tradition, with the Sog society, or else with a peripheral extension of Southern Rub influences into those areas.

Finally, scattered throughout the Great Lakes region, and coexisting in various fashions with the several food-producing societies, there persisted for several centuries longer gatherer-hunter communities about which the language evidence has as yet little to tell us. Through the eastern and southern portions of the Nyanza Basin, Wilton-like microlithic tool assemblages prevailed into the last millennium B.C. indicating the more ancient historical connections of their

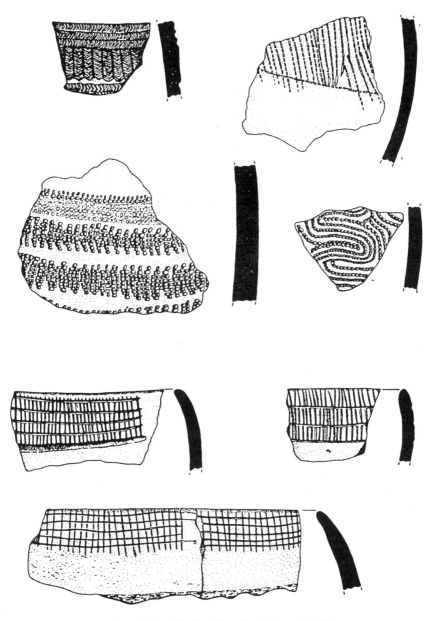

Figure 1. Ceramics of the Early Classical Age, I. Oltome pottery, *top*; Elmenteitan pottery, *bottom* (Robertshaw 1991).

makers with the older foraging societies of Tanzania, eastern Kenya, and other regions to the east and south.[17] The collective name we can give to these stone tool industries is the "Eastern African Microlithic." The existence in central Tanzania today of two relict Khoisan speech communities—the Sandawe, who cultivate and herd animals, and the Hadza, who until very recently still just gathered and hunted—together with the presence of Khoisan loanwords in early Southern Cushitic languages show that all the regions marked by Eastern African Microlithic cultures formerly were the lands of Khoisan-speaking societies.[18]

In the region of Rwanda and Burundi, in contrast, the food collectors would have been peoples with earlier historical connection to the gatherer-hunters of the equatorial rainforest to the west. Their descendants today are the BaTwa of those areas. The existence there before the iron age of a different ancient stone tool tradition, with affinities to the Tshitolian of the Congo Basin, confirms that connection.

## Transformations of the Early Classical Age

Over the course of the last millennium B.C., a new and expanding ethnic and economic presence, composed of early Mashariki communities, made itself felt over progressively wider parts of this region, stimulating a series of interethnic encounters that transformed the demography and economy of the Great Lakes region itself and set in motion changes that in the longer run would rearrange ethnicity and economy all across the eastern side of Africa. We can envision these developments as a series of overlapping periods of cultural and economic interaction.

Initially, roughly between 1000 and 500 B.C., came two successive periods of change involving the early Mashariki communities. In the first period, the Early Mashariki era, three different societies came into contact across a region extending possibly from Lake Rweru on the north to the north parts of Lake Tanganyika in the south, and from the west side of the Mitumba Range to the Katonga-Kagera Basins. In western parts of this region, and probably beginning first, Central Sudanians were influential neighbors of the Mashariki; on the eastern side of this expanse, Sog peoples held the same kind of position. As the first period progressed, dialect differences began to take shape within the proto-Mashariki language. At the same time the Mashariki communities would gradually have been expanding their territories, especially southward down the Western Rift through the

Lake Tanganyika region and away from the early contact areas. This development had the consequence of splitting the early Mashariki into two wider areal groupings of communities, the Kusi, composed of those who spread to the south, and the Kaskazi, consisting of those remaining close to the region of initial settlement (see map 3).

With this development the first period came to an end, and the Middle Mashariki era, in which the Kaskazi communities continued to be influenced by Central Sudanians and Sog peoples, took shape. Meanwhile the dialect differences, already incipient in the first period, continued to grow among the Kaskazi peoples. By the end of the period, well before the middle of the last millennium B.C., as many as eight distinct dialects had appeared (see chapter 2). For a time at least four of the more southerly of these dialects formed a Southern-Kaskazi cluster. The later overall positioning of Kaskazi communities suggests their initial habitation of areas along and just eastward from the Western Rift, not improbably from south of Lake Rweru to Burundi; and thus the Central Sudanic people with whom they had important contacts are also best placed in areas distinctly to the east of the Western Rift, possibly in or around the Kigezi region and perhaps in parts of northwestern Rwanda. The Lakes community arose near or to the north of Kigezi, while the Southern-Kaskazi communities resided probably in more southerly parts (see map 5).

Once again, the end of a period can be defined by the breaking up of the wider areal grouping of communities. In the case of the Kaskazi cluster, two processes were apparently taking place. One was the entire moving away from the region of several dialect communities—the Rufiji-Ruvuma, Kilombero, Mwika, and Rungwe—who spread southward, perhaps initially along the west of Lake Tanganyika but ultimately, by the close of the last millennium B.C., into southern Tanzania. The second was the wide spreading out of the remaining Kaskazi, apparently from the east side of the Western Rift toward the southern shores of Lake Nyanza. Four groupings of communities occupied different portions of this expanse. The Lakes cluster resided somewhere between Ruwenzori and Bukoba; the Kati, perhaps in or near modern Geita area; and the Upland and the pre-Langi possibly near western Mwanza.

These two eras can be projected back broadly to the first half of the millennium: the Early Mashariki period perhaps as early as 1000–800 B.C., and the Middle Mashariki era to somewhere in the centuries 800–500 B.C. During this span there may have been some absorbing of particularly Central Sudanic speakers into early Mashariki society. But the weight of the vocabulary evidence (see tables 4–7) indicates that acquisition of new agricultural and other technology and of new knowledge of the natural world were the primary outcomes of these encounters. The early Mashariki, down to the end of the Middle Mashariki period, it can be proposed, largely expanded by taking up lands, especially the more heavily forested areas below about 1,600 or 1,700 meters that had not been extensively used by the earlier food-producing societies. The Bantu more often moved between and around the areas of the other cultivating peoples than came into direct territorial conflict with them.

What should be expected from the Great Lakes archeology of these eras is a gradually emerging mosaic of the different populations, with the distributions of the Mashariki Bantu, Central Sudanians, Sog, and Rub within the Great Lakes region showing considerable correspondence to the varieties of environment. The Central Sudanians especially should be found near the edges of montane forest at the far west, making a pottery yet to be identified. Sog societies, with or without pottery, should be looked for in drier areas between the Western Rift and Lake Nyanza. The early Mashariki, with several pottery wares belonging to the Chifumbaze Complex, should appear first along the immediate west of the rift and soon afterward in western Rwanda and Burundi, spreading out thereafter through a growing number of areas, in, around, and among the lands of the other two sets of peoples.

To the south of the western Great Lakes region, a different pattern would have emerged contemporaneous with the Middle Mashariki period. There a southward spread of Kusi communities should nearly everywhere have overlapped with gatherer-hunter assemblages. An early grouping of closely similar Chifumbaze potteries dating to the latter first half of the last millennium B.C., possibly yet to be excavated along the west of Lake Tanganyika, can be expected to account for Kusi divergence out of the early Mashariki communities (see chapter 7). The subsequent southward spread, in the Late Mashariki period, of the Rufiji-Ruvuma, Kilombero, Mwika, and Rungwe peoples from the Kaskazi cluster should similarly show up in the appearance of Chifumbaze wares to the south, perhaps at first along the east side of Lake Tanganyika and then, late in the millennium, in or near the Mbeya region and elsewhere to the north and northeast of Lake Nyasa (Lake Malawi).

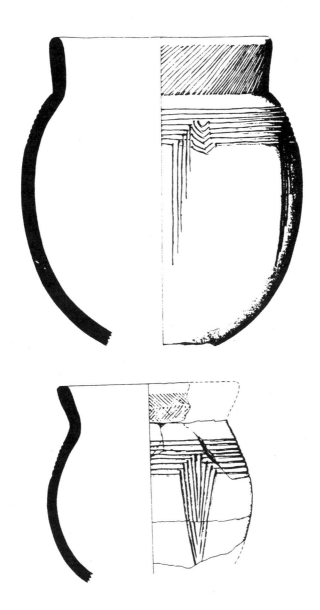

Figure 2. Ceramics of the Early Classical Age, II. Pottery from Mbuga, Burundi (early Kaskazi peoples of the Western Rift region) (van Grunderbeek et al. 1983).

Developments in the Southern Nyanza Basin

Within the Great Lakes region proper, the Late Mashariki period, as we have called the closing phase of the Early Classical Age, had one particularly notable regional manifestation, the Southern-Nyanza era of multifaceted cultural contacts. The transition to the Southern-Nyanza period began a bit after mid-millennium with two roughly concurrent developments. One was the settlement, already described, of the Kati, Upland, and pre-Langi dialect communities along the south or southwestern side of Lake Nyanza. The second was the expansion and resulting divergence of the Lakes society into four dialect communities, the Western-Lakes, West-Nyanza, East-Nyanza, and pre-Luyia. Out of this divergence came the movements of the East-Nyanza and pre-Luyia, who followed the Kati, Upland, and pre-Langi into the lands to the south of Lake Nyanza and, in so doing, completed the formative stage of the Southern-Nyanza era.

The Southern-Nyanza era was characterized above all by the appearance of a major new set of actors on the Great Lakes historical stage, the Tale Southern Cushites. Their presence was strongly and extensively asserted across the expanding Kaskazi territories of the second half of the last millennium B.C. All in all, the evidence gives the impression that the Tale were themselves a recently intrusive group, expanding westward from north central Tanzania not long before or even as Kaskazi communities spread eastward. Their initial influences appeared at the very inception of the Southern-Nyanza era, in a set of loanwords restricted to proto-Lakes and its emerging dialects and dating perhaps to around the fifth century, give or take a century. Thereafter, for probably two or three centuries, the major focus of Tale influence lay among the shifting mosaic of Southern-Nyanza Bantu communities, most centrally influencing the speakers of the Upland, pre-Langi, and Kati dialects (see map 6).

One notable feature can be expected in the archeology of the immediate post-Kaskazi era west of Lake Nyanza. The proto-Lakes period in all probability marks the beginning of the end of environmental correlation with ethnicity. All three loanword sets adopted into the proto-Lakes dialect and its major daughter dialects (see tables 8–9) include some basic words, and no longer consist overwhelmingly of the vocabulary of knowledge new to Bantu speakers. They indicate that Central Sudanians and Eastern Sahelians, and probably Tale people as well, were widely being assimilated into the Lakes society, as part of the process of its divergence into several daughter societies. And the territorial implications of that contemporaneous division of proto-Lakes into daughter dialects are fully in keeping with this conclusion. The Lakes communities, these data require, rapidly spread out over most of the western Nyanza Basin after the end of the Middle Mashariki period. In the archeology these developments should be marked by both a major proliferation of sites attributable to the Urewe variety of Chifumbaze and a rapid decline in sites attributable to other traditions, including surely those of the remaining gatherer-hunters.

How the Tale Southern Cushitic populations will be manifested in the archeological record is less clear. As West Rift Southern Cushites, their pottery should belong to the Oldishi tradition described above. Their presence should be looked for across the lands extending west from Serengeti through the Mara plains to as far east as Bukoba, to account for their impact on the late Lakes society; and the beginning of their expansions westward toward the Great Lakes region would have to belong to the first half of the last millennium B.C. In the currently known archeology, only some of their early, more easterly sites can yet be given probable identification: these occur specifically in the Mara region, dating from the ninth to the fifth century B.C.,[19] just as the language evidence would require.

But for the areas around to the south and west of Lake Nyanza, Tale Southern Cushitic sites may, in two respects, be more problematic to identify. The first has to do with the strength of their specialization in pastoral pursuits, as indicated in their loanwords to both the Lakes society and the Southern-Nyanza areal grouping of communities. Might they have become transhumant pastoralists who left relatively ephemeral sites, at least in some parts of their territories? The second has to do with the kinds of economic relations they established with their more cultivation-oriented Bantu neighbors. If they were very mobile people, or if the sort of symbiosis of herders and cultivators seen in the later western Great Lakes history emerged very early, then the Tale may already have found it more convenient to trade for pottery with their neighbors than any longer to make their own.

## The Close of an Era: Further Archeological Expectations

As the last millennium B.C. drew to an end, the continuing territorial spreading out of Southern-Nyanza communities took them eastward into new contact situations, and created a new areal grouping, probably located at the southeast of Lake Nyanza, composed, from north to south, of the pre-Luyia, East-Nyanza, and Upland dialect communities. Together they entered for a time into bidirectional con-

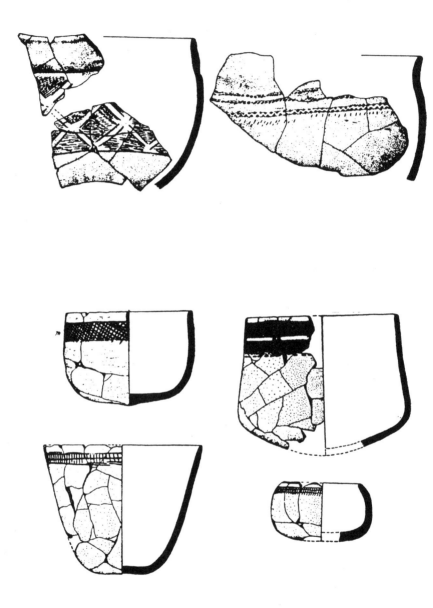

Figure 3. Ceramics of the Early Classical Age, III. Olmalenge pottery, northern Kenya, *top* (Ma'a Southern Cushites?) (Barthelme 1977). Oldishi pottery, southern Kenya, *bottom* (Rift Southern Cushites) (Odner 1972).

tacts, continuing to interact with a Tale people but at the same time being deeply influenced by Southern Nilotes in their livestock-raising and apparently, to some extent, in their initiation customs. These latter contacts place the Southern Nilotes, who can be identified with the makers of the Elmenteitan tradition,[20] in the Mara plains, as eastward-extending neighbors of the Bantu groups. This Southern Nilotic society, the archeology reveals, had displaced the earlier Tale Southern Cushitic populations of those areas by around 400 B.C.[21] Also toward the close of the millennium, farther to the west and probably to the immediate south of Lake Nyanza, the Kati dialect community continued to have very important relations of their own with Tale Southern Cushites, but with a somewhat different Tale community than they did during the immediately preceding Southern-Nyanza era.

Finally, around the last century or two B.C., the Southern-Nyanza connection came fully to an end, with the East-Nyanza and pre-Luyia moving northward into areas of significant Southern Rub populations. These people, it has been argued here, would have made pottery belonging to the Oltome tradition. The Upland and pre-Langi also each briefly encountered Southern Rub people, possibly in the southeast Lake Nyanza region, but possibly in other areas of northern Tanzania, after moving eastward out of the Nyanza Basin. Two sets of Kati communities also passed eastward across Tanzania during the same centuries, leaving the Great Lakes behind. Loanwords in the Takama language, spoken by those Kati populations who stayed in the southern Nyanza Basin, show that Tale Southern Cushites and a Southern Rub population continued to exist for some time in those areas before finally being absorbed by the Bantu speakers. Along the east side of the lake, Southern Rub, Southern Nilotic, and Southern Cushitic peoples persisted, sometimes down to recent centuries, as significant historical actors.[22]

Together, these later eras of encounter between Central Sudanians, Sog, Rub, Cushites, and Bantu speakers map a situation of some diversity in ethnic background and therefore in expected archeological correlations. Tale Southern Cushites, though a declining factor, probably continued as a distinct group just south of Lake Nyanza for some centuries into the first millennium A.D. Extending across the Mara plains south of the Mau Range, almost as far east in some cases as the southeastern shore of the lake, would have been Southern Nilotes. Their presence will be attested in sites belonging to the Elmenteitan tradition and showing extensive, probably specialized livestock raising.

Northward up the east side of the lake, sites attributable to the early Luyia and East-Nyanza Bantu settlers, with Urewe pottery, should be found after the beginning of the first millennium A.D., while away from the lakeshore, Oltome sites, indicative of Southern Rub communities, should also be present. Word evidence from the North-Mara subgroup of the East-Nyanza Bantu shows as well that another Southern Cushitic people resided in the region, probably in the higher country to the east of the lake and possibly toward the modern Kisii and Kericho areas.[23] In Robertshaw's excavations at Gogo Falls,[24] we have already tangible evidence of the ethnic complexity that the linguistic analysis so strongly requires for the southeastern Nyanza region. Much the same variety of cultures also characterized the areas north of the Wami Gulf during the first millennium A.D.,[25] but even less of that complexity has yet been given archeological visibility.

These latter developments belong more properly, however, to the Later Classical Age, and so we will have more to say about their consequences for the evolution of pre-Luyia and East-Nyanza societies in chapter 6.

To this point the trends and patterns of human settlement in the formative centuries of the Classical Age, c. 1000 up to about the third century B.C., have been our primary concern. Of the varieties of human cultural encounter that resulted across western parts of East Africa, and of the often sweeping realignment of lives and livelihoods that emerged in those centuries, we have said relatively little. It is time now to speak to these issues. The shifting material circumstances of life in the Early Classical Age draw our attention first, in chapter 4. In chapter 5 we move on to explore the history of custom and belief among the Eastern African peoples of that age.

# Notes

1 Schoenbrun 1990.
2 Ehret, Okihiro, et al. 1973.
3 Crazzolara 1950–54; Atkinson 1994.
4 Schoenbrun 1990.
5 The reconstructed Central Sudanic root words, as before, are from Ehret 1992.
6 A majority of the borrowed words attributable to these Southern Rub are specifically attested in the present-day Rub languages, and a number of them show specifically Rub innovations in meaning or phonology. For example, the Nilo-Saharan ejectives *ṱ', *t', and *c' were all collapsed into one sound, either *ts' or

*c' in different dialects of the Southern Rub language, just as they were in Rub. The resulting consonant was therefore reinterpreted in Bantu languages as the nearest similar Bantu sound, the fricative *s (or in Guthrie's transcription as *c) when the sound was pronounced [ts'] in the particular Southern Rub dialect, and *j when the sound was pronounced [c'].

[7] The separate borrowed forms of the word for "wild dog" in table 3B indicate, for instance, that one Southern Rub society had *ts' and the other *c' for the consonant just discussed in the previous paragraph. Similarly, two different outcomes characterized the Southern Rub versions of non-initial proto-Nilo-Saharan *ḷ, one result seen in table 33 and the other in the data of tables 34 and 35.

[8] A Nilotic or, for that matter, Rub provenance for the loanwords in tables 5, 7, and 8 is specifically ruled out in a considerable number of instances by phonological criteria, such as the attestation of *t in a loanword where a Nilotic source would have had *d, or of *g where Nilotic or Rub would be expected to show *k (see tables 5A, 7A, and 8A in the appendix). Several words among the loans are known so far only from Nilotic or only from Rub examples—in particular, the Nilotic words for "mud," "bog," and "porridge" in table 5, and the Rub terms for "cultivated field" in table 8 and for a young male in both tables. But none of these words evinces innovations in pronunciation that would specifically require Nilotic or Rub sources for them. The best solution on present evidence is that the Sog language belonged the Kir branch of Eastern Sahelian, but to a subgroup of Kir distinct from Nilotic. Earlier contacts in northern Uganda between the Sog and the Southern Rub peoples, and between the Sog peoples and the early Nilotes, would sufficiently explain the presence in the Sog language of the several words found today only in Rub or only in Nilotic tongues.

[9] Proto-Rub terms are drawn from Heine 1976, Ehret 1981b, and Ehret in press.

[10] This name was proposed in Schoenbrun 1990.

[11] Ambrose 1986.

[12] Ehret 1993.

[13] Hamilton et al 1986; but cf. Taylor 1990.

[14] Saxon 1980.

[15] Robertshaw and Collett 1983.

[16] Ehret 1982c.

[17] Ambrose 1982.

[18] Ehret 1980b.

[19] Robertshaw 1993.

[20] This correlation was first established in Ambrose 1982.

[21] Robertshaw 1993.

[22] E.g., Ehret 1976a.

[23] Ehret 1974b.
[24] Robertshaw 1991.
[25] Ehret 1976a.

# 4. Regional Trends and Developments

The cross-cultural encounters of the Early Classical Age set in motion a variety of historical processes of wide, regional scope across most parts of western East Africa. Of particular importance over the course of the last millennium B.C. were changes in demography, residential practices, and subsistence economy. Population grew overall, especially among the Bantu-speaking societies; new kinds of residential layout and construction and new sorts of household equipment were adopted in many areas; and new combinations and distributions of agricultural activities took shape. It was a period also of increasing shift all across the Great Lakes region from stone to iron-tool technology—the age of metals had begun.

## Economic Geography and Demographic History

### Population Distributions in Early First Millennium B.C.

The Central Sudanians and the Sog and Rub at 1000 B.C. need not have been numerous peoples. The Central Sudanic communities, it has been suggested, made use of only a limited range of territories in or around the Western Rift; and environments in the Nyanza Basin that were well suited to the settlement of cattle-keeping Sog communities may have been still scattered and not extensive at that period. Limited clearing of wooded land had already a long history in some areas of the basin.[1] But in general the heavier forest remained in place, and the savanna of the western Nyanza Basin was probably not yet the kind of open grassland that would have been largely free of tsetse-fly.

The older gatherer-hunter societies in this kind of situation may still have formed the majority population element across the Great Lakes region as a whole; and indeed Oltome pottery may, in a majority of the sites discovered so far, actually have belonged to gatherer-hunters who obtained it through trade from food-producing Eastern Sahelian neighbors. In addition, at such an early period in the opening up of land to agriculture, the food producers themselves, as the example of Meso-America indicates, are likely still to have relied on collected foods for a considerable portion of their own caloric intake. And, finally, because of environmental constraints, the ratio of live-stock to people in both the Sog and Southern Rub, and even more so in the Central Sudanic, societies may often have been low. With so few Oltome sites so far discovered, none more than sparsely investi-gated, it should thus not be surprising that the issue of whether any of them show unequivocal evidence of cattle raising remains contentious.

The earliest Mashariki settlers, too, must at first have been rela-tively few. They, as well as their Central-Savanna Bantu neighbors to the west, probably followed cultivating practices—similar to those identified by Mary McMaster as historically old among the Buans of the Congo Basin—that depended on very long fallow times and fol-lowed tilling techniques that made a minimal intrusion into the surface of the land.[2] The range of crops cultivated among those Bantu of three thousand years ago was not wide: it included several kinds of yams as the staples, supplemented by a legume, probably the black-eyed pea, the Voandzeia groundnut, the castor bean, and apparently two kinds of cucurbits, the bottle gourd and the edible gourd (*Cucumerops edulis*).[3] They bred and raised just two animals, the goat and the guineafowl (Table 16).[4] Hunting and, above all, fishing re-mained extremely important subsistence activities (table 22 below).

Of the two domestic animals, goats have been kept by Bantu-speaking peoples from their earliest period as a distinctive set of so-cieties. The tending of the guineafowl seems likely to have been just as old among them. These fowl are raised today in just the kind of wide, relict scatter through the Bantu-speaking regions, including parts of East Africa, that is typical of old features of material culture; and they must be considered therefore to have been a feature of the Early Classical economies of the Mashariki communities. The guineafowl is likely, like the chicken of later eras, to have often been allowed to for-age for itself. It would have been in that sense, then, a partially rather than a wholly domestic creature, capable on occasion of interbreeding with wild forms. That kind of relationship between human and animal makes intelligible the shift by many Mashariki communities to the rearing of an Eastern African species of guineafowl different from the species looked after by their West African and Savanna-Bantu cultural forebears. The old feature of culture, seen in this light, was the eco-nomic reliance on tending the guineafowl, whereas the choice of guineafowl species to be kept could change in keeping with a chang-ing environmental context of human settlement.

104

---

### Table 16. Early Bantu food-production terms

a. *Proto-Bantu terms*

(cultivation)

| | | | |
|---|---|---|---|
| *-kùá | "yam" | *-bòndò | "raffia palm" |
| *-pàmá | "yam" | *-làgù | "palm wine" |
| *-kúndè | "black-eyed peas" | *-gùndà | "cultivated field" |
| *-jùgú | "Voandzeia groundnut" | | (domestic animals) |
| *-bónò | "castor bean" | | |
| *-súpá | "bottle gourd" | *-búlì | "goat" |
| *-bɨ́là | "oil palm" | *-boko | "he-goat" |
| *-bá | "oil palm" | *-kángà | "guineafowl" |
| *-gàlɨ́ | "oil palm nut" | | |

b. *Additional terms of Savanna-Bantu provenance*

(crops)                                    (domestic animals)

| | | | |
|---|---|---|---|
| *-lungu | "yam" | *-samba | "young female kid" |
| *-lògù | "palm wine" (by irregular sound shift < PB *-làgù) | *-jamba | "guineafowl cock (?), he-goat (?)" |
| *-lèngè | "edible gourd" | *-kómbò | "guineafowl cock (?), he-goat (?)" |

c. *Additional terms in earliest proto-Mashariki*

(crops)

| | | | |
|---|---|---|---|
| *-siabe | "kind of edible tuber" (see also table 44) | *-úngù | "gourd plant" |
| *-lagi | "kind of yam" | | (domestic animal) |
| *-sikisi | "oil palm" | *-pòngó | "he-goat" |

---

Two kinds of trees, the oil and raffia palms, probably also had a domesticated or semidomesticated status in the agricultural economies of the early Bantu—individually owned and tended once they sprouted, and often, but not necessarily always, deliberately planted from seed. Oil palms in particular depended on human agency in rainforest regions because they require sunny, cleared areas to be able to take root and grow: their "natural" environments in such places would have been the abandoned farms and gardens of previous years.

Raffia palms were anciently valuable among the Niger-Congo ancestors of the Bantu as sources of sap for palm-wine brewing; but the widepread use in the Congo Basin of their fibers for raffia cloth weaving probably developed later than 1000 B.C., since this kind of cloth appears to have been unknown to Mashariki communities at any period of their history (table 21 for early Mashariki fabrics and garments). East of the Western Rift zone, the suitable environments for oil palms, even with human agency, and for the raffia palm also, were relatively few. The oil palm thus ceased to be an important plant among most of the Kaskazi and Kusi communities of later times, although palm-wine making survived among a number of those communities where suitable kinds of palms could be found.

But although the first Mashariki communities to enter into the far western edge of East Africa may have been few in number, they also had an initial environmental advantage. Ahead of them lay an area of intermixed savanna and forest, in which the forested lands suitable to their kind of agriculture were, at that time in history, far more extensive than the savanna. Little utilized previously by the other food-producing peoples of the Great Lakes and Western Rift regions, the forested areas would have constituted essentially virgin land for agricultural expansion. In that kind of situation of demographic and economic opportunity, as a wide range of historical examples show us, human fertility tends to increase and population growth to accelerate.

## Bantu Expansion: A Proposal as to Cause

Over the early and middle centuries of the last millennium B.C., then, the Mashariki societies built up their numbers and gradually expanded their territories. During the same period, they began to gain acquaintance as well, through their contacts with the Central Sudanians and Eastern Sahelians, with new kinds of agricultural production, especially the cultivation of African grain crops. For a long time they made little use themselves of this knowledge. But by the last three or four centuries of the era, it has been proposed here, Mashariki farmers had settled throughout the warmer, lower-lying forested areas that extended from the Western Rift valley to Lake Nyanza and from the Kivu Basin southward to the southwestern side of Lake Tanganyika, and they had begun to reach a kind of critical population density across those regions. It would have been a density that, in absolute terms, was still extremely low in comparison with modern agricultural population densities across many of those same areas. But with re-

106

spect to the expectations of the time, it would have been felt by the people themselves as a critical pressure on the viability of their very long-fallow type of agriculture.

The reaching of this demographic stage can be proposed to have had two kinds of consequences. First, it triggered off a series of expansions out of many parts of the Late Mashariki lands, each population movement seeking out new areas farther afield where their accustomed livelihood might be carried on. These movements surely did not all begin at the same point in time, but probably developed over a period of a few centuries, toward the close of the millennium, as the perceived pressure of population growth began to make itself felt in different areas. And second, it led to the fuller putting into practice of that knowledge of grain cultivating technology which the cultural interactions of the earlier centuries of the last millennium B.C. bequeathed to the Mashariki societies. This second consequence allowed a continuing growth and expansion of the Lakes Bantu populations who remained in the Nyanza Basin itself,[5] and it allowed the Bantu communities who left the region to resettle in a variety of environments, especially in east-central and southeastern Africa, where grain cultivation often was essential to farmers' survival. What is argued here, in other words, is that the fundamental factors that explain the vast expansion of Bantu peoples at the turn of the era lie not, as scholars have often argued, in the emergence of ironworking technology, but in the long-term developments of agricultural history.

The growth of the Bantu societies may have had unexpected consequences also for the expansion of another people, the Tale Southern Cushites. Rather than the impetus for expansion being generated by developments within Tale Southern Cushitic society itself, it may well have been the clearing of forest and brush for cultivation by Lakes communities on the east of Lake Nyanza, and by Southern-Nyanza peoples around the south and southwest of the lake, that allowed the Tale to spread eastward, with their cattle, during the second half of the last millennium B.C. Cattle keeping may thus, in the last few centuries B.C., have increased greatly in importance among both the Lake and Southern-Nyanza peoples (see more on this topic below) primarily because of the efforts that these Bantu communities made on behalf of their own nonpastoral agriculture. The Tale moved in as opportunity provided by Bantu farmers allowed and became in the process the major contributors of the new knowledge and expertise in animal husbandry.

# Tool Technology

The most widespread development in tool technology in the last millennium B.C. was the establishment and spread of iron-working. The evidence of language validates the appellation Early Iron Age for the centuries whose history has been explored here. The use of iron in some form or another goes back a long time in the Great Lakes region, as early probably as the start of the last millennium B.C. (see tables 4–7).[6] But the evidence also takes direct issue with any prejudgment of history that allows the title Early Iron Age to be given specifically to the Chifumbaze complex of cultures made by the early Mashariki Bantu. Knowledge of iron arrived early in the period among the proto-Mashariki-speaking communities, and by late in the millennium ironworking was an important activity among most of the later Mashariki societies, notably, it appears from the archeology, among the Lakes peoples living in Bukoba.[7] But the early Mashariki were not the only iron users of the Great Lakes region, and indeed the language evidence indicates specifically that they gained their first acquaintance with the new technology through Central Sudanian and Eastern Sahelian communities already resident there.[8] Interesting archeological discoveries apparently await us in the regions to the north and northwest of the Nyanza Basin. The language evidence suggests, as well, something of the stone toolmaking antecedents of the peoples involved in this history of technological change.

## From Stone to Iron among the Sudanians and Sahelians

The Central Sudanians fashioned a variety of stone tools. Words for axes, adzes, and two kinds of knife blades can be reconstructed for the proto–Central Sudanic language, and a further four names for types of blades or points are known from the ancestral language of the East branch of Central Sudanic. Separate verbs for grinding a tool, apparently for striking off flakes, and for hammering suggest that the PCS people applied a range of lithic skills in their tool making (table 17).[9]

With the development of ironworking, these terms often found new functions in different of the Central Sudanic subgroups. The nouns for different stone blades might or might not be reapplied to their equivalent iron forms. The word for an ax (*-kɔngɔ) continued to name iron axes in West Central Sudanic and in the Mangbetu subgroup of East Central Sudanic, for example, but became a term for

108

Table 17. Tool terms in early Central Sudanic

*a. Proto–Central Sudanic words*

| | | | |
|---|---|---|---|
| *Kɔ | "to fashion (implement)" | *ca | "to shoot bow" |
| *pa | "to shape to a point (by knocking off pieces)" | *(e)re | "arrow" |
| | | *mba | "knife" |
| *ndɔ | "to hammer" | *ngɔ | "kind of knife" |
| *'u | "to grind (tool)" | *kɔngɔ | "ax" |
| *Sei | "point (of tool)" (generic) | *ba | "adze" |
| *ju | "to spear, stab" | | |

*b. East Central Sudanic words*

| | | | |
|---|---|---|---|
| *rɛ | "to strike off pieces" (< PCS "to tear off pieces"; yielded words connected to forging in Moru-Madi and Balese) | *le | "long blade" (Moru-Madi *ele "knife") |
| | | *tɔ | "spike (of spear)" |
| | | *osu | "bow" |
| *lɔ | "ax" | *ɓuɔ | "canoe" |
| *mbɛ | "(large?) blade" | | |

adze in the Moru-Madi subgroup. An older East Central Sudanic term for a long blade (*le) was converted into the word for knife in Moru-Madi, but in a number of other cases the proto–Central Sudanic root words for the earlier kinds of knife blades continued to denote iron knives. And although new verbs for the fashioning of iron into iron tools were widely innovated in different Central Sudanic subgroups, in several instances the older stone-working words were shifted to forging. The term for "to hammer" (*ɔndɔ), for example, was the source of a Moru-Madi word for blacksmith and separately, in Kara of West Central Sudanic, took on the meaning "to forge."

The course of such developments among the Eastern Sahelian societies of the last millennium B.C. remains much more obscure. The Sog people were themselves surely participants, along with the Central Sudanians, in the first developments of metallurgy in the Great Lakes region, because their language was the apparent source of several Mashariki words of ironworking connections, notably *-gèlà "iron" (see table 5) and *-tapo "iron ore" (see table 7). But we lack as yet any direct or indirect testimony from language as to the kinds of stone tools the Sog might have made before the iron age.

## Developments in Toolmaking among Mashariki Peoples

The earliest Mashariki settlers along the west side of East Africa, their toolmaking vocabulary implies, produced polished stone blades, among other kinds of points for their implements. A key Mashariki term *-tíán- for "to forge," which came into use in that meaning by the Kaskazi era, derives from a verb stem and a verb suffixation that in tandem originally conveyed "to grind or rub together."[10] Now this is a meaning not at all descriptive of the smith's pounding of heated metal, but quite evocative of the process of forming a polished stone blade. Evidently we have here a verb for toolmaking transferred from stone- to ironworking in the Late Mashariki era. Its testimony tells us that archeologists should expect to find polished stone blades on the earliest Mashariki sites, with ironworking only subsequently appearing. The major lithic shapes not improbably would take the form of polished stone axes, resemblant to those known between 3000 and 1000 B.C. in the early Bantu sites of the equatorial rainforest, the region to which the cultural ancestry of the early Mashariki can be traced.

Polished stone would by no means exhaust the tool forms to be looked for on sites of the earliest Mashariki. Two other old Bantu verb roots of toolmaking application—(1) *-túl-, meaning in proto-Bantu "to strike (a thing) repeatedly" and producing in proto-Mashariki a secondary sense "to forge";[11] and (2) *-sòng- "to shape to a point"—probably orginally referred respectively, it can be proposed, to striking off flakes in lithic work and to forming points in softer materials, such as wood or bone. At least seven root words of relict distribution among the Bantu societies identify particular cutting and piercing tools of pre-proto-Mashariki provenience, most likely made of stone, that remained in use into the Early Mashariki period. The ranges of meaning attested today for each of the seven words suggests that their namesakes probably included a small thin point for piercing, a very small cutting blade or point, larger stabbing and cutting blades, and at least three composite tools, one a knife, a second an adze, and the third an axlike instrument (table 18).

Some interesting differences, both collective and individual, distinguished the Central Sudanian and Bantu tool kits of stone-age times. For one thing, the Central Sudanic terms seem generally to refer to blades, while the pre-proto-Mashariki words allow for microlithic forms (in particular, see *-pamba and *-keto in table 18) in addition to blades.

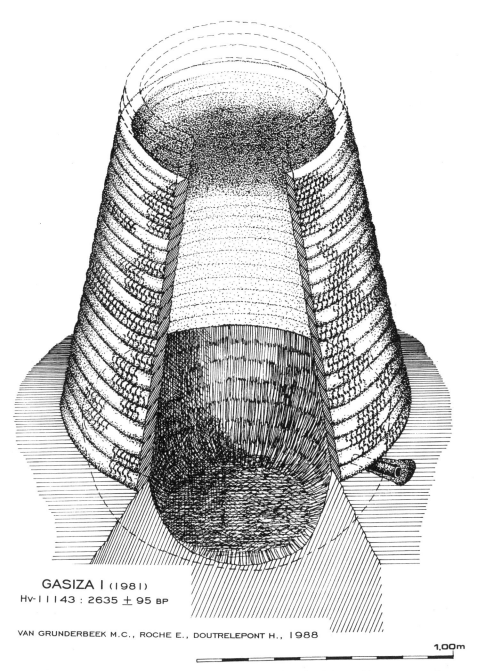

GASIZA I (1981)
Hv-I I I 43 : 2635 ± 95 BP

VAN GRUNDERBEEK M.C., ROCHE E., DOUTRELEPONT H., 1988

1.00m

Figure 4. Iron technology in the Early Classical Age. Reconstruction of earliest known African iron-smelting furnace, Gasiza, Burundi, tenth century B.C. (calibrated date). (Graciously provided by the excavator, Marie-Claude van Grunderbeek).

111

Intriguingly also, the Bantu before the iron age may not have possessed a tool that was simply an ax for chopping trees and branches. The scattered, relict application today of the PB root word *-sòká (see table 18) to axes, wherever that term has been preserved, indicates that the stone-age tool to which it referred must greatly have resembled an ax and may indeed have had chopping as one of its functions. But the word itself derives from a proto-Bantu verb *-sòk- "to poke," a quite different action from chopping.

There is an explanation, however, that more than satisfactorily accounts for these seemingly contradictory indications, namely, that the *-sòká was the primary cultivating tool of early Bantu-speaking societies—that it was what might be called a "planting-ax." Mary McMaster has argued convincingly that the early forest farmers, so as to minimize the destructive effects of direct rain on lateritic soil, would have planted by first poking or slicing into the ground with a suitable tool and then inserting her cutting or seed into the resulting small crevice (see also the discussions below of agricultural change). In modern times among the Buans of Congo (Zaire), the suitable tool for that kind of farming has been a large iron knife blade; it can both cut into the ground and slice off any remaining twigs obscuring the planting site.[12] But a stone knife lacks the same density of mass and fineness of its cutting edge, and thus requires more force from its user, to be as effective as a metal knife. In the stone age only a blade hafted like an ax, in the same plane as but perpendicular to its handle, would have generated sufficient torque to have allowed easy piercing of the ground as well as efficient hacking off of branches or twigs that interfered with planting.

So the *-sòká in all probability functioned originally as an all-purpose agricultural tool, as Jan Vansina has already posited. But it was surely not a digging stick as he has also suggested.[13] Its derivation from a verb for "to poke" is accounted for by its proposed use in planting. Its original form as an ax, presumably a polished stone ax, and its probable complementary use as a chopping tool for clearing fields is required by the consistent reapplication of the word *-sòká, in three disparate sets of Bantu peoples after the coming of the iron age, to an iron ax and not to any other tool.

As iron technology took hold, all these stone-age terms began widely to be replaced across the Bantu field by new words for iron-bladed cutting and chopping tools. The newer terms more often than not took on the sort of extended areal distribution in language after neighboring language—that is overtly indicative of their having spread by diffusion, in concert with the spread of the instruments they

Table 18. Pre-proto-Mashariki terms for blades

| | | |
|---|---|---|
| *-tía | "point, blade" (generic term) | PB; originally a ground or polished point because of the derivation of this noun from PB *-tí- "to grind, rub" |
| *-pamba | "small thin point or blade" | proto-Bantu (PB)—attested meanings: Bobangi "kind of knife"; Kaskazi (Swahili "palm-tapping knife"; Yao, etc., "arrow") |
| *-keto | "very small blade or point" | Savanna and Mashariki Bantu—attested meanings: C.Sav. (Luban "arrow"); Mashariki (Sukuma "awl"; Njombe subgroup of Kati, Gogo "razor"; Nyanja "barbed arrow") |
| *-palu | "long stabbing blade" | PB; attested meanings: Bobangi "large spear"; Kaskazi (East-Nyanza, Luyia "knife"); Kusi (Shona "stabbing spear") |
| *-pata | "large cutting blade" | Kongo and Mashariki Bantu; attested meanings: Kongo "sword"; Mashariki: Nyiha (Rungwe) "blade (generic)"; East Ruvu of Kati "sheath, "scabbord"; Kusi: Venda "quiver") |
| *-píó | "knife" | PB; relict distribution: far northwestern rain-forest languages; W.Sav. (Herero); Kaskazi (Lakes subgroup; Langi); Kusi (SE-Bantu); see Ehret 1995/96 for further discussion |
| *-bàgò | "adze" | PB; relict distribution: far northern rain-forest languages (variously "hoe," "ax," "adze," "knife"); Kaskazi: Luyia ("hoe"), Gusii ("hoe-handle"); Rufiji-Ruvuma ("adze" or "ax": Ehret 1995/96) |
| *-sòká | "planting-ax" | PB; relict distribution as a word for "ax": in some rainforest Bantu languages; in Kaskazi (only the Upland group); and in Kusi (only SE-Bantu) |

113

named.[14] The older tool terms, left over from the Stone Age, have survived, in contrast, only here and there among the Bantu languages, reapplied in different places to different tools of the newer technology.

## Iron Technology: An Overview

Overall, iron technology would appear to have become established gradually in the Great Lakes region. The language evidence indicates its presence first among Central Sudanians and Sog peoples, probably even before 1000 B.C. For this reason, its earliest archeological manifestations should be sought in northwestern parts of Uganda and adjacent parts of Congo and also in areas farther to the northwest along the Nile-Congo divide. By the tenth or ninth century, iron forging and smelting had begun to take hold among the Kaskazi peoples residing just east of the Western Rift in such areas as modern-day Burundi (fig. 4). The Kaskazi communities in some areas would have became users of iron tools early on, but in most areas iron would still several centuries later have been a relatively rare material, used for adornment but often too valuable to be wasted on tools. By mid-millennium, ironworking began to diffuse westward into the rainforest of the Congo Basin[15] and, over the next few centuries, southward to the Kusi cluster of Mashariki communities.[16] During the second half of the millennium, there may have been, as well, advances in furnace building that helped make the Lakes Bantu settlers of the southwestern Nyanza Basin into important iron producers.[17]

# Developments in Residential Patterns

A second regionwide set of developments, covering the last millennium B.C., took place in housing styles and residential layout. An initial situation in which particular residential features characteristically belonged to particular populations can be expected to have broken down in various ways over the course of that period.

## Changing House Styles

The very earliest Mashariki would have built rectangular houses with gabled roofs, arranged these houses in small village-sized settlements of probably a single street, and had few kinds of out-structures. During the last millennium, their cultural descendants began to adopt round styles of houses, reflective of the influence of the Central Sudanians and the Sog. The beginning of this changeover is probably attested in the development as early as the Early Mashariki period of an additional word for house, *-umba, which eventually displaced the original proto-Mashariki term, *-ju, in most of the Mashariki languages.[18] Another root word, *-lìlì "sleeping place" (see table 5), borrowed apparently from an Eastern Sahelian language, may indicate changes as well in the internal layout of the dwelling.

A further indicator of changing house styles was the development in the Middle Mashariki period of a new, specialized meaning "to thatch" for an older verb *-bìmb- "to cover up." The pitched roof of the proto-Bantu house was composed of woven panels, as is shown by the semantic derivation of PB *-túng- "to build"[19]—the original sense of that verb was "to weave" or "to plait." This style prevailed among the earliest Mashariki as well, and in those parts of East Africa where the old Bantu rectangular, pitched-roof house has been preserved, the roofs in some areas even today are fashioned of woven palm material. The word *-túng- itself must have lasted into proto-Mashariki as the verb for the making of such roofs, because at least one Mashariki language, Xhosa, still uses it, although in the meaning "to thatch."

The changeover to thatched roofs probably appeared initially among the Kaskazi areal grouping of Mashariki communities. The distribution of *-bìmb- "to thatch" coincides largely with the descendant languages of that grouping, although it also includes today Kusi languages spoken in northern Mozambique and Malawi and has an overlapping spread into languages of Zambia and Katanga (Shaba) that suggests the subsequent diffusion of thatched roofing westward across the southern savanna zone. The conclusion that this meaning spread from the Kaskazi Mashariki communities, after the initial breakup of the early Mashariki society, is verified by the reflexes of the root in Mashariki languages spoken south of the Zambezi. There the application of the word to thatching did not develop, and it retained instead a nontechnical sense, "to hide," directly derivable from the reconstructed meaning "to cover up." Some of the Kusi communities of the Late Mashariki era, from whose dialects these languages-derive, apparently continued to use *-túng-, as its preservation in Xhosa shows, and perhaps therefore were still weaving roofs even while many of the Kaskazi peoples had began to adopt thatching.

Figure 5. House styles dating to the Early Classical Age. Round house with conical roof, *top*; rectangular house with palm-thatch gable roof, *middle*; rectangular house with flat roof (tembe), *bottom*.

How early the round house with a thatched roof became the usual style remains for archeology to determine, and the timing may well have been different in different areas. The rectangular, gabled-roof style continued apparently to be built by some Kaskazi Bantu communities along the south or southwest of Lake Nyanza as late as the close of the Southern-Nyanza era, because that kind of house is still constructed at present among descendants of one of the three early Kati communities, the Northeast-Coastal Bantu. Among other Kati, however, a third style of house building, the flat-roofed rectangular *tembe*, may have begun to be built already toward the close of the Southern-Nyanza era. The sources of this building style were surely the Tale Southern Cushites—flat-roofed houses can be argued from their relict distribution in East and northeastern Africa to have been the most ancient Cushitic style. And, up until its adoption by early Kati peoples, this style would in all probability have been diagnostic of Tale Southern Cushite settlements south of the lake.

## Developments in Residence and Village Layout

Major shifts in residential layout can also be expected to have appeared among Bantu-speaking societies of the last millennium B.C. in the Great Lakes region. But changes in house style are likely to have appeared well ahead of other change in residence patterns. For the Early Mashariki era, the adoption of the word *-ba "enclosure, yard of residence" (see table 4) may betoken some changes in the spacing and separation of dwellings within villages. At least two new proto-Mashariki root words referred to fences and fence building. A noun *-bígo, from a verb *-bíg- "to build a fence," denoted probably a pole fence. A distinct root word *-bág-, of borrowed origin (see table 5), appears in the proto-Mashariki noun *-bágò, "fence" (of an uncertain type; its reflexes include Gusii *orobagɔ* "fence" and Lamba *uluβago* "game-fence").

The same word also produced a second proto-Mashariki noun *-bágá, referring to an enclosure for livestock and used today for "cattle pen" in such widely scattered groups as the Thagiicu (of Upland), Kinga (of Njombe), and Nguni. But *-bágá and *-teba, *-tiba "animal pen" (see table 5), were both so widely displaced by later words that each probably most often referred to the observed features of neighboring peoples' habitations, rarely or not at all found among the Bantu communities. The specific meaning of *-bágá in its Langi

117

reflex, "outlying cattle pen" (one not located in one's village or homestead), gives overt support to that conclusion.

For the immediately subsequent Late Mashariki period, indirect evidence suggests that single-street villages remained the norm, but a norm modified in one notable respect. The proto-Mashariki word for "ridge," *-gòngò,[20] became in the northern and central Kaskazi dialects (but not in the southern dialects) a word that also applied to the local settlement. This datum implies it was the Middle Mashariki period, roughly dating to the second quarter of the last millennium B.C., that saw the inception of the practice, still followed among Thagiicu peoples in Kenya today and in parts of the Great Lakes region and elsewhere, of laying out the local settlement along a ridge, with the individual farmsteads on each side of the ridge and with the top of the ridge forming the single street of the settlement. The various implications of this inference for archeological investigations need not be belabored. Such a development would be in accord with the proposed locating, already argued, of Kaskazi communities along and to the east of the Western Rift, in highland areas.

Not until the end of the last millennium B.C., however, can we argue for the replacement of villages by neighborhoods of scattered homesteads, and even then this development took place among only some of the Bantu communities. A major possible area for such a changeover could have lain along the south of Lake Nyanza, among some but not all of the member communities of the Southern Nyanza areal grouping. The proto-Kati speakers who were heavily influenced by Tale Southern Cushites would be likely candidates, in particular any Kati people who might have begun to make *tembe*-style houses. The Upland people, who moved thereafter to the eastern side of East Africa, would seem to have maintained the earlier ridge-village type of settlement, and the pre-Luyia and East Nyanza communities, although eventually shifting for the most part to neighborhoods of homesteads, probably made that changeover only during the subsequent centuries of strong Southern Nilotic and Southern Rub influences, during and after their spread northward up the east side of the lake (discussed in chapter 6).

## Developments in the Everyday Items of the Household

Another area of material culture where significant developments took place was in furnishings. The adoption, around the turn of the eras, of certain kinds of beds by Kati peoples from Southern Cushites is overtly indicated in the vocabulary evidence presented here (e.g., see table 2B). The semantic specification, during the Late Mashariki period, of *-lìlì, originally "sleeping place" in proto-Mashariki Bantu (see table 5), to a bed of some kind pushes back the first Mashariki use, or at least knowledge, of beds as alternatives to sleeping mats to probably the middle of the last millennium B.C. The subsequent diffusion of bed making to peoples and regions west of the Western Rift and Lake Tanganyika can be inferred from the occurrence there of *-lìlì in its historically secondary meaning "bed."

Three-legged carved wooden stools are an additional item that the evidence shows to have been newly spreading to Bantu-speaking societies in these eras, probably not earlier than the middle of the millennium and possibly not till late in the millennium. This type of seat was sculpted from a single large block of wood. The adoption of such stools by the Lakes society was marked by the borrowing into the proto-Lakes language of the word *-tébè, itself a noun deriving from the old Eastern Sahelian verb root *te:b "to sit, stay." From this fact we know that the making of such stools came to the Lakes communities from an Eastern Sahelian people. The source in this case may have been the Southern Rub society, since in the Sog language the particular noun derived from this verb had rather a different meaning (see table 5). The extended block distribution of *-tébè southwestward of Lake Tanganyika into parts of Congo (Zaire) and Zambia, it can be argued, traces the subsequent spread of the stool beyond the Great Lakes region and into central Africa.

Among the containers and utensils of the household, too, a variety of developments can be discerned from the vocabulary record. Southern Cushites, Eastern Sahelians, and Central Sudanic peoples all had somewhat differing emphases in their utensilry, and they produced a number of items not apparently part of the background that the Mashariki Bantu settlers brought with them into Eastern Africa.

All the food-producing societies of the last millennium B.C. surely made pots for cooking, and the Southern Cushites, Bantu, and Central Sudanians produced pots for water carrying and storage as well (see tables 19 and 28). But interestingly, only in a single instance so far identified (see table 8A.f), was a word for a kind of pot borrowed. Apparently the potting styles of the different societies tended not to spread to other peoples, and the archeology of differing ceramic wares of the last thousand years B.C. can therefore be expected for the most part to correspond with ethnicity and language.

The weaving of mats and basketry appears to have been an especially important craft among the Bantu communities of the last mil-

Table 19. Early Mashariki woven goods

*a. Proto-Bantu terms*

| | | | |
|---|---|---|---|
| *-pìnd- | "to plait" | *-kéká | "palm mat" |
| *-tùngá | "basket" (bamboo?) | *-sásá | "reed (?) mat; |
| *-túndù | "large, tall basket" | | open-sided shelter |
| *-tètè | "wicker hamper" | | originally with |
| | of palm or bamboo) | | palm-mat roof" |

*b. Proto-Savanna term*

| | |
|---|---|
| *-titi | "small basket dish" (of liana fiber) |

*c. Proto-Mashariki terms*

| | | | |
|---|---|---|---|
| *-tándà | "reed sleeping mat" | *-tumba | "woven sack" |
| *-pe | "flat basket" | *-làgò | "reed mat" |
| *-pìndà | "woven bast sack" | | |

*d. Kaskazi terms*

| | | | |
|---|---|---|---|
| *-ibo | "large open basket" | *-kapo, | "small basket" |
| *-sege, | "basket" (probably | *-kapu | |
| *-seke | of palm fiber) | *-ambị | "large palm mat" |

lennium B.C. The typical Mashariki household throughout the period would have made use of several kinds of baskets, of different sizes and shapes and fashioned from a variety of materials, including probably bamboo, palm leaves, and lianas, and also of several types of mats, plaited from palm leaves and reeds. To the Early or Middle Mashariki period can also be traced the making of woven bast sacks. The Central Sudanians, too, anciently wove baskets; and during the Late Mashariki period, two Central Sudanic names for different kinds of baskets were adopted by some of the northern Mashariki communities, reflecting their adoption probably of new basket types from their Sudanian neighbors (*-ibo and *-kapo, *-kapu in table 19d; see also table 6).

The Eastern Sahelian peoples in this history seem to have had a different influence on early Mashariki utensilry. From the Sog society came a kind of vessel not traceable back earlier in Bantu history, a deep wooden bowl or jug (tables 5 and 20). Utilized in several Mashariki societies of more recent eras as a milking jug, that may well have been its original function among the Sog people too.

120

Another practice not found among the earliest Mashariki people was the making of leather containers. For a long time, it appears, this kind of manufacturing remained the province of the earlier East African farmers. The earliest adoption of a word for a leather sack in Mashariki cannot be dated until after the Middle Mashariki era. It rather seems that the making of leather containers became common among Bantu-speaking East Africans only as their expansions of the late last millennium B.C. and early first millennium A.D. began to get underway, as the example of the West-Nyanza group's adoption of *-tago "small leather sack" from Tale Southern Cushitic (see table 9) illustrates.

The archeologist quickly discovers pots, and so their importance tends to get strong play in archeological appreciations of early African history. The material evidence of the more perishable bits of household culture—the baskets, the wooden and leather containers, the furniture of the house—so rarely preserved in the physical record, may be rather difficult to find. But the language evidence tells us that their practical significance in the evolving patterns of daily life in the last millennium B.C. was surely every bit as great as that of pottery (table 20).

---

### Table 20.  Early Mashariki containers

*a.  Proto-Bantu and other pre-proto-Mashariki terms*

| | |
|---|---|
| *-búmb- "to make pot" | *-gayenga "potsherd" (reduced |
| *-bìgá "water (?) pot" | shape *-gaye in Kati |
| *-(j)ùngú "cooking pot" | group of Kaskazi) |
| | *-súpá "bottle gourd" |

*b.  Proto-Mashariki terms*

| | |
|---|---|
| *-tụba "deep wooden bowl" | *-beela "calabash shell |
| *-kụlụ/u "calabash" | or sherd" |

*c.  Kaskazi term*

*-kolo "small calabash"

---

# Clothing among the Early Mashariki

The emphasis amongst the earliest Mashariki Bantu communities on fibers as fabricating materials, so visible in their house construction and their containers, affected their apparel making as well (table 21). Both barkcloth garments and grass or leaf skirts trace to before the Early Mashariki era, and as Vansina's evidence allows, barkcloth making was surely a proto-Bantu skill already in the third millennium B.C.[21] The weaving of raffia cloth, an old trait in some of the westerly Bantu-speaking regions, does not appear, however, to have been known among the early Mashariki people, and its technology may therefore have spread among the western populations of equatorial Africa only after the close of the proto-Bantu period.

Leather, although probably not a favored material in early times, was used by the Savanna-Bantu ancestors of the Mashariki to make at least one kind of garment, possibly worn around the waist. Baby-slings for carrying a mother's infant on her back were probably originally fashioned from leather also. Leather was prepared apparently, as among some more recent East Africans, by pegging out the hide to dry (see verb *-bàmb- in table 21), after which it would have been softened by rubbing and kneading.

Over the course of the last millennium B.C., leather became a successively more important clothing material among the evolving Mashariki communities. At least one new term for a man's garment

---

### Table 21. Early Mashariki garments

*a. Terms of Savanna and Mashariki distribution*

| | | | |
|---|---|---|---|
| *-bàmb- | "to peg out (hide)" | *-samba | "leaf or grass skirt" |
| *-gùbò | "leather garment (worn at the waist?)" | | |

*b. Proto-Mashariki terms*

| | | | |
|---|---|---|---|
| *-sani | "barkcloth" | *-beleko | "baby-sling" |
| *-sambi | "girl's leaf apron" | | |

*c. Terms of Kaskazi distribution*

| | | | |
|---|---|---|---|
| *-lolo | "(leather?) apron" (girl's?) | *-limba | "man's garment" (leather shawl?) |

---

122

of leather, worn apparently at the waist, came into use at the Early Mashariki era. Two additional leather garments, one worn by women or girls, were adopted among the Kaskazi group of communities before the middle of the last millennium B.C., and still other items of leather clothing were probably added late in the millennium by different subgroups of Kaskazi people. The sources of these changes in styles of clothing may at first have been Sog Eastern Sahelians, but that possibility remains to be directly demonstrated. In later centuries the Southern Cushites and Southern Nilotes clearly became important sources of new forms of processed leather among the different Kaskazi groups (note examples in table 9A.c and table 3B).

## Hunting and Fishing in Early Mashariki Economies

The earliest Mashariki had their historical roots in a world in which hunting and fishing probably were every bit as important as food-producing activities. Their food-collecting pursuits depended on a variety of techniques, as the reconstructed vocabularies of methods and implements show (table 22).

The developments of apparently new vocabulary distinctions, both in the pre-proto-Mashariki period and in the proto-Mashariki era itself, imply continuing developments in hunting and fishing technology that deserve their own closer investigation in the future by historians and archeologists. In fishing, for instance, the shifting of an older verb, originally meaning "to dip," to a new technical usage, "to fish (with a basket)," suggests that the use of fish baskets to scoop up fish from streams took hold long before the Early Mashariki age, very early in the history of Bantu differentiation and spread, but apparently not until somewhat after the proto-Bantu period. (An opposite meaning shift, from the narrowly technical to the general, would be highly implausible.) A further development, of fish traps (or at least of a particular kind of fish trap), can be placed in the Early Mashariki period. Similarly, the change of terminology for "arrow" at the proto-Savanna stage would seem to reflect a changeover already in pre-proto-Mashariki times from using palm-frond midribs as arrowshafts to the use of some other kind of material—a shift that may have been encouraged by the changing environment of Bantu settlement at that point in time, from rainforest to woodland savanna.

By the end of the Early Mashariki era, with Bantu settlement verging often on more open country, the bow and arrow may have begun to be a more centrally important implement of hunting. In the

Table 22.  Mashariki hunting and fishing vocabularies

*a.  Terms of proto-Bantu distribution*

(hunting)                                        (fishing)

| | | | |
|---|---|---|---|
| *-bìng- | "to hunt, chase" | *-lób- | "to fish with hook |
| *-támbò | "snare" | | and line" |
| *-tá | "bow" | *-lóbò | "fish-hook" |
| *-bànjí | "arrow; mid-rib of palm" (alternate shape *-bànjá) | | |

*b.  Terms dating before Savanna-Bantu emergence*

(hunting)                                        (fishing)

| | | | |
|---|---|---|---|
| *-sàk- | "to hunt" (by driving animals?) | *-lùb- | "to fish with a fishbasket" |
| *-tég- | "to set trap" | | |

*c.  Terms of Savanna and Mashariki distribution*

(hunting)

| | | | |
|---|---|---|---|
| *-bind- | "to hunt" | *-gʉí | "arrow" (displaced PB *-bànjí) |
| *-líbá | "falling trap" | *-gomba | "kind of arrow" |

*d.  Proto-Mashariki terms*

(hunting)

| | | | |
|---|---|---|---|
| *-tulo | "arrowshaft" | *-pongolo | "quiver" |
| *-tíngà | "tendon bowstring" | | |

*e.  Words of Kaskazi distribution*

(hunting)

| | | | |
|---|---|---|---|
| *-lás- | "to shoot arrow" | *-ábʉ | "(hunting) net" (table 6) |
| *-pìnd- | "to pull bow" | | |
| *-sàalé | "arrow" | (fishing) | |
| *-bànò | "arrowshaft" | | |
| *-gai | "tendon bowstring" | *-gònò | "fish trap" |

*f.  Words of Kusi distribution*

(hunting)

| | | | |
|---|---|---|---|
| *-koka | "kind of trap" | *-sèbè | "arrow" (table 38) |

124

making of bows, a possible technological innovation of the late Mashariki period was the increasing use of tendon in place of fiber bowstrings, as suggested by the appearance of several terms with that specific meaning. The sources of such an innovation remain unclear because both Southern Cushitic and Khoisan peoples earlier used tendon bowstrings in East Africa.[22] New varieties of arrows in the Late Mashariki period, perhaps adopted from their neighbors, seem also probable—note, for example, Kusi *-sèbé "arrow," a loanword from an Eastern Sahelian langauge (see table 38)—and additional kinds of traps were coming into use by the end of the Middle Mashariki era or shortly thereafter (sections d and e of table 22). Most interestingly, the early Kaskazi adopted a new element of hunting technology, a net, apparently from their Central Sudanic–speaking neighbors.

The Mashariki were by no means the only food-producers of the last millennium B.C. who practiced hunting and fishing in the Great Lakes region. Both the Eastern Sahelians and the Central Sudanic communities hunted. As we have seen, Sog people in particular seem to be the source of at least one new word for "arrow," suggesting that in part at least the developments in archery among the early Kusi communities were influenced by the Eastern Sahelian practices, whereas the Central Sudanians bequeathed the hunting net to the Kaskazi. The Central Sudanians were, like the Mashariki, notable fisherfolk, although different in their particular techniques. They seem, for instance, to have made no use of the hook and line in their fishing, but did have old root words for fish traps, barbed harpoons, and weirs (see table 12).[23] Conceivably the use by Bantu communities of fishtraps, traceable in vocabulary reconstruction no earlier than the Late Mashariki period, may owe in some way to contemporary Central Sudanic example; but since the proto-Mashariki word does not appear on the surface to be a Central Sudanic loanword, such a connection remains to be demonstrated.

The gathering of honey was another collecting activity of ancient standing all across eastern and sourthern Africa. Among the Khoisan gatherer-hunters and the Southern Cushites, this facet of livelihood is reflected in a considerable array of reconstructible vocabulary.[24] The difficulty of reconstructing any early apiarial vocabulary among Nilo-Saharan languages suggests, however, that honey may not been as significant a product among the Eastern Sahelians and Central Sudanians.

The Mashariki Bantu settlers of the early last millennium B.C., like the Southern Cushites, must have made considerable use of honey, as their complex honey terminology implies (table 23). It ap-

125

Figure 6. Developments in woodworking technology. Three-legged stool (from central Tanzania)

pears, though, that they did not brew mead. And they probably were
the introducers of actual beekeeping, as opposed to the collecting of
wild honey, to the eastern side of the continent. Specifically, the
Kaskazi communities sometime before 500 B.C. invented the round,
barrel-like beehive so generally used across East Africa today, calling
it by the root *-lìngà, derived from a proto-Bantu verb *-lìng- "to
wind round; to surround," descriptive of the hive's shape. This kind
of hive then spread from Kaskazi peoples south to the early Nyasa
communities of Malawi, probably in the first few centuries A.D. and
thence later to the Shona of Zimbabwe, whose borrowed shape of the
word *-lìngà has undergone a meaning shift, to the contents of the
hive, the honeycombs.

---

Table 23. Beekeeping vocabulary in early Mashariki Bantu

*a. Words of Savanna-Bantu provenance*

| *-ókì, | "bee; honey" (PB) | *-saila | "empty honeycomb" |
| *-úkì | | *-púlá | "beeswax" |
| *-tàná | "natural beehive" (PB) | | |

*b. Additional terms in early Mashariki*

| *-sa | "honeycomb" (empty?) | *-kìndà | "cell of honeycomb" |
| *-sapa | "honeycomb" | *-ánà | "bee larva" (sing. *li-ánà, pl. *ma-(li-)ánà) |

*c. Additional term in Kaskazi*

*-lìngà  "barrel-shaped beehive"

---

## Crops and Society

### Developments in Grain Cultivation

From the beginning of the Early Mashariki period, the Bantu-speaking communities must have observed the practices of grain cultivation
among their food-producing predecessors of the Great Lakes region.
Along with words for porridge and flour (see tables 4–7 in chapter 2

127

and table 24 below), a fairly full range of terms for the processing of grains trace to the Early Mashariki period: particular root words for "mortar," "threshing floor," and "winnowing tray," as well as verbs for the specific processes of threshing and winnowing all occur common to Kaskazi and Kusi (see table 24).[25] But the full conversion of this knowledge into established agricultural practice, it must be argued, took place only after the divergence of the early Mashariki into the distinct Kaskazi and Kusi clusters of communities.

Several strong indicators appear in vocabulary that the Mashariki peoples remained throughout the first half of the last millennium B.C. primarily yam cultivators whose methods of tillage emphasized minimal disturbing of the soil and soil cover. Most notably, the development among the early Mashariki communities of a new verb \*-pànd- to express the meaning "to plant" confirms directly that they continued to plant by slicing into the ground, presumably with the planting-ax (as argued above). This verb had existed earlier in Bantu, but it had previously meant "to split." Its particular semantic shift makes sense only if the planting process among the early Mashariki peoples still in fact centered around an action of slicing into the ground.

Still another notable lexical indicator is an old Savanna verb that continued in common use in proto-Mashariki, \*-sàkul-, normally translatable as "to weed" in modern languages. This word can be derived from the proto-Savanna noun \*-sàká "thicket, secondary forest" by addition of the Bantu verb suffix of reversive meaning, \*-ul-. Its original literal meaning was thus "to take away brush" or "to debrush," an action not at all implying the fine clearing of the ground connoted by the usual modern meaning "to weed," but rather the broad clearing of heavier cover that Professor McMaster reconstructs for the early Bantu cultivation.[26]

A third development in lexical history that specifically shows the early Mashariki to have been still preeminently the raisers of planted, rather than sown, crops was their development of a new word, \*-bègú, commonly translated as "seed" in present-day languages. Derived from the proto-Bantu verb \*-bèg- "to snap/break (off)," its primary reference in proto-Mashariki had to have been to a shoot, a cutting, or a section of tuber broken off a plant. Like the proto-Bantu root word \*-bútò, which \*-bègú displaced entirely from use in proto-Mashariki, the new term may soon have been extended by analogy to seeds, but its original application would have been to crops propagated, like yams, from cuttings or snapped-off pieces of the plant.

Still another indicator of the continuing focus of the early Kaskazi and Kusi communities on root crops is provided by the earliest word we can yet reconstruct depicting their harvest ritual. That word, *-lìmbul-, which before the Late Mashariki period took on the ceremonial sense "to eat the first of the new crop," had previously been the verb for a concrete agricultural activity, "to dig up root or tuber crop."[27]

Other vocabulary developments of the Late Mashariki period (see table 24, sections b and c) reinforce the impression that grain cultivation remained for several centuries something observed rather than participated in. The taking up of grain raising in a small way before the middle of the last millennium may be indicated in the adoption separately by the Kaskazi and Kusi groupings of communities of distinct pairs of names for the grain crops, sorghum and finger millet. A second, still more telling indicator that grains nonetheless remained minor crops, if grown at all, is the consistent nonpresence of any early terms, even at the Kaskazi and Kusi stages, for a grain storage structure, a "granary."

---

Table 24. Developments in proto-Mashariki cultivation

*a. Words of proto-Mashariki distribution not in Ehret 1974a*

| | | | |
|---|---|---|---|
| *-pu(e/a) | "sorghum" | *-selo | "winnowing tray" |
| *-tàngà | "an edible cucurbit" | *-bùgà | "threshing floor" |

*b. Other crop terms of proto-Mashariki provenance*

| | | | |
|---|---|---|---|
| *-lumbu | "Plectranthus sp (?)" | *-úngù | "edible gourd" |

*c. Words of Kaskazi distribution*

| | | | |
|---|---|---|---|
| *-pémbá | "sorghum" | *-gàlì | "porridge" |
| *-gimbi | "finger millet" (S'n-Nyanza areal) | *-tele, *-tili | "prepared grain" |
| *-legi | "finger millet" (S'n Kaskazi areal) | *-pùngò | "winnowing tray" (S'n Nyanza areal) |
| *-lo | "finger millet" (Lakes; Temi of Upland) | *-taalo | "winnowing tray" (N'n Kaskazi: Lakes, Upland groups) |
| | | *-sì- | "to grind grain" |

*d. Words of Kusi distribution*

| | | | |
|---|---|---|---|
| *-pila | "sorghum" | *-poko | "finger millet" |

The Kusi communities may have begun to make grain cultivation a more significant element in their subsistence by not long after 500 B.C., since on the whole they tended to preserve older proto-Mashariki grain terms. The Kaskazi took the same step apparently still later, after their own initial expansions and their gradual divergence into several clusterings of communities. Among the indicators favoring this solution are the development of new, regionally occurring grain cultivation terms among the various Kaskazi groups, such as for "winnowing tray," and their adoption of not one, but several different regional names for finger millet (see table 24c). The verb *-pànd- remained the general verb for "to plant" among the Kaskazi, but apparently soon lost that usage in the Kusi groups, and this outcome also argues for a longer-lasting maintenance of the older planting techniques among the Kaskazi than among Kusi.

With respect to archeological expectations, the sites of Kusi communities, when eventually found, may well show increasing evidence of grain cultivation early in the second half of the last millennium B.C. Even so, yams must still have remained the major source of carbohydrates for most of the Kusi. The sites of Kaskazi people in the Nyanza Basin should present more irregular evidence for the development of grain cultivation until probably quite late in the millennium.

## Environmental Consequences of Adopting Grain Crops

These proposed developments in cultivation have significant implications for the palynology as well as the archeology of the period. The earliest Mashariki farmers, if McMaster's proposals and the arguments made in this chapter are right,[28] would have cultivated using minimal clearing of land, cutting larger vegetation (*-sàkul-) but leaving stumps in place, and branches and leaves on the ground to protect the surface from the potentially destructive effects of tropical downpours. They would have planted using small incisions in the soil made by slicing into it (*-pànd-) with a bladed tool, the planting-ax (see table 18: *-sòká). This set of techniques would have continued to be important among many Mashariki communities till late in the last millennium B.C.

Grain cultivation required a rather different technology, involving a more thorough clearing of the land (as reflected in the verb *-tém- in table 5), probably along with a burning of the cut-down vegetation in order to kill the seeds and stems of potential weeds, before the sowing of the grain took place. One new tool associated with grain cultivation, the long digging stick (see table 6: *-(u)lo), was adopted from the Central Sudanians by the Kaskazi grouping of communities probably before the middle of the last millennium B.C. Yet the overall evidence makes it clear that grain cultivation did not become a major activity among most Kaskazi peoples till centuries later. The tool most capable of turning the soil over, the iron hoe, also did not become general knowledge, the language evidence shows, till very late in the millennium, just before the wider East African expansions of Bantu people began (see table 6).[29]

The spread of the Mashariki into the Western Rift and western Great Lakes regions in the first half of the last millennium B.C. can therefore be expected to have had only limited effects on the fossil pollen (palynological) record, and for some of the areas settled by Kaskazi communities this consequence should have lasted through much of the second half of the millennium as well. Not probably before the end of last millennium B.C. did the Luyia and East Nyanza descendants of the Lakes people add to their vocabulary a new verb, adopted from an Southern Rub language, indicative of their move to more intensive cultivation (see *-bus-, verb for second weeding, in table 33). But once the raising of grains started to grow in importance, forest clearance of a broader and more lasting kind would have begun. For some areas of early Mashariki settlement, this new kind of effect should be visible in the pollen evidence by or before the middle of the last millennium; for other areas, only toward the end of the era or in the early first millennium A.D.

## Beer Brewing as an Accompaniment of Grain Cultivation

The tardy adoption of grain cultivation among the early Mashariki is mirrored in the history of their alcoholic beverages. The proto-Bantu made palm wine (table 16), and the practice of brewing wine from palm sap has persisted as a sporadically encountered feature of Mashariki culture, even though the Eastern African settlers after 500 B.C. were moving into lands with most often different species of palms from those previously used for brewing. Notable preservers of the tradition have been the Northeast-Coastal Bantu societies and the Tsonga of the southern Mozambique lowlands. The fact that new words have been drafted into use to name "palm wine" in such regions suggests that although the idea may been retained, perhaps through such a medium as folklore, the actual making of the drink

131

may have ceased for a period of generations, as Bantu communities of the turn of the eras moved far to the east and south, to areas where new suitable species of palm for wine had first to be identified.

The replacement of palm wine by beer among Mashariki peoples probably did not begin in earnest until the Late Mashariki era, probably fairly close in time to the respective establishments of significant grain cultivation among Kaskazi and Kusi communities. Two words for "beer," which may be separate derivatives of a single underlying root word, have wide distribution.[30]

The first of them, *-àlùà, appears in a nearly continuous spread from the Lakes group of languages southward through western Tanzania and the Lake Tanganyika area to central and western Zambia, and also separately in central Kenya in the Thagiicu languages of the Upland group of Kaskazi. It had thus to have come into use among Kaskazi communities before the movement of Upland communities out of the Great Lakes region, hence before the end of the last millennium B.C. But the rest of its distribution has the appearance of a diffusionary spread of the word and therefore of the item it names, beer, from the Kaskazi communities of western Tanzania. It is a spread that in fact almost precisely parallels that of the generic terms for the grains finger millet and sorghum, respectively *-lè and *-sàká, confirming the conclusion (see chapters 2 and 8) that the introduction of grain crops into the woodland savanna areas of southern Congo (Zaire) came from the Great Lakes region via the areas around northern Lake Tanganyika.

The second term, *-álà, appears in a broken distribution in Kusi languages and with a second area of occurrence to the west, in languages of the far southern parts of the savanna of western Zambia and eastern Angola. Its relict pattern in the Kusi languages conforms to its reconstructibility back to the Kusi cluster of communities of the late Late Mashariki era, while its use in languages such as Luvale and Mbunda can be understood as marking the later spread of beer making westward from the early Kusi settlers of southeastern Africa. Like the grain terms *-pú and *-bèlé, its distribution charts a separate, more southerly diffusionary route of grain crops, from Kusi societies westward through the dry savannas just north of the Kalahari (as is argued in chapter 8).

In sum, the evidence of generic terms for beer favors a late adoption of that grain beverage—probably after the middle of the last millennium B.C. for the Kusi, and at a point very late in the millennium for Kaskazi communities, at a time when the wider eastward scattering out of Kaskazi settlements was already beginning. Again, as for

132

grain cultivation, the evidence suggests that the Kusi grouping of Mashariki communities resided in a region where the factors favoring a shift to greater reliance on grains were more strongly present than for the Kaskazi farther north. Subsequently, probably during the early centuries of the first millennium A.D., the making of beer diffused southward from the Bantu peoples of the Great Lakes to Central-Savanna Bantu peoples in western Zambia and southwestern Congo (Zaire), and from Kusi settlers in southeastern Africa westward as far as southeastern Angola. Still farther west, in southwestern Angola, the older term for palm wine was reapplied in non-palm-wine-producing regions to the new kind of alcoholic beverage.

Whether the shift to brewing of beer will have easily visible archeological manifestations or not remains to be investigated. Possible consequences of the making of beer could, for instance, have included the development of particular kinds of pots for the cooking stages in beer brewing, or of large storage calabashes to hold the beer once brewed. Another feature encountered in a number of northern Mashariki societies is the beer straw, used by men to drink from a common pot, but like a beer calabash it is also an item unlikely often to be preserved in the archeological record.

# Livestock Raising

## Developments in Cattle Keeping

The later last millennium B.C. was, it appears, a time too of considerable change in the distributions and practices of herding. The earliest Mashariki were already keepers of goats, with a full breeding taxonomy of reference specifically to goats,[31] but to goats only. Through their encounters with the Eastern Sahelian peoples they surely gained some acquaintance with cattle, but an acquaintance that apparently did not translate into significant cattle raising. They developed a generic term for the cow, *-gòmbè, a word of as yet unknown origin.[32] But a breeding terminology specifically bovine did not develop. Two terms with breeding implications, *-kambako or *-kambaku, widely "bull," and *-buguma, *-bogoma "bearing female (of any livestock)," were present among the Kaskazi areal grouping of communities. The first of these two terms can be traced back to the preceding Early Mashariki period, because it is known also at present from a single Kusi language, Tsonga. There, however, it means "male hippopotamus." A fourth root word, of early proto-

Mashariki provenance, \*-puiḷi, perhaps meant simply "animal of breeding age." In Rundi its reflex refers today to "bull," but in the Botatwe languages of Zambia its meaning is "heifer," and in Shona "sheep."

Only late in the last millennium B.C. can significant raising of cattle by communities that spoke Mashariki dialects be expected to turn up in the archeological record. Southern Cushitic loanwords probably signal the beginnings of this process among the peoples of the Southern Nyanza areal grouping of Kaskazi Bantu (table 1B). Its full working out lay, however, in the immediately succeeding era, at the turn of the millennium, as the various dialect communities moved into their own separate encounters variously with Southern Nilotic, Southern Rub, and West Rift Southern Cushitic societies (see tables 31–36 and tables 3B and 4B). Even then, intensive or specialized cattle keeping should not be expected among the Bantu who settled eastward or southward of Lake Nyanza during the first few centuries A.D.—despite the influences visible in their vocabularies.

For the early Lakes societies that emerged west of Lake Nyanza after 500 B.C., the process may have taken a rather different turn, with the cattle raisers themselves in time adopting the language and most other features of the Lakes cultures, but maintaining their distinctive pastoral economic specialization. The origins of pastoral specialization by certain segments of Lakes Bantu societies, so evident during the past thousand years, may trace back, in other words, as early as the later stages of Lakes expansion.[33] Loanwords diagnostic of intensive cattle utilization (notably "blood" in table 9), together with the differing economic implications of Sog, Central Sudanic, and Southern Cushitic loanwords in the proto-Lakes language (see above), favor the conclusion that the originators of specialized pastoralism in the Great Lakes region were people of Tale Southern Cushitic ancestry (see table 9).

The milking of cattle was known to early Mashariki societies but is not likely to have been a significant source of sustenance. Some sort of knowledge of the practice is required by the application of the same verb, \*-kám-, to milking all across the Mashariki-speaking regions. The tenuousness of this acquaintance is suggested, however, by the fact that \*-kám- continued everywhere to maintain also its original connotation of squeezing in general. One proto-Mashariki noun, \*-sile, \*-seli, \*-sele "fresh milk" (see table 5) and one other possibly late Kaskazi term, \*-(y)aba "cream" (recorded so far only from Takama and Botatwe languages and of uncertain source) also support an acquaintance by Middle or Late Mashariki times with milk and milk fat from animals. A third root word, *-piu(piu) for fresh milk (from Mashariki *-píù "warm, hot," itself deriving from the proto-Bantu verb *-pí- in its senses "to be ripe" or "to be hot"), has a wide, scattered occurrence across the Kaskazi grouping of languages. But the complete lack of nouns for milk in soured form until much later times, after Bantu communities spread out across eastern and southern Africa, suggests that milk and milk fat were products more often obtained from or known among neighboring peoples than produced and processed in the Bantu communities themselves.

The Mashariki acquaintance with the bleeding of cattle, in contrast, probably dates no earlier than the very end of the Late Mashariki period, since the verb *-lás- denoting the practice is linked to cattle bleeding only in the northern and some central East African languages. Even in these instances, the verb generally also preserves its primary meaning, "to shoot with an arrow," showing as for *-kám- "to milk" that the trait was probably initially observed among neighboring societies rather than adopted by the Mashariki communities themselves. The practice was most likely a contribution specifically of Southern Cushites, for the bleeding of cattle does not occur among Central Sudanians, nor is it a probable ancient feature among Eastern Sahelian peoples, except among the Nilotes. That conclusion is corroborated by a roughly contemporaneous development in noun vocabulary, the adoption of the Tale Southern Cushitic word for blood in the Southern Nyanza areal grouping of dialects (see table 1B) and separately in early Lakes Bantu (see table 9)—the combined distributions of the two borrowed forms of the noun broadly correspond to that of *-lás- in its secondary meaning "to bleed." A corollary inference from the particular Kaskazi choice of *-lás- as the verb for "to bleed" is, of course, that the cattle-bleeding observed by these early Mashariki communities would have been performed even then by ahooting a special kind of arrow, with a blunt wooden point, into an ox's jugular vein, as has continued to be the custom in East Africa down to recent times.

The generic term *-gombe "cow" diffused westward across the southern savanna, in concert presumably with the spread of knowledge of the animal from Kusi Bantu peoples. An additional root word, *-tàngá "cattle pen; herd" (see table 38), also charts that course of spread. It is found scattered in several meanings (cattle pen, outlying cattle post, herd), a pattern typical of old root words, among the languages that derive from the Kusi areal grouping of Mashariki communities, and in a block distribution, typical of spread by borrowing, farther west across Zambia into parts of far southern Congo

(Zaire). But these distributions across the southern savanna zone, while partially paralleling that of grain terminology, probably betoken a westward spread of cattle later in time than the grains, possibly not until well into the first millennium A.D. (see chapter 7).

## Sheep and Donkeys

Another late addition to Mashariki livestock keeping was the sheep. This animal was certainly raised by Eastern Sahelian peoples much earlier than the last millennium B.C., and by that time had surely become known to many of the Central Sudanic people. The adoption of words for sheep in the early Mashariki dialects place the *effective* raising of the animal by Bantu speakers, however, surely no earlier than the late parts of the millennium. To that period can be attributed an array of separate word borrowings, from variously Southern Cushitic, Eastern Sahelian, and Central Sudanic languages into the Southern Nyanza regional grouping of dialects and into the southerly Kaskazi tongues (see tables 7, 10, 39, and 1B).

One additional root word, *-kondolo, names the sheep today in some of the southern Tanzanian languages and in Swahili. In Nyam-wezi-Sukuma it refers more narrowly, however, to wethers and goat wethers; and since this root can be derived from an earlier Bantu verb *-kond- "to strike"[34]—and because pounding the testicles is a wide-spread method of gelding in East Africa—it must be presumed originally to have been a word of technical reference to goat wethers. Its distribution dates it to the Late Mashariki period in that meaning, with its later application to sheep in general taking place first in proto-Rufiji-Ruvuma, a descendant language of the Kaskazi cluster, spoken in southern Tanzania at around the turn of the era.

For the spread of sheep beyond East Africa proper, the conclusions presented previously still generally hold:[35] namely, (1) that sheep (of the fat-tailed kind) were spread via East Africa into southeast-central, southeastern, and southwestern Africa ahead of Bantu expansion there, and (2) that, to the west of East Africa, sheep (of non-fat-tailed type) followed several lines of spread southward through the forest to the western southern savanna belt subsequent to the initial Bantu settlements in those areas.

One other animal, the donkey, apparently became well known to Bantu speakers at about the same time as sheep, that is to say, toward the close of the Southern-Nyanza era. An earlier acquaintance of some sort with the donkey belongs to the very first stage of the

136

Southern-Nyanza period, at perhaps about the the fifth to fourth century B.C., when the West-Nyanza subgroup of the Lakes Bantu still had a part in the interactions of the Southern-Nyanza communities with the Tale Southern Cushites. That first knowledge is reflected in the Southern-Nyanza adoption of the Tale root word for "donkey," *-dogowe, still used today in a Ganda of West-Nyanza and in many Kati languages (table 1B).

But the actual keeping of the animal by Kaskazi communities themselves should be dated two or three centuries later, to the late Southern-Nyanza period, when new regional names for "donkey" came into use. The areal grouping of pre-Luyia, East-Nyanza, and Upland communities adopted, with slight variations in pronunciation, the proto–Southern Nilotic term for "donkey" table 1B). The Kati contemporaneously applied, curiously, an earlier Eastern Bantu root, *-jóbé "marshbuck," to the new animal; this usage persists to the present in languages spoken at the extremities of the Kati distribution, such as Giryama and Sukuma. But they also maintained the earlier term *-dogowe and, as the donkey apparently gained importance in their economies, developed a separate word for the jackass, calling it by the root word *-póngó, which had previously meant "billy-goat" in the Early Mashariki period. That particular meaning for *-póngó may also have been taken up by the pre-Langi at about the same time. At probably a much later era, after the settlement of Kati and Upland speakers to the east of the Eastern Rift Valley, that same usage was borrowed into the Upland language, proto-Chaga, from a Kati language spoken in northeastern Tanzania (see chapter 6). This kind of limited breeding terminology, composed of a generic term and a term for a breedable male, is typical of animals raised for purposes other than their subsistence value,[36] and it suggests that, among at least some of the late Kati people, the donkey had already become an important beast of burden.

The generic term *-dogowe itself underwent a secondary spread much later, possibly as late as the eighteenth or nineteenth century, as a sometimes supplementary, but clearly borrowed word for the animal, to languages such as Nyamwezi-Sukuma, Rundi, and Safwa, spoken around the western and southwestern fringes of modern-day Tanzania. The probable explanation of this occurrence is that the animal did not survive well in the areas settled by these particular Mashariki peoples and thus remained little known to them until the commercial developments of recent centuries.

# Summing up the *Longue Durée*

We can begin now to see, incompletely and often dimly, something of the long-term trends and the major transitions in life and livelihood in western East Africa over the period of the last thousand years B.C. At 1000 B.C. farming populations who spoke Nilo-Saharan languages occupied a relatively restricted range of environments. These farmers depended principally on seed agriculture, with grains as the staples, supplemented in varying degrees by the raising of goats, sheep, and cattle and by hunting and, especially among Central Sudanians, fishing. Central Sudanic communities resided in areas as yet undiscovered archeologically but, from the coinciding indications of different kinds of language evidence, best placed in the long north-south belt of lands along the Western Rift. To the east of the Rift, most probably in drier parts of western Uganda, could be located another food-producing society, the Sog. Still farther to the east, the Southern Rub people, an offshoot of the Rub of northeastern Uganda, had perhaps already spread south along the immediate east of Lake Nyanza as far as the modern Mara and Musoma regions. Wherever farmers had not yet settled—and probably in many of the areas they had settled—food-collecting peoples continued to carry on their own kind of economy, as yet little disturbed by their agricultural neighbors.

During the next several hundred years, a new population increasingly made its presence felt. Bantu communities, speaking the proto-Mashariki language, intruded first into the lands on the immediate west of the Western Rift zone and then into the countries along the east of the Rift, extending in the north from the Kivu Basin to probably the southern end of Lake Tanganyika. Their arrival triggered off a wide range of new developments.

First and foremost, their settlements began to open up large new areas to farming. The Mashariki communities sought out a different range of environments than had been used before by the food-producing peoples of western East Africa. They had come from a high-rainfall, wooded region, and they began their settlement in the same kinds of environments, although a little higher in altitude and slightly cooler, in western East Africa. They were able to do so because they brought with them a wholly different kind of farming, dependent on relatively high rainfall—a planting rather than seed agriculture, with yams as its staples. They also raised goats and guineafowl, made considerable use of collected and hunted food resources, and fished extensively.

Their choice of areas to settle had two further probable consequences. First, unopposed by established farming communities, the Mashariki communities are likely to have entered into a period of accelerated population growth, a common consequence elsewhere in world history when mature cultivating economies have intruded into lands previously occupied by purely food-collecting peoples. Second, their expansions by stages would have overwhelmed and eliminated independent hunting and gathering as a viable economic option, not only because of population growth among the Mashariki communities, but because the Mashariki people supplemented their farm-produced foods with hunting, fishing, and collecting on a considerable scale. In other words, they competed strongly for resources with the previous gathering peoples.

At the same time, a wider regional process of technological shift began gradually to take hold, as the knowledge and practice of iron-working spread among the peoples of the western Great Lakes. It appeared first among the Central Sudanian and Eastern Sahelian communities before 1000 B.C., and probably well before mid-millennium had become common among the more northerly Mashariki communities as well. Gradually, it can be expected, the adoption of iron drove into disuse the different stone toolmaking traditions of each of these sets of peoples, much later in some areas than in others.

Up to mid-millennium, these developments built up across western East Africa probably an irregular patchwork of different cultural and economic approaches to life, with sizable areas of Mashariki settlement interspersed, especially in the Western Rift zone and just to the east of there, with Central Sudanic and Sog territories. The interactions across ethnic lines created a new body of widely shared technological knowledge, not only of ironworking but, especially among the Mashariki communities, of agricultural practices quite different from those their forebears had brought with them into East Africa. As yet, however, the new agricultural knowledge had had little practical effect; local economic orientations still probably largely coincided with ethnicity.

Over the second half of the last millennium B.C., this patchwork of culture and economy began to break down. A number of particular features of material culture of Sudanic, Eastern Sahelian, or Cushitic origin gained wide currency among the Bantu-speaking societies. Increasingly, it seems probable, Mashariki communities gave up their old style of rectangular, gable-roofed houses in favor of the round, conical-roofed houses of the Nilo-Saharan-speaking societies. By late in the millennium, new kinds of furnishing, too, notably beds

139

of some kind and carved wooden stools, had attained wide use across the region. Iron took on increasing importance in toolmaking even before the fifth century B.C., and the knowledge and practice of iron-working began also to spread out of the Great Lakes region, westward to Bantu peoples of the Congo Basin and to the more southerly, Kusi communities of the Mashariki Bantu. Meanwhile the faster growth of Mashariki populations had shifted the demographic advantage away from the earlier farming societies. The Mashariki communities spread into more and more areas, and as a consequence the Central Sudanic and Sog people began progressively to be assimilated into the societies of their Bantu-speaking neighbors.

The pace of human-induced environmental change must also have increased in several areas, as a number of the Mashariki began adding grain cultivation to their agriculture, adopted new agricultural tools such as the long digging stick and the iron hoe, and started practicing in consequence a more extensive clearing of land. In the areas along the south or southwest of Lake Nyanza, the clearing of land may already, as early as 500 B.C., have helped open the way to the settlement for the first time of specialized cattle raisers, the Tale Southern Cushites, in the region. Later in the millennium the cutting back of forest probably further accelerated in some areas, notably in Bukoba at the southwest of Lake Nyanza, to meet the charcoal requirements of extensive iron smelting.[37]

Toward the close of the millennium, these various developments converged to set off a new series of events. Population growth commenced in more and more areas to threaten the ability of Mashariki people to sustain, unmodified, the very-long-fallow, yam-based agriculture that their ancestors had brought with them into western East Africa in the early parts of the millennium. One response, to add grain crops and increase the portion of the diet obtained from cultivation, had already been underway among some Mashariki communities. This step probably helped fuel the wider spread of Lakes people within the Nyanza Basin. The adoption by various Mashariki people during the same centuries of sheep and, where environment allowed, cattle contributed a further increment to subsistence productivity— and an additional factor, grazing, in the sustained decline of forest.

A second response was a more drastic one: to move entirely out of the western side of East Africa and to seek out suitable environments far afield in which to pursue the old livelihood or to carry on a mixture of yam raising and increased grain cultivation. This option was taken up particularly among the Kaskazi communities in the south and southwest of the Nyanza Basin, and among the Kusi groups

140

residing still farther to the south. Thus began the events that mark the inception of the Later Classical Age—the far-flung expansions of Bantu societies that within a period of four or five centuries, from perhaps 300 B.C. to A.D. 200, scattered Mashariki peoples from the coasts of Kenya at the north, to the woodland savannas of Malawi and Mozambique and the varied environments of Zimbabwe, Natal, and the Transvaal at the south.

But that is a topic for chapters 6 and 7. For now, we have still another important set of themes to explore that relate to the Early Classical Age of Greater Eastern African history, and so we move on to chapter 5, in which we take account of social and political institutions and of custom and belief among the East Africans of the early and middle last millennium B.C.

# Notes

[1] Hamilton, Taylor, and Vogel 1986; Schoenbrun 1990.
[2] McMaster 1988.
[3] Ehret 1974a; Vansina 1990.
[4] Ehret 1980a.
[5] This topic is dealt with extensively in Schoenbrun 1990.
[6] This evidence is developed at length in Ehret 1995/96.
[7] Schmidt 1978.
[8] Ehret 1995/96.
[9] Central Sudanic root words in table 17 are taken from Ehret 1992.
[10] Ehret 1995/96.
[11] Ehret 1995/96
[12] McMaster 1988.
[13] Vansina 1990: 45.
[14] Ehret 1995/96.
[15] McMaster 1988.
[16] Ehret 1995/96.
[17] Schmidt 1978 and elsewhere.
[18] The term *-umba may possibly be from a hypothesized Central Sudanic root word *omba, built on the proto–Central Sudanic root *mba, "to sit, stay," hence, "to dwell, reside"; the derivation proposed in Ehret 1973b is any case wrong.
[19] Vansina 1990 identifies it as a "Western" Bantu root.
[20] This usage may conflate this word and another Bantu root word of the same segmental phonology, *-gongo, "country, locality," found in some non-Mashariki Bantu languages.

[21] Vansina 1990.

[22] Ehret 1980b: 300.

[23] See Saxon 1980 for a first development of this evidence.

[24] See Ehret 1980b for the relevant data.

[25] See also Ehret 1974a; Guthrie 1967–72, for primary data.

[26] McMaster 1988.

[27] Schoenbrun forthcoming.

[28] McMaster 1988.

[29] See Ehret 1995/96 for further argumentation.

[30] Contra Ehret 1974a, the sources of these two root shapes remain to be satisfactorily identified.

[31] Ehret 1980a.

[32] The proposal in Ehret 1973b of a Central Sudanic source for this root word cannot be sustained.

[33] Schoenbrun 1990.

[34] Contra the mistaken etymology in Ehret 1968.

[35] Ehret 1974a.

[36] As argued in Ehret 1980a.

[37] Schoenbrun 1990.

# 5. Aspects of Social History

While wide-ranging changes in both the specifics of material life and the broad orientations of economy and technology were taking place among the societies of western East Africa, especially during the second half of the last millennium B.C., new developments in social relations and religion may have been rather fewer. Quite different social institutions and religious systems characterized the best known cultures of the era, those of the Central Sudanians, the Mashariki Bantu, the Southern Nilotes, and the Southern Cushites. And more often than not, change in these portions of culture came about through the shifting of people from one cultural system and ethnic identification to another. The building of composite social and religious traditions, which blended Sudanic and Bantu features, much more characterizes the social history of the first millennium A.D. than of the first millennium B.C.

## Social Institutions and Religion among the Sudanians

### Central Sudanian Kin and Authority

It has been argued that segmentary kinship systems prevailed among early Central Sudanic peoples, and certainly there is comparative evidence in several geographically separate Central Sudanic societies for that kind of social structure.[1] Segmentary systems are ones in which people identify themselves as belonging to a series of kin groupings of successively wider scope: for example, to a lineage of a subclan of a clan of a tribe, with the legendary founders at each step up the scale being siblings of a common parent to whom is ascribed the founding of the next higher level in the scheme. The vocabulary evidence so far available does not, however, require such a system. It supports only the single level of a clan among early East Central Sudanians; and for the still earlier proto–Central Sudanic period even a reconstructible word for "clan" has as yet to be identified.

The usual pattern of descent among Central Sudanic societies today is patrilineal, but the situation of the early East Central Sudanic

143

societies is not so clear. The single reconstructible word for a kin institution, *ďi "clan," has conflicting applications in modern languages. Among the solely patrilineal Moru-Madi peoples it refers simply
to a clan, which, naturally enough, is patrilineal; for the Balese, who
live today in the Ituri region of Congo (Zaire), surrounded by
patrilineal societies, it identifies, in contrast, a matriclan. The possibility is thus a strong one that the proto–East Central Sudanic people had
matrilineal clans in the third millennium B.C. But whether such a rule
of descent might still have existed among the particular East Central
Sudanians who interacted with the early Mashariki peoples in the last
millennium B.C. cannot presently be determined.

Chiefship in the sense of a hereditary leadership role did not exist among the early East Central Sudanic societies. One named position, *opi, passed down within a particular family or lineage, appears
among the Moru-Madi and neighboring Balendru groups of East
Central Sudanic, but it was a status originally of religious rather than
of political significance. Among the modern Lugbara, it identifies a
functionary whose role it is to tend the shrine of the spirit of an important founding ancestor of a kin group.[2] Known only among the
two neighboring Central Sudanic populations, the term may well have
spread in use from one group to the other after the proto-East Central
period of 4,000-plus years ago. As argued below, the *opi probably
originally had some more general role as a religious intercessor or
perhaps prophet of Divinity.

Only the most preliminary of proposals can be made as to the
social order that might have existed among the Sog and Southern Rub
societies. Among the Rub, and among other Eastern Sahelian peoples
of East Africa, such as the Southern Nilotes, patrilineal clan institutions can be traced back to at least the early last millennium B.C. The
probability, therefore, is that clans, presumably patrilineal, would have
been found also in the last millennium B.C. among the Sog and
Southern Rub communities of the Great Lakes region. It should be
kept in mind, however, that direct, determinative vocabulary evidence
for this conclusion remains to be identified. The comparative Eastern
Sahelian cultural evidence, in addition, strongly supports the proposition that the Southern Rub and Sog societies got along quite well
without any positions of hereditary, chiefly political authority.

## Sudanic Religion

Many Eastern Sahelian as well as the Central Sudanic peoples partake of a common religious tradition of ancient standing across large parts of the eastern sudan geographical zone, which lies to the north of East Africa. From its geographical distribution, we can call this tradition the "Sudanic religion." It is a religion that spread widely thousands of years ago to encompass the Cushitic peoples of the Horn of Africa as well as the Nilo-Saharan-speaking peoples of the sudan proper. The evidence of vocabulary implies its presence among the Cushites probably as early as the proto-Cushitic period of the eighth or seventh millennium B.C.[3] It may have spread to the Central Sudanians during the proto–Central Sudanic era, at a time somewhere around 5000 B.C.[4]

In this Sudanic religion there is but a single level of the preternatural, a single spiritual Force or Presence associated symbolically and perhaps literally also with the sky and rain. Recent scholarly studies have translated the African names for this conceptualization of spirit as "Divinity."[5] Its initial capital letter expresses the global equivalence of Divinity to the Christian and Muslim ideas of God, but the particular choice of the word is meant to convey the less theistic ontology of its subject. Another term in English that might serve almost as well would be "Spirit." Divinity (or Spirit) was one, although it could have different particular hypostases: in more recent history, Divinity in a number of societies has come to express itself in the form of named lesser manifestations of spirit.

Two basic religious concepts are encoded in the reconstructed early Central Sudanic vocabulary. One of these is the sky-Divinity connection, denoted in proto–East Central Sudanic by two words, *dra and *ore, and the other is a metaphor of the shadow as the life-force, *nẓi, that departs the body at death.[6] No role for ancestor spirits appears in the early evidence, and the generality of comparative cultural testimony confirms the nonpresence of this feature in early Central Sudanic religion. Certain spirits of the dead do figure in the considerations of some recent Central Sudanic societies, as for instance the founding ancestors ministered to by the *opi among the Lugbara. But these aspects of belief seem all to be historically recent additions to religion. The Lugbara language, which has reapplied the old root word *ore for Divinity to the ancestor spirit looked after by the *opi, is a case in point. The meaning shift of *ore took place probably during the last 1,000 years, since even in the very closely related Madi language the word still today denotes Divinity. And for that reason, it must also be argued that the *opi originally had a broader role, perhaps as an intercessor or seer of Divinity or its particular hypostases.

How that great human philosophical concern, the problem of evil, was accounted for in early Central Sudanic thought remains to be studied. In many Nilotic societies, which also subscribe to the basic concepts of this Sudanic religion, evil as well as good stem ultimately from Divinity. Bad happenings are divine retribution for wrongs that one, or one's recent forebears, have committed. All that can be said at present is that the early Central Sudanians may well have held the same view.

## Polity and Society among Bantu Communities

### Kin and Authority among the Early Mashariki

To the Mashariki Bantu who began to settle in far western East Africa in the early last millennium B.C. can be attributed a quite different set of institutions and beliefs. Their social historical background can be outlined in considerably greater detail as well.

Professor Jan Vansina in his study of the early history of the equatorial rainforest has raised some interesting issues for the reconstructing of the institutions of political authority among the earliest Bantu-speaking societies.[7] He postulates an original pattern in western Bantu areas of households grouped together in "Houses," in effect sections of a village, composed of people linked by a variety of relations including bilateral, noncorporate kinship. The Houses were headed by "Big Men," who gained their positions at least in part through their wealth and not necessarily by inheritance.

But authority among the early Mashariki probably had a rather more formal connection to kinship institutions than Vansina's model allows for. Moreover, the set of ideas which constitute that connection can be traced back to the earlier proto-Savanna period and even perhaps still earlier, to the original proto-Bantu society. Four noun roots widely tie in with conceptions of chiefship in Mashariki languages: *-àmì, *-kúmù, *-éné, and *-kósì.

The first, *-àmì, appears to have applied in earliest Mashariki times to the chief of a clan or a grouping of closely connected clans. With this meaning it has a rare, relict distribution—occurring in the Lakes group of the Kaskazi division of Mashariki and, outside Mashariki proper, in the Botatwe group (and in some adjacent lan-

146

guages much influenced in recent times by the Botatwe). This distribution is consistent with this position's having come into being among the easterly participants in the Savanna-Bantu expansion, not long before the start of the Early Mashariki period. The person who bears this title, wherever kingship has not evolved, has above all ritual functions, especially with respect to the ancestors and in matters related to planting and the harvest, and, though influential, is certainly no ruler. And it is this kind of role we must also envision also for the *mu-àmì* of the early last millennium B.C.[8]

The second noun root, *-kúmù, similarly has a relict distribution in Mashariki languages, occurring in the Lakes subgroup and in some contiguous Takama tongues in the meaning "diviner-doctor" ("medicine man") and in the Nyasa subgroup (Tumbuka, Sena, and the Nyanja-Chewa language) as "chief, king." Outside Mashariki this root word often denotes a role loosely translated into European languages as the position of "chief," and it is the term that Vansina interprets as "big man." The historically original sense of the word, however, was "honored person," as its derivation from the PB verb *-kùm- "to be honored" clearly requires. To project back to earlier eras the "big-man" role, as envisioned by Vansina, that may have existed in certain westerly Bantu societies during the past 1,000–1,500 years is surely to mischaracterize the less politicized social position connoted by the noun *-kúmù. Social influence and ritual importance rather than material authority are implied in its derivation.

The overall semantic history of *-kúmù fits best with its having originally applied to a ritual leader of a defined kin group or set of related kin groups. It would, in other words, have identified a position much like those found often among Bantu and other Niger-Congo societies in which political kingship did not evolve (Bantu languages belong to the Niger-Congo language family), such as the office of *nri* among the Igbo of Nigeria, or the *okumo*, the ritual chief priest of the Krobo of Ghana. The latter example is a particularly telling datum for this interpretation because *okumo* is visibly cognate with the proto-Bantu term *-kúmù, although separately derived from the underlying verb *-kúm-. The verb itself continued to convey a connotation of kin-connected ritual leadership in the early Mashariki languages, as is demonstrated by the separately derived term, *mfumwa* (from earlier *-kúmua), found in the Asu and Seuta languages of the Kati subgroup and applying to a clan chief with important ritual functions. Even within the Mashariki branch of Bantu, the comparative evidence clearly thus implies that an originally ritual, rather than political, role in society was encoded in this verb and its derived nouns.

147

The probable kin group to which the *-kúmù̠ was connected in early Mashariki society would have been the lineage. In a scatter of Mashariki and Central-Savanna-Bantu languages, the word has that kind of application today, for example, in Nyiha of the Rungwe subgroup, where it designates a subchief. The higher Mashariki level of ritual authority over the clan can, in any case, already be attributed to the *-àmì̠. The *-kúmù̠, it is proposed here, would have fulfilled for the lineage the same roles, of presiding over planting and harvest ceremonies (*-lì̠mbul-) and mediating between the local community and its ancestors, as the *-àmì̠ performed for the clan as a whole. In the more ancient eras of Bantu history, before the development of the position of *-àmì̠ among the immediate ancestors of the Mashariki, the only kin-chiefly role would have been that of the *-kúmù̠.

A third member of the PB set of nouns of authority, *-éné, has the primary meaning of "owner, master" through most of its wide Savanna and Mashariki Bantu distribution. But in several areas, especially in parts of the southern savanna geographical belt, it serves as a word for "chief" or "king." It is not at all improbable that a major portion of this southerly distribution stems from the diffusion of new political ideologies during the Later Iron Age, roughly since 1000 A.D. But sporadic occurrences of the word with chiefly meanings elsewhere, as in the northern Swahili towns, where it appears in the skewed shape *mwinyi* or *mwenyi*, suggest that the connection of this term to clan-chiefly authority may be quite old, at least as a secondary conceptualization of such roles in society. Further support for the very early existence among Bantu societies of this conception of kin leadership can be also be seen in the use far to the west of the Mashariki lands, in the Kongo language, of the verb *-vw-* "to own" to express the relationship of kin leaders to their dependents. And the connection of *-éné to leadership may go back to even earlier periods of Niger-Congo history if it is indeed cognate, as various scholars have suggested, with Akan (of Ghana) *-hene "chief."

And finally, the fourth term, *-kósì̠, appears with several regionally distributed meanings—in the Kati languages of Tanzania, as "elder; married man; family head"; in the Southeast-Bantu subgroup, as "chief"; in Shona, as "senior wife"; and in savanna languages extending inland from the Atlantic coast and southward from the western equatorial rainforest, as "lion." These meanings together suggest its original implication to have been "strong or mature person, particularly (though not necessarily only?) male, having authority over a small group of kin." Its original scope of reference is most likely to have been to heads of the extended families that made up a lineage.

148

The cumulative implication of these data is that not long before the Early Mashariki period, a new level of hereditary kin chief (*-àmì) emerged among the Mashariki communities and some of their Savanna-Bantu relatives. An earlier position, traceable back to proto-Bantu, of "honored person" (*-kúmù)—most probably a hereditary ritual head of a narrower, lineage grouping of households within the wider kin—continued to have a leadership role in society. A subsidiary conceptualization of leadership viewed the *-àmì and *-kúmù as owners (*-éné) of their kin in some socially symbolic fashion. An additional formally recognized role may have been that of an extended-family head (*-kósì).

## Mashariki and Savanna-Bantu Kin Institutions

What was the nature of the "kin" of which we speak here? Vansina, in dealing with the more westerly Bantu societies of the forest, argues for an originally bilateral reckoning of kinship, with clans and lineage organization evolving later in response to particular regional historical conditions.[9] But for the early Mashariki, and even for the wider Savanna-Bantu grouping that includes Mashariki as one of its subgroups, the evidence is consistent with a different picture.

Two reconstructible words sketch out the primary outlines of the picture for the early Mashariki communities.

The less widely found of the two, *-kòlò, can be traced back to the Late Mashariki era. It appears in Luyia dialects of the Lakes subgroup and widely through the other Kaskazi languages. It consistently connotes "clan"; and among the Ruvu peoples, the one subgrouping of the Kaskazi who have both matrilineal and patrilineal descent groups, *-kòlò specifically carries the meaning "matriclan."

The second term, *-lòngó, recurs in languages of both the Kaskazi and Kusi divisions of the Mashariki group and in some Central-Savanna languages as well. Its Mashariki occurrences are relict ones. In the language of the patrilineal Venda of Southeast-Bantu it has been glossed as "family group," while the Ruvu subgroup of Kaskazi provides key evidence on its original meaning—there it designates an institution of only relict role in Ruvu societies, a "patrilineage," as opposed to *-kòlò for the more centrally important "matriclan." (In the single patrilineal society of the Ruvu group, the Gogo, *-lòngò now refers to a patrilineage within the patrilineal clan.) Interestingly the Ruvu patrilineage is associated, as the matriclan connection is not, with the food avoidances an individual should observe.[10]

Moreover, in the meaning "lineage," *-lòngò needs also to be traced back still earlier than the Early Mashariki period, to the preceding proto-Savanna era. "Lineage" for our purposes here is defined as the group of people who descend by known genealogical connections from an earlier common ancestor; a "clan" is a wider grouping of lineages claiming, usually without being able to recite the specific genealogical connections, a still earlier common founding ancestor. The Lega, Central-Savanna, and Western-Savanna reflexes of *-lòngò have a somewhat different range of meanings from those found in Mashariki. These include "tribe" (in some Southwest-Bantu dialects and in Lega), "family" (in Luba of Kasai), and "blood relationship" on either the mother's or father's side (in Luba of Katanga). Were only this evidence available, one might assume an originally broad Savanna-Bantu meaning "kinship" for *-lòngò, with the senses "family" and "tribe" as different specifications, in particular languages, of the distance of that kinship.

But there is another and clinching consideration for choosing "lineage" as the word's original kinship referent: *-lòngò began in proto-Bantu with the concrete meaning "line (of objects)," and it is that meaning for the root which is still found widely all across the Bantu-speaking world today. Its tangible referent was not, in other words, an amorphous or loose grouping, but a sequentially ordered set. And its only logical analogue in kin relations is the line of forebears that leads back to a founding ancestor, in other words, a lineage. The derivation of *-lòngò makes sense only if it started its career in the arena of kin relations with the specific meaning "lineage."[11]

A lineage level in the kin structure of early Mashariki society, and of earlier Savanna-Bantu society as well, is also evoked by widely recurring, reconstructible old metaphors encompassed in the words that translate today as "lineage" across a wide variety of Bantu languages. One metaphor for lineage recurs in scattered, relict distribution among Kaskazi languages, and must therefore be reconstructed back to the Late Mashariki period: to wit, "doorway," most often expressed by proto-Bantu *-lìàngò.

Two other metaphors for the lineage, "belly" and "house," have much wider occurrences. The first of these, "belly," appears in such disparate languages as Kongo and Ila of the Botatwe group, in Nsenga of the Sabi group, and, among Mashariki languages, in Luyia and Soga of the Lakes subgroup. The second image, "house," evokes the lineage across a parallel geographical spread of Bantu lan-

150

guages, but in a much larger number of those societies. These latter two metaphors both show the kind of scattered distribution indicative of their great age among Bantu societies, their specific range of occurrences tracing their use to well before the Early Mashariki period, to at least the proto-Savanna language. "House" stands out as the principal term for "lineage"; "belly" may have been a less-favored alternative idiom. The "doorway," as a feature of the house, may reflect a Kaskazi reworking of the house-lineage metaphor.

Finally, and most importantly, what kind of lineage do these metaphorical names depict? The metaphor of "belly" is overtly matrilineal in its implication. But what may not be recognized by European or American commentators is that "house" in its African milieu is commonly also an idiom of female connotation. Widely in tropical Africa, possession of a house is the characteristic feature of being a wife and a mother. "A woman's home is her castle," as one might restate the English saying. The lineage unit named by the metaphor "house" among the early Savanna and Mashariki societies was, one can argue, originally matrifocal and matrilineal.

What of the second term for "lineage," *-lòngò, which must also be reconstructed back to some point in the Savanna-Bantu era? Its recurrent connections in Mashariki languages to patrilineal kinship favor its original application to a patrilineal descent group, in contrast to the matrilineal connotations of Kaskazi *-kòlò and of the old metaphor "house." The surprising intimation of the evidence is therefore that a dual descent system, consisting of matrilineages (conveyed by the Savanna-Bantu root, *-jú, *-jó, literally "house," from earlier Bantu *-júbò, "house," by loss of medial *b) and patrilineages (*-lòngò), would have been present both in the early Mashariki society and in the earlier proto-Savanna period. The operations of dual descent found in such Southwest-Bantu societies as the Herero and among the Ovimbundu of Angola no longer need, in that case, special historical explanations of their own. They can be simply understood as historically modified survivals of a much more ancient system that embraced both matrilineages—which governed residence as they do among the Herero, for instance—and patrilineages, of some other, as yet to be determined, social role.

A third old term for a formal kin grouping needs to be reconstructed as well, namely, *-gàndá. Vansina, who as we have seen also postulates the very early Bantu development of "House" as a metaphor of social structure, connects the "House" with this particular PB root word, although envisioning it as an unstructured institution of bilateral kin and other social connections.[12] But the semantic evidence does not support that connection. In the westerly Bantu areas, to which Vansina's arguments most directly pertain, the recurrent concrete references of the root *-gàndá are to residential units larger than the house but, as often as not, smaller than the whole village: to "village" in a number of languages, to a "chief's compound" in other cases, to a "quarter of a village" in a few languages, and even to "fishing camp" in the central Congo Basin.

The word consistently takes on the meaning "house" only in a quite different part of the Bantu field, in a relict occurrence in just the Kaskazi languages—appearing thusly in the Mwika subgroup, in a few Upland languages (where it actually names a ruder shelter than a house), and in the West Ruvu sub-subgroup of the Kati languages. It also appears as the word for "house" in certain Sabi dialects and in the Botatwe group, where its use probably owes specifically to influences from Kaskazi languages spoken in Zambia in the early first millennium A.D. (see tables 37 and 44).

Clearly, then, *-gàndá originally named a residential grouping subordinate to, or forming an offshoot of, a village. Only later, among the Kaskazi dialects of Mashariki, did it take on the narrower meaning "house." Neither "house" nor "village" can, in any case, have been the original concrete reference of this root, because strongly reconstructible proto-Bantu roots for both these meanings exist: *-júbò "house" and *-gì̀ì "village" (usually reconstructed as proto-Bantu and proto-Mashariki *-gì̀, with an alternate Mashariki reflex *-jì̀).

From these two kinds of considerations—of competing root words and of actual semantic outcomes—it can be argued, in sum, that *-gàndá originally named a residential unit larger than an individual house, most probably a section of a village; that it became, by meaning shift dating no earlier than Middle Mashariki times, a synonym for *-júbò/*-jú/*-jó "house"; and that, finally, both terms were widely, but not universally, displaced from use over the course of the Middle and Late Mashariki periods by a new root word *-ùmbá for "house." The probable reason for this displacement (as already proposed in chapter 3) was the wide replacing at that period of the earlier Bantu rectangular, gable-roofed houses by a round, conical-roofed style of dwelling. Not surprisingly, one especially notable relict Mashariki retention of *-gàndá for "house" is in the East Ruvu languages of eastern Tanzania, whose speakers often still build rectangular, gable-roofed houses.

In two ways, then, the interpretation offered here departs from Vansina's reconstruction. First, it posits that while the concept of a

"House" did appear as an early formative principle among Bantu societies, it was a "House" differently founded—on a more formal kin basis, that of the lineage—than Vansina implies. Second, the particular root word that expressed this linkage was most probably not *-gàndá, but rather *-júbò, the actual oldest Bantu root word for a tangible house, the reflexes of which are still used to express the lineage-house metaphor today in Kongo and in many of the Lakes languages. As other words took on the concrete meaning of "house," they too became susceptible to expressing the additional meaning "lineage," originally "matrilineage." Examples include *-ùmbá used for both "house" and "lineage" in Gusii and *-gàndá applied in the same range of meaning in Bemba and other Sabi dialects.

To what kind of kin group did the term *-gàndá originally apply, then, if not to a "house" in its metaphorical extension to a lineage? As a kin term, *-gàndá appears today in a relict distribution—among a block of matrilineal peoples centered around the lower Congo River region, where it denotes "clan"; in Herero in Namibia, where it specifies a matriclan, as opposed to a patriclan, within a system of dual descent; and in the Lakes subgroup of the Kaskazi Mashariki, to designate "clan," today patrilineal. The areal distribution of *-gàndá in the lower Congo region, crossing the lines of subgroup relationships, indicates that in that particular zone it may have spread, at least in some instances, by diffusion long after the original Bantu settlement of these regions had taken place. It may thus represent, as Vansina has argued, a development in a few societies there of matrilineal clanship subsequent to the early Bantu eras.

But the remaining distribution of *-gàndá as a kin term cannot be explained away as a late development. Overall, it has just the kind of relict distribution that makes sense historically only if we reconstruct it as having taken on a kin meaning at least as early as the proto-Savanna period. The most telling evidence that *-gàndá anciently identified a matriclan comes from Herero, where the word specifically defines a matriclan in opposition to a patriclan. The Lakes societies today attach *-gàndá to patrilineal clans, but these peoples can be shown from their preservation of the "house" and "belly" metaphors for "lineage" to have once been matrilineal.

Might *-gàndá have originally referred to a lineage and been later separately expanded in meaning in different regions to apply to a clan? Its concrete application, to a section or offshoot of a village, argues strongly against this idea, for the following reason. The metaphor of the "house" does not identify as a lineage the group of people who constitute a literal household. Rather, it comprises those belonging to different present-day households who can trace their ancestry to *a particular household of the past*—to a particular founding, historical "house." It was and is a term of historical content. Similarly, *-gàndá, as the next residential level wider than the household, should not have referred in its kin sense to the particular collection of households that constituted an existing residential *-gàndá. Rather, as for "house," its social metaphor would have been historical. Its expected referent would have been the next wider level in society, namely, the collection of metaphorical "houses," that is to say, the collection of lineages, whose members thought of their distant lineage ancestors as having belonged to a particular association of founding households—as having belonged, in a metaphorical or perhaps literal sense, to a single residential *-gàndá of an earlier time. The abstract meanings of "house" and *-gàndá make historical sense only if they developed in tandem, during a single era of social development in which the concrete term "house" took on the added meaning "lineage" and the concrete word for a "collection of houses" began to apply to a "collection of lineages," that is, a clan.

In sum, by both lines of argument, it seems probable that by the proto-Savanna-Bantu period, society was structured around matriclans (*-gàndá). each composed of matrilineages ("houses": *-jú/*-jó/ *-júbò). The matriclans and matrilineages coexisted with an alternative social reckoning, of patrilineal descent, the patri-kins probably having a single level of structure and having a less fundamental importance in societal organization than the two levels of matri-kin.[13]

Before the Early Mashariki era, as was shown above, there had emerged also the role of kin chief (*-àmì). In the context of the kin-group evidence, the *-àmì is best interpreted as most likely having been a role of principally ritual importance. Judging from the attributes of the position among the Luyia and the Botatwe peoples, the *-àmì probably carried out the same sorts of ritual functions directed toward the ancestors, but simply for a larger grouping of kin, as had lineage heads previously. The earlier position of "honored person" (*-kúmù), judging from its recurrent connection to lesser chiefly roles among later Mashariki subgroups, probably continued to fill the role of that lineage head, whereas the extended family within the lineage looked to the *-kósí as its senior member.

During the Early Mashariki era, the patrilineage may have become the social locus of particular food avoidances or taboos, if indeed it had not already possessed this feature. The modern-day distributions of such traits fit that conclusion well. Clan or lineage avoidances tend to be rare in the Mashariki societies that remain matrilineal today, but recur among distantly separated Mashariki peoples, such as the Sotho of Southeast-Bantu and the Lakes communities, who have shifted entirely to patrilineal descent. Moreover, in the Ruvu societies, which have both patrilineages and matriclans, such avoidances are specifically patrilineal features. The matriclans, on the other hand, probably continued throughout the last millennium B.C. to provide the primary basis of inheritance, succession, and residence. The term for matriclan, *-gàndá, was, however, eventually displaced from use during the Late Mashariki period by a new term *-kòlò, with the older word surviving only among some of the Bantu communities of the Great Lakes region, where it was reapplied to an emerging new social grouping, a patrilineal clan.

The structure of society depicted by *-gàndá, *-àmì, and related terms can be proposed to have engendered a particular kind of material expression during the proto-Bantu era. The typical early Mashariki settlement was composed, it can be argued, of people who in theory belonged to a particular matrilineage, although in practice their numbers would presumably have included affines and people allied by ties of friendship or other common interest. The individual settlement by at least the Late Mashariki period, as already argued in chapter 3, may often have taken the form of a ridge-village, overseen by a ritual head, the *-kúmù. The effective larger social unit comprised, at most, a few such settlements, tied together by their shared acceptance of a particular kin chief (*-àmì) as their overall ritual leader and by their sense of a deeper-level, clan connection among their respective matrilineages.

## Age Sets and Rites of Passage among Bantu Communities

A second kind of early Mashariki social institution probably had its source in male rites of passage from boyhood to manhood. Boys, it can be shown from the language evidence, were initiated at adolescence into age sets of some sort. The custom itself appears today in a rare, relict distribution among the Mashariki societies. Age sets are found at the far northeast, among several of the Kaskazi peoples whose ancestors during the first millennium settled in Kenya or far northern Tanzania and assimilated into their societies considerable numbers of Southern or Eastern Nilotes, both of which had their own kinds of age-set systems. They are found also in the far southeast, among the Southeast-Bantu subgroup of Kusi. The retention down to the present of the proto-Bantu root word for age set, *-kúlà, in the

155

Luyia and the Southeast-Nyanza subgroups of Kaskazi confirms that the institution was not an adoption from Nilotes, but a preserved older feature in early Mashariki society, and a feature, at that, which traced back all the way to the proto-Bantu era. The transparent derivation of the root word *-kúlà from PB *-kúl- "to grow (up)" demonstrates the ancientness of the conceptual linking of age sets to coming of age.

The original functions and social roles of Mashariki age sets remain to be established. Their disappearance among so many of the later Mashariki peoples suggests that they were of secondary importance to the social order. They probably lacked the sort of corporate status that age sets often took on among those Kaskazi societies that were influenced by the Nilotic example. They were surely recruited from a local clan-based community and served mostly as a means of socializing adolescent males to community norms and mobilizing their labor for community projects.

The outward sign of initiation into manhood and into an age set was circumcision. Again this custom has widely been lost among recent Mashariki societies, but the reconstructed culture vocabulary resoundingly confirms its salience in early Mashariki society. At least three root words dealing with circumcision and its ceremonial aspects can be reconstructed not only back to proto-Mashariki but to the earlier proto-Savanna-Bantu period; two more root words can be traced to proto-Mashariki; while an additional important verb came into use apparently toward the end of the Late Mashariki period (table 25). The connection of circumcision to age-set formation is reconfirmed in these data, notably by a noun root *-líika, the reflexes of which in northerly Bantu languages mean "age set" and in Southeast-Bantu, specifically Sotho, signify "boy undergoing circumcision rites."

The ceremonies surrounding the operation itself were long and elaborate, covering a period of possibly as much as three months. The comparative ethnographic evidence, drawn from the far separated examples of the Luyia and East-Nyanza peoples of the Kaskazi division of Mashariki[14] and of the Southeast-Bantu of the Kusi division, is remarkably consistent in its testimony as to the major steps in the process. The boys to be circumcised first bathed in a stream and then were taken to a circumcision camp. There they were circumcised. They were also smeared with mud, but just when is unclear: the evidence of Xhosa practice places the smearing immediately after the cutting itself, but in Luyia societies it preceded the event. Soon after—in the Xhosa example as soon as the initial healing had taken place—the initiated boys were smeared with white clay, and the covering of white clay was renewed throughout the seclusion period. As

Vansina has shown, white clay had a long and ancient association in Bantu thought with ritual observance.[15]

During the seclusion period, the boys were not allowed to bathe, they probably each had an older male sponsor or tutor, and for a portion of the period they were taught various kinds of cultural and social lore. Shortly *before* leaving seclusion, the boys had their heads shaved. (Shaving also preceding circumcision is found in some Luyia and East-Nyanza societies, but this appears to be a trait adopted from their Southern Nilotic neighbors.) There may also have been a bathing ceremony at the end of seclusion, in which the white clay was finally washed off. The boys then left the seclusion camp, which was burnt.

The evidence from Bantu societies of the western savanna indicates that many of these features of the circumcision rites go back still further into the Bantu cultural past, well before the Early Mashariki era. An interesting difference in western savanna areas was the importance of masks in the rites, and this difference highlights another development that probably began in early Mashariki times, namely, the decline of maskmaking. Masks were a very ancient feature of Niger-Congo cultures. They have remained immensely important in

---

### Table 25. Bantu age sets and circumcision

a. *Words of certain or probable proto-Bantu (PB) usage*

   *-kúlà   "age set"
   *-tịb-   "to circumcise"

b. *Words of Savanna and Mashariki distribution*

   *-alik-   "to enter circumcision rites"
   *-alam-   "to engage in circumcision observances (during seclusion period)"
   *inkunka "circumcision observances"

c. *Words of Mashariki distribution*

   *-lịịka   "initiate, boy undergoing circumcision rites"
   *-aluk-   "to finish circumcision rites and leave seclusion"

d. *Word of northern areal Kaskazi distribution*

   *-taban- "to perform circumcision rites"

---

many of the more westerly Bantu cultures and surely were, the comparative cultural evidence tells us, a notable element of early Bantu material culture. Among the numerous Mashariki societies, however, the making of masks is rare and may thus already have been dropped by many of the Mashariki communities during the last millennium B.C., not only for circumcision ceremonials but in other social contexts as well.

Girls in the Mashariki communities of the last millennium B.C. apparently underwent initiation rites of their own. The particular forms of such observances remain to be properly investigated, but it seems clear that female "circumcision" was *not* among them.

The really fascinating social historical issues here, though, are ones that for now cannot be resolved. We have begun the historical process of trying to reconstruct certain institutions of social cooperation and authority among the early Mashariki peoples. But historians have yet to explore the ways in which these various levels of custom and belief may have intertwined among those communities in the first half of the last millennium B.C. We can see that kin chiefship held a powerful centrality in the expression of community identity:   the *-àmì would have been the focal figure in the ceremonies of both planting and harvest and in other community ritual directed toward the ancestors. The *-kụ́mụ̀ may well have laid claim within the localized lineage unit to a similar and potentially competing range of roles. And chiefs had access to an idiom of ownership over the people of their kin group. But the practical ways in which authority would have been exerted, and the symbols and rites through which kin-group leaders would have expressed such authority, remain matters about which we know almost nothing. How did the idiom of ownership, for example, figure in the legitimization of kin chiefship? Where did age sets fit into this scheme of things? These are only some of the questions that future historical study of this period will need to tackle.

## Religion and Society among the Mashariki Peoples

The early Mashariki communities recognized two levels of the preternatural, God and the ancestors. A third level, of what might be called territorial spirits, whose powers operate across a particular area or region and can be approached via priestly intermediaries, can be found rather widely today among the more westerly Bantu and appears among some Mashariki people in east-central Africa. But the language evidence gives no indication that this dimension of belief

158

existed among proto-Mashariki speakers and, where it is found today, it probably usually reflects developments that date since the last millennium B.C.[16]

At root, the Mashariki religion was profoundly different from Sudanic religion. Its basic categorization of spirit was sharply different, and so was its fundamental conceptualization of the roles of spirit in religious observance. God was recurrently treated as a distant figure in actual religious practice among Bantu-speaking societies, evoked as the Creator but indirectly prayed to if at all. Day-to-day religious observances, it can be argued from the generality of more recent example, focused among the early Mashariki on the ancestors of the community (*-lɨ́mù). Such observances may have been carried out at several levels—for the wider clan community as a whole by the *-àmì, for the lineage by the *-kúmù, and for the family by the family head. There is some comparative cultural evidence that familial ancestors may have been venerated at small shrines, in the form of small round huts, behind the main house. But the apparent lack of any reconstructible proto-Mashariki word for such a shrine makes this proposition a tenuous one.

The issue of soundly demonstrating the existence or the absence of a concept of Supreme Being for early Bantu societies has been a vexed one. It appears, however, that when one allows for the recent spreading of particular terms for God by Christian missionaries, there still remains a solid core of lexical evidence for the ancientness of the concept.[17] The proto-Bantu root word for God was *Nyàmbé. It is found widely across the western side of the Bantu-speaking regions of Africa, and it almost certainly is cognate with the Akan (of Ghana) word for God, *Nyame, implying its use far back in Niger-Congo language history, long before the proto-Bantu period.

The derivation of the word *Nyàmbé is an issue that has not been much studied so far. But one proposal, especially deserving of further consideration, is that it comes from an old Niger-Congo verb root the early Bantu reflex of which was *-àmb- "to begin." That etymology identifies *Nyàmbé as "Beginning," or in other terms, as First Principle, a conception in keeping with the view of *Nyàmbé as Creator that one must attribute to the early Bantu and presumably to their earlier Niger-Congo forebears.

A solution to the philosophical problem of evil very different from that common in Sudanic religion prevailed among the early Bantu societies. Evil had its source for the earliest Mashariki communities, not in divine judgment, but much closer to home. For one thing, neglect of one's responsibilities toward the ancestors could bring bad consequences for the community or the family.  For another, evil came from the forces of individual envy and ill-will, in the form of *bu-logị or "witchcraft," as it has been translated into European languages.  Because of this understanding of evil, the Mashariki communities maintained a particular part-time occupational specialization not found among the other East Africans of the last millennium B.C., the position of the *-ganga, the doctor-diviner (or, to use a term no longer in favor, the "witch-doctor"), whose responsibilities focused above all on diagnosing the causes of sickness and other bad happenings and on prescribing a course of treatment directed toward rooting out the *bu-logị or correcting the neglect of the ancestors that had brought the evil about.

# Social History among the Southern Cushites and Southern Nilotes

Two other sets of players in this history, the Southern Cushitic and the Southern Nilotic societies, each had still different institutions from those found among the Central Sudanian and Eastern Sahelian societies or among the Bantu of the last millennium B.C.  Inhabiting territories that lay for the most part to the east of the Nyanza Basin, and not having moved south into western Kenya much before 700 B.C., the Southern Nilotes took on a limited role in the history of the Great Lakes region only at the end of the millennium.  The Tale Southern Cushites, as we have seen, had a longer and somewhat wider impact on developments in the region, from probably as early as the middle of the last millennium.

## Southern Cushitic Culture and Society

Southern Cushitic peoples typically resided in neighborhoods of dispersed, extended-family homesteads.  Patrilineal clans are a feature so widely attested among Cushites that they can provisionally be reconstructed far back before the proto–Southern Cushitic period.  The comparative cultural evidence also favors the idea that each clan was territorially based, encompassing the populations of several nearby neighborhoods.

The old Cushite root word for such a localized kin group remains to be discovered.  But another ancient Cushitic term indirectly testifies to their existence:  the word used in proto-Cushitic, as well as proto–Southern Cushitic, for the hereditary headman of such a clan, *wab-, can already be identified.[18] For West Rift peoples, an alternate Iraqw term *kahamusmo*, literally "speaker," captures a probably old conception of this kin chief as one who articulated the general sense of community meetings and acted as spokesperson for the community in its dealings with its neighbors. Among the Ma'a and some of the East Rift peoples, another idiom, of the clan head as the figuratively senior figure of the community (proto–Southern Cushitic *dil-), prevailed.

To judge from the examples of such disparate Agaw and Eastern Cushitic peoples of the Horn of Africa as the Kemant and certain Soomaali groups, both of whom also call clan chiefs by forms of the old root *wab-, the clan head originally held a central position in community religious observances. An additional probable function of the clan head was to act for the community in allotting cultivating land to those in need of it. Overall, the evidence suggests that the Cushitic *wab- was a person of less actual and potential authority than the early Bantu kin chiefs; a comparable metaphor of the *wab- as the "owner" of the kin group would have been inconceivable.

Like the Mashariki communities, the Southern Cushitic societies all practiced circumcision, but unlike the Bantu they practiced, in addition, female circumcision in the mild form of clitoridectomy. And again unlike the early Mashariki peoples, they apparently did not form their young men into age sets, even though circumcision was apparently considered to mark the passage into adulthood for both males and females.

The Southern Cushites of the third and second millennia B.C. held religious beliefs that contrasted the Sudanic concept of Divinity associated with the heavens, with an opposing category of dangerous spirits as their solution to the problem of evil. A probable additional feature of Sudanic connection, known at the least among the West Rift peoples, was the identification of the life force that left the body at death by a term that also meant "shadow" (see above for this same idea among the earliest Central Sudanians).

Among those same West Rift people, but not apparently among other Southern Cushites, one major shift in religious conceptualization came into being by probably early in the last millennium B.C., a shift in the associations of nature that attached to Divinity, from "sky," as represented in the proto–Southern Cushitic term *Waak'a, to an alternative metaphor, "sun." Why did this shift come about? What kinds of change in religious belief and practice might lie behind it? These questions are ones we cannot answer at present, but they deserve serious historical study in the future.

## Southern Nilotic Society

The Southern Nilotes of the second half of the last millennium B.C. were deeply influenced by the Southern Cushites who had preceded them in highland Kenya. This impact showed most strongly in Southern Nilotic vocabulary and in certain aspects of material culture,[19] such as their adoption of stone bowls, long a feature of the Savanna Pastoral Neolithic cultures of the Southern Cushities.[20] But in many key aspects of culture the Southern Nilotes continued to differ considerably from their Cushitic neighbors.

Like the Cushitic communities, they possessed patrilineal clans, but this feature of society surely traced back to their earlier Nilotic and Eastern Sahelian heritage. They did not have any sort of hereditary position of leadership, even of the clan-head variety. Among the Kalenjin of more recent times, clan membership has often tended not to be accompanied by specific territorial claims, and members of different clans could usually be found widely dispersed through a society. It seems probable, however, that in the last millennium B.C. and the early first millennium A.D., Southern Nilotic clans, or at least different clusters of associated clans—what we may call tribes—did coincide with particular territories. The "tribe" and the territory it occupied were called *e:m.

The Southern Nilotes, like the Southern Cushites, practiced both circumcision and clitoridectomy in connection with the rites of passage into adulthood. The evidence of words shows, however, that these Southern Nilotic traits originated from the influence of Eastern Cushites, at a time no later than the early first millennium A.D., before the Southern Nilotes had moved south into western Kenya.[21]

Most unlike the Southern Cushites, but a bit like the early Mashariki peoples, the Southern Nilotes initiated circumcised young men into age sets. The age sets, though, were of an entirely different kind from those found among the Bantu of those centuries: they formed a cycling system. A cycling system is one in which a regularly recurring order of age-set names is used. The society applies the names to the successive age sets initiated over a period of many years, and when the last name on the list has been used, they return to the beginning of the cycle of names and start over again. In the proto–Southern Nilotic system, the age-set cycle, it is believed, consisted of a

sequence of eight named sets (see table 26 for names currently reconstructed.) The original gap of time between the initiation of one age
set and the initiation of the next on the cycle was probably around ten
years, with the whole cycle of names starting over again after about
eighty years.[22]

The early form of the age system in Southern Nilotic society had
in addition a generational component. Most probably the eight age
sets of the cycle originally were grouped into two generations, each
comprising four of the sets. A man and his son had to belong to alternate generations in this system. The son of a man who had been
initiated into any of the four age sets that made up one generation
could be initiated only into one of the four age sets that comprised the
next and alternate generation.[23]

Alongside the age sets there existed an age-grade system, a
set of formal statuses by which social and political responsibility were
distributed among the men of the Southern Nilotic communities. At
the time young men were circumcised and initiated into one of the
age sets, they were simulaneously initiated into the first age grade, that
of the young men—in later Kalenjin society, and possibly in the
proto–Southern Nilotic society as well, the *muren* grade. Among the
Kalenjin of the past 1,200 years, there has been only one other grade,
that of *payyan* or elder. A man would graduate, together with the rest
of his age set, into the *payyan* grade at the time of initiation of the
next younger age set of the cycle and would then remain a *payyan*
through the rest of his life. But it would not be surprising if among
the still earlier Nilotes of the later last millennium B.C., a somewhat
more complicated system with four grades, one for each of the four

### Table 26. Southern Nilotic age sets and circumcision

| (circumcision) | | (age-set cycle) |
|---|---|---|
| *mʊraːt | "to circumcise" | 1. *sɔːwe |
| *tuːm | "to dance at circumcision" | 2. *koronkoro |
| *kaːremaːn | "circumcised boy" | 3. (unknown) |
| *soːm- | "uncircumcised child" | 4. *kini (?) |
| *muren | "young man" | 5. (unknown) |
| *ipin | "age set" (Kalenjin) | 6. *nyɔːnki |
| *saika | "age-set band (?)" (Tato) | 7. *maina |
| *sakaːlam | "generation-set" (Tato) | 8. *cuːma |

age sets that made up a generation, might have existed. Evidence is lacking as yet, however, for resolving this matter.

Like circumcision, the cycling age-set system, along with its associated generational and age-grade components, entered into Southern Nilotic culture during the earlier era of Southern Nilotic contacts with Eastern Cushites around 1000–700 B.C., all probably as part of the same cultural package. In later times the full complexity of the proto–Southern Nilotic age organization broke down in different fashions among different Southern Nilotic peoples. In the proto-Kalenjin society of mid-first millennium A.D., the generational component was entirely lost; among Tato peoples by contrast, it was the cycle of eight named age sets which instead dropped from use, while generation sets remained central to social cohesion. But during the first half of the first millennium A.D., the early Southern Nilotic system in all its complexity probably continued to function among all of the Southern Nilotic peoples.

One especially notable feature of intangible culture did pass from Southern Cushites to the early Southern Nilotes, however. The proto–Southern Nilotic society of the second half of the last millennium B.C. adopted the specifically West Rift religious linkage of Divinity to the sun. Not only can the metaphor be reconstructed back to the proto–Southern Nilotic period, but the very word used in the proto–Southern Nilotic language for both Divinity (or God) and the sun, *as(i:s), is a direct borrowing from Southern Cushitic (we will have more to say on this topic below).[24] There is as yet, however, no evidence that the idea of attributing evil to dangerous spirits took hold along with the changed metaphorical association of Divinity. Divinity may still among the Southern Nilotes have been the ultimate source of both good and evil, as was true among their earlier Eastern Sahelian forebears.

## Social and Religious Change in the Last Millennium B.C.

The social historical trends of the last thousand years B.C. appear to have been constrained, much more than the developments in the history of material culture, by cultural boundaries among the peoples who resided in western East Africa and the Great Lakes region. Even within the compass of Mashariki culture, social institutions and religious beliefs may have changed little for most of the period. Nevertheless, it was not an era of social or intellectual stasis. At least four different instances of significant change in beliefs or social relations are revealed in the evidence so far available to us, and in three of those instances a significant input from non-Bantu cultures shaped the course of change among the Bantu.

## Social and Political Shifts among the Kaskazi

One of these developments emerged before mid-millennium among the Kaskazi cluster of communities. For the northern and central members of that cluster, a new kinship metaphor arose. To an older Mashariki term for "taproot, lower trunk," *-kòlò (see above), was attributed an additional meaning, "matriclan." Lacking a precedent among the reconstructibly earlier Bantu kin idioms, the new metaphor can plausibly be explained as the loan-translation of a common Central Sudanian metaphor for a kin grouping, seen, for example, in the Lugbara (Moru-Madi) word ólá "root; descendants of a particular ancestor." Whether this possibly Sudanian contribution to vocabulary reflects a significant practical change in kin structure or conceptualization among the Kaskazi, or only a supplementary metaphor expressing the significance of clan membership, remains to be seen.

A second notable change, a shift in the distribution of clan authority, appears to have been developing among just the Lakes communities in the early second half of the millennium. Its outward sign was a conversion of the meaning of the word *-kúmù, from kin-group leader to doctor-diviner. That shift of meaning, overleaping a deep conceptual chasm between the two roles in both nature and scope, seems inexplicable unless it reflects an actual transformation of the position of the *-kúmù, with the *-kúmù losing all temporal authority in kin-group affairs and sharply changing in his or her sphere of religious action, from ancestor rites to divining and medicine. Among the Lake communities living to the west of Lake Nyanza, a new position of lesser standing than the *-ámì, that of the *-kúlù, probably replaced the *-kúmù as the local kin and community head.[25]

The causes and course of this transformation remain a topic for future debate. How did such a change in sociopolitical structure come about? Did, perhaps, large clan polities of several thousand members evolve in the different locales settled by the Lakes people of the second half of the last millennium B.C.? Might the top level of kin authority, the *-àmì, have then accummulated sufficiently greater material and social power to be able to depoliticize the potentially competing position of the *-kų́mų̀—instituting in its place a new, locally recruited set of *-kúlù as community and kin heads?

And if so, what means to greater power might have appeared in those eras? Might increased population density and hence competition for resources, or control over access to the newly important iron technology, have provided a material basis for a widened clan-chiefly authority? Both are possible factors. Growth in population density surely took place among the Lakes communities west of Lake Nyanza; and, at least along the southwest of the lake, much increased iron production has been proposed for the latter parts of the last millennium B.C.[26]

A third cultural development, dating to the second half of the millennium, comprised the spread of certain ideas of bodily marking from Tale Southern Cushites to the Southern-Nyanza areal cluster of communities. Two borrowed words in the languages that derived from the Southern-Nyanza areal cluster of communities attest to this particular influence (see table 1B). One of these, *-sàr-, consistently applies to markings made by cutting into the skin of a person. Its particular uses in modern languages do not fit with its having been adopted as a term for decorative scarification, but do allow an interesting alternative possibility, that it originally connoted an incision made for medicinal purposes. The second root word, *-lam-, more often than not refers to livestock marking; its original application may have been to identificatory marking of cattle, perhaps to the notching of the animals' ears since branding was not present in the areas and period in which the Kaskazi communities adopted the word in the first place.

## New Developments in Religious Thought

At two points in the last millennium B.C., significant modifications in religious belief apparently also came into being among some, but not all, of the Kaskazi.

The first of these developments appears in the adoption in the Middle Mashariki period, c. 800–500 B.C., of a new word *Mu-lùngù for "God." Leaving aside very recent spreads of this name caused by missionary use (for example, to the Thagiicu languages of Kenya), we note that *Mu-lùngù has the kind of distribution—widely through the Kati and Rufiji-Ruvuma languages—that would trace its origin back to the short-lived Southern-Kaskazi clustering of communities of

166

the time just before mid-millennium. The word occurs also in languages of the Nyasa and Makua subgroups of Kusi, but there is suspect as a very early loan spread from southern Kaskazi dialects (see chapter 8 for this history).

The new term for God seems very probably to be derivable from the old Bantu verb *-lùng- "to become fitting, become straight." Such a derivation, if correct, would imply that, during the first half of the last millennium B.C., certain of the Kaskazi communities took up an additional conceptualization of the Creator God of earlier Bantu religion, as the exemplar of what is right or suitable. This view might superficially seem similar to the concepts of Divinity we attribute to the Eastern Sahelian neighbors of the early Mashiriki, who saw Divinity as the source of judgment or retribution for wrong-doing. But the implication of direct divine intervention in human life is not necessitated in the Kaskazi semantics of the word *Mu-lùngù. On comparative cultural grounds, the older Bantu conception of a distant Creator seems still to have been widely present, and if any Sudanian influence was present in this particular religious development among the Kaskazi communities, it must have been very indirect in its effects.

Relatively late in the last millennium B.C., a second significant change in religious beliefs, of visibly Southern Cushitic inspiration, began to take effect among a limited number of the Kaskazi societies. In particular, as early perhaps as 300 or 400 B.C., a further reconceptualization, identifying the Bantu Creator God with the sun-linked Divinity of the Southern Nilotes and Southern Cushites, began to be taken up by peoples of the Southern-Nyanza clustering of communities. This new conceptual shift revealed itself initially in the reapplication, among certain Southern-Nyanza communities, of the ancient Bantu term for "sun," *lį-úbà, as an alternative for the earlier Southern-Kaskazi word for God, *Mu-lùngù.

Underpinning the naming change was a new relevance for God in religious rites and a view of God as more actively accessible Spirit than had been allowed for in the earlier Mashariki and proto-Bantu religion. The new idea took hold in particular among the incipient pre-Luyia and East-Nyanza peoples of the Lakes group, the Upland communities, the ancestors of the Langi, and the early Takama of the Kati group. The initial sources of this conception of God would have been the Tale Southern Cushites of the Southern-Nyanza areas. But its meaningfulness to the Upland, Luyia, and East-Nyanza peoples was surely further enhanced by their mutual interactions, toward the very close of the era, with the Southern Nilotic cattle raisers of the Mara region (see also chapter 2), among whom the same concept of Divinity was present.

The interesting feature of this particular religious change is that the linkage of Divinity and the sun was very much a regional, cross-cultural development. As we have already seen above in our survey of Southern Nilotic culture history, this idea of the divine certainly appeared first, as the language evidence certifies, among the West Rift peoples, possibly no earlier than the early last millennium B.C. These peoples included the various Tale communities, who lived at that period all across the Mara plains, and the Highland West Rift society of the nearby Mbulu highlands of north central Tanzania. Its subsequent spread in the second half of the millennium encompassed a large contiguous stretch of country extending northward from the Mara plains to the Uasingishu plateau—all lands of the Southern Nilotes by the fourth century B.C.—and westward at the same from there to the southern shores of Lake Nyanza, where the late Southern-Nyanza areal cluster of Kaskazi Bantu resided. Whatever the ethnic and language affiliations of the newly emergent societies of the time, all across the region the same religious idea took hold. And that raises intriguing issues of causation and the dynamics of religious change in preliterate eras, issues that remain to be explored by historians of Africa.

## Looking Ahead to the Later Classical Age

With the winding down of the last millennium B.C., the time of relatively slow change in the patterns of belief and social relations came to a close. In the ensuing Later Classical Age, as Bantu societies spread out into far-flung new regions of settlement, a variety of different regional histories, much more often characterized by deep and lasting social change, would take shape. With the developments of that period we must now engage ourselves.

## Notes

[1] Murdock 1959.
[2] Middleton 1965, 1987.
[3] Ehret 1976b, 1979, 1980b, 1987: 85.
[4] See Ehret 1993 for this dating.

[5] After Lienhardt 1961 and elsewhere.

[6] For these and other Central Sudanic root words, see Ehret 1992.

[7] Vansina 1990.

[8] This root word is also present in the name of the Bami society of the Lega people; there its application to those who belong to this secret society can be understood as derived meaning, reflective of the ascription to the members of the Bami society of a high status and influence.

[9] Vansina 1990.

[10] Guthrie 1967–72 cites several cases also of the more abstract meaning "kinship" for this root in Mashariki languages of the Lake Nyasa region, but here confusions with a tonally-distinct root *-lòngó "brother" probably account for that gloss. The Mang'anja dictionary (Scott 1957), in fact, specifies the relationship between sister and brother as the meaning of its reflex, not simply "kinship" in general as Guthrie's citation claims.

[11] PB *-lùngù, glossed by Guthrie 1967–72 as "tribe" (i.e., the wider societal grouping, which includes many clans), must be considered a distinct root, despite its superficial resemblance to *-lòngò. It derives from PB *-lùng- "to join together by tying"—hence its reference to those joined together by their common membership in the same society—whereas *-lòngò, as noted, comes from an older word for a line of objects. The coexisting presence in early Savanna-Bantu of the term *-lùngù may well have influenced the occasional meaning shifts of *-lòngò to "tribe," however.

[12] Vansina 1990.

[13] This conclusion is supported not just by the Ruvu example of *-lòngò already described, but by the similar relict retention in the Ila (Botatwe) culture of southern Zambia of the same sort of patrikin of minor importance within an overall matrilineal system, there serving especially as a cattle-owning group. Ila uses the distinct but resemblant root word *-lùngù for this institution today, but can be argued to have originally called it *-lòngò (see arguments in note 11 above).

[14] For an excellent culture historical analysis of these, see de Wolf 1983.

[15] Vansina 1990.

[16] Werner 1979.

[17] As Vansina 1990 also seems to agree.

[18] Ehret 1987.

[19] Ehret 1971.

[20] Ambrose 1982.

[21] Ehret 1971.

[22] The pattern of around fifteen years between sets, common among the Kalenjin of recent centuries cannot be reconstructed back to proto-Southern Nilotic times because the early system was constrained by the division of the age sets into two

generation sets comprising four age sets each. Generation sets, to judge from later historical examples from a variety of societies, normally cover a span of time very close to forty years, and thus each of the four age sets in a generation would need to have lasted somewhere around ten years.

[23] Among the Kalenjin peoples of Kenya, the generational component had already dropped from use more than twelve hundred years ago, thus leaving an opening for the longer span of about fifteen years between the initiation of age sets to come into vogue.

[24] Ehret 1971.

[25] Schoenbrun, personal communication, 1994.

[26] Schmidt 1978; Schoenbrun 1990.

# 6. East Africa in the Later Classical Age, to A.D. 400

## Broadening the Historical Stage

The Later Classical Age of Greater Eastern Africa spanned the turn of the era, from around the third century B.C. up to the fourth century A.D. In those centuries a sweepingly new historical dispensation, rooted in the developments of the Early Classical Age of the Great Lakes region, rapidly took shape all across the eastern side of the African continent. In East Africa proper, in the lands which today comprise Kenya and Tanzania, the transformation of life and livelihood began in about the last two centuries B.C., as various Kaskazi communities scattered out to new areas of settlement, often hundreds of miles away from the Nyanza Basin. In southeastern and east-central Africa, parallel developments began to take hold even earlier, in some areas as early as the fourth century B.C. There the stimulus for change came principally from the Kusi communities spreading south out of the Lake Tanganyika region, although Kaskazi peoples also had a role to play in east-central Africa.

Already by the second and third centuries A.D., these far-flung population movements had left their scattered but lasting archeological mark on lands as far apart as the Kenya coast and the coastal zones of Natal. By the fourth century A.D., a new distribution of peoples and cultures had come into being across the hundreds of thousands of square kilometers from the Great Lakes region in the north, to the Indian Ocean seaboard on the east, and to Transvaal and Natal on the south. In addition, these movements of Kusi and Kaskazi peoples helped set in motion a series of technological changes that spread westward to the early Central-Savanna and Western-Savanna-Bantu, who themselves were expanding southward during those same five or six centuries, into the central and western parts of the savanna belt.

We will consider this complex history in three parts, turning our attention first, in this chapter, to the new developments in ethnicity and society in East Africa proper. As in chapter 2, the discussions here focus on identifying and locating the human actors in the historical

171

drama, and the evidence of language thus again, as in chapter 2, takes a prominent position in our historical arguments. Then, in chapter 7, we expand our considerations to the historical transitions occasioned farther to the south, especially by the settlements of the Kusi peoples. Finally, in chapter 8, we lay out the broader patterns and trends of technological, social, and economic change that give substance and moment to the human developments of the Later Classical Age.

## Historical Background: Kenya and Tanzania

The Later Classical Age began for Kenya and central and northern Tanzania with the breakup of the Southern-Nyanza cluster of communities late in the last millennium B.C. With the winding down of the contacts between Bantu-speaking and non-Bantu communities that had marked that period (see chapter 2), the territorial contiguity of the proto-Luyia, East-Nyanza, Upland, pre-Langi, and Kati societies came definitively to an end. It came to an end because many of the members of these communities moved into new areas to the east, often far away from the Nyanza Basin and the Western Rift. In southern Tanzania at about the same time, other Kaskazi communities were undertaking similar long-distance shifts of residence, settling in several parts of southern Tanzania and far northern Mozambique and Malawi. The more drastic option for the Mashariki communities of the later last millennium B.C., of responding to the growing demographic pressures of the age by seeking out entire new areas for settlement, had begun to be taken up.

### Southern Cushites in the Last Millennium B.C.

In northern and central East Africa a long economic history of food production preceded the developments of the turn of the era. Southern Cushites, as we have seen, introduced the earliest livestock raising and cultivation to many parts of modern-day Kenya and Tanzania. Three major divisions evolved among the first Southern Cushitic populations of the late fourth and early third millennium B.C., the Dahaloans, the Mbuguans, and the Rift peoples. Here the term "Rift" has reference to a different rift valley feature from the great Western Rift, which has figured so prominently in our story so far. From central northern Kenya southward into north-central Tanzania, lies another long, north-south extending double rift, the Eastern

Rift Valley system. The Rift Southern Cushites are so named because of their early historical locations in and around this region.

During the first half of the last millennium B.C. the Mbuguans probably resided in territories that included the plains along the Eastern Rift in central Kenya. The Rift societies inhabited the wide grasslands on both sides of the Eastern Rift in southern Kenya and northern Tanzania, and the Dahaloan lands may have extended from the eastern highlands of Kenya down to the Kenya coastal zone.[1] The Mbuguan territories before 2000 B.C.—or so the evidence of Mbuguan loanwords in the Yaaku language, spoken just north of Mount Kenya today, indicates[2]—included also the dry grazing lands of northern Kenya, north of Mount Kenya and east of Lake Turkana. Mbuguan archeology is best identified with the Olmalenge variety of the Savanna Pastoral Neolithic, which is found through those same regions.[3] The archeology of the Dahaloans remains still to be identified, however.

The Rift Southern Cushites, the makers surely of the Oldishi versions of the Savanna Pastoral Neolithic, comprised at least three different societies at the start of the last millennium B.C.—the proto–West Rift people on the high plains to the west of the Eastern Rift Valley, the proto–East Rift society in the Kilimanjaro and Maasai Steppe regions to the east of the rift,[4] and the Bisha in areas to the east of Kilimanjaro near the Taita hills.[5] By the second half of the last millennium, the early West Rift society had diverged into two sets of communities. One was the Highland West Rift people from whom the present-day Iraqw, Burunge, and Alagwa of Tanzania descend, and the other formed the Tale pastoral society, which played, as we have seen, a major role in the economic developments of late last millennium B.C. in the Nyanza Basin.

Although the Southern Cushites combined cultivation and the herding of livestock, their pastoral pursuits seem in most cases to have predominated in actual subsistence practice. This emphasis seems clear for the Tale peoples, from their extensive influence on the herding vocabularies of their Kaskazi neighbors (table 9A, tables 1B and 2B). It is reconfirmed for other early Southern Cushites in central Kenya, whose diet has been shown, through studies of the chemistry of their bones taken from burial sites, to have consisted predominantly of meat and milk.[6] They raised cattle, sheep, and goats, and kept donkeys as well.

Interestingly, though, the reconstructed vocabulary of cattle and other livestock breeding gives no indication that the Southern Cushites of those centuries attributed any esthetic or special social valuation to cattle. Few words of the kinds indicative of a special cultural status of cattle, such as words for cattle colors or horn shapes, trace back before the last 1,000 to 1,500 years. Only the everyday breeding distinctions—such as bull, heifer, calf, and the like—which testify to the practical subsistence importance of an animal, seem to have been present in the early Southern Cushitic languages.[7]

Unquestionably, cultivation contributed some portion of the diet of most of the Cushites, including apparently the Central Tale people, whose vocabulary provided to certain northerly Kaskazi communities the only three Southern Cushitic loanwords in early Mashariki Bantu that relate even indirectly to grain cultivation table 1B.a-c). The crops known to the Southern Cushites were relatively few: apparently sorghum in a couple of varieties and one other grain species, presumably finger millet, along with black-eyed peas, the Voandzeia groundnuts, and calabashes (table 27). But the wealth of reconstructed supporting vocabulary indicates that cultivation was more than just an activity the Southern Cushites witnessed among their neighbors.

The Cushites brewed mead only, it seems, and not beer.[8] Beer is

## Table 27. Southern Cushitic cultivating vocabulary

### a. Proto–Southern Cushitic roots

| | | | |
|---|---|---|---|
| *kur- | "to cultivate" | *bot$^y$'oro | "gruel (?)" |
| *man$^y$- | "enclosed, cleared area" | *salak$^w$- | "black-eyed peas" |
| *buʕ- | "to harvest" | *koog- | "Voandzeia |
| *yomb- | "large digging stick" | | groundnut" |
| *sem- | "small digging stick" | *hon- | "calabash pulp and |
| *mus- | "pestle" | | seeds" |
| *tuʔ- | "to pound grain" | *k$^w$'aad- | "kind of calabash" |
| *ʔaal- | "to sift grain" | *xib- | "calabash (bowl?)" |
| *bur- | "flour" | *pareh- | "calabash sherd" |
| *bila | "grain ear (?)" | *honto | "calabash bowl" |
| *hʌʌmpi | "grain husks (?)" | | |
| *mee | "granary" (in house) | | |
| *ʕaag- | "grain (generic)" | **b. Proto-Rift roots** | |
| *mušange | "grain sp." | | |
| *mag$^w$ale | "(red?) sorghum" | *gubar- | "flour" |
| *ʕʌl- | "white sorghum" | *sor- | "grits (?)" |
| *dlak$^w$- | "porridge" | *ʕam- | "calabash plant" |
| *ʔax$^w$- | "gruel" | *waʔ- | "calabash" |

a common drink among Highland West Rift peoples today, but the complete lack of any reconstructible beer terminology earlier than the proto-Highland period of c. 700–1000 A.D. suggests that most if not all Southern Cushites, including the Tale peoples, were probably still mead- rather than beer-drinkers two millennia ago.

The earliest Southern Cushitic societies in East Africa likely built flat-roofed houses of a rectangular floor plan, and, as suggested above (chapter 4), the tembe-style of flat-roofed house constructed by many of the Bantu societies of central and western Tanzania today probably owes to the preservation of that style among the Tale communities of the second half of the last millennium B.C. In hilly areas, but probably not in the plains favored by Tale communities, the house must often have been set onto a platform of flat land dug into a hillside (called *ʕas- in proto–Southern Cushitic), and this practice has been carried on down to the present among the Iraqw people of the Highland West Rift group.

Among the Rift Southern Cushites of the last millennium B.C., beds were part of the household furnishings. The making of both slat and rope beds seems to have passed from these peoples to the Kati communities at the close of the last millennium B.C. Beds had been invented among the Southern Cushites as early as the proto-Rift period of the second millennium B.C., as the existence of proto-Rift words for beds indicate (see table 28). Words indicative of Southern Cushitic stool making are, however, entirely lacking until much later centuries, and that accords with the evidence in the Great Lakes region, that stools were an Eastern Sahelian contribution to the material culture of the home in eastern Africa (see chapter 4).

The Rift peoples kept their cattle in round pens, probably originally encircled by pole fences. The derivation of the proto-Rift word for cattle-pen, *kʷ'ama, from an earlier verb meaning "to be round," attests to the pen's general layout. Judging from the residential patterns found among the tembe-builders of more recent centuries, we believe that the extended-family households (*wayaʔo) of at least the Tale Southern Cushites may have been composed of houses grouped in a square around the circular pen. A large and scattered grouping of homesteads formed the *lawa, the local community. In addition to the houses of the homestead, a separate structure (*ʔaɬ-) was built for the calves or smaller stock. Separate granary huts, however, do not seem to have been a feature of early Southern Cushitic households; rather, stored grain probably was placed in a loft or bin (*maay) within the house. Only in the late centuries B.C., among some of the Tale people, does evidence for a granary hut turn up (table 1B).[9]

In contrast to the emphasis on woven fiber in container and clothing manufacture among the Mashariki and Central Sudanic societies of the last millennium B.C., the contemporary Southern Cushitic peoples especially used leather, a perhaps not surprising difference considering the much greater scale of their livestock raising. Whereas several kinds of baskets would have been woven in a typical Central Sudanic or Kaskazi household, and among the Kaskazi a variety of mats as well, probably only a single kind of basket was made by the early Southern Cushites. Instead, leather sacks, a rarity among Mashariki peoples before about 2,000 years ago, and string bags, unknown to either the Bantu or the Nilo-Saharans of those eras, must have served most of the needs for lightweight, flexible containers among the Cushites (see table 28). The Southern Cushites also, uniquely, utilized segments of the mountain bamboo of East Africa, *Arundinaria alpina*, as quivers for carrying their arrows (table 30b).

---

Table 28.  Southern Cushitic containers and furniture

*a. Proto–Southern Cushitic words*     *b. Proto-Rift words*

| *saaŋ- | "water pot" | *hitl- | "large pot" |
|---|---|---|---|
| *loob- | "leather sack" | *lakaba | "small cook pot" |
| *ŋak'- | "basket" | *ʔam- | "leather pouch" |
| *dah- | "wooden (?) vessel" | *k'atin- | "bed" |
| *haanka *or* | | *buru | "bed(-frame)" |
| *haanka | "string bag" | | |

---

An especially intriguing element of Southern Cushitic material culture, at least among those who lived in the Kenya Rift region, was the fashioning of stone bowls. These containers are intriguing for several reasons. For one thing, we are not sure what use they were put to. In addition, stone bowls seem to have been a transcultural item, common among not only the Southern Cushites of that region, but also the Eburran gatherer-hunters of the forests adjacent to the Rift;[10] and they were adopted as well by the Southern Nilotes who arrived in the region in the earlier last millennium B.C. Then, too, we do not know what the words for "stone bowl" might have been. People ceased to make stone bowls during the early and middle centuries of the first millennium A.D., and when things are dropped entirely from

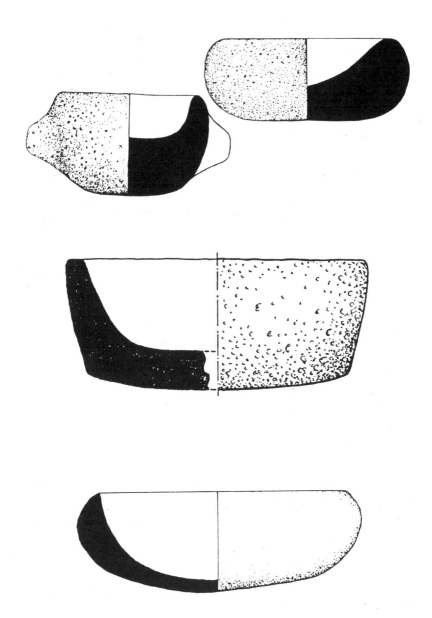

Figure 7. Stone bowls. Bowls from Olmalenge sites, *top* (Ma'a Southern Cushites?) (Barthelme 1977). Bowl from an Oldishi site, *middle* (Rift Southern Cushities). Bowl from northern Cape, South Africa, *bottom* (Morris 1991).

177

use, so are the words for those things. Even more interesting, another region of stone–bowl making existed in southern Africa, possibly associated with the first era of livestock raising in that part of the continent. We will have more to say on that topic in chapter 7.

A variety of nontangible features found in Southern Cushitic cultures of the last millennium B.C. have already been discussed (in chapter 5), but deserve a brief review here. Localized patrilineal clans with hereditary clan heads probably formed the predominant basis of the social order, while Southern Cushitic religion combined the Sudanic religious concept of Divinity with a differing view of the problem of evil (see chapter 5). Among the West Rift peoples, a new metaphorical association of Divinity with the sun replaced the earlier association of sky and rain sometime before 500 B.C. Both male and female circumcision marked the passage of Southern Cushitic children into adult status, but no age-set systems apparently existed in their societies, as they did among the contemporary Mashariki Bantu.

## Southern Nilotes in the Last Millennium B.C.

The Southern Nilotes had a shorter historical presence in the region, having moved southward into western Kenya apparently sometime in the first half of the millennium. Makers of the Elmenteitan archeological tradition, they settled in the highlands to the west of the Eastern Rift valley, in what is today Kenya. They cultivated grain crops at the lower margins of the montane forests, at around 1,800 meters elevation, where forest gave way to highland grassland; and they grazed cattle, sheep, and goats both below the forest zone and also above it, on the high moorlands above 2,600 or 2,700 meters.[11]

During the second half of the millennium, two major divisions developed among the Southern Nilotes. The proto-Kalenjin took shape among those residing to the north of the Mau range; from their language the modern Kalenjin dialects of Kenya derive. The Tato society emerged among other Southern Nilotes who expanded onto the plains to the south of the Mau. The present-day Datoga dialects spoken in north-central Tanzania descend from the proto-Tato language.[12]

The historically most prominent Southern Nilotic people of the time we can call the Mara Southern Nilotes.[13] The Mara people spoke probably a dialect of the proto-Tato language.[14] Specialized cattle raisers on a considerable scale, they spread their settlements westward, after 400 B.C., across the Mara plains of southwestern Kenya as far as southeastern Lake Nyanza. Their reliance on a livestock-based economy is resoundingly apparent from their loanwords in the East-Nyanza, pre-Luyia, and Upland dialects of the late Southern-Nyanza clustering of Kaskazi Bantu communities (see table 10). That emphasis is amply confirmed in the archeology of their residential sites.[15]

The Southern Nilotes of 2,000 years ago, as we have seen (chapter 5), drew on a varied cultural historical background. They possessed patrilineal clans, a heritage that may trace to their more distant Eastern Sahelian ancestry. Regional clusterings of clans, it can be proposed, cooperated in loose supra-clan groupings, called *e:m. The Mara people probably formed one such *e:m. The Southern Nilotes initiated their youths into age sets belonging to a cycling system, a set of customs that dated back to a period of intensive interactions with Eastern Cushitic peoples, probably around 1000–700 B.C., before the Southern Nilotic settlement in western Kenya;[16] and they practiced both male and female circumcision, features that owed to those same interactions of their ancestors with Eastern Cushites.[17] And from their Southern Cushitic neighbors in central East Africa came a major philosophical contribution to the Southern Nilotic worldview, the conceptual linking of Divinity with the sun. Through their close relations with Southern Cushites, the proto–Southern Nilotes also added the keeping of donkeys as pack animals.

Like the Southern Cushites, the Southern Nilotes put major emphasis in their economy on livestock raising. But for the Nilotes, cattle had apparently, in addition, a much more potent social significance. Already in the late last millennium B.C., the Southern Nilotic vocabulary contained a number of cattle-color terms and possibly, although not at all certainly, terms for different deliberate deformations of cow horns.[18] This terminology reveals the presence, even then, among Southern Nilotes of the status that cattle ownership confers today in the interfamilial and peer relations of Nilotic societies, and the kind of esthetic and affective qualities with which Southern Nilotes even then imbued their animals.

The proto–Southern Nilotes also introduced a new feature of livestock raising to central East Africa, the branding of cattle. The term used for the branding tool, *meceR, came from an Eastern Cushitic language and thus shows the earlier diffusion of this trait from the direction of Ethiopia.

Cultivation seems to have held a subsidiary role for most Southern Nilotes of the last several centuries B.C. Just two grains, sorghum and finger millet, and two kinds of calabashes make up the presently reconstructible crop vocabulary of the proto–Southern Nilotes.[19] We

179

may suspect their knowledge of another crop or two, such as black-eyed peas, but cannot prove it from the available language evidence. And like the Southern Cushites, the Southern Nilotes brewed mead but probably were not yet beer drinkers during the last millennium B.C. Even today among the Datoga of Tanzania, mead remains the preferred drink.

The Southern Nilotes of that period built round houses with conical roofs, as befitted their more distant Eastern Sahelian cultural roots. Neither beds nor stools had apparently yet become established parts of their household furnishings. Wherever cattle raising was a significant activity, as among the Mara people, the houses lay within thorn-fenced cattle pens (*pe:R). Within the pen a separate enclosure (*sa̰Rma̰) for milk cows and their calves could usually be found.

Even more than the Southern Cushites, the Southern Nilotes relied on leather for clothing, containers, and other uses. Besides leather sacks, they constructed large, barrel-shaped honey storage containers, made of leather wrapped around a slat framework. Their early sleeping mats were probably of leather, and they utilized a piece of leather as a catchcloth (*ra:ro) to put under a grindstone when grinding their grain. They made no baskets at all during the late last millennium B.C., and even string bags (*kerep) can be traced back among them no earlier as yet than the proto-Kalenjin society of the period 500–1000 A.D. The Southern Nilotes did use pots, but probably, as the evidence of both vocabulary and archeology indicates, possessed very little variety in pot shapes, less than among the Mashariki Bantu and even the Southern Cushites. Calabashes formed an another important class of containers for the early Southern Nilotic societies, as they did also among the Southern Cushites and the Central Sudanic and Southern Rub peoples of the Nyanza Basin (see tables 11 and 29 and table 38A in appendix); but the use of carved wooden bowls or jars may not have spread among them till after the turn of the era.

---

### Table 29. Proto–Southern Nilotic containers

| | | | |
|---|---|---|---|
| *mɪlʸɔ(:t) | "large leather sack" | *ter | "pot" |
| *sampʊ:r | "small leather sack" | *toi(u:t) | "pot" |
| *lʸɔ:r | "kind of leather sack" | *sot | "calabash" |
| *tokol | "leather honey-storage barrel" | *kutu:ŋ | "calabash" |

Environments of the Cushitic and Nilotic Economies

A subsistence emphasis primarily on livestock raising and only secondarily on grain cultivation meant that both the Southern Cushities and the Southern Nilotes favored open grassland and the fringes of the montane forests for their settlements. At the turn of the era, the heartland of the Southern Cushitic territories extended from the highland plains of the Eastern Rift Valley region in central Kenya, across the grassland and steppe of central southern Kenya and far northern Tanzania, to the dry savannas of seasonally deciduous tree cover extending south through central Tanzania to the northern parts of Southern Highlands. One offshoot of the West Rift Southern Cushites, the Tale peoples, as we have already learned, had spread west into the southern and southwestern Nyanza Basin, while other Southern Cushites, of the Dahaloan branch, probably inhabited a scatter of areas in eastern Kenya and southern Somalia where cattle raising was possible.[20] The Southern Nilotes occupied a variety of grassland and highland areas in western Kenya, from the west slopes of the Eastern Rift Valley to the Mara plains of southwestern Kenya.

Everywhere they lived in Kenya and Tanzania, the Southern Cushites and the Southern Nilotes coexisted with gatherer-hunters. A combination of two factors explains the continuing success of food-collecting economies in southern Kenya and central northern Tanzania. For one thing, the population densities of the dominant herding societies of those areas were still very low; wild animals thus survived in large numbers and could support specialized food-collection. But probably more important, neither the Nilotes nor the Cushites seem to have possessed a significant cultural commitment to hunting, of the kind that comes forth so prominently in Bantu folklore, in which, for instance, founder-heroes are so often credited with having been great hunters. Neither the Cushites nor the Southern Nilotes fished at all; both considered fish to be creatures unsuitable for eating, a trait of very ancient provenance among Cushites and apparently adopted by the early Southern Nilotes under either Eastern or Southern Cushitic influence. The proto–Southern Nilotic herders and farmers, from the meagerness of their reconstructible vocabulary of the chase, may have hunted not at all; the Southern Cushites seem to have had a bit more developed hunting knowledge (see table 30). On the whole, it would appear, the Nilotes and Cushites of those regions did not significantly compete with the gatherer-hunters for the same resources.

Moreover, one can detect among the Southern Cushites and Southern Nilotes the long-term persistence of a social perception that

## Table 30. Hunting terms in early Southern Nilotic and Southern Cushitic history

*a. Proto–Southern Nilotic terms*

| | | | |
|---|---|---|---|
| *lʸąkạ:t | "to hunt" | *(y)ąk- | "specialized gatherer-hunter" |
| *ko:Ra:ŋ | "bow" | | |
| *kạ:t | "arrow" | | |

*a. Early Southern Cushitic terms*

| (proto–Southern Cushitic) | | (proto-Rift) | |
|---|---|---|---|
| *xʷafaal- | "to hunt" | *łakat- | "to hunt" |
| *k'oos- | "bow and arrow" | *gaʕar- | "bow" |
| *ʕaasol- | "wooden-tipped arrow" | *mah- | "arrow" |
| *k'ad- | "arrow poison" | *tlan- | "arrows" (loan from Khoisan) |
| *has- | "bowstring of sinew" | | |
| *daʔa | "quiver, of bamboo" | *ts'ah- | "arrowhead" |
| *ʔog- | "specialized gatherer-hunter" | *ts'axʷ- | "to trap" |

the food-collecting way of life was a distinct and separate sphere of existence from their own. In the proto–Southern Cushitic language of over 5,000 years ago, already there existed a term for gatherer-hunters conceived of as a distinct category of people, *ʔog-. The proto–Southern Nilotes of the last millennium B.C. adopted from their Cushitic neighbors both the term, as *ɔk-/*ąk- (seen in the modern name of the Okiek people of the Mau forest of Kenya) and the socioeconomic distinction it represented.

Over much of Tanzania and in significant portions of Kenya, too, however, food-collecting livelihoods persisted simply because of the ecological selectivity of the the Cushites and Nilotes. In environments where cattle could not be raised because of tsetse-borne sleeping sickness, there the herders did not settle—in the wooded savannas of most of western Tanzania; in the similar vegetation zones found in the southeastern third of Tanzania and extending southward from there through northern Mozambique; and in the wooded hinterlands of the Tanzanian and Kenyan coasts as far north as the Tana River. The forested mountain ranges of northeastern Tanzania and eastern Kenya sheltered significant populations of food-collectors as well. The Eburran gatherer-hunters, of whose language relationships we remain uncertain, exploited the montane forests of highland Kenya that lay surrounded by the open grazing country of their food-producing neighbors. Other food-collectors who spoke languages of the Khoisan family, of whom only the Hadza lasted into the twentieth century, inhabited large parts of Tanzania and still probably could be found in areas along the Kenya coast as late as 2,000 years ago. Earlier, in the third millennium B.C., Khoisan food-collectors had apparently been a prominent population also in the east-central parts of northern Kenya.[21]

In consequence, large portions of western, far eastern, and southern East Africa remained, in the second half of the last millennium B.C., lands of only gatherer-hunters, living in very small communities with exceedingly low population densities. Many of these regions had relatively good rainfall, often above 1,000 millimeters of precipitation a year. They were entirely suited to agriculture, but to a kind of farming that was not constrained by an accompanying strong commitment to cattle raising.

## Patterns of Kaskazi Settlement, 100 B.C. to A.D. 400

Into just those kinds of lands flowed the Bantu expansions of the turn of the era. Faced—if the proposals of chapter 4 are correct—with an increasing demographic pressure on their abilities to carry out the low-population-density, very long fallow, yam-based agriculture of their forebears, the Kaskazi had either to adopt shorter-fallow systems and turn to greater use of grain crops or to find countries somewhere else that were suited to their accustomed farming practices. In the highlands of the Songea and Njombe districts in southwestern and southern Tanzania, in the hinterland of the Tanzania and southern Kenya coasts, and in the lower montane zones in northeastern Tanzania, need and opportunity conjoined. There could be found just the sort of warm, well-watered lands in which yam cultivation would thrive. Such areas, too, lay open to relatively easy agricultural settlement, because there the Kaskazi peoples did not have to face competition for land from already established food-producing communities.

A long initial jaunt had to be undertaken, it was true; and intelligence about such beckoning lands probably accumulated only over a period of generations, acquired by the more easterly Kaskazi groups at secondhand from the Southern Cushites or the Southern Nilotes who inhabited the intervening territories. But before the close of the last millennium B.C. the necessary information, vague and misleading as it must often have been, together with the cultural expectations that

183

would allow longer-range population movements, must have been in place among the eastern and southern outliers of the Kaskazi populations of western East Africa. For by the beginning of the first millennium A.D. the eastward scattering out of Kaskazi peoples was already well underway. The Upland communities, the Northeast-Coastal and Njombe communities of the Kati grouping, and the Mwika, Rungwe, Rufiji-Ruvuma, and Kilombero communities all resettled in new areas, far to the east or south of the Great Lakes region.


## Early Upland Communities

The Upland people moved completely of out the eastern Nyanza areas, passing right across the drier lands of central northern Tanzania to settle in the highlands and adjacent coastal hinterland of northeastern Tanzania and eastern Kenya. From the evidence of language, several early Upland populations can be mapped. Their very first settlements, accounting for their close contacts with both Southern Nilotes and Southern Cushites (tables 3B and 4B), probably lay well inland from the Indian Ocean coast. The North Pare Mountains provide the most probable locus of these events. A further extension of Upland groups then took place eastward to the Kenya coastlands and the Usambara mountain region of far northeastern Tanzania, while a somewhat later offshoot of the Upland communities moved to the south slopes of Mount Kenya by around the fourth century. The northern fringe of the coastal arm of this settlement may have reached the riverine areas of southern Somalia, where the former presence of Bantu speakers may be attested in a few rare Upland loanwords in the riverine Soomaali dialects.[22]

Two sets of loanwords, one from a Southern Nilotic language and the other from a Southern Cushitic tongue were adopted into the Upland dialects while the Upland communities still formed one closely associated grouping of people, living in northeastern Tanzania. The phonological and other characteristics of those loanwords show that the agents of this influence were Southern Cushites certainly different, and Southern Nilotes probably different, from those residing in the southeastern Nyanza regions. Both these sets of influences are thus best understood as taking effect after Upland communities arrived east of the Eastern Rift Valley, by or before the first to third centuries A.D. The Southern Nilotes most likely spoke a dialect of the Tato language (table 3B). The Southern Cushites certainly did not

184

speak a Rift language, but whether their language belonged to the Ma'a or Dahaloan group remains unclear as yet (table 4B).[23]

A third set of cultural contacts of the Upland people, with a Rub-related community (see table 31), has an uncertain historical setting. It may have taken place before the turn of the era, just before the eastward movement of Upland communities out of the Lake Nyanza Basin. But if the attribution of early pottery in one locale of the Eastern Rift region to the Oltome tradition is correct,[24] then the Rub' loanwords restricted to the Upland languages may instead have been borrowed earlier in the period of Upland settlement in far northeastern Tanzania. The Southern Rub dialect or language that influenced the proto-Upland vocabulary was, in any case, distinct from the one that affected the pre-Luyia and East-Nyanza peoples.[25]

The linguistic case for the early presence of Upland people in the North Pare mountains and on Mount Kenya is particularly strong, because these postulated settlements have direct historical links to the more recent populations in those regions. The communities that remained in the North Pare mountains evolved into the Chaga-Dabida society of c. 700–800 A.D., itself ancestral in language to the modern-day Gweno and Chaga communities of North Pare and Mount Kilimanjaro and to the Dabida society of the Taita hills.[26] The Upland people who moved north to southern Mount Kenya gave rise in subsequent centuries to the early Thagiicu society of the Eastern Highlands of Kenya, whose linguistic descendants, such as the Gikuyu, Embu, Chuka, and Meru, still occupy those regions today.

---

Table 31. Eastern Sahelian (Rub) loanwords in Upland

| (peripheral basic) | | (livestock) | |
|---|---|---|---|
| *-Biu | "entire(ly)" | *-Boro | "cattle pen" (only in Dabida; also as Dabida loan to Saghala) |
| *-Turu- | "to pierce" | | |
| (wild animals) | | *-sara | "hedge, thorn fence" (Chaga-Dabida only) |
| *-ceege | "porcupine" (attested only in Thagiicu) | | |
| *-cuui | "wild dog" | | |

The Northeast-Coastal Bantu people, an offshoot of the earlier Kati people, settled originally at the turn of the eras in the hinterland of the central Tanzanian coast (see below in this chapter). But by about the fourth or fifth century A.D., two of the early Northeast-Coastal communities were spreading their territories northward. One, the Seuta, pressed into far northeastern Tanzania, and the other, the Sabaki, advanced along the coastal belt into Kenya.[27] The early Upland communities of those two regions have left behind only an indirect linguistic record of their former existence, confused by the presence especially in two Sabaki languages, Mijikenda and Pokomu, of loanwords adopted from the Thagiicu languages of the Upland subgroup in very recent centuries.

Nevertheless, small but significant sets of very early Upland loanwords in Sabaki and Seuta can be given provisional identification, because of their distributions or their phonological characteristics. Apparently as the Upland dialects of those regions gradually dropped out of use in favor of the languages of the incoming Sabaki and Seuta peoples, a number of older Upland words were adopted into the early Sabaki and Seuta tongues and, somewhat later, into the proto-Mijikenda dialect of Sabaki (see table 5B).

Proto-Mijikenda itself began to diverge in North and South Mijikenda dialects no later than about 1000 A.D., well before the arrival of Thagiicu settlers in the sixteenth century. Some of the Upland loanwords can probably be explained as having been borrowed separately by either North or South Mijikenda speakers from their historically recent Thagiicu neighbors, or else as having been borrowed first by one branch of the Mijikenda, with secondary borrowing spreading those words to the other Mijikenda groups. But other words of apparent Upland source are not easily explained in this fashion and seem best understood as reflecting a much earlier era of interactions between Upland and Northeast-Coastal communities.

On the economic side, the kinds of meanings found in the proposed loanwords suggest that Upland peoples of the first few centuries A.D., perhaps because of their interactions with Southern Cushites and Southern Nilotes, had already developed a significantly stronger interest in livestock raising than their Northeast-Coastal Bantu neighbors and successors.[28] They would seem also to have had a fundamental influence on the development of age-set organization structures among the early Seuta and the proto-Mijikenda. But this history belongs to the centuries after A.D. 400. In the fourth century the older Mashariki customs of initiation probably still held true among Northeast-Coastal communities.

A much more recent stratum of Upland loanwords comprises borrowings that appear variously in Mijikenda, Saghala, Asu (Pare), Shambaa, and a few dialects of the East Ruvu group (notably in Zalamo). This stratum is not to be confused with the sets of early Upland loanwords in Sabaki and Seuta. The numerous recent loanwords can be specifically traced to Thagiicu immigrants arriving from the Mount Kenya region since about 1500. Between the fifteenth and the eighteenth centuries, different Thagiicu dialects came for a time to be spoken in parts of the Taita hills, the Pare Mountains, the Usambara range, and the coastal hinterlands of Kenya and far northern Tanzania. Of these, only Daiso, spoken in the Usambara region, has survived in use down to today. But as a consequence of these population movements, in each area loanwords from the immigrant Upland dialects were adopted in significant numbers by the local Bantu languages. Because this evidence in the Northeast-Coastal languages relates to much later eras of history, it has not been specifically identified in the tables here.[29]

The locations required for the earliest Upland settlers accord in every case with their having been the makers of Kwale ware.[30] Kwale sites have been found in the North Pare mountains and adjacent areas on Kilimanjaro, on southern Mount Kenya, near the Kenya coast, and in the Usambara mountains and Ngulu Hills of northeastern Tanzania. There remain immense gaps in our archeological knowledge of the history of Kwale ware. Nevertheless, a provisional outline history can very tentatively be proposed, and it matches up very well indeed with historical implication of the linguistic record of Upland peoples.

Both in the North Pare region and on the southern slopes of Mount Kenya, archeological continuities have been argued to hold from the earliest Bantu settlements into later times. In North Pare the later Kwale wares continued to be made alongside a second style of pottery, Maore ware, which eventually superseded it during the second half of the first millennium. On southern Mount Kenya a large gap of time separates the known occurrences of early Kwale ware, attested from around the fifth century A.D., from the Gatung'ang'a wares, found in sites dating to around the twelfth century. Yet Gatung'ang'a pottery appears to carry on Kwale motifs, differing principally in a decline in the variety of decorative elements used.[31] The societal continuities required by the linguistic evidence are matched, in other words, in North Pare and in the southern Mount Kenya region by parallel continuities in the archeology.

In the Usambara region, in contrast, the Kwale wares of the second and third centuries A.D. were replaced by the fifth and sixth centuries by varieties of a distinct pottery, Tana ware. The ceramic tradition is much too different to be directly derivable from the Kwale potteries of only a couple of centuries earlier, although some decorative motifs of Kwale ware may have been adopted into Tana pottery. Along the Kenya coast, the same changeover may have taken place a century or two later. Moreover, new settlement patterns appear in conjunction with the archeological shift. The Kwale settlements known from the Usambaras were placed on ridges. Their makers, it is clear, carried on the old Kaskazi innovation of ridge-villages,[32] a tradition still found among the recent Upland societies of the Chaga and the Thagiicu. With the arrival of Tana ware in the Usambaras, and presumably of the Northeast-Coastal peoples who made Tana pots, this pattern came to an end. The displacement of Upland peoples apparent in the language evidence for far northeastern Tanzania and coastal Kenya is thus paralleled in the pottery record and in the archeology of settlement.

We need to digress briefly at this point, to make clear the chronological tack taken here and in subsequent chapters in the correlating of particular peoples with particular radiocarbon-dated archeological cultures. The radiometric dates so far available for the first period of the Mashariki Bantu diaspora tend everywhere to be relatively few, and the number of sites as yet excavated and dated for each incipient society oftentimes form a very, very small sampling. In most regions the chances that archeologists, in their few dated excavations, have already happened upon sites from the very beginning of settlement are slight. In one or two instances, such sites may have been found. But in most cases the earliest sites so far dated probably belong not to the first two or three generations of settlement, but to a time at least *several* generations later. By then the number of habitation sites of the early communities would have grown considerably in number, and their remains would have become thus easier for archeologists to come across.

The earliest currently available Kwale date, from near the Kenya coast, falls in about the third century A.D.; by the reasoning followed here, the actual first settlement there of the Upland people, who are proposed to have made Kwale pottery, would therefore have to be placed at least a century or two earlier than the third century A.D. The proposed initial arrival of Upland groups, in the North Pare Mountains region, should date still a bit before that, at or before the turn of the era—hence the dating of Upland expansion offered above.

To sum up, the overall evidence indicates that the Upland communities moved across the plains of central northern Tanzania to settle, perhaps as early as the beginning of the first millennium A.D., in wooded highland areas in northeastern Tanzania, most probably in the North Pare Mountains. The correlative archeological and linguistic mappings best identify them as the makers of Kwale pottery. From North Pare they spread eastward to the Usambara Mountains and the warm, forested Kenya coastlands before the third century and to the lower montane forest of the south slopes of Mount Kenya by the end of the fourth century. The Upland communities nearest the coast were displaced and absorbed during the middle first millennium by Sabaki Bantu settlers coming from the south with a new style of pottery. But in two areas of the interior a longer-term cultural continuity prevailed. The communities on southern Mount Kenya evolved into the later Thagiicu grouping of peoples, such as the Gikuyu, while the dialect of the Upland people in the North Pare Mountains developed into the languages of the latter-day Chaga and Dabida societies.

## Antecedents of the Langi

Unique among the emigrants who moved eastward at the close of the Southern-Nyanza period, the pre-Langi found a place for themselves in the middle of north-central Tanzania. The ancestors in language of the modern Langi are likely to have been the makers of Lelesu ware. Their principal food-producing neighbors over the next centuries were West and East Rift Southern Cushites, and these contacts are much in evidence in the Langi vocabulary (and deserve their own separate investigation). But Langi also has its own set, not large, of Eastern Sahelian loanwords (see table 32). The smallness of the set suggests that, like the Eastern Sahelian loans in proto-Upland, these words might derive from the last interactions of the pre-Langi with a Rub community before their movement westward out of the Southern-Nyanza region. But as with the Upland interactions, the possibility that they reflect a Rub population located farther to the east, in or around the modern Mbulu district of Tanzania, cannot yet be entirely ruled out. What strengthens this possibility is the occurrence of Ol-tome pottery in the Lake Eyasi area, just northwest of Mbulu.

Not surprisingly, considering the dry climate of the regions settled by the distant linguistic forebears of the Langi, a few notable influences from the Eastern Sahelians appear in their vocabulary of grain growing (see table 32).

Table 32.  Eastern Sahelian loanwords in Langi

| (wild animals) | | (cultivation) | |
|---|---|---|---|
| ntinyi | "small black ant" | idoŋa | "granary (hut)" (also in Gogo) |
| kęcoci | "insect" | | |
| | | lǫfęre, | "porridge stirrer" |
| (livestock) | | (pl. fęre) | |
| mǫholo, | | | |
| pl. *mę holo* "dewlap" | | | |

## Northeast-Coastal and Njombe Societies

By the beginning of the first millennium A.D., the Kati people had already begun to diversify into three dialect communities. And, like the proto-Upland people, two of the Kati speech communities, the proto-Northeast-Coastal and the proto-Njombe, traveled across the drier intervening lands of central East Africa. The language evidence places the Northeast-Coastal people as settlers in the immediate hinterland of the central Tanzanian coast, while the Njombe society would have taken shape in the Southern Highlands of Tanzania.[33] Each of these societies entered into its own history of interaction with different Southern Cushitic communities resident or soon to be resident in their respective regions.[34]

The Northeast-Coastal society had important relations with an Mbuguan Southern Cushitic people, the Ma'a, whose descendants today live in parts of the Usambara Mountains, but who probably resided in the early first millennium A.D. in the central Maasai Steppe and in or near the inland parts of the Ruvu and Wami River watersheds of central eastern Tanzania. The early Ma'a seem to have had a rather peripheral influence on Northeast-Coastal culture history; their loanword set (table 6B) overall is a small one.

The Northeast-Coastal communities, in settling in eastern Tanzania, met up with a new yearly rainfall regime characterized by a short as well as a long rainy season. They maintained the old word *-tíkà for the long rains of northern and central coastal Tanzania, which fell at approximately the same months of the year as the *-tíkà rain season of their early Mashariki ancestors. The short rains, which came around October and November, partially coincided with the proto-

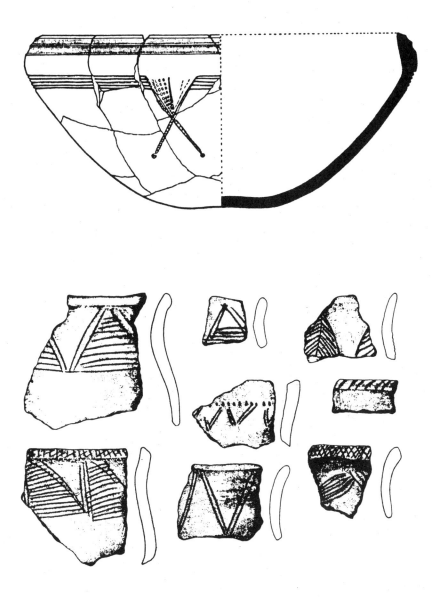

Figure 8. Ceramics of the Later Classical Age in northern East Africa. Kwale ware, *top* (Soper 1967). Tana ware, *bottom* (Haaland 1995/96).

191

Mashariki season *-lìmò. Some of the Northeast-Coastal people thus reapplied that term to the short rains. Others communities, however, instead adopted the Ma'a name (see *-bu̟li, table 6B) for the season. The name or names they gave to the intervening hot season, from December to February, and to their cool season between about June and September, remain to be discovered.

As direct cultural forebears to the Sabaki and Seuta societies, the Northeast-Coastal people would have been the makers, too, of Tana pottery. Some of their early sites, characterized by just such ceramic wares and dating to the early centuries A.D., have already been located by archeologists near the central Tanzanian coast. The early Northeast-Coastal settlers cannot be connected up with the Kwale ware sites of the first few centuries A.D., known farther north from the Kenya coastal region and from the Usambara Mountains. These, as we have already seen, were most probably made by the eastern outliers of the Upland Bantu communities.

Already by the fourth and fifth centuries A.D., Northeast-Coastal people had spread over a considerable span of territory, extending from the Rufiji delta north to the Pangani Valley. Within that span four separate societies were beginning to emerge out of the original Northeast-Coastal society. Along and just inland from the coast can be located the Ruvu, centered on the drainage basins of the Ruvu and Wami Rivers, and the Seuta, residing in parts of the modern Handeni district. The pre-Asu society would have been taking shape about the same time among Northeast-Coastal communities who had moved inland to the South Pare Mountains. (Later, by the fifth and sixth centuries, the pre-Asu may have begun to enter into close interactions with an Upland people, the Chaga-Dabida, of North Pare.) At the coast a fourth incipient Northeast-Coastal society, the Sabaki, was coming into being in the areas just north of the lower Pangani River.[35]

The early Njombe communities, whose settlement took them southward into the modern-day Njombe district of Tanzania, were influenced deeply by the Iringa Southern Cushites, an East Rift society that had expanded by or before the early first millennium A.D. into the northern parts of Tanzania's Southern Highlands. The loanwords so far identified indicate a broad general influence of these East Rift people on Njombe history, including a particularly strong impact on cattle-keeping ideas. The adoption, even, of a few basic vocabulary items from the Iringa language shows that the erstwhile Iringa Cushites probably composed a major element in the ancestry of the later Njombe society (table 7Ba). The archeological cultures that correlate with the early Njombe settlers and with the Iringa Southern Cushitic society remain to be identified.[36]

## Developments among the Luyia and East-Nyanza

While the Upland and Kati communities were striking off across the central regions of East Africa and settling far to the south and southeast of the Nyanza Basin, the proto-Luyia expanded into new areas within the basin. In the late Southern-Nyanza era, around probably the last two or three centuries B.C., they can be argued to have formed, along with the East-Nyanza and Upland peoples, the northeastern outliers of the Southern-Nyanza cluster, inhabiting areas along the southeastern side of Lake Nyanza. The shared Luyia and East-Nyanza adoption, after the Upland peoples had left the region, of a number of loanwords, especially livestock terms, from the Mara Southern Nilotes (table 33a) indicates that the pre-Luyia remained for a short time longer in that region, continuing to be neighbors of the East-Nyanza community.

At the same time, they and the East-Nyanza entered into new relations with a Rub-related society (see table 33b). A notable contribution of these Southern Rub peoples to the early proto-Luyia and East-Nyanza communities is visible in the borrowed verb *-bus-, denoting a second clearing of a field. The adoption of this word surely reflects a first shifting of agricultural emphases among these Lakes Bantu communities, away from a still yam-based agriculture toward more use of seed crops.

By the third or fourth century, if not before, the Luyia had settled to the immediate north of the Wami Gulf. There they began a long and complex history of relations with a variety of Nilo-Saharan peoples. Around the northeastern side of Lake Nyanza they also soon entered into centuries of cultural and social encounter with another set of Lakes Bantu, the North-Nyanza peoples, whose expansions had carried them around the northern side of the lake by or before mid-first millennium A.D.[37]

A notable feature that must be added to the picture developed in earlier studies of Luyia history is the occurrence of a major body of loanwords restricted to Luyia that come from a Southern Rub language. The earliest stage of this contact surely dates to the very beginnings of Luyia settlement in the areas north of the Wami Gulf, at around the first to fourth century A.D. (see table 34a and table 34A.1). But the interactions probably went on for several more cen-

Table 33.  Southern Nilotic and Eastern Sahelian (Rub) loanwords
common to Luyia and East-Nyanza

a.  *Southern Nilotic loanwords*

(wild animals)

*-tiaaŋį  "wild animal" (also
    isolated in Temi
    of Upland)

(livestock)

*-(h)iili  "bull, ox"
*-giluki,
  *-guluki  "bull"
*-sųbiinį  "ewe-lamb"
*-suunu  "barren animal"
    (also isolated in
    Temi of Upland)

b.  *Rub loanwords*

(parts of body)

*-teŋe  "elbow" or "back
    of knee"

(cultivation)

*-bus-  "to dig field a second
    time"

(wild animals)

*-biiji  "bushpig" (also
    spread to Ganda)
*-suuji  "wild dog"
*-tuuju,
  *-tuuyu  "hare"
*-jaalia  "tick bird"

Table 34.  Samples of Eastern Sahelian (Rub) and
Southern Cushitic loanwords in proto-Luyia

a.  *Rub loanwords*

(basic word)

*-ŋeenį  "fish"

(wild animal)

*-jegeje  "porcupine"

(livestock)

*-migu  "ram"

b.  *Southern Cushitic loanwords*

(basic vocabulary)

*-gòkè  "ashes"
*-gálí  "big"

(wild animals)

*-tàlàŋì  "lion"
*-sàsà(n)gè  "spotted carnivore"

turies before the Southern Rub language of the region finally died out.[38]

Another set of actors who had some importance in the earliest period of Luyia settlement north of the Wami Gulf spoke a Southern Cushitic language. Only a small number of Southern Cushitic loanwords can yet be securely traced to proto-Luyia (see table 34b). But a number of other such loanwords, not cited here, have been recorded from the North and the South Luyia dialects, and it seems likely that Southern Cushitic communities continued to persist also for some centuries after the Luyia arrival.[39] The relationships of these Southern Cushites remain unclear.

# Further Developments in the Southern Nyanza Regions

As the diasporas of the Upland, Kati, pre-Langi, and pre-Luyia proceeded, two other societies took shape during the early first millennium A.D. among those Bantu speakers who stayed behind and continued to reside in the southern and southeastern Nyanza regions.

### The Formative Era of the East-Nyanza Society

At the southeast of the lake lay the lands of the early East-Nyanza society. That region, like the areas to the north of the Wami Gulf, had a history of varied intercultural contacts. As we saw in chapter 3, a Southern Cushitic society occupied areas located perhaps in parts of the Kisii district of Kenya, while the Mara Southern Nilotes probably long remained important inhabitants of the areas to the immediate east and south, on the Mara plains. In addition to those Southern Nilotes and Southern Cushites, on whom considerable evidence has been published previously,[40] a Southern Rub people remained significant actors for a time, too, in the developments of the region (table 35).

The kinds of words borrowed reveal a surprisingly strong Rub influence on livestock raising among the early East-Nyanza communities but, unlike the preceding era before the turn of the era, as yet no visible contribution to cultivation practices (such can be seen in table 33). In addition, the adoption of a number of basic words shows a Rub impact limited not just to cultural imitation but involving a considerable assimilation of former Southern Rub speakers into the East-Nyanza society. The last stage of this process, during which the re-

> ### Table 35. Sample of Eastern Sahelian (Rub) loanwords in East-Nyanza languages
>
> *a. Proto-East-Nyanza words*
>
> (basic words)    (livestock)
>
> \*-salu    "cloud"    \*-gaini    "bull"    \*-juuru    "ewe-lamb"
>                       \*-taaŋana    "o x"    \*-korope    "he-goat"
>
> *b. Proto-Mara words (branch of East-Nyanza)*
>
> (basic words)         (parts of the body)         (material culture)
>
> \*-sense    "sand"    \*-tururu    "buttock"    \*-siri̧    "rope"
> \*-tukia    "hair"    \*-boto    "cheek"

maining Southern Rub were absorbed into Gusii society, is marked by the significant set of loanwords, including basic vocabulary, taken into early Gusii. This stage might possibly date as late as the first half of the present millennium.

As we saw in chapter 3, Robertshaw's excavations at Gogo Falls give us a tangible sample of the ethnic complexity revealed so strongly in the evidence of language for the southeasten Nyanza Basin. But the interactions among the East-Nyanza Bantu peoples, Southern Rub, Southern Nilotes, and Southern Cushites that date to the first few centuries A.D. form only the first round in a much longer and more variegated history of cultural encounter. The longer run of that story belongs to the subsequent middle eras of eastern African history rather than to the Classical Age, and lies outside the scope of the story we tell here.

## The Emergence of the Takama Society

A second society that evolved in the Southern-Nyanza Basin in the first few centuries A.D. were the Takama. In essence, the early Takama comprised those Kati communities who remain behind in the old lands of the Southern-Nyanza areal cluster, to the immediate south of Lake Nyanza, and who did not trek eastward as did the Northeast-Coastal and Njombe peoples. In the first few centuries A.D., the Takama continued for a time to interact with Rift Southern Cushites (see table 36a). These Cushites were probably closely related to the

Central Tale people who had so influenced the Southern-Nyanza communities. The Takama seem to have dealt to some extent also with a still persisting Southern Rub society, itself presumably located to the south or southeast of the lake (see table 36b).

As late as the fifth or sixth century A.D., the Takama still formed one people. Only thereafter did they evolve into three sets of descendant communities—the Wembere, who probably moved off to the southeast to settle near the Wembere River and from whom the present-day Ilamba and Rimi derive; the pre-Kimbu; and the West Takama, whose present-day representatives are the numerous Sukuma and Nyamwezi communities of western Tanzania. The Tale Southern Cushites may have continued for a time to have an influence on West Takama history before they ceased to be notable actors in the events of the Southern-Nyanza Basin (see table 36Ab in appendix).

Still later, probably from the early second millennium A.D., both West Takama expansions to the west and southeastward movements of the Western-Lakes communities of the Lakes group brought the West Takama societies increasingly into the cultural orbit and under the strong cultural influences of different Lakes societies. The extreme example of this kind of impact is provided by the most northwesterly of the West Takama peoples, the Sumbwa. But these contacts relate to

---

Table 36. Sample Southern Cushitic (Central Tale) and Eastern Sahelian (Rub?) loanwords in early Takama

*a. Tale words of proto-Takama provenance*

(wild animals)

*-duulu "zebra"
*-longi "black-tipped mongoose"

(domestic animals)

*-gulyati "he-goat"
*-dogootįa "young goat, ewe-lamb"

(other culture)

*-lugu "war" (also areal spread to Gogo, Rungwe group)

*b. Eastern Sahelian loanwords in early Takama*

(peripheral basic)

*-buubu "dust"

(wild animals)

*-pusi "wildebeest"
*-laala "Thomson's gazelle"

---

later periods of history and are not of direct further concern here.[41]

Neither the Rub nor the Tale peoples, on the one hand, seem on present evidence to have greatly reshaped the livelihood of the developing Takama society of the early centuries A.D. On the other hand, there remains a considerable body of agricultural vocabulary (not cited here) found in the West Takama language, Nyamwezi-Sukuma, the origins of which have yet to be traced. Among the words of this vocabulary there may be important clues to the developments of those centuries that are still to be uncovered.

## Developments among the Southerly Kaskazi Peoples

Four other groupings of Kaskazi communities had come into existence before the close of the last millennium B.C., the Rufiji-Ruvuma, the Kilombero, the Mwika, and the Rungwe. None participated directly in the interactions that so forcefully shaped the histories of the Kaskazi communities who formed the Southern-Nyanza regional cluster, and none seems to have had any further significant interactions with the Sog or Central Sudanic societies who had been such important neighbors of their Mashariki ancestors earlier in the millennium.

Where then, during the second half of the last millennium B.C., did their initial divergence into separate sets of communities begin? The eventual settlement of each in central and western parts of southern Tanzania, by or before the first two or three centuries A.D., suggests strongly that their origins lay among the southerly members of the early Kaskazi cluster of communities. They may thus have resided to the south of the Nyanza Basin proper and east of the Western Rift, but in districts where rainfall and other environmental conditions allowed them to pursue their accustomed agricultural economy. Possible settings for their evolution into distinctive groupings of communities thus include a variety of forested and wooded savanna areas, extending from Burundi on the north to the southern end of Lake Tanganyika.

Whatever the locations of their ancestral communities at the middle of the last millennium, by the first or second century A.D. they had each emerged as distinct societies in different adjoining countries around the north end of Lake Nyasa, all with rainfall of 1,000 millimeters or more a year and all suitable to yam-based, long-fallow cultivation. The Rufiji-Ruvuma society took shape somewhere on the upper Ruvuma River watershed, in or around the modern Son-

198

gea district of Tanzania, while the Kilombero had moved into areas close to the Kilombero valley.[42] The Rungwe people occupied parts of the highlands probably near modern Mbeya, while the Mwika settled to the west of the Rungwe.

One other emerging Kaskazi society can be placed in an adjoining area. The Njombe, an offshoot of the Kati group, settled, as described previously, in high-rainfall areas of the Southern Highlands of Tanzania, most probably in the modern Njombe district. The Kilombero people were their immediate western neighbors; and the Rufiji-Ruvuma and Rungwe, their respective neighbors to the southeast and to the west.

The southern outliers of Kaskazi settlement in the first few centuries A.D. reached probably as far south as the modern-day Tumbuka country in Malawi. We must argue for this southerly extension of the Kaskazi because of the presence of a considerable number of apparent Kaskazi loanwords in the Nyasa languages (Nyanja-Chewa, Sena, and Tumbuka), the ancestral form of which was most probably spoken in central or southern Malawi (see chapter 7). This outlying Kaskazi society apparently had earlier connections with the Southern-Kaskazi areal cluster of communities of the early mid-first millennium B.C. and may have been an offshoot of the Rungwe settlement (see table 43 for a selection of apparent Kaskazi loanwords in the Nyasa group).

Rather different histories of growth and expansion occupied these several sets of farming communities. The Mwika, from whom the modern Nyamwanga, Mambwe, Fipa, and other closely related societies of the Tanzania-Zambia borderlands derive, emerged along the highland corridor extending west from Mbeya area toward southern Lake Tanganyika. The Rungwe society developed among those residing around the almost 3,000-meter-high Rungwe Mountain, hence the name given that people. The Rungwe themselves diverged within a very few centuries into two different sets of communities. One of these, the proto-Nyika society, ancestral to the present-day Nyiha and Safwa, developed north of the mountain. The other, the proto-Konde-Ndali, from whom the Nyakyusa, Ndali, and Konde peoples derive, took form among the Rungwe communities who filtered into the valleys and plateaus south of the mountain amd around the north end of Lake Nyasa.

Moreover, there are strong indications in the language evidence that other Kaskazi peoples, who may have been closely related to the early Mwika societies, spread their settlement southwestward across Zambia by or before the turn of the era (see chapter 7 for an extend-

ed discussion of this history). Support for this conclusion comes
from the significant substrata of early Kaskazi root words that recur in
the Sabi (Bemba, Bisa, etc.) and Botatwe language groups, both of
which intruded into Zambia no earlier than the second half of the first
millennium A.D. (a sample of these words are cited in table 37; others
appear in table 44).[43]

The Njombe peoples, in contrast, although surely growing in
population, found scope for their expansions within the territories
they had already laid claim to, and apparently remained still a single
society till the second half of the first millennium. The Kilombero
people, who may initially have settled in the Mahenge highlands just
west of the seasonally flooded Kilombero valley, probably also remained one society till after 500.

The Rufiji-Ruvuma communities, in contrast to the rest, began
rapidly to spread out over extensive new territories possibly as early as
the first and second centuries A.D., expanding eastward down the Ruvuma River toward the Indian Ocean seaboard and probably also into
the northern parts of Mozambique as far south as the latitude of Mozambique Island.[44] The priority of Rufiji-Ruvuma settlement in these
latter areas is reflected in a number of words found in the Makua dialects spoken there today, but which are apparently of Rufiji-Ruvuma
origina. An especially notable case is the word *-sese "four," a spe-

Table 37. Sample of Mashariki words overlapping
into Sabi dialects

| *-tòb- | "to hit" | see table 5 |
|---|---|---|
| *-gàlì | "porridge" | see table 7; specifically Kaskazi |
| *-tò | "gravy" | early Mashariki root, but possibly Kusi source instead of Kaskazi |
| *-pùlí | "edible cucurbit" | same as for *-tò "gravy" |
| *-sikisi | "oil palm" | see table 16 (only in Bisa?) |
| *-tapo | "iron ore" | see table 7; specifically Kaskazi |
| *-pe | "flat basket" Rungwe | see table 19; specifically Mwika or |
| *-gàndá | "house" | probably specifically from Mwika; meaning "house" is Kaskazi innovation with relict retention in Mwika and Ruvu subgroups (see chapter 5) |

cifically Rufiji-Ruvuma word found in northern, but not southern, Makua dialects (see chapter 7)

As this expansion proceeded, the original cluster of Rufiji-Ruvuma communities diverged into two regional clusters, the Ruvuma, who established themselves at first, as their name implies, in the lands about the middle Ruvuma River, and the Mbinga, who emerged among those communities whose country lay in the modern Mbinga and western Songea districts, around the upper Ruvuma watershed.[45] The continuing spread of Ruvuma settlement down the river toward the Indian Ocean coast commenced, as early as the fourth century, to bring about a further split within the Ruvuma society between the Yao-Mwera communities, located along and to the south of the middle Ruvuma, and the pre-Makonde who had moved into the coastal hinterland, around the lower stretches of the river.

Probably also no later than about the fourth century, the Mbinga cluster of communities began its divergence into two successor societies, the Ruhuhu whose territory lay in the region of the Ruhuhu River of the modern-day northern Mbinga and northwestern Songea districts, and the Lwegu, whose earliest territories probably occupied the areas running eastward from Lake Nyasa into the far upper Ruvuma River watershed. Their name is taken from the spread of many of their descendants northeastward, late in the first millennium A.D., through the drainage basin of the Luwegu River as far as the delta of the Rufiji River. In those regions they eventually gave rise to the well-known Matumbi, Ngindo, and Rufiji societies of recent centuries.

As yet, just three archeological cultures belonging to this region and dating to the first few centuries A.D. have been given clear definition. The Kalambo tradition can be identified as the work of Mwika peoples. It occurs over exactly the regions where the early Mwika and Mwika-related peoples must, on linguistic grounds, be placed, namely, in northeastern Zambia and in the areas south and immediately southeastward of Lake Tanganyika. The second, Mwabulambo, is known from northern Malawi sites that fit in well with the proposed early locations of some of the Rungwe peoples. A third culture, the Monapo, as yet excavated only from sites in northern Mozambique, appears most probably to have been made by communities of the Ruvuma branch of the Rufiji-Ruvuma (see chapter 7). The archeologies of the other early Kaskazi communities of 2,000–1,700 years ago in southern Tanzania—the Kilombero, Njombe, and the Mbinga—remain to be identified.

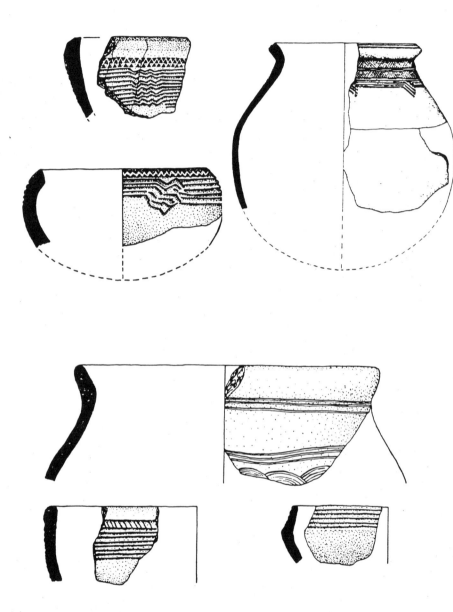

Figure 9. Ceramics of the Later Classical Age in southern East Africa. Kalambo ware, *top* (Clark 1974); Mwabulambo ware, *bottom* (Robinson and Sandelowsky 1968; Robinson 1976).

## An Overview of Kaskazi Resettlement

All across East Africa, then, from the highlands of Kenya in the north to the watershed of the Ruvuma River and its tributaries in the south, a wide reshaping of human population distributions took place from the last two centuries B.C. through the third and fourth centuries A.D. In perhaps no more than a four-hundred-year span, agricultural people planted their ways of living, as well as ways of subsistence, in a set of environments little if at all penetrated before by food-producing societies. A single broad grouping of societies, all of them descendants of the Kaskazi cluster of Mashariki communities who had established themselves along the western edge of East Africa in the first half of the last millennium B.C., precipitated this sea change in life and livelihood. The prime motive force behind their expansions may have been no more than the need for land in which to be able still to carry out their livelihood in the manners and forms to which their history had accustomed them.

Across this range of territories, their settlement initially built up a new mosaic of cultures and economies (map 7). The pre-Langi did settle in dry north-central Tanzania as an island of Bantu-speaking farmers who must already have adopted grains as their staple crops; otherwise they would have been unable to have competed successfully with the Southern Cushitic farmers and the Khoisan food-collectors who were their neighbors. But the remainder of the Kaskazi diaspora passed initially beyond central East Africa, eastward into areas of higher rainfall. The Upland Bantu communities formed islands of yam-based planting agriculturists in northeastern Tanzania and southeastern Kenya, surrounded by Southern Cushitic and Southern Nilotic pastoral farmers, with gatherer-hunter groups able for a long time to persist in the higher, colder forests and the marginal pasture lands. Pursuing the same kind of agriculture practices as the Upland groups, the Northeast-Coastal communities settled to the east of the dry savannas and grasslands of central Tanzania, near the Indian Ocean. Southward in far southern Tanzania, areas of middle-level highlands and well-watered lowlands accommodated an extended clustering of several Kaskazi communities, the Njombe, the Kilombero, the Rufiji-Ruvuma, the Mwika, and the Rungwe. The Njombe territories lay adjacent to those of the Iringa Southern Cushites, raisers of livestock and cultivators of grains. But in many other parts of southern Tanzania, the Kaskazi settlers moved in on gatherer-hunter communities, whom they probably fairly soon dispossessed and displaced as the dominant populations.

203

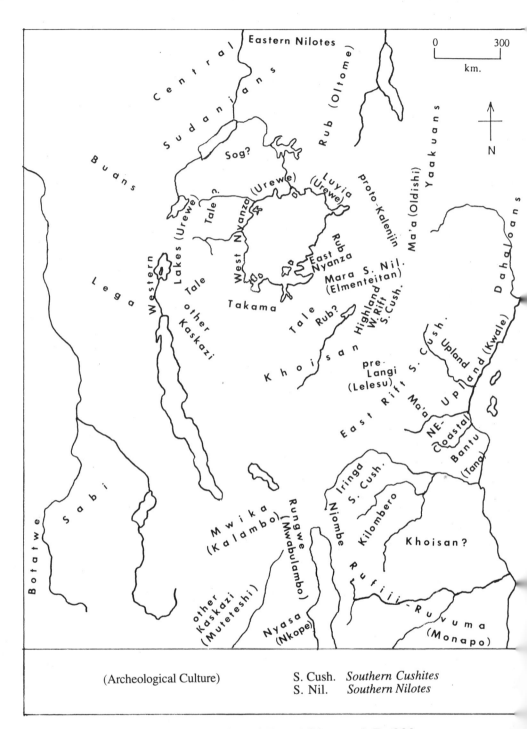

Central Sudanians

Eastern Nilotes

Buans

Rub (Oltome)

Yaakuans

Sog?

Lakes (Urewe)

Luyia (Urewe)

proto-Kalenjin

Ma'a (Oldishi)

West Nyanza (Urewe)

Tale?

Lega

Western

Tale

East Nyanza

Rub

Mara S. Nil. (Elmenteitan)

Dahaloans

other Kaskazi

Takama

Tale

Rub?

Highland W. Rift S. Cush.

S. Cush.

Upland (Kwale)

Khoisan

pre-Langi (Lelesu)

Ma'a

East Rift S. Cush.

NE-Coastal Bantu (Tana)

Botatwe

Sabi

Mwika (Kalambo)

Rungwe (Mwabulambo)

Iringa

Niombe

S. Cush.

Kilombero

Khoisan?

Rufiji-

other Kaskazi (Muteteshi)

Nyasa (Nkope)

Ruvuma (Monapo)

0          300
km.

N

(Archeological Culture)

S. Cush.  *Southern Cushites*
S. Nil.   *Southern Nilotes*

Map 7.  Peoples of East Africa, c. A.D. 300

These developments form only half the picture, however. Southward from East Africa proper—in Malawi, Mozambique, southern and central Zambia, and far southeastern Africa during just those same centuries—an equally sweeping recasting of the form and content of social and economic history was taking place. Once again the expansions of Mashariki Bantu peoples, sometimes Kazkazi but most often descendants of the early Kusi cluster of communities, gave direction and shape to those developments. To the laying out of that history we now direct our efforts.

# Notes

1 Nurse 1983, 1988b.

2 Ehret 1974b.

3 Robertshaw and Collett 1983, see also chapter 1.

4 Ehret 1974b.

5 Ehret and Nurse 1981 and n.d.

6 Ambrose 1986.

7 Ehret 1979, 1980b.

8 Ehret 1980b.

9 Ehret 1980a.

10 The modern-day Okiek of the highland Kenya forest areas, the direct cultural heirs of Eburran people, speak Kalenjin dialects, but language of the Eburrans of last millennium B.C. is not known. One scholar has proposed that they may have spoken a Khoisan language (Ambrose 1982), but the considerable differences in tool kits between Eburrans and other hunter-gatherers in eastern Africa make that a very uncertain postulation. By the later last millennium B.C., they may well have adopted the Southern Cushitic language of their food-producing neighbors, but this too is a matter for future investigation.

11 Ambrose 1982.

12 The key historical linguistic study of the Southern Nilotes, much relied on here, is Rottland 1982, with additional useful materials from Rottland 1989.

13 The Mara Southern Nilotes were misappropriately called the "Victoria Southern Nilotes" in Ehret 1971.

14 Contra Ehret 1971, which puts them in a third subgroup of their own.

15 Robertshaw 1993.

16 Ehret 1982c.

17 Ehret 1971.

18 Ehret 1971.

19 Ehret 1971.

20 Ali 1985.

[21] Ehret 1971, 1974b.

[22] Ali 1985.

[23] Note in particular the word for "black-eyed peas" in table 32, which may be of Dahaloan source. The distinct sound found in the loanwords, written as *T*, was probably originally the Southern Cushitic dental *$t$, which is pronounced like French *t*. The inherited Bantu *t was alveolar and pronounced like English *t*. Note also that the Bantu sound that has been reconstructed here as *l (but in Guthrie 1967–72, as *d) had already become an *r in the Upland dialect group and that, lacking an *l, the Upland dialects converted Southern Cushitic *l to an *r.

[24] Robertshaw and Collett 1983.

[25] As the Upland term for "wild dog" (*Lycaon pictus*), *-cuui, shows, their word borrowings came from a language that retained proto-Rub *c (pronounced similarly to English *ch* ) as a palatal sound (see table 31), whereas the Luyia and East-Nyanza form of the same word, *-suuji, shows a shift of proto-Rub *c to *ts or *s, either of which would yield the attested *s of the borrowed shape (see table 31A). The loanword set in Langi may have come from the same dialect as influenced early Upland, because it too renders proto-Rub *c as a palatal *j (see "insect" in table 32 below). The other differences in pronunciation are explainable outcomes of the phonologies of the Bantu languages involved.

[26] Ehret and Nurse, n.d.

[27] These datings are based on glottochronological arguments. The basic vocabulary retention rate centers around mid or low 70 percents between North and South Mijikenda dialects, indicating a divergence beginning around 1,000 years ago. The lowest range of figures between the different Sabaki subgroups lies in the mid-60 percents, in keeping with the archeological dating of their initial spreading out northward along the Kenya coast, with Tana ware, after 500, while the lower median figures between the Sabaki and Seuta subgroups of Northeast-Coastal Bantu run in the high 50 percents, indicating a beginning for their divergence from each other in the Tanzania coastal hinterland at possibly around 200 or 300 A.D.

[28] The materials here draw in part on Nurse and Hinnebusch 1993 but offer an alternative explanation of some of the early Sabaki and Mijikenda root words. Those cited in table 34 all have phonological characteristics that suggest them to have been borrowed from Upland languages other than the particular Thagiicu dialects brought to the coast in the last 500 years, or else their distributional features or phonology favor their adoption before divergences among the Sabaki or Seuta languages that began about 1000 years ago, such as between North and South Mijikenda. If this interpretation is correct, they reflect interactions of Sabaki and Seuta with Upland communities that may have lasted several centuries as the Upland groups who preceeded the Northeast-Coastal peoples in the

region were gradually assimilated into the already distinct early Sabaki and Seuta societies.

[29] For goodly selections of these data, see Nurse 1979, 1983, and 1988b; Ehret and Nurse 1981.

[30] Soper 1982; Ehret 1984, 1988.

[31] Soper 1982.

[32] This archeological information was conveyed most recently in the paper and accompanying slide presentation of Dr. Felix A. Chami at the Conference on East African Agricultural Origins, Cambridge University, July 1994.

[33] Ehret 1984.

[34] Ehret 1974b, 1984, 1988.

[35] Ehret 1988.

[36] Several of the Iringa loanwords occur outside the Njombe languages, but with areal distributions indicative of their having spread relatively recently by secondary borrowing from Njombe peoples to other Bantu communities (see examples in table 7B.B-D). The solidly old occurrence of each such word lies in the Njombe languages. These words then have partially overlapping spreads into one or another language spoken adjacent to modern-day Njombe tongues. These include several Rungwe languages of far southwestern Tanzania; some of the Ruvu dialects of Northeast-Coastal Bantu such as Gogo or Kami; and certain Takama languages, specifically Kimbu, Rimi, or Ilamba. The distributions can be understood to reflect the various northward movements of Njombe peoples of the past several centuries, known from the oral traditions.

[37] For a survey of this history, in some respects dated, see Ehret 1976a; for North-Nyanza history see Schoenbrun 1990.

[38] Many of the word distributions indicated in the tabling of Southern Rub loans in Table 34A.1 are no doubt incomplete; they represent the occurrences of the words as thus far recorded. Several that are currently known from just South or North Luyia, for instance, probably occur more widely among the Luyia dialects and thus will eventually have to be attributed to proto-Luyia.

[39] This case is also made in Ehret 1976a.

[40] Ehret 1971, 1974b; Schoenbrun 1990.

[41] Abundantly documented by Hinnebusch, Nurse, and Mould 1981 and further supported by Schoenbrun 1990.

[42] Waite and Ehret 1981.

[43] So numerous are the words of Mashariki origin in the Bemba-Bisa dialect group that Guthrie (1967–72) included Bemba and Bisa in his M zone, which also includes Mashariki languages.

[44] Waite and Ehret 1981.

[45] Waite and Ehret 1981; Nurse 1988a calls this group with less historical appropriateness "Rufiji."

# 7. Southeastern Africa in the Later Classical Age, to A.D. 400

## Broadening the Historical Stage

In the southern parts of Greater Eastern Africa, just as in East Africa proper, sweepingly new directions of historical development characterized the centuries of the Later Classical Age. In those more southerly regions, the inception of the transformative developments of the time may have begun in some areas as early as the fourth century B.C. A different set of Mashariki Bantu, the various early Kusi societies, took center stage in the reshaping of life and livelihood in the southeastern regions of the continent, and they played out their history against a different cultural and economic backdrop than in East Africa. Still, in very broad terms, a similar range of consequences ensued in southeastern Africa from the scattering out of the Bantu-speaking communities: first, the wide establishment of agricultural economies—to a greater extent than in East Africa, in areas that entirely lacked food production previously—and, second, the rise to economic and demographic prominence of communities whose cultural values, ideas, and practices traced in large part back to the Mashariki people of the formative era of the Classical Age.

## Introducing the Historical Actors

### The Early Centuries of Kusi History

The early Kusi cluster of the middle of the last millennium B.C., like their contemporaries the Kaskazi, can be understood as a wide regional grouping of contiguous communities with already several incipient dialects emerging among them. At least four distinct Kusi dialects had evolved by the close of the millennium; we can call these dialects respectively proto-Sala-Shona, proto-Southeast-Bantu, proto-Makua, and proto-Nyasa. Probably one or two other Kusi dialects were spoken, of which we have as yet only indirect knowledge.

209

The Kusi clustering of Mashariki communities first emerged, as we have seen (chapter 2), as a southerly extension of the early Mashariki populations of the first half of the last millennium B.C. Their later directions of settlement, south and southeastward out of the far west of East Africa, certify their location to the south of the contemporaneous Kaskazi cluster. Their nonparticipation in the interactions of the Kaskazi communities with such undoubted East African peoples as the Tale Southern Cushites, the Southern Rub, and the Southern Nilotes place them also outside of the Nyanza Basin.

Where, then, in particular did the Kusi cultural world first begin to take shape? Climate and topography favor the areas along the west side of Lake Tanganyika. It was the lands at the west of the lake, rather than the east, that most constituted a biological and geographical continuation southward of the early Mashariki environments. From the Mitumba Mountains at the north to the Malimba Range at the southwest side of the lake runs a chain of highlands, heavily forested in those times, that, with only a few breaks in elevation, rise to above 1,400 or 1,500 meters. Positive indications, in the form of apparent Mashariki loanwords in such Central-Savanna tongues as the eastern Luban dialects and in the Sabi language, Malungu, spoken to the immediate west of southern Lake Tanganyika,[1] also point to these areas as having been occupied before the past thousand years by speakers of early Mashariki dialects.

The highlands along Lake Tanganyika form a long but very narrow and limited extension southward, however, of the western Great Lakes environments, and the terrains initially attractive to settlement would probably have formed only a small part of the whole area. These conditions in themselves may have helped to accelerate Kusi spread southward and to create a perception of land shortage rather earlier among the Kusi communities than among the Kaskazi. The overall history of agricultural vocabulary fits in, in any case, with the idea that the Kusi during the second half of the millennium already may have shifted toward a more effective and sustained use of their grain agricultural knowledge than many of the Kaskazi were to do until early in the first millennium A.D. (as argued in chapter 4). Such a direction of development, toward agricultural diversification, would make eminent sense, of course, as a response to a need to produce more food on the same amount of land.

Other evidence, of the natural world, confirms that the centers of Kusi expansion in the last half of the last millennium B.C. shifted as far south as southern Lake Tanganyika. Kusi faunal vocabulary shows them to have resided near to regions where they might commonly have encountered zebras and wild dogs, but probably rarely if at all any wildebeests, giraffes, or ostriches. They had also developed a term for a more open, lightly wooded plain (see tables 2 and 3). The nearest country that fits these requirements encompasses both the regions of miombo savanna to the immediate southwest and south of southern Lake Tanganyika, stretching southward through eastern Zambia, and the similar savannas of Tanzania to the east of the lake.

Reflective of their movement into the edges of the two-season climatic regime of the southern savanna zone, the Kusi communities also developed a new climatic term, *-gìnjá (in Shona *-gènjá) to denote a wet season that centered around the months from December to March. They continued for a time to use proto-Mashariki season names *-lìmò and *-tíkà. The first, *-lìmò, initially referred among the Kusi communities to the period from about September to November, months that in the Kusi lands were probably hot and preceded the rains, rather than initiated them as they had among the earlier Mashariki. The second old seasonal term, *-tíkà, may have been retained at first to distinguish the relatively cool months immediately following the rains.

Subsequently, among those Kusi communities who settled south of the Zambezi in the very early first millennium A.D., and among the Nyasa of Malawi, the more complex seasonal situations to be found in those regions generally led to the retention of both older terms. For instance, *-lìmò came to refer to a hot season in proto-Nyasa and to the Southern Hemisphere's rainy summer in some Southeast-Bantu languages. The term *-tíkà in similar fashion shifted its application to the cool, dry southern-hemisphere winter among the Southeast-Bantu languages.

The Kusi communities of the second half of the last millennium B.C. may also have faced a different kind of challenge in some areas: the competing presence of an Eastern Sahelian food-producing people. The loanwords in the Kusi languages that reflect the interactions with this Sahelian society (see table 38) may just possibly have entered the Kusi dialects earlier and farther north, in the western Great Lakes region, as a southerly counterpart to the Eastern Sahelian influences evident in the Southern Kaskazi dialects of the Late Mashariki period (see table 7). But the rest of the evidence we have looked at for the locations of Eastern Sahelian societies places them distinctly to the east of the Western Rift. If indeed the early Kusi lands lay on the other side of the Rift, along the west side of Lake Tanganyika, then the Eastern Sahelians would hardly have been in a position directly to influence the earliest emerging Kusi communities. For that reason the

Table 38.  Eastern Sahelian loanwords in Kusi

| (wild animals) | | (cultivation) | |
|---|---|---|---|
| *-bílà | "hyrax" (also found in Botatwe group | *-poko | "finger millet" |
| | | *-pila | "sorghum" (highly tentative attribution, however; also found in Botatwe group) |
| (livestock | | | |
| *-tàngá | "herd; cattle pen" (also found in Botatwe group) | (other material culture) | |
| *-kola | "small pen, fold" (variant: Venda *-kolo) | *-sèbè | "arrow" |

small general set of Eastern Sahelian loanwords limited to the Kusi languages can be suggested to derive from cultural interactions dating to the latter half of the last millennium B.C., when the centers of Kusi settlement had probably already shifted southward into the regions near southern Lake Tanganyika.

The proposed locating of Eastern Sahelian communities to the south of East Africa proper, in the regions near to southern Lake Tanganyika, turns our attention toward the second crucial set of considerations in laying the background for southeastern African developments of the early first millennium A.D.—toward identifying the wider cultural and economic setting of that part of the continent during the Early Classical Age.

## Gatherers and Herders:  Southern Africa, 1000–100 B.C.

Southeastern Africa in the last millennium B.C. contained a great variety of natural environments—woodlands and woodland savanna in Malawi and northern Mozambique; drier savanna in much of central and southern Mozambique; high rainfall woodland in a narrow band along the southern Mozambique coast and again farther south along the Natal coast; montane forest in eastern Zimbabwe; interior plateaus with zones variously of savanna, grassland, and steppe in eastern Zambia, Zimbabwe, interior South Africa, and Botswana; and finally subtropical grassland and steppe south of the Orange River. The gatherer-hunter peoples of those regions made stone tool industries belonging to the Wilton tradition or to related traditions that shared a still more ancient, common ancestry with Wilton.

The more ancient archeological tradition from which Wilton and the other resemblant assemblages derive has been called the Eastern African Microlithic;[2] its origins go back 17,000 to 20,000 or more years ago in eastern Africa.[3] We have encountered this tradition before in surveying the historical background of the Classical Age farther north in East Africa proper (see chapter 3). In each case where the varieties of this long-lived tradition can be traced down to the last millennium B.C. or more recently, including its Wilton versions of the past 7,000 years in southern Africa, the Eastern African Microlithic can be identified as the accomplishment of peoples who spoke languages of the Khoisan family.

A great variety of Khoisan-speaking, gatherer-hunter societies occupied the lands of southern Africa in the first half of the last millennium B.C. In the far northern Kalahari region and possibly extending northward even then into Angola, could be found the Ju, among whose modern descendants are the well-known !Xu (Kung) people. Somewhere in the northeastern or north-central parts of the Kalahari lay the lands of the proto-Khwe society. Their descendants of later times included most notably the Khoikhoi, of whom we will have a good deal more to say shortly. Across the southernmost parts of the continent stretched the then numerous and diverse communities of the Southern Khoisan group, their territories covering most of the present-day Cape province of South Africa and extending northward into the southern Kalahari and, on the east, across the High Veld. The latter-day heirs of the Southern Khoisan tradition include the !Xoo of the southern Kalahari and also the /Xam, who in the eighteenth and early nineteenth centuries inhabited parts of the northern and central Cape. Still other Khoisan peoples, whose languages are now entirely extinct, resided in Natal, Mozambique, Malawi, and the southern and eastern portions of Zambia.

Thirty years ago historians and archeologists viewed these gatherer-hunters as the sole occupants of the southeasterly parts of Africa before the advent of Bantu settlement. Increasingly, however, it has become evident that, already to a limited extent, a particular kind of food production, livestock raising, had commenced spreading toward far southern Africa some centuries before any hint of Bantu communities in those regions. Outside the southernmost parts of the Cape province of South Africa, the archeology of this first spread of food

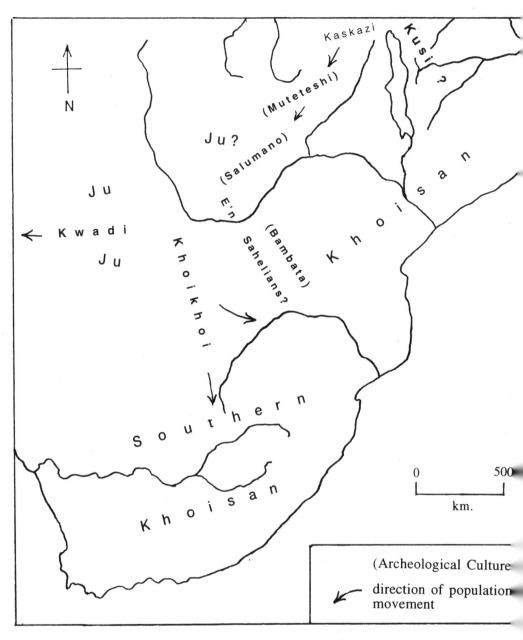

Map 8. Peoples of southeastern Africa, c. 200 B.C.

production remains elusive. Only to the south of the Zambezi River have the material remains of this history begun to be identified at all, and even there some of the locations of the early pastoralism required by the vocabulary evidence have yet to be verified in the archeology. The historical resources of language need a great deal more study, but their indications even now allow at least a provisional outlining of the rough course of developments in southeastern Africa over the last millennium B.C.

Previous works that made use of language data to probe this history were seriously mistaken in certain points of interpretation,[4] notably in arguing that Central Sudanians were the intermediaries of the transmission of livestock raising from East Africa southward to the middle Zambezi areas. The establishment of a sound, systematic phonological reconstruction of the Nilo-Saharan language family allows, as it does for the history of the Great Lakes region, a reformulation of this work on a much sounder basis, the result of which has been the discarding of the putative Central Sudanic role.[5] What remains is, instead, a distinct body of materials pointing to an Eastern Sahelian presence in several regions.

The strongest indications for southerly Eastern Sahelian populations places probably several such communities in the Corridor region between southern Lake Tanganyika and northern Lake Nyasa and just south of there in northern and north-central Malawi. It has already been proposed that the Eastern Sahelians whose influence appears in the general Kusi set of word borrowings (see table 38) may have lived between the south end of Lake Tanganyika and the north end of Lake Malawi. In the languages of each of the Kaskazi and Kusi peoples who settled in that region about 2,000 years ago, there also appear small loanword sets of distinctly Eastern Sahelian provenance. The Mwika, as well as the Rungwe and the later Nyakyusa descendants of the Rungwe, and also the Nyasa each had their own separate interactions with Eastern Sahelian communities (see table 39).

The word borrowings in those several Bantu languages and dialects spoken twenty to sixteen centuries ago reveal the proposed Eastern Sahelians of the Corridor region and northern Malawi to have been raisers of sheep and probably cultivators of grains. The evidence is as yet insufficient to fully resolve the issue of whether these Sahelians were connected most closely to the Sog or the Southern Rub societies. But the rarity of Rub attestions of the borrowed words so far discovered favors the conclusion that the Eastern Sahelians of those regions came from a Sog rather than Rub ancestry.

Table 39. Evidence for Eastern Sahelians in the Corridor
and northern Malawi regions

*a. Eastern Sahelian loanwords in proto-Nyasa*

(wild animal)

(cultivation, livestock)

*nguele "hippopotamus"

*-kebele "pearl millet"
*-bila "sheep"(Nyanja-Cewa;
also spread to Lomwe)

*b. Eastern Sahelian loanwords in early Rungwe*

(peripheral basic words)

(livestock)

*-tulu "testicle"
*-oβe "finger"
*-gola "skin" (Nyiha-
Safwa subgroup)
*-sepe "hair, fur" (Nyiha
subgroup)

*-gole "sheep" (Nyiha-
Safwa subgroup)

*c. Eastern Sahelian loanword in Nyakyusa*

(peripheral basic word)

*-tapatapa "thigh"

*d. Eastern Sahelian loanwords in early Mwika*

(body part)

*-tulu "testicle" (also in
proto-Rungwe)

(cultivation)

*-kolo "hoe" (Mambwe-
Fipa subgroup)

(livestock)

*-fuele "sheep"(from pre-
sumed earlier *-kẹele;
PB *kẹ > Mwika *fu)

*-aaβo "udder"

Southwest from Malawi, in far northeastern Botswana and far western Zimbabwe, lay another region in which sketchy Eastern Sahelian influences dating to the last millennium B.C. can be discerned. The proto-Khwe language, a member of the Khoisan language family spoken in that region in the early second half of the millennium, adopted a small but highly salient set of word borrowings relating to economy from an Eastern Sahelian language.[6] The characteristics of this loanword set (table 40), like those found in the languages of the

---

Table 40.  Eastern Sahelian loanwords in early Khwe dialects

*a.  Khoikhoi words with overt Eastern Sahelian parallels*

(grains)

| | (livestock) | |
|---|---|---|
| *pere- "grain food (in general)" (applied in recent Khoikhoi to "bread") | *aro- | "ram" (recorded so far only from Nama) |
| | *oro- | "milk ewe" (recorded so far only from Nama) |
| *topo- "porridge" (recorded so far only from Nama) | *kuro- | "young ram" (recorded so far only from Nama) |

*b.  Early Khoikhoi subsistence words of uncertain source*

(food preparation)          (livestock)

*suro- "broth"                *komo- "cow (generic)"
                             *gu-   "sheep" (proto-Khwe)

---

Corridor region (see tables 38 and 39), best fit with its having been related to the Sog languages of the Great Lakes region.  The southern outliers of Eastern Sahelian settlement apparently had reached as far, by sometime between 500 and 300 B.C., as the edges at least of the Khwe country, in the dry savanna and steppe south of the middle Zambezi River.  Archeological manifestations of this era of economic interaction may possibly be represented by sites in far southeastern Zimbabwe and adjoining parts of Botswana, which contain livestock remains and a type of pottery called Bambata ware and date as early as the fourth or third century B.C.[7]

The most direct routes from such movements of people and animals south from East Africa to central southern Africa lie along the mostly tsetse-free corridor that extends south-southeast from the Rungwe Mountains, along the west side of the Lwangwa River valley, to the Batoka Plateau of southern Zambia.  But the archeological evidence of such a community has not yet been identified.  There remains a missing geographical link in our mapping of the transfer of livestock raising to the south of the Zambezi that very much deserves close archeological investigation.

From northeastern Botswana southward, the further spread of livestock raising was carried forward by the descendants of the early Khwe.  Their encounter with Eastern Sahelians, it can be suggested, precipitated the adoption of domestic animals, possibly initially sheep only but, certainly soon afterward, cattle, by at least some of the Khwe and by their Khoikhoi descendants.

Some investigators have suggested that we have one set of possible indirect indicators in the material record of the presence of herders of East African origins in areas south of the Zambezi. These are the stone bowls excavated in a wide spread of areas settled early by the expanding Khoikhoi and Kwadi in the Cape and Namibia.[8] Stone bowls, as we have previously learned (chapter 6), were a prominent feature of culture among the Southern Cushites, early Southern Nilotes, and Eburrans of the Kenya Rift regions. Did the Khoikhoi and Kwadi adopt the making of these bowls from Eastern Sahelian communities, who had in turn adopted this technology farther north and brought it south with them? The archaeological contexts of such finds in southern Africa remain to be fully worked out, and so far we lack, once again, evidence of such bowls from the intervening countries. Nevertheless, the resemblance in forms of the bowls found at the two ends of Greater Eastern Africa are close, and so they remain an intriguing matter for future study.

## Social and Political Consequences of Khoikhoi Herding

In the beginning, the Khwe keeping of livestock formed probably simply an adjunct to their more ancient gathering and hunting pursuits. But the adoption of herding had an unintended transforming effect on demography and society. Animal generations are far shorter than those of human beings; and protected and nurtured by people, livestock populations can begin to grow rapidly, creating a pressure on local grazing resources and causing the herders to seek to expand their lands. Multiplying the amount of food available to their keepers, the growth of domestic animal populations at the same time relieves their owners of the need for such cultural restraints as the late weaning of children by which gatherer-hunters keep their own numbers in check. And so the human population begins to grow as well.

One descendant society of the Khwe, the Khoikhoi, already by no later probably than the third century B.C. were expanding southward through the good grazing lands of eastern Botswana and far southwestern Transvaal toward the confluence of the Orange and Vaal Rivers, and probably also eastward into parts of the Limpopo River watershed.[9] By the first century A.D., they had diverged into at least three societies. The sites of the southernmost of these peoples, the Cape Khoikhoi, appear at that point in time in the archeology of the coastal areas of the present-day east-central Cape province. From there the Cape Khoikhoi communities spread rapidly westward in the first four centuries A.D. toward the Cape of Good Hope and probably also eastward toward southern Natal. The Orange-River Khoikhoi society, whose later descendants were the Nama of Namibia and the !Kora of the lower Vaal River region, took shape during those same centuries in the areas around the confluence of the Vaal and Orange Rivers. A third people, the Limpopo Khoikhoi, apparently settled in several parts of the Transvaal, reaching as far east perhaps as far southern Mozambique by the close of the last century B.C., but the archeological expression of their proposed settlements remains to be discovered.[10]

An additional expansion of Khwe-speaking people, that of the ancestral Kwadi society, progressed eastward across the northern fringe of the Kalahari region and carried a mixed herding and collecting economy into northern Namibia by or before the third and fourth centuries A.D.

The Khoikhoi on the whole were raisers of cattle and sheep, but not apparently of goats, while at the same time they maintained much of the gathering and hunting knowledge of their Khwe ancestry. Whether the Limpopo Khoikhoi might in addition have cultivated some grains, since their lands had suitably warm growing seasons for the African grain crops, remains to be investigated. Most of the Cape Khoikhoi, who settled in areas lacking sufficient rain in the warm times of the year, did not cultivate at all, it seems. The earliest Kwadi certainly raised sheep in northern Namibia, but whether or not they kept cattle or grew any crops remains also unknown as yet.

The adoption of livestock and the subsequent growth of the human population surely had consequences for the social and political order among both the Khoikhoi and the Kwadi. Only for the Cape and Orange River Khoikhoi, however, can even a partial picture of this history as yet be sketched out. From the meager preservation of bits of the Khoikhoi oral tradition, it appears that the growth and expansion of the early Cape-Orange communities led to a replacement of the bilateral, noncorporate reckoning of kinship found among their Khwe ancestors with a patrilineal, segmentary system.

As the first step in this process, we can hypothesize, the small set of close relatives by birth and marriage, who had formed the core of the earlier local Khwe gathering-hunting band, evolved into a more formal patrilineage around which a significantly larger local herding band coalesced. The older, informally recognized Khwe position of semihereditary local band headman at the same time evolved into a more formal position of lineage chief. The earlier typical food-collecting band, comparative cultural evidence suggests, probably had consisted of no more than twenty to thirty-five or forty people; the larger local herding band among the Khoikhoi came normally to comprise as many as a hundred or more.

In such a larger community the nearest kin connections of many of its members must often have lain several generations back into the past. No longer could an informal, common knowledge of extended-family relationships be counted on to provide a sufficient social glue for the band, and no longer could group decision making be left to an informally reached concensus. The claim to shared patrilineal descent provided a new constitution for social allegiance among the early Cape-Orange Khoikhoi, able to sustain cohesion among a grouping of persons whose actual points of common kin connection were often no longer close. The lineage chief evolved in tandem with this development into a leader able to act as the moderator over community meetings and as the enunciator, and thus also the major influencer, of the legal and political decisions that emerged from such meetings.

In time, as the herding community continued to grow in population, the original lineage-based band would successively break up into a number of bands, each now forming a separate lineage-based local residential unit, but each also recognizing their common historical connection and considering their core patrilineages to belong to the same wider clan grouping. For the Cape Khoikhoi this second stage in the growth of social and political complexity probably began to emerge as early as their settlement in the modern southeastern Cape Province of South Africa, at around the turn of the era.

As the Cape Khoikhoi expanded farther eastward and westward in the first several centuries A.D., still larger political groupings began to emerge among them, each viewed by its members as a supraclan chiefdom composed of several clans that could each trace their origins back to an earlier clan-grouping of related patrilineages. The chiefs of these chiefdoms held inherited positions as the chiefs of the senior clans within the polities, seniority being based in this case on the historical claim of a senior clans to having been the group from which the other clans of the chiefdom had diverged. The chiefs of the individual clans of the polity, including the historically senior clan, in turn apparently filled the roles of lineage chiefs over the senior lineages of their respective clans.

If the evidence of seventeenth-century practice is any guide to fourth-century culture (and it may be a very weak guide at best), these chiefs had more a potential than a practical authority over the populations of their chiefdoms. In day-to-day affairs their influence and authority tended to be exerted at the level of their own lineage and secondarily at the level of their clan. Only now and then would issues have arisen that would have brought into effect their roles as the adjudicators of interclan disputes or as leaders in conflicts with other chiefdoms. They seem to have had little if any role in communal religious observances, and their historical claims to chiefly ancestry and their ability to maintain a fitting degree of personal wealth in livestock appear to have been the fundamental pillars of their authority and influence.

A similar growth in political scale, from lineage-size polities to chiefdoms composed of several clans, apparently took place among the Nama of Namibia, whose cultural ancestry derived from the Orange-River Khoikhoi society of the early first millennium A.D. But among the Nama this development may belong to much later centuries than the fourth or fifth.

## Overview: Early Livestock Raising in Southeastern Africa

To sum up, the evidence of language scantily but on fairly solid grounds places an Eastern Sahelian settlement, most probably of scattered, small Sog communities, with cattle and sheep and some grain cultivation, in parts of the Corridor region between Lake Tanganyika and Lake Nyasa, possibly as early as the middle of the last millennium B.C. These people subsequently expanded southward into areas in northern or north central Malawi. The highlands to the west away from Lake Nyasa, too high and cool to harbor tsetse flies and thus bovine sleeping sickness, provide the most likely environment for this settlement. No later than the third century B.C., another strand of Eastern Sahelian expansion had passed, probably southwestward from the Corridor region, as far as the edges of far northeastern Botswana and far western Zimbabwe, conceivably reaching there via the higher lands to the west of the Lwangwa River valley of Zambia.

In Botswana local Khoisan communities, speaking the proto-Khwe language, added a livestock-raising component, under Eastern Sahelian influence, to their existing gathering and hunting livelihood, setting off a new period of rapid spread of cattle and sheep raising, carried south to the southern Cape regions, southeastward into the Transvaal, and eastward to Namibia by different cultural heirs of the Khwe. For several of the areas of early pastoral spread south of the Zambezi, archeological verification is available, although quite uneven

221

in its coverage. For the intervening areas over which this pre-Bantu livestock raising had to have spread in order to reach southern Africa at all—in southwestern Tanzania, northern Malawi, and Zambia—the relevant archeology remains to be discovered.

# Social Transformation in Southeastern Africa, to A.D. 400

During the centuries around the turn of the era, Kusi Bantu communities began to scatter out across southeastern Africa, bringing new subsistence practices and different ideas and kinds of social organization into a world then largely Khoisan in language and civilization and still in a majority of instances inhabited principally by gatherer-hunters. Encountering in most areas only food-collecting peoples, of very low population densities, the Kusi populations expanded fairly rapidly in numbers and with little opposition into a great variety of regions.

## Kusi Communities and the Archeological Record

Four major groupings of Kusi settlers can presently be identified from the linguistic-historical evidence—the Sala-Shona, the Southeast-Bantu, the Nyasa, and the pre-Makua. The archeology of the period allows for a somewhat larger number of Kusi societies. Five of the archeological cultures known from the Later Classical Age of southeastern Africa will be argued here to correspond to particular groupings of Kusi communities. The Lydenburg culture in several facies, from Transvaal south to Natal and Transkei, can be attributed to the Sala-Shona people; the Matola culture in lowland southern Mozambique and far eastern Transvaal, to the early Southeast-Bantu; the Nampula in the southern half of northern Mozambique, to the pre-Makua; and the Nkope culture of central and southern Malawi, overlapping into adjoining parts of Zambia and Mozambique, to the Nyasa; and the Gokomere-Ziwa culture of the Zimbabwe Plateau, to Kusi peoples probably closely related in language to the Nyasa.

Three further archeological manifestations, Kalambo, Monapo, and Mwabulambo—the combined distributions of which cover a span of territories running from northeastern Zambia through northern Malawi to northern Mozambique—have been discovered from sites dating also to around and just after the turn of the eras. But each is

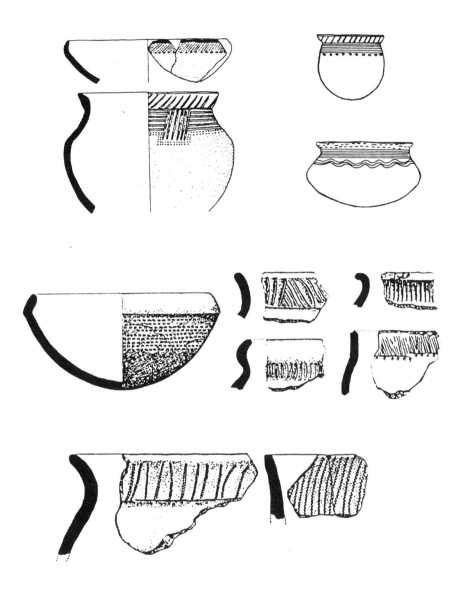

Figure 10. Ceramics of the Later Classical Age in east-central Africa. Nkope ware, *top* (Robinson 1976). Nampula ware, *middle* (Sinclair et al. 1993). Monapo ware, *bottom* (Sinclair et al. 1993).

best identified as the accomplishment of a different southerly outlier of the Kaskazi peoples of East Africa proper. The Kalambo tradition, widespread in northeastern Zambia by the first three or four centuries A.D., can be attributed to the Mwika; the Mwabulambo, to the Rungwe or to a closely related people; and the Monapo, to early communities belonging to the Rufiji-Ruvuma cluster (see chapter 6).

A sixth culture, Muteteshi of central Zambia, seems very possibly to represent a southward extension of Kaskazi rather than Kusi settlement, but the language of its makers would have died out with the diappearance of the Muteteshi tradition not long after mid-first millennium A.D. The basis for connecting it up with Kaskazi-speaking people will be dealt with later in this chapter. Another culture, the Salumano of far southern Zambia, may be connected as well with Kaskazi Bantu settlement.

## Subsistence Developments among the Early Kusi

Most of the Kusi communities of the opening phase of the Later Classical Age, it can be suggested, had already begun to make more significant use of grains and perhaps other seed crops than had the contemporary Kaskazi peoples. The Kusi settlers of the very early first millennium did tend more often than not to move to areas of moderately high rainfall. But more commonly than the contemporary Kaskazi, and usually much sooner than their East African relatives, the Kusi societies expanded into nearby drier country. Yams, it can thus be argued, were still important crops for the Kusi societies at the threshhold of their scattering out across southeastern Africa, and remained so among peoples such as the Nyasa, who moved into high-rainfall areas in Malawi. But in many other Kusi communities grain crops must quite soon have eclipsed yams in importance. The Kusi peoples may also fairly early have made another kind of adaptation to drier environments, one that at the same time applied the expertise of the older Bantu agricultural ancestry: they may have been among the peoples who domesticated an indigenous southeastern African root crop, *Plectranthus esculentus,* sometimes called the "Livingstone potato."

As for livestock, only the goat was well known and raised among all the Kusi who moved out southward at the turn of the era. Sheep they had not yet acquired.[11] Cattle, though, were part of the food-producing knowledge of the earlier Kusi communities of the second half of the last millennium B.C., and the existence of a variety of Kusi terms relating to milk or cattle, some retained from the Middle Mashariki period (see especially table 5) and others specifically adopted by the Kusi cluster of communities (table 38), suggests at the least that the Kusi peoples of those centuries were close neighbors of Eastern Sahelian cattle raisers and may have kept a few of the animals themselves.

But among most of the Kusi who scattered out across southeastern Africa at the turn of the era, the actual raising of cattle must still have been a relatively uncommon activity. The Nyasa and pre-Makua moved into regions where cattle raising, because of tsetse-fly and sleeping sickness, would not usually have been possible, and their loss of all the earlier Kusi cattle terms, except the generic word *-gòmbè, reflects this history. The Sala-Shona, in contrast, preserved one older Kusi breeding term of specific reference to domestic bovines, *-pulu "calf," along with the old generic term *-gòmbè, the word *-tàngá for "herd" or "cattle pen," and one proto-Mashariki domestic animal term, *-puilị, probably originally meaning "bearing domestic animal."[12] They resettled in regions where cattle raising was possible, and their retentions of these terms suggests that they themselves kept some cows, although surely relatively few. At the inception of their expansions southward, they appear unlikely to have yet milked such cattle as they did possess, or their goats for that matter.[13]

## The Early Sala-Shona Communities

The Sala-Shona society took shape south of the Limpopo River, among immigrant Bantu communities who by the third century A.D. had spread over a scatter of good rainfall environments extending from the east central Transvaal south to the coastal areas and lower river valleys of Natal. The argument for this identification conjoins archeological and linguistic evidence.

In the first place, the archeological remains of the early centuries A.D. all across that span of settlement belong to the Lydenburg tradition, which includes among its regional varieties the Msuluzi and other sites of coastal and near-coastal Natal, along with the Sixini culture, which derives from a farther southward extension of these peoples, during the later first millennium A.D., from Natal to the Transkei and Ciskei regions. In other words, a single group of related communities, speaking closely related languages or dialects of one language, can be invoked as the makers of Lydenburg. In addition, it is apparent from the particular motifs and designs of Lydenburg pottery that its affiliations were to the Chifumbaze complex and that its makers therefore formed one offshoot of the wider scattering out of Bantu communities through Greater Eastern Africa in the Later Classical Age.

The case from linguistic evidence for identifying the makers of the Lydenburg tradition with the Sala-Shona can be made directly in the instance of Natal. In the modern-day Nguni languages of that part of South Africa and of the far eastern Cape province, as Carolan Ownby has shown, there are very large sets of loanwords adopted from some other Bantu language. The diagnostic phonological characteristics of these loanwords, wherever the evidence is sufficient, show them to have been adopted into Nguni from a language different from, but especially closely related to, modern Shona. Given the name Sala by Ownby, this extinct language appears to been a sister language to proto-Shona, from which all the extant modern-day Shona dialects derive.[14] For that reason the term proto-Sala-Shona has been applied here to the common mother language, spoken the early first millennium A.D., that was ancestral to both Sala and proto-Shona. The great number and semantic variety of the loanwords in the Nguni dialects show that Sala communities were established in Natal long before the beginning of Nguni expansion there around A.D. 1000, and that the descendants of the Sala formed a majority element in the actual human ancestry of many later Nguni societies.[15]

The case for an earlier Shona-speaking population in the Transvaal must be more indirectly made, since no investigation of similar interpretive depth to Ownby's has yet been made of Shona loanwords in the Sotho and Venda. We have thus to begin with recent data and work backward in time. Specifically, the material culture of the speakers of the later dialects of the Shona language, found in Zimbabwe and adjoining parts of Mozambique, shows an unbroken connection back to the "Kutama" tradition, which spread across Zimbabwe in several varieties from the tenth to the thirteenth centuries. The Kutama tradition in turn can be derived directly from late versions of the Lydenburg tradition, found at sites in the Transvaal that date to around the eighth and ninth centuries.[16] In both Natal and the Transvaal, then, the local facies of the Lydenburg tradition can, in one manner or another, be linked to speakers of early forms of the Sala-Shona languages.

The two early Sala-Shona societies of the second to fourth centuries A.D. had different histories of contact with other peoples. The Sala of the Natal region had moved into areas apparently previously inhabited only by Khoisan gatherer-hunters. Both the archeology and the language evidence reveal a history for the Sala communities of long-term coexistence with food-collecting peoples, lasting into the later centuries of the first millennium A.D. The Sala language eventually became extinct, but only in the early second millennium in the face of the expansions of the early Nguni into the region.[17]

The northerly set of Sala-Shona communities in the Transvaal, who spoke the proto-Shona language, appear to have entered into important relations with a Khoikhoi herding society. The extent to which these Khoikhoi were incorporated over the course of time into the Shona society is as yet unclear. The Shona language has not properly been investigated for Khoikhoi loanwords in its vocabulary. Only a few very striking such word borrowings are as yet known, notably for "udder, breast" and "year" (table 8B). These words have meanings that cause them rarely to be borrowed unless a significant additional range of loanwords of less basic meanings were adopted into the language along with them. But until a deeper study of Shona has been made, the expectation that more early Khoikhoi loans in proto-Shona remain to be discovered cannot properly be tested. Were considerable numbers of erstwhile Khoikhoi people assimilated into the early Shona society? The kind of borrowings known suggest that the answer might very possibly be, "Yes"; but the available data is insufficient to argue the case.

## The Early Southeast-Bantu Peoples

A second Kusi society, the Southeast-Bantu, evolved in areas adjoining fairly closely to those of the Sala-Shona. Several root words innovations uniquely shared by the proto-Southeast-Bantu and proto-Shona languages—the two most notable examples being the basic words *-jebe for "ear" and *-ganda for "egg"—probably reflect the close contacts between the two societies during the early first millennium. The language data as a whole strongly favor southern Mozambique and the eastern Transvaal as the broad region of Southeast-Bantu settlement.[18]

Exactly those regions saw the establishment of the Matola culture in the archeology of the first three to four centuries A.D. The closeness of the geographical fit between the sites of the Matola tradition and the placement of the early Southeast-Bantu people implied by the linguistic inferences makes a very strong case for the correlation of the two lines of argument.[19] That correlation will be assumed without further argument here, leaving aside the possibility for now that future archeological investigations may require modifications of this proposition. The route of the Southeast-Bantu movement southward to southern Mozambique probably passed through the areas to the immediate east of Lake Nyasa during the last century or two B.C.

Already by the fourth century, or so the language evidence indicates, the spreading out of the Southeast-Bantu society over larger areas had begun to lead to their divergence into five sets of communities. The Nyambane society from which the modern-day GiTonga-speaking peoples derive, emerged in the high rainfall areas along the central coast of southern Mozambique. A second people, speaking the dialect ancestral to present-day Chopi, developed near to the Nyambane, but perhaps inland from the coast in areas of drier climate.[20] A third incipient Southeast-Bantu society, the Tsonga, developed out of those communities resident in the lowlands around and to the south of the lower Limpopo River. Three other Southeast-Bantu societies arose among those who had settled in the early first millennium to the immediate east, above the escarpment in the far eastern Transvaal. The early Nguni are most probably to be looked for in the southeastern Transvaal and parts of modern Swaziland;[21] the linguistic forebears of the Venda, in the northeastern Transvaal;[22] and the earliest Sotho between them, in central eastern Transvaal.[23]

The predilections among some southern African archeologists, toward eschewing broad synthesis and downplaying linguistic techniques unfamiliar to them, has meant that the potential archeological correlations of the language evidence for these regions have yet to receive in full the kind of knowledgeable attention they deserve. Despite these drawbacks, a first, partial archeological confirmation that some of the early Southeast-Bantu did indeed settle in the first millennium in the eastern Transvaal has long been available in the work of the archeologist N. J. van der Merwe. More than two decades ago he argued that, in the Palaborwa lands of central eastern Transvaal, unbroken archeological continuities extend from the present right back to the later first millennium A.D.[24] Palaborwa, a Sotho language still spoken there today, provides the corresponding language continuity: it traces back to the particular early Southeast-Bantu dialect, proto-Sotho, that would best be placed on linguistic-geographical grounds in that same general region by the second half of the first millennium.

The Southeast-Bantu communities of the first three or four centuries A.D. seem even more notably than the early Shona to have been culturally indebted to their interactions with a pastoral Khoikhoi society. The most potent impact of the Khoikhoi appears in Southeast-Bantu herding vocabulary, where not only the generic term for sheep,

\*-gú, but also a new generic term for cattle, \*-kòmò—almost completely displacing older Mashariki Bantu \*-gòmbè from use—and a word for milk drawn from a cow, \*-pị, came from the Limpopo Khoikhoi language (table 9B). These data imply that the Southeast-Bantu at the beginning of their settlement in southern Mozambique most likely kept few cattle or sheep themselves and that only later, under Khoikhoi influence, did they begin seriously to raise cattle and to adopt the practice of milking. Cattle raising probably did not become a significant economic activity for the Southeast-Bantu for still some centuries more, since the different subgroups of the Southeast-Bantu seem each to have developed their own more technical breeding and herding vocabularies subsequent to their divergence out of the original society. That conclusion is also in keeping with the currently known Matola archeological evidence, in which cattle raising is not certainly attested till after 500.

Besides their practical economic impact, as represented in their loanwords, the Khoikhoi over a period of centuries were probably themselves increasingly absorbed, through marriage and cultural assimilation, into the expanding Southeast-Bantu communities. The initial stage of these cultural interactions dates to the first two or three centuries A.D., before the Southeast-Bantu society began to diverge into several daughter societies. But the Limpopo Khoikhoi probably continued to be influential in the early developments among some of the daughter societies, especially the early Sotho and, above all, the very early Nguni, who eventually started to adopt even the unusual click sounds of Khoikhoi into their language.[25] That adoption is likely to have started, contrary to the usual scholarly view, in parts of the eastern high veld region, well before the expansion of the Nguni into Natal from 1000 onward.[26]

## The Nyasa Society

To the north of the Zambezi River, in the Lake Nyasa region, a third major grouping of Kusi communities coalesced by about the beginning of the first millennium A.D. into the Nyasa society. The territory in which this society first took shape lay between the Lwangwa River on the west and Lake Nyasa on the east, for it is there that the split of the Nyasa group into two primary branches took place early in the millennium. One branch of the Nyasa group is composed of the Tumbuka language, which is restricted to northern-central Malawi and adjacent areas of Zambia today. A second branch, Southern

Nyasa, comprises the remaining dialects and languages of the group. These spread by several expansions during the past 1,500 years across a wide run of territories, extending today from the Nyanja-Chewa of central and southern Malawi, through the Kunda, Sena, and other related peoples of the lower Zambezi drainage basin in Mozambique.

Two neighboring peoples had a particularly visible impact on the Nyasa. One group was Eastern Sahelian in language and livestock -raising and grain cultivating in economy (see Nyasa word borrowings for "sheep" and "pearl millet" in table 39) and resided possibly in higher areas of north-central Malawi. The scope of Eastern Sahelian influences on the Nyasa society remains to be more fully investigated. The second people who greatly influenced the Nyasa, although Mashariki Bantu in language like the Nyasa, had their historical origins in the Kaskazi rather than Kusi cluster of communities. Their lands should thus be looked for in northern Malawi, adjacent to the other Kaskazi settlement communities of the Later Classical Age (as noted in chapter 6).

The Kaskazi contribution to the makeup of early Nyasa culture and society was a significant one and is evinced in a large number of Kaskazi word innovations that were taken into the proto-Nyasa vocabulary (table 41 lists a small, but culturally significant selection of these). The Nyasa people may have been influenced to some extent in their religious and social ideas by the Kaskazi immigrants, as their use of the Kaskazi root word for "God" would seem to indicate. The nature of that influence remains to be studied, however.

But to a much greater extent the Nyasa seem to have benefited in clear technological ways from their encounter the Kaskazi settlers. From their Kaskazi neighbors, for instance, the early Nyasa adopted the cylindrical style of beehive and perhaps in consequence their first deliberate keeping of bees, in place of the collecting of wild honey. They also may have taken up a new kind of arrowsmithing, as well as adopting hunting nets from the Kaskazi communities. Most important of all, it appears to have been from the Kaskazi immigrants into northern Malawi that the early Nyasa gained a lasting and accomplished command of the skills of smelting and forging iron.

The archeological distributions of the first four centuries A.D. in Malawi offer a clear correlation with the language inferences. The Nyasa people are proposed here to be identifiable with the makers of the Nkope tradition, present in the archeology of the central areas, in a few places in the north, and all through the southern parts of that country. The northern Malawi counterpart of Nkope was a different contemporary facies of the Chifumbaze Complex, the Mwabulambo

Table 41. Kaskazi culture words in proto-Nyasa

(intangible culture)

| | | |
|---|---|---|
| *-lùngù | "God" | see chapter 5; also spread early to proto-Makua |

(technology)

| | | |
|---|---|---|
| *-òmbò | "vessel, boat" | see table 6 |
| *-lás- | "to shoot (with bow)" | see table 22 |
| *-bànò | "arrowshaft" | see table 22 |
| *-ábù | "(hunting) net" | see table 22 |
| *-zinga | "round beehive" | see table 23; loanword phonology (expected *-dzinga) |
| *-tapo | "iron ore" | see table 7 |
| *-sul- | "to forge" | loanword phonology (expected outcome *-ful-) |
| *-lùkut- | "to work bellows" | (see Ehret 1995/96) |

tradition. The location and dating of Mwabulambo fills the bill of particulars for its having been the accomplishment of the particular Kaskazi people who so greatly influenced the proto-Nyasa language and culture. In chapter 6, the makers of Mwabulambo are suggested to have been speakers of an early dialect of the Rungwe subgroup of Kaskazi. Farther to the northeast, toward southern Lake Tanganyika lay a third facies of the Chifumbaze Complex, the Kalambo tradition, which from its location surely was the work of another Kaskazi group, the early Mwika society.

## The Historical Roots of the Makua Communities

A fourth early Kusi society, the pre-Makua, evolved among immigrants who moved in the first few centuries A.D. into areas most probably to the immediate east of southern Lake Nyasa. The Makua languages today are spoken across much of northern Mozambique, but the differences among them are relatively small. They can all in fact be considered, with the single possible exception of Chuabo, as dialects of one language. The northern dialects of Makua are so closely related that their spread into the hinterland of the northern

Mozambique coast may well have been the ethnic accompaniment of the Zimba invasions of the late sixteenth century.

Farther inland to the south and west, however, the Makua presence was a markedly older one; the split between Chuabo and Lomwe and the rest of Makua dialects may date as much as 1,000–1,200 years ago. The directions and timings of later Makuan expansions thus place the earliest Makuan settlements in the southerly and southwesterly portions of the present-day Makua-speaking regions. Peoples of the Rufiji-Ruvuma subgroup of the Kaskazi Bantu of East Africa, as previously proposed in chapter 6, probably accounted for much of the initial agricultural settlement of northern Mozambique in the early first millennium A.D., and the Makua spread to the north only much later in time.

The Makuans, residing at around the third and fourth centuries eastward and southeastward of Lake Nyasa, appear to have been influenced, both economically and socially, by their encounters with the Nyasa society to the west and with the expanding Rufiji-Ruvuma peoples to their north. In both instances certain word distributions appear to reflect those contacts: the later proto-Makua language, for instance, maintained the Kaskazi word for God, \*-lùngù, in a pronunciation that shows the word to have been adopted from either Rufiji-Ruvuma or the Nyasa societies during that period. A particular contribution of probable Rufiji-Ruvuma provenance to early Makua material culture can be seen in the proto-Makua use of \*-sàâlé "arrow," a root word otherwise entirely restricted in its occurrence to Kaskazi languages.

Interestingly, no linguistic evidence has yet been discovered requiring Makuan relations with peoples other than the early Rufiji-Ruvuma and Nyasa communities. Non-Bantu food-producing peoples do not seem to have been present in their region of settlement. Presumably the first Makuan immigrants encountered gatherer-hunters in the course of their expansions in the early centuries A.D., but if so the linguistic traces of that encounter remain to be identified, and within a relatively few centuries a solely food-collecting way of life had probably ceased to be a viable economic alternative.

Extensive blanks remain in the archeological knowledge of northern Mozambique. In fact, at present only the areas inland from central parts of the northern coast, north and south of the latitude of Mozambique Island, have been surveyed. From the standpoint of language evidence, however, this region is an especially interesting one, because it is in just those areas that the expanding Makuan and Ruvuma territories would be expected to have overlapped each other by around the fourth century A.D.

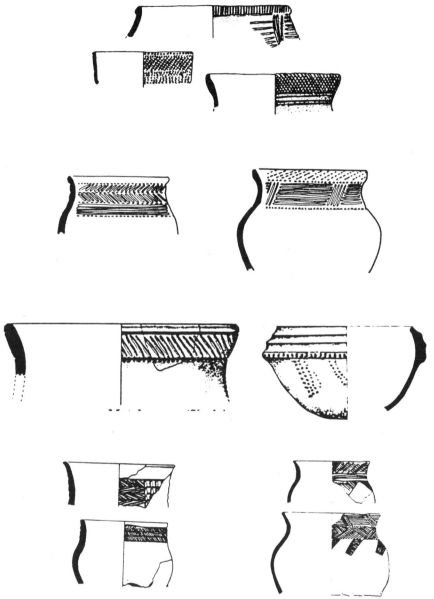

Figure 11. Ceramics of the Later Classical Age in southeastern Africa. Bambata ware, *top* (Robinson 1966). Gokomere ware, *upper middle* (Huffman 1976). Matola ware, *lower middle* (Sinclair et al. 1993). Lydenburg wares: from Transvaal, *left bottom* (Inskeep and Maggs 1975), from Natal, *right bottom* (Maggs and Michael 1976).

And in the archeology of northern Mozambique, just such a situation of cultural overlap seems attested for the two different facies of the Chifumbaze Complex that have been discovered so far. The Nampula tradition, dated to as early as the second century A.D., extends inland and southwestward in the direction of Malawi. From its geographical distribution, it has to be attributed to the early Makuans, and that link is confirmed by long-term continuities in material culture extending from Nampula times down to the modern-day Makua peoples.[27] The Monapo tradition, its earliest dates so far falling in the fourth century A.D., occurs northward from the latitude of Mozambique Island.[28] Its location and its dating make it the prime candidate for the material expression of the expanding Ruvuma people, who by about the second or third century would have been spreading south from the Ruvuma River region (see chapter 6).

# Other Mashariki Peoples of the Later Classical Age

Besides the Sala-Shona, Southeast-Bantu, Nyasa, and pre-Makua, several other Mashariki Bantu peoples can be identified as important actors in the Later Classical Age of southeastern Africa. But these societies gave way in the post-Classical period before the spread of new Bantu settlements into their areas. Their descendants were incorporated into the newly expanding communities of those later times, and their languages dropped from use, although often bequeathing to their successors a set of loanwords that allows us to rediscover this history.

### Kaskazi Settlement in Central and Southern Zambia

One such notable region of Mashariki settlement, dating possibly as early as the fourth century B.C., but more probably a century or two later, lay in central and southern Zambia. Interestingly, the societies that first carried the culture of the Later Classical Age into those lands seem most probably to have been of Kaskazi rather that Kusi affiliation. The evidence of their former presence in that region has been preserved in the modern-day Botatwe languages of those areas. It consists of a significant set of words—some of them previously borrowed in the Great Lakes region from Central Sudanic or Southern Cushitic into the Kaskazi dialects of early last millennium B.C.—that are specifically limited to Kaskazi languages except for their overlapping spread to the Botatwe group (see table 42 for a partial listing).

The archeology identifies two peoples to whom this Kaskazi connection might be attributed, the makers of the Muteteshi and Salumano cultures. Both peoples fashioned potteries of close relationship to other Classical Age wares of the Chifumbaze tradition. The Muteteshi and Salumano ceramics seem, in fact, close enough in decorative motifs and arrangements that it can be argued that both communities had connections to a single earlier period of expansion of Mashariki groups coming from western East Africa and spreading southwestward across central Zambia in the late last millennium B.C.

Muteteshi sites, located in the heart of central Zambia, and dated from the first century A.D. to the sixth,[29] are the best candidates for the immediate Kaskazi predecessors of the Botatwe in the region. The archeological remains of economic activities among them include evidence for the raising of seed crops and livestock as well as a considerable contribution of hunting and gathering to the diet.[30]

For the early Salumano culture, found just north of the Zambezi River in the southern parts of western Zambia, there is available at present one radiocarbon date of the fourth century B.C. The gap in time between then and the dating of the second stage of the culture, Salu-

Table 42. Sample of Kaskazi words found also in Botatwe

| | | |
|---|---|---|
| *-líílà | "umbilical cord" | Kask: Lakes, Takama, Upland; Botatwe; Southern Cushitic loanword (table 1B) |
| *-inie | "liver" | Kask: Lakes, NE-Coastal, Rungwe; Botatwe; Central Sudanic loanword (table 6) |
| *-kondį | "hartebeest" | Kask: Lakes, Upland, Langi groups; Botatwe; overlap into some Sabi (table 3A) |
| *-umbu | "wildebeest" | Kask: Kati; Botatwe; also overlap into Lamba of Sabi group (table 3A) |
| *-gàndá | "house" (semantic history: see chapter 5) | Kask: Ruvu of NE-Coastal, Kilombero, Mwika, Upland (hemispherical shelter); Botatwe; also overlap from Mwika areas into Sabi languages of Zambia |
| *-ba | "cattle pen; thorn fence" | Kask: "yard of home" (see table 6) |
| *-puilį | "cow" | Kask: Western-Lakes ("bull"); also in Kusi: only Shona ("sheep"); Botatwe, with overlap into Lamba of Sabi group as "cow"[31] |

mano B—to the fifth to the eighth centuries A.D.[32]—is quite large. It seems thus probably that the fourth-century B.C. date provides us with no more than a terminus post quem for the Salumano A society, The first stage of Salumano settlement might therefore have begun closer to the turn of the era and nearer in time to the currently known dating of the Muteteshi culture. More dates for Salumano A are needed to resolve this issue, however.

Two particularly intriguing features of the early Salumano culture are, first, the extent to which its economy apparently depended on the herding of cattle and on hunting and, second, the ephemeral nature of the sites. This combination of characteristics raises an interesting possibility about the Salumano A people. The economy and habitation style it implies resemble very little what we would expect from the linguistic evidence for a Kaskazi or Kusi society dating to around the turn of the era, but it is a good deal like what we would expect from Eastern Sahelians or from the Khwe of the last several centuries B.C. Might the Salumano people, residing as they did just across the Zambezi from the Khwe lands in Botswana, have been an Eastern Sahelian community, or else an early Khwe people, whose pottery belonged to the Chifumbaze tradition of the Mashariki Bantu because they either obtained their ceramic wares in trade or had adopted the technology from a Kaskazi people? And in that case, might the dating of Salumano A as early as the fourth century B.C. be right after all?

The same questions can be raised for the Bambata culture found south of the Zambezi in western Zimbabwe and eastern Botswana. Like the Salumano pottery, Bambata ware occurs in sites dated as early as the third century B.C., and these sites are ephemeral and marked by clear evidence of reliance on both livestock raising and hunting.[33] Do these two sets of data together finally give us our first archeological evidence for the spread of livestock ahead of Bantu expansion into southern Africa? Or, alternatively, might they have been made by some very atypical Mashariki?

Between then and now, all across Zambia, there have been periods of major ethnic shift. These developments have displaced the Kaskazi cultures and societies of the early first millennium A.D. in all but the far northeastern fringes of the country, where Mwika peoples still persist. This varied history of ethnic shift postdates the Classical Age, but it needs at least a brief discussion here if we are adequately to round off our understanding of the prior spread of the Classical Mashariki tradition and its influences.

236

The Muteteshi culture probably came to end by the sixth or seventh century, at the time that a new population, the Botatwe (see chapter 2), would have been moving into west-central Zambia from the direction of the Katanga (Shaba) region of Congo (Zaire).[34] Along with words of apparent Kaskazi origin (see table 42), a strong Kusi component also appears in the vocabularies of the modern-day Botatwe dialects, Ila, Lenje, and Tonga. Some of these Kusi elements belong to a middle Zambezi areal word set, found outside Botatwe in the Shona and Nyasa languages. They appear to reflect a set of wide regional interactions dating to the past 1,500 years rather than the presence of a specific earlier Kusi peoples in southern Zambia.[35]

But other vocabulary of Kusi origin in Botatwe (see table 38 for a few examples) are better understood as the relics of early Botatwe interaction with a particular Kusi society. One major new culture, Kalundu, appearing after the fourth century A.D. all across the areas from Kabwe through the Batoka Plateau, is the probable candidate for this Kusi influence on the proto-Botatwe language. After the eighth century, the Kalundu culture progressively gave way everywhere to the expansion of several new closely related cultural facies, most notably Namakala, Fibobe, and Gundu, that are clearly attributable to the ancestors of different of the modern Botatwe societies.[36]

The Salumano tradition continued to evolve and develop, it appears, till as late as the thirteenth century. But over most of farther western Zambia a different set of cultures, of probable Western-Savanna-Bantu affiliations, began to predominate after the fourth century. In and around the Zambezi flood plain of far western Zambezi, a continuity from the Sioma culture of the fifth century down to the present-day Luyana group of peoples seems to have been maintained.[37]

Reflective of this long history of cultures in contact, a variety of Kusi and probably Kaskazi influences spread early and strongly to the Luyana-related societies of the Zambezi flood plain and indirectly farther westward from there through southern Angola and eventually to northern Namibia. To a more modest extent, some of these influences passed early to other eastern languages of the Western-Savanna group, such as the Luvale and Ndembu of far western Zambia.[38] Western-Savanna influences may well have similarly spread eastward to the early Kusi societies. The ethnic divide is, in any case, likely to have been a porous and shifting one in the first millennium A.D.[39]

## Kusi Expansions around Lake Nyasa

Another important Mashariki society of the Later Classical Age, in this case a Kusi people, appears for a time toward the close of the last millennium B.C. to have occupied some of the areas to the immediate north or northeast of Lake Nyasa. The presence of this early Kusi population in the north Lake Nyasa region is indirectly implied by the occurrence in certain far southern Kaskazi languages of words that would otherwise appear to be strictly Kusi innovations. The particular root words of this set occur widely and only in the Kusi languages, with one exception—that they also turn up restricted to certain Kaskazi languages that derive specifically from the dialects spoken by the earliest Kaskazi settlers of far southwestern Tanzania, most notably the Njombe languages and to a lesser extent some of the Rufiji-Ruvuma languages (table 43). They have, in other words, distributions that fit best with their having been original Kusi terms that were then adopted by slightly later-arriving Kaskazi communities from the Kusi people who preceded them in the region.

This proposed Kusi settlement, best located somewhere in the present-day Njombe and Mbinga districts, very possibly formed a first stage in the expansions by which Kusi populations eventually established themselves farther south in Africa. Seen in that light, the more easterly Kusi groups, the Makuans and Southeast-Bantu, could be understood to have spread, probably late in the last millennium B.C., from the northeastern side of Lake Nyasa southward through the areas

---

Table 43: Sample of proposed Kusi substratum words in the southernmost Kaskazi languages

| | | |
|---|---|---|
| *-sómbá | "fish" | Kusi (Makua, Shona, Nyasa); also Rufiji-Ruvuma, Kilombero, with additional spread, probably from Rufiji-Ruvuma, to Ruvu subgroup of Kati |
| *-gàlà | "feather" | Kusi (Nguni); also Njombe; also Botatwe |
| *-pìkò | "wing" | Kusi (Nyasa; SE Bantu); also Njombe; spread to some Sabi; also Comorian |
| *-lùmb- | "to praise" | Kusi (Nyasa; Shona); also Njombe; also Botatwe; earlier proto-Mashariki meaning "to thank" |

---

238

to the east of the lake. Scattered archeological traces of Matola culture, seeming here and there to underlie the Nampula materials of the early Makuans,[40] may provide direct evidence of just such an easterly route for the Southeast-Bantu movements in particular. The other early Kusi groups, the Nyasa and Sala-Shona, presumably would have moved south by different, more westerly routes, possibly through Malawi itself.

In the archeological context of southeastern Africa, such a two-pronged movement of Kusi peoples may account in part for the tendency of archeologists to discern eastern and western "streams" in the material evidence of the early centuries A.D. Other confusing factors include the presence of distinct Western-Savanna-Bantu cultures, notably Sioma, farther west. Which cultures constitute which stream seems to differ according to the archeologist involved, however,[41] and it is probably time, in view of the varied history of human encounter unveiled here, to jettison the whole concept of streams.

## Additional Kusi Settlements South of the Zambezi

A very large blank on our language map of the Later Classical Age encompasses modern Zimbabwe and the areas adjoining to the east in Mozambique. Two lines of evidence support the idea, however, that the Zimbabwe Plateau was home during most of the first millennium to communities that spoke a language especially closely related to the Nyasa subgroup. One is the archeological finding that the pottery in early Gokomere culture, found all across the plateau from just before 200 up to 900, often bears especially close resemblance to that of the contemporary Nkope tradition immediately to the north of the Zambezi, in Malawi: the Nkope and Gokomere may have been two facies of one common underlying variety of the Chifumbaze complex (see figs. 10 and 11 for striking examples of this resemblance).[42]

The second indicator that a Kusi language of the Nyasa group was spoken in Zimbabwe in the first millennium is a set of Nyasa words occurring widely in the Central Shona dialects, which are spoken all across the Zimbabwe Plateau today. For instance, the proto-Shona word for fire, *-lìlò, was replaced in the Central Shona dialects during the era of their spread across the plateau, 900–1200, by another word, *mu-ótò, otherwise found outside the Kaskazi languages only in the Nyasa subgroup of Kusi. And this is only one of a number of words having this type of distribution in the Shona dialects.[43] As a basic word, it is the kind of item typically borrowed in a historical situation in which the borrowing language displaces the source language from use over a period of generations. A second feature of this kind of borrowing is that the speakers of the source language of the loanwords originally much outnumbered the borrowers of the words. Thus the language and archeology both seem consistent with the hypothesis that Zimbabwe in the first millennium was largely occupied by a southern extension of the Nyasa peoples.

As for lowland Mozambique south of the Zambezi River, the language evidence remains to be adequately studied. It is not at all improbable that the central coast of southern Mozambique, and not just the far south of the country, was inhabited by Southeast-Bantu communities; and this idea is reinforced by indications of Matola culture sites, attributed above to the early Southeast-Bantu, found northward toward the Nyambane region of Mozambique. The high-rainfall climate of the Nyambane area would have made it a particularly attractive location for the earliest Southeast-Bantu settlement—a possibility deserving of closer archeological investigation.

## Southeastern Africa to A.D. 400: A Summing up

The Later Classical Age for southeastern Africa was an era of transformation in demography and culture. Much more than East Africa proper, the southeastern areas in the later last millenium still served as the home to a great many Khoisan peoples of deep historical roots in the region. The establishment of food-producing economies started far more recently there. The first herding and probably also cultivating peoples, apparently Eastern Sahelian in language, did not press southward from East Africa proper till after 500 B.C. South of the Zambezi, in northeastern Botswana and adjoining areas, a Khoisan people, the Khwe, subsequently took up sheep and cattle raising, and between 300 B.C. and A.D. 100 their descendants carried a mixed herding and gathering-hunting livelihood to the far southern coasts of the Cape region, apparently also into parts of the Transvaal, and westward as well, to far southern Angola and northern Namibia.

Close on the heels of these first exopansions of food production into southern Africa came the scattering out of the Kusi communities, around and just before the turn of the era, into a large variety of environments in Malawi, Mozambique, Zimbabwe, and eastern South Africa. In Zambia equally early movements of Kaskazi peoples seem to have pressed into northeastern as well as central and possibly southern parts of the country (map 9). These new settlers brought with them

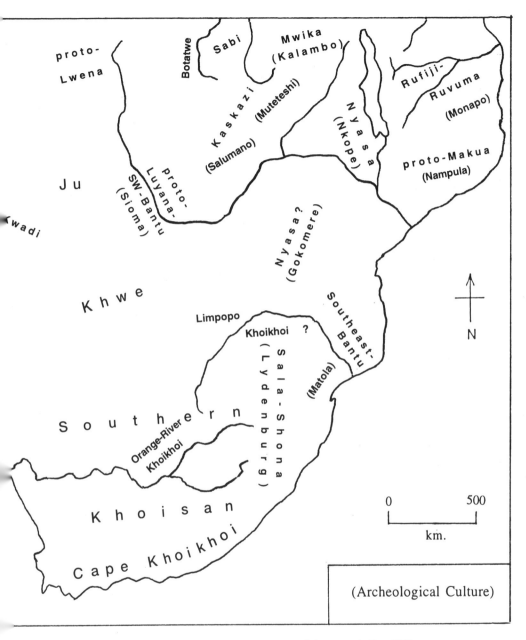

Map 9. Peoples of southeastern Africa, c. A.D. 400

241

an acquaintance with a wide variety of agricultural approaches, melded together from different historical backgrounds over the course of the last millenium B.C. This knowledge led to their practical development of cultivating systems that combined the raising of yams with the growing of grains and other seed crops, such as calabashes, black-eyes peas, and Voandzeia goundnuts. Both sets of peoples may have contributed to the domestication of an additional crop, *Plectranthus esculentus,* indigenous to the region. The Kaskazi communities, settling in what is today eastern and southern central Zambia, already gave considerable attention to cattle raising, but the Kusi in contrast kept few if any cows.

Armed with the economic advantage of a sedentary agricultural base and with the demographic advantage that came from residing in village-sized units—and over the first three centuries A.D. attaining a growing mastery of iron technology—the Kusi communities of the southeastern regions and the Kaskazi in the present-day Zambia quickly set in motion trends of social and cultural change entirely new to those regions. To these new historical directions, in East Africa and Zambia among the Kaskazi peoples and their neighbors, as well as in southeastern Africa among the Kusi—and also to the consequences of such developments for other Bantu peoples residing to the west of Greater Eastern Africa—we now direct our considerations.

# Notes

[1] Unpublished fieldwork of Douglas Werner.

[2] As proposed by Munson 1977.

[3] Phillipson 1977, 1985.

[4] Ehret 1968, 1982c.

[5] Ehret in press.

[6] In Ehret 1982b these words were wrongly attributed to Central Sudanic.

[7] Walker 1983. Most scholars have assumed this pottery to be connected to the Chifumbaze set of traditions and thus made by Bantu speakers; Walker takes implicit note of this issue but sidesteps drawing any conclusions about it.

[8] Morris 1991, along with references in his article provide a range of sources on these matters.

[9] Ehret 1982b.

[10] Ehret 1982b.

[11] The findings in Ehret 1968 remain valid on this point.

[12] This term appears in the Botatwe languages in the meaning "cow (female)" or "heifer" (see table 44) and, in a relict Kaskazi occurrence, in certain Western-

Lakes languages in the meaning "bull." In the later descendant language Shona of proto-Sala-Shona, this term has taken on the meaning "sheep."

[13] The arguments in Ehret 1967 still hold on this point.

[14] Ehret and Kinsman 1981; Ownby 1985.

[15] Ownby 1985.

[16] Huffman 1974, 1978.

[17] Ownby 1985.

[18] Ehret, Bink, et al. 1972.

[19] Ehret and Kinsman 1981.

[20] Laumann 1995.

[21] Ownby 1985.

[22] Gonzales 1995.

[23] Ehret, Bink, et al. 1972.

[24] Van der Merwe and Scully 1971 and elsewhere.

[25] On the Sotho see Ehret, Bink, et al. 1972.

[26] Ownby 1985.

[27] P. Sinclair, personal communication, July 1994.

[28] Sinclair et al. 1993.

[29] Robertson 1991, cited in Katanekwa 1994.

[30] Katanekwa 1994.

[31] Corrects reconstruction and distribution of Ehret and 1974a.

[32] Katanekwa 1994.

[33] Walker 1983.

[34] Ahmed 1995.

[35] Ehret, in preparation.

[36] Katanekwa 1994.

[37] Katanekwa 1994.

[38] Ehret, in preparation.

[39] Cf. indications in Huffman 1989.

[40] Sinclair, personal communication, July 1994.

[41] Phillipson 1977; Huffman 1989 and elsewhere; Denbow 1986; etc.

[42] As indirectly implied in Soper 1982.

[43] Ehret and Kinsman 1981.

# 8. Social and Economic Transformation in the Later Classical Age, 300 B.C.– A.D. 400

## Long-Term Trends of Change

Tracking the various settlements of Kaskazi and Kusi communities, our task of chapters 6 and 7, affords us one prospect on the developments of the mature Classical Age of East and southeastern African history, but a rather limited one. It identifies key players of the period from the third century B.C. up to the fourth century A.D., but misses much of the wider sweep of regional social change and the interregional spread of ideas, practices, and new inventions, as distinct from the movements of people themselves.

Three major themes of wide consequence for life and livelihood across East and southeastern Africa emerge from a closer consideration of social and economic history, and two of these had repercussions as well for the peoples of the savannas and rainforests to the west of eastern Africa. For one, the expanding Kaskazi and Kusi communities of those centuries often shed, to differing extents, a number of key social practices and institutions of their early Mashariki ancestors, reformulating their social relations even when there was little cultural impact as yet from the peoples into whose lands they moved. Second, over the same period the immigrant Bantu communities had a far from uniform experience with the major technological changeover of those centuries, from a mainly stone-using to a more fully ironworking tool technology. Nevertheless, it was from the Kaskazi societies in the Great Lakes region and Kusi peoples of the middle Zambezi that the knowledge of iron and ironworking spread west toward the Atlantic to the other Bantu societies of those regions. Third and equally important, the spread of new agriculture elements all across the savanna zones to the south of the equatorial rainforest owed specifically and almost wholly to the Kusi and Kaskazi example—to developments in food-producing technology and practices that had taken on increasing importance among the various Mashariki societies as the last millennium B.C. wound toward its close.

# Themes in Social History, 300 B.C. to A.D. 400

The scattering out of Kaskazi and Kusi Bantu communities in the Later Classical Age had several recurrent social and demographic consequences. To begin with, their settlements tended in much more rapid and thoroughgoing ways to encroach on the livelihood and independence of gatherer-hunter communities than did those of the Southern Nilotes or Southern Cushites in northern East Africa. And, most interestingly, the very fact of having moved house over long distances seems to have created conditions that encouraged significant changes in the Kaskazi and Kusi social order.

## Subsistence and Social Demography

The new Bantu settlements of the turn of the era and the first few centuries A.D. seem, in some respects, almost to have replayed the developments of the first half of the last millennium B.C. The Kaskazi communities, like their earlier Mashariki ancestors, moved principally into areas of forest or well-wooded savanna not previously utilized by food producers. The Kusi communities, too, tended often as not to resettle at first in well-watered areas—the Nyasa initially in the high-rainfall lands of central and southern Malawi, the pre-Makua in similar, somewhat drier environments to the immediate east and southeast of Lake Nyasa, the Southeast-Bantu possibly at first along a high-rainfall strip of southern Mozambique coast, and the Sala-Shona in environments that included the moist Natal coastal region. But the Kusi communities also, more quickly it appears than the Kaskazi of the turn of the era, soon moved into drier areas. The Gokomere sites, attributed to Nyasa-related settlements south of the Zambezi, on the Zimbabwe Plateau, came by the fourth and fifth centuries to include not just the wetter northeastern side of the region but also the open savannas of the central plateau; the Sala-Shona countries early encompassed the central Transvaal as well as the Natal coastlands; and the people who made the Muteteshi culture had moved apparently right away into savanna country in Zambia.

Preceded in many areas only by gatherer-hunters of very low population densities, the Kaskazi and Kusi peoples of the early centuries A.D. acquired the same kinds of demographic advantage and economic opportunity as their early Mashariki forebears before them. Among both the Kaskazi and Kusi communities similar propensities toward population growth, as well as similar pressures for territorial expansion engendered by their very long fallow agriculture, can be expected to emerge from the archeology of those centuries.

And because the Kaskazi and Kusi economies supplemented their agricultural production to such an extent by gathering, hunting, and fishing, they would have competed directly in most areas with the pre-existing gatherer-hunter populations for many of the same subsistence resources. Their settlement in a region would have tended, in ways that the Southern Cushitic and Southern Nilotic economic perceptions did not, to force the preexisting gatherer-hunter societies to make a relatively rapid accommodation to the new economic order. Across the southern half of Tanzania, only in those areas where Kaskazi settlement would not at first have been attracted—where annual rainfall fell below 1,000 millimeters, such as in the vast, lower-lying interior areas of southeastern Tanzania and much of western Tanzania—can purely food-collecting economies be expected to have persisted much beyond the middle of the first millennium. Similar environments in southeastern Africa where lower rainfall allowed gathering-hunting livelihoods to survive into considerably later centuries included interior Natal, interior southern Mozambique, the grasslands of the Orange Free State, and western Zimbabwe. Contrastively, where Southern Cushites or Southern Nilotes long remained the dominant populations, as in much of central northern Tanzania and in most areas of Kenya, the gatherer-hunter communities often continued to maintain considerable economic autonomy for many centuries and, in some cases, right into the twentieth century.

## Developments in Residential Practices

A variety of different reshapings of society arose among the Kaskazi communities who moved eastward out of western East Africa, and among the Kusi peoples who scattered out across southeastern Africa; and to a lesser extent changes appeared in other areas of culture as well.

In residential patterns, the developments of the Later Classical Age tended more to consolidate earlier, incipient trends than to institute new kinds of change. The Kusi societies, it seems probable, had shifted generally by or before the turn of the era to the making of thatch-roofed round houses. The situation among the contemporary Kaskazi communities seems to have been a more mixed one. Round houses with their conical roofs, already present among some Kaskazi peoples by perhaps the middle of the last millennium B.C., became probably the universal pattern among all the Lakes societies and among the Upland communities by the turn of the era. And among most of the various Kaskazi settlers of southern Tanzania, round houses also probably became the norm. The Takama and the pre-Langi instead may early have shifted to the building of rectangular, flat-roofed houses. The most conservative builders were the North-east-Coastal Bantu. Settling in far eastern Tanzania, they alone among the Kaskazi communities of the early first millennium A.D. appear to have preserved the old rectangular, gabled-roof style of house of the earliest Mashariki society, but even they more often than not probably fashioned their roofs of thatch rather than of woven palm strands.

Villages consisting of a set of households situated along a ridge remained important among more northerly Kaskazi communities, such as the Upland and probably many of the Lakes groups. Village layouts among some of the settlements of far southern Tanzania may for a time have preserved this same pattern; while among the early Northeast-Coastal Bantu communities of eastern Tanzania, single-street villages, but not ones laid out along a ridge, may have been the early custom. In still other instances, in particular among the pre-Langi and the Takama, it is possible that neighborhoods of scattered homesteads may already have become common. The various early Kusi communities probably at first maintained villages as the common residential pattern in all their new areas of settlement, but the pattern of laying out the village along a single street may have lapsed early on and been replaced by various more irregular layouts of the constituent households.

## Reconfiguring Chiefship and Kinship

The most notable recurrent consequence of the long-distance Kaskazi and Kusi resettlements was the reshaping of kin chiefship into a lesser-scale and less structured form of authority. Amongst Kaskazi societies, only the Lakes peoples, most of whom expanded contiguously out of their earlier areas of habitation, retained the highest level of kin authority, the *-ámì, and only among certain of the Lakes societies did a larger scale of polity emerge (see chapter 5). Everywhere else, it seems, the scale of kin authority tended to be downsized.

The Northeast-Coastal communities, whose resettlement near the Indian Ocean required a long-distance move across the center of Tanzania, lost without trace both terms for kin authorities, *-ámì and *-kúmù. But rather than dropping the institution of clan chief, they seem to have renamed and perhaps in some ways revised their concepts of clan authority. The persistence of clan chiefship in one form or another would hardly be surprising for the Northeast-Coastal peoples. For, as was seen previously (chapter 5), the old kin structures of the early Mashariki society, of which kin chiefs were a part, were probably preserved little changed among the early Northeast-Coastal people and, in later times, among their Ruvu-speaking descendants. The conceptualization of kin authority encapsulated in the verb *-kúm- "to be honored" apparently remained strong and reemerged in the construction of a new word for clan chief, *-kúmùà, found among both the Seuta and the Asu descendants of the Northeast-Coastal people.

A second term for clan chief, *-témì, came to be used among the early Takama. This word derives from the earlier Mashariki Bantu verb *-tém- "to cut down," especially in clearing land for farming. A dual symbolism may have inhered in this term. First, an old metaphor among Kaskazi peoples expresses "to render a judgment" with verbs bearing the concrete meaning "to cut." At the same time, the allocating of new land for farming can be argued to have been anciently a responsibility of clan or lineage chiefs, and so the *-témì could also be understood as the one who authorized the clearing (*-tém-) of new fields.[1] Perhaps the multiplicity of different societies, of Eastern Sahelian as well as Tale Southern Cushitic background, which over the long term were absorbed into the evolving Takama people, placed a premium on the role of a chief as as an ajudicator of disputes over land as well as customary behavior. Whatever the shorter-run historical causes of the name change, the comparative cultural evidence shows that the old ritual importance of the clan chiefship in matters concerning the ancestors continued as its core function among the early Takama communities.

For the Upland communities of the early first millennium A.D., the evidence is still more severe in its indications: kin chiefs of the earlier Mashariki types may have disappeared entirely from the historical stage. Not one proto-Mashariki term for such roles remains today in any of the Upland languages. The most satisfactory explanation, because it requires a single historical development, is that kin chiefship disappeared among Upland peoples at the very beginning of their settlement east of the Eastern Rift Valley. But it could also be that developments later in the first millennium separately led to its decline or reformulation in the Chaga-Dabida and Thagiicu societies.

Among the several sets of Kaskazi communities who settled in far southern Tanzania, the proposed lineage level of kin authority, the

*-kúmù̧ (see chapter 5), persisted as an apparently viable institution in the first few centuries A.D. It maintains relict occurrences as the word for "chief" in general in a scatter of Rufiji-Ruvuma languages, notably in Mavia of the Ruvuma subgroup and in Ngindo of the Mbinga subgroup. Among the Rungwe people it remained the term for a second-level position of authority: in the Nyiha language today its reflex denotes a subchief, and in Nyakyusa a counsellor of a prince. The word, it can thus be argued, still retained in the Rungwe communities of the first to fourth centuries its older Mashariki application, to a lineage head. The higher level of clan authority, the role of *-ámì̧, was apparently not maintained, however.

For the Njombe, both higher levels of kin chiefship appear to have been lost entirely. Chiefship was reconstituted during the early or middle centuries A.D. around a new and different concept, symbolized by the use for "clan chief" of a new root word, *-túá, the former Bantu meaning of which had been "aboriginal inhabitant." Clearly, claims to chiefship in the Njombe society began to be legitimized by priority of settlement. Chiefs were the putative descendants of the first Kaskazi settlers of a locality;[2] and clan membership at that crucial defining period, it can be suggested, may have been recreated out of people's relations to the founding family or their adoption of that familial connection.

What, finally, of the early Mashariki clan chief, the *-ámì̧? Did such a higher level of authority still exist among those who moved into southern Tanzania 1,800–2,000 years ago? Widely in the Rufiji-Ruvuma group and also in some Mwika and Rungwe languages, a distinct root word *-ènè has taken over as the term for a hereditary "chief." Its solid distribution through the center of the modern-day Rufiji-Ruvuma territories, in contrast to the broken, peripheral occurrence of *-kúmù̧, best fits with a history of its having diffused as a subsequent replacement term for earlier *-kúmù̧, its spread reflecting the rise of a new prominence for the conceptualization of a kin chief as "owner" of his or her kin, but surely at a date after the fourth century A.D.

Taken as a whole, the evidence suggests that, amongst the Rufiji-Ruvuma, only the lesser level of kin authority represented by the lineage head survived the transference of communities from western East Africa to southern Tanzania. For the Rungwe, the same kind of argument can be made, that only the position of lineage head survived into the early centuries A.D. and that the creation of other levels of political authority in Rungwe societies belongs to times much more recent than the fourth century. Among the Njombe a still more thoroughgoing change took place; clan chiefship in its older form disappeared completely and was constituted anew in accord with a different set of principles.

Similar contractions of the scope of kin chiefship eventuated also among the expanding Kusi communities of the first few centuries A.D. The Nyasa settlers retained only the lineage level of kin chiefship, that of the *-kúmụ̀. As for the pre-Makua, evidence that would allow the reconstruction of their first-millennium A.D. institutions of authority remains to be identified. The Makua of more recent centuries applied the metaphor of *-ènè "owner" in their word for a chief or king, but that usage probably derived from the wider regional spread of *-ènè among the contiguous Rufiji-Ruvuma societies and, if so, is reflective of changes in chiefly authority that diffused in periods since A.D. 400 (see discussion just above).

The most severe change took place in the societies that moved farthest south, the Southeast-Bantu and the Sala-Shona. There both of the higher positions of kin authority disappeared without trace. What kind of institutions took their place among the Sala-Shona peoples of the first three or four centuries A.D. is entirely unclear. (In the later first millennium, well after the close of the Classical Age and thus not germane to our considerations here, an entirely new kind of rulership emerged among the Shona, evolving after 1100 into the kingships of later Zimbabwe history. But that is a topic for another book.) Among the very earliest Southeast-Bantu settlers, of perhaps the first couple centuries A.D., the cultural connection of the old verb *-kúm- to authority surely persisted for a time, since that word took on the meaning "to rule" in later centuries among the people of the Chopi and GiTonga branches of Southeast-Bantu and formed the root for a new word for "chief," *-kúmò, in those languages.

But among the rest of the early Southeast-Bantu, a new basis for chiefship apparently quickly emerged. The root word *-kósị̀ became the general term for hereditary authority, and the verb *-kúm- came to mean "to be rich" rather than "to be honored" for one's intangible attributes. Apparently only the role of the extended family head, the *-kósị̀, remained in existence among the communities that coalesced into the Southeast-Bantu society; and as new, larger local social units began to take shape by the third or fourth century, chiefship was reconstituted among most of the Southeast-Bantu as an institution whose legitimacy resided in its traceability back to a founding family head. The term *-kósị̀ enlarged its scope to the leader of a larger local grouping of people, metaphorically invoking but no longer literally connoting the role of head of a family. This reconstituted

251

chiefship probably lacked the same close ties to clanship; it may from the beginning have taken on the character of a very small territorial chiefship for which chiefly wealth, to judge from the changed meaning of the verb *-kúm-, mattered more than kin legitimization. Only among the communities along the central coastal zone of southern Mozambique did *-kúm- maintain its direct linkage to chiefly authority, and even there the verb itself came to connote the exercise of rule rather than the attracting of respectful support.

Why did such shifts in the structure of kin authority take place? The most plausible cause lay in the differing scales and organization of the individual resettlements that composed the overall population movements. Among the Rufiji-Ruvuma, the establishing settlers, it can be proposed, arrived in small groups, perhaps of the size of several related families. Their highest level of leadership, in that case, would have been a lineage head, a *-kúmù, as the word evidence attests. A similar scale of settlement may account for the courses of change observed in the several early Northeast-Coastal societies and among the Rungwe and the Nyasa. The Njombe and the Southeast-Bantu, among whom only the status of senior family member, the *-kósì, was preserved, can be expected, by the same line of argument, to have settled in still smaller groups, of little more than extended-family size, with chiefship reemerging with new bases of legitimization as more settlers joined the local community and as it grew by natural increase.

The higher level of kin chiefship would, in any case, have been an institution exceedingly difficult to move over great distances. The authority and ideology of the institution depended in considerable part on the chief's maintenance of a relation with the ancestors, and the spirits of those ancestors continued to reside where their mortal forms had been buried, in the old lands of the community, As long as a community expanded into new lands nearby, the chiefship could follow. The role of the *-ámì survived among most of the Lakes societies because the spread of the Lakes peoples extended gradually outward across mostly contiguous parts of the Nyanza Basin. Nearly everywhere else, the Kaskazi and Kusi expansions of the Later Classical Age set off into faraway lands, where the ancestors had not previously lived and where kin authority needed to be built anew.

The kin basis of society probably underwent modifications as well in many of the Kaskazi and Kusi communities who settled far afield from western East Africa during the first three or four centuries A.D. A tendency toward the loss of the distinction between lineage and clan levels of relationship surely accompanied the simplification or, in some areas, loss of kin chiefship. Clan or lineage relations also

252

were probably often reconstituted, built up around local groupings of immigrants whose earlier forebears in western East Africa might have come from quite different clan or lineage backgrounds.

Matrilineal descent continued for long time to be probably the predominant basis nearly everywhere for determining residence and reckoning inheritance in these Bantu communities. Patrilineality took hold eventually among most of the northern East African Kaskazi societies and amongst the Southeast-Bantu and the Shona. But there is no reason as yet to suppose that any of the shifts to entirely patrilineal descent, except possibly among some of the Lakes societies, had been completed as early as the fourth century. The adoption of patrilineality is very likely instead to have begun no earlier the later first millennium A.D., at first in just a few societies, as the consequence of new social and economic factors, such as the changeover to extensive cattle raising in several of the Kaskazi societies of northern East Africa. In the very early Shona and Southeast-Bantu territories south of the Limpopo, too, the shift to patrilineality may first have emerged in the later first millennium as a consequence of the growth in cattle raising, although the example of Khoikhoi patrilineal descent there may have been an additional contributing factor. Even today, however, all the Kusi peoples north of the Zambezi and most of the Kaskazi peoples of eastern and southern Tanzania remain matrilineal in descent.

## New Developments in Age Organization

Another key area of social structure, where sweeping and widespread change may have gotten underway among the Kusi and Kaskazi societies already during the period between 100 B.C. and A.D. 400, comprised the intertwined customs of male circumcision and age-set formation. Before the turn of the era, both traits were probably still universal among the Mashariki Bantu peoples, and for some Kaskazi and Kusi communities they retained a central social importance into much later times. Among the Southeast-Bantu of the first few centuries A.D., for instance, the sort of circumcision observances reconstructed for the early Mashariki continued to have a lively social presence, and both age sets and circumcision continued to be important among a number of Southeast-Bantu societies right down to the twentieth century. The proto-Shona also may have maintained circumcision, and this custom apparently lasted into recent centuries among a few Shona-speaking communities. Whether age

253

sets continued for very long to be formed among them is unclear, however.

In East Africa proper, among the proto-Luyia, the East-Nyanza, the Upland, the pre-Langi, and the Northeast-Coastal societies, the association of circumcision and formation of age sets also remained strong probably throughout the first half of the first millennium, and most of the later descendant societies of these particular Kaskazi peoples, just like the Sotho and Nguni among the Southeast-Bantu, retained both customs as central features of the life cycle right down to the twentieth century. Wherever these elements of early Mashariki culture were preserved, the main features and observances of the old circumcision rituals often remained current for many centuries, and only gradually did particular elements get added or deleted from the overall set of customs.

Nevertheless, between the beginning of the first millennium A.D. and the middle of the second millennium, a widespread and wholesale disappearance of circumcision and age sets did take place. The details of this history escape us. Considering that the removal of foreskins lacks archeological visibility and that the relevant language evidence tends to consist of the loss of old, rather than the gain of new, vocabulary, the details will probably always escape us. One broad observation can be made at this point, however. The areas where circumcision and age sets have been lost form a vast contiguous region running right through the middle of the overall span of the present-day Mashariki Bantu territories, from the western Nyanza basin and the Western Rift valley south into all of southern Tanzania, northern Mozambique, and Malawi and much of Zimbabwe and eastern Zambia. This kind of distribution suggests an early, single, extended era of the diffusion from society to society, for reasons unknown to us now, of a view that saw circumcision as lacking social or ideological salience.

How the coterminous decline of age-set institutions was connected to the disappearance of circumcision may always remain uncertain. But there is in fact one possible history, quite speculative, that might both plausibly and elegantly account for the dual loss of those practices. It starts with the idea that age sets disappeared first, and for a practical reason: as an ordered complex of features, age-set systems may have proved difficult to maintain continuously as the older Kaskazi and Kusi communities broke up and the former members of those communities moved far away and resettled among the new groupings of people. With the withering of age-set observances, circumcision as, above all, the rite of initiation into an age set would have lost its raison d'être and so dropped from use too. Age sets and consequently circumcision would, on that hypothesis, have been mutual casualties of the disruptions of social continuity occasioned by the distant Kaskazi and Kusi population movements of the turn of the era.

In a few places, for particular historical reasons, the associated customs would have survived among the expanding Mashariki populations. In Kenya and northern Tanzania, circumcision may have gained in significance because of its presence also among the neighboring Southern Cushites and Southern Nilotes, while age-set institutions were reinforced by the parallel existence of age sets, although of a rather different kind, among the neighboring Southern Nilotes. Amongst the Southeast-Bantu, circumcision and age sets of course persisted also, but for historical reasons that may prove a bit more difficult to uncover.

This hypothesis does not satisfactorily account, however, for the loss of these linked customs in the Western-Lakes and West Nyanza subgroups of the Lakes peoples, whose history did not involve early population movements of such great distance. Perhaps there age sets came up against different kinds of opposition. Again, however, we can only speculate about possible courses of events. The lack of both age sets and circumcision among the Central Sudanians and among nearly all Eastern Sahelian peoples, as well as the lack of age sets among the Southern Cushites, all of whom were assimilated over the long run into the Lakes societies, might have been one factor, of significance particularly in the last millennium B.C. and early first millennium A.D. Conceivably also, the rulers of early protostates in the region, if they found themselves unable to coopt age sets as instruments of their own power, might have sought to suppress them and the circumcision ceremonies that legitimated them.

## Art and Music in the Classical Age

A further area where someday our understanding of society and culture during the Classical Age of Greater Eastern African history will be greatly enriched lies in the history of the arts. The available lexical and archeological evidence poorly serves these topics; there remains so much more information still to be searched out and recovered from both these kinds of historical resources. As a result only a few, usually broad developments in the history of art and music emerge as yet to view.

The Mashariki communities, from the beginning of their settlement in the far west of East Africa, carried with them a strong tradition of figure sculpture in wood, a kind of artistry that may have been almost entirely new to eastern Africa. Their attention to sculpture derived from their more ancient roots in the Niger-Congo civilization of western Africa, and it served not just to fulfil human esthetic drives, but had roles in their religious observances and in other ceremonial occasions. An important additional, and ancient, aspect of this art was maskmaking—the sculpted heads of animals or mythical beings providing the essential core element of the masks. Masks had notable use, or so it appears from the comparative cultural evidence, in circumcision and initiation ceremonies among the earliest Mashariki and probably among many of the later Kaskazi and Kusi communities.

As Kaskazi and Kusi communities scattered out across Greater Eastern Africa around the turn of the eras, they tended to carry aspects of their earlier sculpting tradition along into their new areas of settlement. Masks may often have continued to be made, especially, one suspects, in those places where the old circumcision and other initiation customs remained strong. A new development in figure sculpture appeared among the Sala-Shona of the Transvaal, who molded fine terra cotta heads that in their styles show historical links to the wood sculpting of Bantu-speaking societies elsewhere. The known examples of these "Lydenburg" heads date to about the fifth century A.D., but the genesis of the technique may well lie back in the second or third century.

The artistic impulse tended to be differently centered amongst the various other societies of the Classical Age. For Southern Cushites—and also the Southern Nilotes, who were strongly influenced in the latter last millennium B.C. by their Southern Cushitic neighbors—the intricate decorating of leather clothing and the fashioning of a large variety of jewelry for both men and women seem the most prominent focus of artistic effort. This interest in the decorative arts also found expression in designs on pottery and calabash containers and very possibly on other tools and utensils of the household. Comparative cultural evidence provides a partial basis for these conclusions, although in the case of clothing and jewelry a considerable amount of vocabulary evidence supports them as well. The evidence of borrowed words shows, for instance, that the decorated leather skirt of women and at least two kinds of metal jewelry were adopted by early Southern Nilotes from Southern Cushitic peoples.[3]

To the far south, in southern Africa, the artistry of Khoisan peoples had long taken a quite different form, rock painting, with strong

Figure 12. Ceramic sculpture in the Later Classical Age. Lydenburg head. (Courtesy of the South African Museum).

connections to healing and religious concerns,[4] and in some areas, rock engraving. An extremely ancient and long-preserved artistic tradition, Khoisan rock painting can be traced back thousands of years before the Classical Age in central parts of East Africa proper as well as in southern Africa, and it only slowly died out with the progressive assimilation of Khoisan peoples into non-Khoisan societies over the past two to three thousand years.

Art history among the Central Sahelian and Eastern Sahelian communities of the last millennium B.C. remains quite obscure. The comparative cultural and linguistic evidence suggests that historians might find it profitable to pay attention to a particular kind of artistic expression of significance among some of these peoples—an old, notable focus on human body decoration, especially on different kinds of intricate scarification. Scarification was, of course, not by any means unique to societies living at the northwestern edges of East Africa 2,000 years ago, but it does seem to have been especially important and varied in its manifestations in those areas.

In music, as in the visual arts, the Mashariki communities of the last millennium B.C. brought with them something entirely new to eastern Africa. Unlike any of the earlier music traditions of the eastern side of the continent, the Mashariki musical performance was basically polyrhythmic and percussive. Like their ancestors in the ancient Niger-Congo civilization, the Bantu communities relied on drums as their principal, and possibly in the early first millennium B.C. their only, instrument. The comparative cultural evidence allows that they may have had as many as three distinct kinds of drums, of different pitches and beaten to different conjoining rhythms. The vocabulary evidence certifies so far to just two kinds of drums, however, among the early Mashariki (table 44). Accompanying this new style of musical performance came a new kind of dancing, also of more ancient Niger-Congo background, emphasizing multiple, often rapid, movements of the body and assigning footwork only a subsidiary role.

Quite different styles for both the playing of music and dancing existed in the other societies of the last millennium B.C. in eastern Africa. Drums seem to have been entirely unknown across the whole of the eastern side of the continent at the beginning of the last millennium B.C., but string instruments of two kinds may have been very old features in different parts of those regions. The comparative cultural evidence suggests that musical bows, of one string, as well as instruments with several strings had a considerable antiquity among the Khoisan peoples who made the ancient Eastern African Microlithic

258

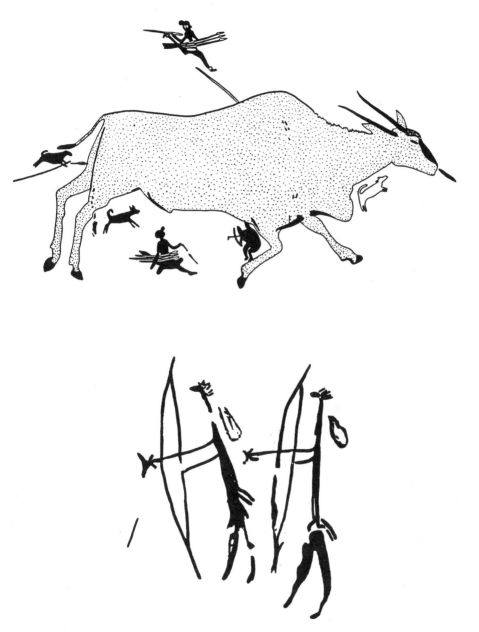

Figure 13. Rock art of Greater Eastern Africa. Wounded and dying eland, Cape Province, South Africa, *top* (Lewis-Williams 1981). Bowmen, Masange, central Tanzania, *bottom* (Sassoon 1967).

259

archeological tradition. The language evidence reveals that a five- or six-string lyre was also in use among Southern Cushitic peoples of the last couple of millennia B.C. (see table 44), and was adopted from them by the Southern Nilotes of western Kenya sometime between 500 B.C. and the mid-first millennium A.D.[5] The lyre seems to have been an instrument of similar antiquity among peoples of the lands immediately north of modern-day Uganda and possibly also among the Central Sudanians of the Western Rift region.

---

### Table 44. Early Eastern African musical instruments

*a. Proto-Mashariki terms*

| (root word) | | (distribution) |
|---|---|---|
| *-goma | "drum" | proto-Bantu (PB); proto-Mashariki (PM); wide general distribution among Bantu languages |
| *-tumba | "large kind of drum" | PM: Kaskazi (Lakes; Takama); Kusi (Shona; Sotho); also in Malungu of Sabi group |

*b. Southern Cushitic terms*

| | | |
|---|---|---|
| *pok$^w$'an- | "lyre" | pre-proto–West Rift |
| *turer- | "flute" | probable pre-proto–West Rift; very widely spread by borrowing |

*c. Nilotic terms*

| | | |
|---|---|---|
| *ture | "horn instrument" | possible proto-Nilotic |
| *ıkɔːntı | "kudu horn" | S'n Nilotic: Kalenjin (loanword from unknown source) |
| *-tar- | "horn instrument" | E'n Nilotic: Lotuko-Maa subgroup |
| *poːkaːn- | "lyre" | S'n Nilotic: Kalenjin (loanword from Southern Cushitic) |
| *ʈum | "string instrument (lyre?)" | early areal spread in far southern Sudan and northern Uganda |

*d. Proto-Rub term*

| | | |
|---|---|---|
| *po'j | "flute" | (Ik meaning "whistle") |

---

The evidence for wind instruments in early eastern and southern African history needs much more study. Comparative cultural data and to a lesser extent the language evidence support a very old fashioning and playing of wooden horns among Eastern Sahelians. Their use of animal horns, often to sound an alarm or herald a ceremonial gathering rather than to make music *per se*, appears also to be a cultural feature of some antiquity. Among the early Southern Cushites a different wind instrument, a flute of some kind, is likely to have been known and used before the first millennium A.D., although the language evidence is more difficult to interpret in this instance (see table 44). The Rub peoples of as early as 1000 B.C. also played a flute or musical whistle of some kind.

One other instrument, the *mbira* or thumb piano, may have been added to the stock of Greater Eastern African musical instruments early in the Later Classical Age. The word evidence implies that the *mbira* originated amongst the Kusi communities who settled in the lower Zambezi and Malawi regions, and that it diffused from those peoples northward into Tanzania and toward the Great Lakes and also northwestward into the Congo Basin.[6] The *mbira* today is typically composed of a wooden or calabash resinator to which are attached keys in the form of different-length, flat iron prongs. The instrument may originally have had bamboo prongs, as could still be found in some areas in the early twentieth century, and its inventors may thus have lived around the end of the last millennium B.C. or very beginning of the first millennium A.D. when iron, as we have learned, was still a relatively rare material among Kusi people.

Little can be said as yet about the early styles of dance among any eastern African peoples other than the Mashariki. Southern African Khoisan dancing, judging from the evidence of comparative performance in different recent Khoisan societies, may from fairly ancient times have emphasized footwork, accompanied by only very restrained movements of the body. Among the societies that spoke Southern Cushitic and the Southern Nilotic and other Nilo-Saharan languages, it would appear, in general and *very* broad terms, that footwork of differing kinds also had considerable importance, that body movements tended to be single and not often rapid, and that the musical accompaniment of dance did not entail drums, although it might include string instruments or clapping and singing. One particular kind of dance, a jumping dance of the young men, often competitive in nature, can be identified from the comparative cultural evidence as an old entertainment among Southern Nilotes and very possibly also the Southern Cushites. But nearly everything else remains to be discovered about this aspect of social history.

With the scattering out of Kaskazi and Kusi peoples from the turn of the era onward, the Niger-Congo styles of music and dance performance began to take hold in most areas where these Bantu-speaking communities and their languages came to predominate. The influence of these styles tended not to spread, though, beyond the Mashariki societies themselves; drums, for example, never were adopted by the Southern Nilotes or the Southern Cushites of the first millennium A.D., and both societies apparently continued to maintain their older kinds of dancing.

Musical influences did quite clearly pass in the opposite direction, however. In several separate regions, the Mashariki societies adopted new instruments from their non-Bantu neighbors. The spread of the lyre to early Kati communities (see *-pango in table 44), for instance, belongs to the same interactions, dating to the close of the last millennium B.C., of the Kati with Tale Southern Cushites that are so evident in the evolution of Kati livestock terminology (see tables 1B and 2B). But, on the whole, the wider adoption of new musical instruments by the Bantu-speaking communities of Greater Eastern Africa and their development of more mixed musicologies would seem to have taken place mostly in the period after the fourth century A.D.

A much rarer, contrary historical trend, toward the loss of an old Mashariki musical instrument under the influence of neighboring peoples who lacked that instrument, can be seen in the decline in the use of drums among the Upland societies. This development was so general among Upland communities of the past 1,000 years that its origins may trace back as far as the turn of the era, to the early Upland interactions with Southern Cushites and Eastern Sahelian peoples. Alternatively, the loss of drums might reflect subsequent musical developments, separately engendered in different later Upland societies by their assimilation of large numbers of erstwhile Southern Cushites and Nilotes into their communities at different points in the early second millennium A.D.[7]

# Developments in Tool Technology to A.D. 400

As for technology, even though ironworking had become established among many of the societies of western East Africa by or before the middle of the last millennium B.C., the scattering out of

Kaskazi and Kusi communities from those regions in the Later Classical Age had mixed consequences for technological history.

## Ironworking in East Africa

In southern Tanzania the Kaskazi settlers apparently brought in with them the first knowledge of iron and ironworking, and they soon transformed their surroundings in tool technology as well as subsistence economy. In northern Tanzania and southern Kenya, in contrast, the Upland peoples instituted new approaches to subsistence production within their immediate neighborhoods. By the fourth century they had established pockets of yam-based, long-fallow planting agriculture in the Pare Mountains and along the south side of Mount Kenya, an emphasis that still can be discerned under the layers of other, later agricultural innovations in those regions. But they did not by themselves revolutionize tool technology.

Already in the earliest first millennium, it is clear that at least the beginning steps toward iron production had been taken by some of the Southern Cushites as well, and this development is overtly revealed in the metallurgical terms adopted from Southern Cushitic into the early Upland dialects. In proto-Upland the verb for hammering iron was taken from a Southern Cushitic language (table 4B), whilst among the Thagiicu settlers of southern Mount Kenya two more Southern Cushitic words, for the blacksmith's bellows (*-bụra) and for iron itself (*-saga), were added as terms that continued to coexist in use with the synonymous earlier Kaskazi root words, *-gùbà "bellows" and *-gèlà "iron." The historical traditions of more recent Thagiicu societies, which credit the Agumba people who preceded them on Mount Kenya with being skilled blacksmiths, surely recall something of this ancient situation.[8]

Where the Southern Cushitic knowledge of iron originated remains unknown. One possibility is that their acquaintance with the new technology came from an entirely different direction, from the east through the sea-borne importation of iron goods at the Indian Ocean coast. This trade was already an important enterprise in the first century A.D., according to the *Periplua Maris Erythraei*, a merchant's guide to Indian Ocean trade.

Iron technology among the Southern Nilotes also apparently owed nothing to the Bantu example, but seems rather to have reached them from the northwest, from a Rub people.[9] The evidence of word histories situates this knowledge among the Southern Nilotes by no later than the late last millennium B.C. The available archeology, however, has yet to verify ironworking among them before around the seventh or eighth century A.D. Among the Mara Southern Nilotes, for instance, the trade in obsidian and obsidian blades remained a major economic activity right into the first few centuries A.D.[10] Part of the problem may be our lack of studies of Elmenteitan sites from the probable centers of Southern Nilotic population 2,000 years ago, in the Uasingishu Plateau of western Kenya. But it may well also be that iron remained a rare material among them for some centuries, used in jewelry perhaps, but not yet common enough to be fashioned very often into tools.[11] Or alternatively, the Southern Nilotes of the first half of the first millennium may not yet themselves have smelted the iron they used, and thus did not leave behind easily discovered by-products of ironworking, in particular, slag.

## The Spread of Ironworking into Southeastern Africa

To the south, the Kusi peoples seem to have had a more tenuous acquaintance with iron in the last few centuries B.C. than did their Kaskazi relatives of the western Nyanza Basin. A bare knowledge of iron as a material can be attributed to Kusi communities probably already early in the second half of the last millennium B.C. But the establishment of actual iron forging and smelting among them waited until the very threshold of their expansions across southeastern Africa. By then marked dialect differences had already emerged among the various communities of the Kusi cluster, and different sets of Kusi communities had slightly different experiences in adopting iron. The Sala-Shona peoples and the Southeast-Bantu, for example, obtained their metallurgical expertise apparently by diffusion from Kaskazi settlers of southeastern central Africa.[12]

Even then, iron may have remained for some time a relatively rare material little used in toolmaking among some of the Kusi societies. The Nyasa provide the particularly striking case; only as they settled in north central or central Malawi around the turn of the era did they begin to take up a full ironworking vocabulary, and they did so then by borrowing several of their key words from a Kaskazi people who about the same time were advancing into Malawi from the north (see chapter 7; also table 42).

Interestingly, although the Sog peoples of the northern Great Lakes region used iron before their Mashariki neighbors, there is no indication one way or the other in the language evidence as to whether the Eastern Sahelians farther south knew of metals before the arrival of Bantu communities at the end of the last millennium B.C. Their expansions southward may well have outpaced the spread of iron-working out of the Nyanza Basin, and their archeology, once it is found, is thus likely to turn out to be of a stone-age type.

## The Diffusion of Iron Technology Westward

The establishment of ironworking first in the Great Lakes region before 500 B.C. and its spread several centuries later into southeastern Africa form one chapter in a two-part story of wider historical setting. The vocabulary of both tools and of ironworking itself identify in multiple ways the seminal position of western East Africa for the spread of metallurgy westward across the forest and savanna belts, and these data sketch out the variety of routes by which this knowledge and practice diffused westward (see map 10; several examples of such vocabulary appear in tables 4–7).[13]

By around 500 B.C., iron smelting and forging had begun to spread directly westward, from the western Great Lakes into the eastern parts of the equatorial rainforest. Mary McMaster dates the appearance of iron among the Buans, who lived northeast of modern Kisangani at around the fifth century B.C., and discerns both Mashariki and direct Central Sahelian influences on the forms of Buan ironworking.[14] From that region the use of iron spread westward apparently following the Congo River toward the Atlantic coast and toward Cameroun. A second early introduction of iron, coming from the Western Rift region, passed westward to the ancestors of such modern peoples of southeastern edge of the rainforest as the Tetela and then southward to the Central-Savanna, Sabi, and Botatwe communities by the beginning of the first millennium A.D.[15]

Across Zambia and far southern Congo, still another area of the diffusion of ironworking can be discerned in the language evidence and, to a lesser extent as yet, in the archeology.[16] All across the southern savanna belt, the major direction of the introduction of iron smelting and forging seems to have been from the middle Zambezi region. The full establishment of ironworking, although relatively late among Kusi people, seems quickly to have developed into an important industry over the first few centuries A.D. From Zimbabwe and eastern Zambia, ironworking once established must have spread rapidly west toward the Atlantic. Already in the first two or three centuries A.D. this westward diffusion of technology would have reached

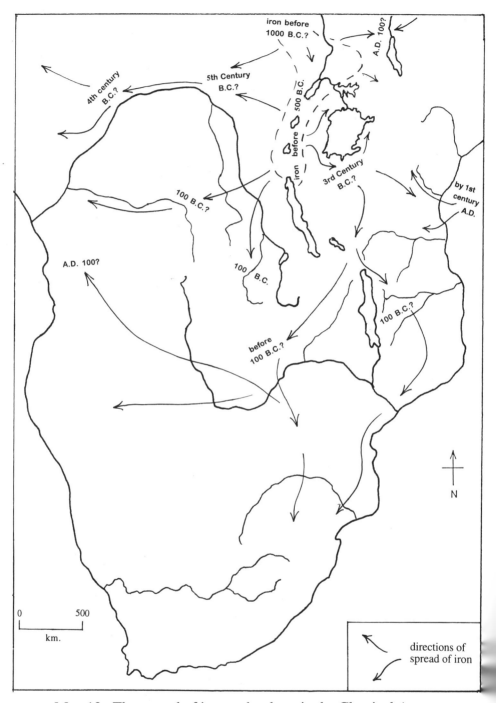

iron before
1000 B.C.?

A.D. 100?

5th Century
B.C.?

4th century
B.C.?

iron before 500 B.C.

3rd Century
B.C.?

by 1st
century
A.D.

100 B.C.?

A.D. 100?

100 B.C.

100 B.C.?

before
100 B.C.?

0        500
km.

N

directions of
spread of iron

Map 10.  The spread of iron technology in the Classical Age

266

western Angola. There, in the areas around the lower Congo River, the evidence of vocabulary suggests, its course overlapped with the earlier spread of iron westward through the rainforest from northern East Africa.

## The Tools of Cultivation

The growth in the variety of the iron tools used by the Mashariki Bantu had mixed effects for cultivation. Iron adzes, axes, and knives began to be produced probably fairly early in the Classical Age in the Great Lakes region, and the distributions of various new terms for these tools reinforce the evidence of the metallurgical terminology. Together these data depict several lines of spread of iron technology westward from its various early Mashariki and Central Sudanic practitioners.[17] But the use of iron hoes appears to have been a development relatively late in taking hold among the Kaskazi and Kusi communities.

The semantic histories of several words that are applied to the hoe among different Kaskazi and Kusi languages consistently imply a particular sequence of changes in what constituted the primary tool of cultivation over the last millennium B.C. Each of these words—most notable among them, *-gèmbè and *-témò—took on the meanings "ax" in some portions of their distribution and "hoe" elsewhere. The second term, *-témò, specifically derives from a proto-Mashariki verb meaning "to cut down," as in clearing a field. The Kaskazi and Kusi communities, it must be argued, passed through a stage, perhaps dating to around the middle of the last millennium B.C., during which they began to replace their earlier stone planting-axes with iron axes. Then, during the later centuries of the millennium, a newly invented tool, the iron hoe, began slowly to take over the digging functions of cultivation, and the iron ax more and more came to be reserved for the cutting and clearing that preceded the cultivation itself. In some cases the term previously used for the iron planting-ax adhered to the newer, although differently hafted tilling implement, the iron hoe. In other cases, it applied to the ax plain and simple, and a new term came into use for the hoe.

The new iron-bladed planting-ax, it thus appears, remained the predominant cultivating tool among Mashariki peoples until the iron hoe drove it from use, at different times in different areas, over the course of the last five hundred years B.C. In at least two early instances, the loanword evidence seems to indicate that iron hoes were

267

initially acquired by the Kaskazi communities from Central Sudanians or Eastern Sahelian people (see table 6d; table 39e). From the more southerly Kaskazi communities, the use of the hoe then passed southward to peoples of the Kusi cluster, by or before the early first millennium A.D. Thereafter, the implement diffused westward to peoples of the western savanna, the most notable line of its spread marked by a distribution of the word *-témò in the meaning "hoe." This distribution shows the hoe to have spread from southeastern Congo through northern Angola and southern Congo to the regions both north and south of the lower Congo River.[18]

# Agricultural Innovation in the Savanna Belt

The Later Classical Age, from the third century B.C. to the fourth century A.D. saw also the full establishment of grain agriculture among the Kusi and many of the Kaskazi societies. That establishment allowed a secondary consequence to emerge—it created the basis for the diffusion of grain crops from Mashariki people all across the the southern savanna belt.

### Westward Diffusion of Grain Crops: Long-Term Effects

During the second half of the last millennium B.C., before the rapid scattering out of Kaskazi and Kusi communities across eastern and southeastern Africa at the turn of the era, Central-Savanna and Western-Savanna communities can be expected to have been spreading somewhat more widely across the more northerly, high-rainfall portions of the southern savanna belt. Their agricultural practices and their crops in those centuries would have been much the same as among the early Mashariki people, emphasizing minimal intrusion into the soil, depending on very long fallow times, and with different yams as probably the principal crops. But as was true for the early Mashariki, their expansion beyond well-wooded savanna environments would have been constrained by the demands and expectations of their agriculture.

For the Central and Western-Savanna societies, then, the westward spread of grain crops open up new possibilities as the first millennium A.D. progressed. It opened up new areas for Western-Savanna settlement as far south as the lands where the dry southern fringes of the savanna merged into the northern parts of the Kalahari steppe,[19] and over the longer term it created a more complex agriculture that contributed in subtle but significant ways to the growth of human populations. That growth of population, especially among the Luban and Lundan peoples of the woodland savanna zones, formed a key element in the major transformations of political and social life in the second millennium. It fed the expansions of Sabi peoples, the makers of the Luangwa tradition, across eastern and central Zambia and far southern Katanga (Shaba) after the tenth century. It provided the concentration of work and productivity on which the Lunda and Luba empires of the second millennium were built.

## The Pathways of Grain Crop Spread

The overall lexical evidence reveals two broadly parallel bands of westward diffusion of grain crops from the Mashariki in the early first millennium A.D. One diffusionary route lay across the northern, better-watered half of the savanna zone; the other, farther to the south along the northern fringes of the Kalahari region.

The northerly line of spread began apparently in the southern Great Lakes region, diffusing via the areas around northern Lake Tanganyika first to the early eastern Luban and the Sabi communities and thence westward toward the Atlantic. A pair of names for the two grains, finger millet and sorghum, that can be grown in these environments appear to map the trans–Lake Tanganyika connection: (1) *-lè "finger millet" (a Central Sahelian loanword: see table 8), which is found in relict occurrence in the Lakes subgroup of Kaskazi and is known also from Malungu of far southeast Congo and Bemba of eastern Zambia; and (2) *-sàká "sorghum," which is used in the Western branch of the Lakes languages and also widely in Sabi languages, such as Malungu, Lamba, and Bemba.[20] The adoption of the Kaskazi word *-(u)nù̀ "mortar" (see table 6), in languages extending all the way from the Luba-speaking regions to northern Namibia and the mouth of the Congo River, probably also reflects this connection, because that term is known among Mashariki peoples only from certain northern member languages of the Kaskazi grouping. A different term for mortar, *-túlí (see table 5), is found through most of the rest of the Mashariki regions.

The specific connection of *-(u)nù̀ to the northern Kaskazi groups would require that this spread of grain crops did not get underway at its earliest until the close of the Late Mashariki era, sometime after 500 B.C. The restricted Mashariki distribution of the grain terms *-lè and *-sàká, to just the Lakes group of languages and, in the case of *-sàká, to just Western-Lakes languages, refines this reasoning, placing the beginning of the westward spread of grain crops no earlier than sometime in the last three or four centuries B.C., at a time when the Lakes group of Kaskazi had itself already spread out and begun to diverge into four subgroupings of communities, one of which was Western-Lakes.

The subsequent diffusion of grains from the upper Lualaba watershed westward to the Atlantic is charted by a second pair of root words for finger millet and sorghum: (3) *-ku "finger millet" and (4) *-sángú "sorghum" (table 46). The first of these, interestingly, may be a Central Sudanic loanword, deriving from the proto–Central Sudanic root word *kwi "grain, seed grain." If this derivation is correct, it would reflect an additional contribution to the spread west of grain crops, coming from perhaps the same Central Sudanic society, which during the first millennium A.D. influenced the history of the Forest society of the Lakes group. This people resided apparently near the northwestern side of Lake Tanganyika (see table 8). The second word *-sángú is visibly, from its lack of regular sound corres-

| Table 45. Words of areal spread from Western-Lakes to Sabi and Luban languages | | |
|---|---|---|
| *-lè | "finger millet" | Lakes (some Luyia); Sabi (Malungu, Bemba, etc.) (Central Sudanic loanword: see table 8) |
| *-sàká | "sorghum" | Lakes (Western-Lakes); Sabi (Lamba, Malungu, Bemba, etc.) |
| *-pèl- | "to grind" | Lakes (Western-Lakes); Luban; Sabi; in Nyanja of Nyasa subgroup of Kusi (possible Sabi loanword); spread to Kuba and to Southwest-Bantu semantic derivation, probably first in Western-Lakes, from verb "to scratch," seen in *-pèlè "scabies" |
| *-ka | "cattle" | Lakes (Western-Lakes, East-Nyanza); Sabi (Lamba) (Eastern Sahelian loanword: see table 8) |
| *-panga | "ram" | Lakes (Western-Lakes); Luban; Sabi |

270

pondence, a borrowing of the old Mashariki Bantu word *-sàngų́ "individual grain (of sorghum or other cereal crop)."[21] In Angola, to judge from the distributions of both *-sángú and *-(u)nų́ "mortar," this spread turned apparently southward, overlapping in northern Namibia with the parallel more southerly spread of grain cultivation west from the middle Zambezi region.

Farther south, the practices of grain cultivation began diffusing from Kusi communities probably by the first few centuries A.D., possibly reaching southern eastern Angola by or before the middle of the millennium. The western outliers of both *-pú "sorghum" (see table 4) and *-bèlé (see table 5), applied to either "sorghum" or "pearl millet," extend along the southernmost parts of the southern savanna zone, to languages of the Luyana-Southwest subgroup of Western-Savanna-Bantu, whose ancestors in the fourth or fifth century were probably the makers (as was proposed in chapter 7) of the Sioma tradition of the Zambezi flood plain.[22] In keeping with the drier climate of that zone, the grain crops of this diffusion were sorghum and probably also pearl millet. The line of spread in this instance probably followed through southern Zambia and the middle Zambezi region.

## The Spread of Cattle Keeping from Eastern Africa

The knowledge of cattle may have passed westward along approximately the same two routes. By far the less significant route, however, would have been via the Lake Tanganyika region, and for an obvious environmental reason, namely, its tsetse-harboring woodland savannas. Not surprisingly, only one word of Kaskazi connection, the specifically Lakes word *-ka "cattle" (see table 8)[23] has a distribution similar to those of the grain terms *-1è and *-sàká. It reappears in the eastern Zambezi-Congo watershed region in a doubly prefixed form *icinka*, "cattle pen," in Lamba of the Sabi grouping of languages.[24] Apparently the initial knowledge of cattle may have come to some of the Luban and Sabi peoples along with the spread of finger millet and sorghum from the western Great Lakes region by early in the first millennium A.D.

But the principal direction of the spread of cattle raising was westward from southeastern Africa, as is evident in the diffusion of the southern Kusi root word *-tànga "herd" or "cattle pen" (see table 39) all across Zambia—for instance, in Lamba and Kaonde—and as far west and northwest as the heartland of the precolonial Lunda kingdom of southwestern Congo. Presumably accompanying this spread of the knowledge of cattle came also the proto-Mashariki root term for "cow," *-gòmbè, a word universally found, sometimes with skewed pronunciations, the rest of the way across the southern savanna to the Atlantic Ocean, from the northern edge of the Kalahari in the south to the southern edges of the equatorial rainforest in the north.

Among the most southerly of the Western-Savanna-Bantu communities of the first millennium A.D., an additional component of pastoral influence came from the Khwe peoples of the northern Kalahari and northern Namibia. Sheep, in particular, seem specifically to have been adopted by the early Southwest-Bantu, the Yeyi, and the Totela from the Khwe peoples of the northern Kalahari and Namibian

---

Table 46. Words reflecting farther westward agricultural spreads

*a. Words of mostly northerly spread in the savanna zones*

| *-ku | "finger millet" | Luban; Lundan; to KiKongo |
|---|---|---|
| *-sángú | "sorghum" | spread to southwestern savanna zone, in meaning "pearl millet"; reapplied to maize in recent centuries in far western savanna areas; from Mashariki *-sàngų́ "individual grain" |
| *-pèl- | "to grind" | (see table 45 preceding) |

*b. Words of southerly distribution in the savanna zones*

| *-pú | "sorghum" | (see table 4) |
|---|---|---|
| *-bèlé | "sorghum" or "pearl millet" | (see table 5) |
| *-sa | "sorghum" | Western-Savanna: Lwena; SW Bantu |
| *-úngù | "chaff" | Kusi: all Kusi groups; Botatwe; also Kwanyama; loan-shape *-jungu in Bemba, Lunda, Luvale |
| *-tàngá | "cattle-pen" | Kusi: most Kusi groups; also Botatwe, Lamba, Luvale, Lunda (crossing distribution from southerly into somewhat more northerly savanna areas); see table 38 |

*c. Word of wide general distribution*

*-gòmbè "cow"

regions. The Khwe, as we have seen, had become sheep raisers centuries earlier, in the latter last millennium B.C. Among the Southwest-Bantu peoples, cattle terminology also reveals this dual impact. The presence in the proto-Southwest-Bantu language of the old generic term for cow, *-gòmbè, links their first acquaintance with the animal to its general spread westward in the early first millennium. But other cattle terminology in their languages suggests a considerable role for Khwe peoples in the subsequent development of a major pastoral component in their economies.[25]

In most of the westerly savanna regions, the practice of milking cattle was never taken up, even in such areas as the southern highlands of Angola where cattle in later centuries became very common. Only along the southern fringes of the savanna belt, among peoples speaking languages of the Luyana-Southwest subgroup of the Western-Savanna-Bantu did milking become an integral part of the pastoral sector of the economy, just as it was among their Khwe neighbors.

The timing of these various developments in livestock raising is not entirely clear. The spread of the bare knowledge of cattle westward to the early Western-Savanna societies may well date to the first few centuries A.D. The effective taking hold of pastoral activities among the Luyana-Southwest-Bantu probably belongs, however, to the centuries after about 400, and the growth of cattle raising among southern Angolans, to still later times. Revelatory of the longer-term consequences of eastern African economic history on events outside eastern Africa, these developments deserve summary mention here, but their fuller explication belongs to another history still to be written. (Map 11 sums up our current ideas about the spread of new crops and animals up to the fifth century).

## Indian Ocean Trade: Its Effects on Economic Change

The Commercial Revolution contributed additional elements to this overall westward flow of ideas and things from Classical East Africa. The direct encounter of Eastern Africans with the new kind of trade was a relatively limited one, but the indirect consequences were extensive in their reach. With commerce there came a variety of new items, the adoption of which by local peoples sometimes had effects that rippled right across the continent. The rise of the Indian Ocean commercial networks also brought one small but historically noteworthy new settlement of people, the forebears of the Malagasy, to the eastern coast of Africa and from there to the island of Madagascar.

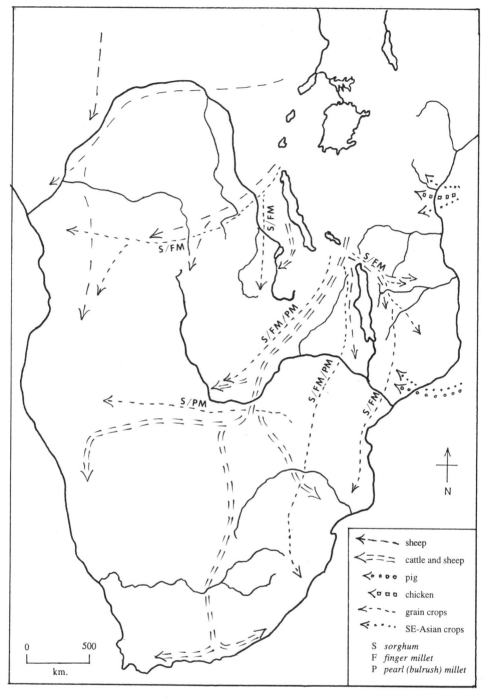

S/FM

S/FM

S/FM

S/FM/PM

S/FM

S/FM/PM

S/FM

S/PM

N

| | sheep |
| | cattle and sheep |
| | pig |
| | chicken |
| | grain crops |
| | SE-Asian crops |

S  *sorghum*
F  *finger millet*
P  *pearl (bulrush) millet*

0        500
km.

Map 11.  The spread of crops and animals
in the Later Classical Age

Commerce and Society

Formal commercial activity built Eastern Africa's first major town, Rhapta. Apparently the only really major trading port on the Indian Ocean seaboad, it lay most probably, from the descriptions we have of it, somewhere along the northern or north-central coast of present-day Tanzania, possibly near the present-day Tanzanian capital, Dar es Salaam.[26] Its archeological remains have yet to be discovered. The local inhabitants of the region imported glass beads and iron goods, such as spears, axes, knives, and small awls, brought by visiting southern Arabian and sometimes eastern Mediterannean merchants, while exporting ivory, rhinoceros horn, and tortoise shell.

Rhapta originated, like Carthage in the Mediterranean region, as a trading settlement founded by outside commercial interests, in this case South Arabian merchants. The town and its trade are reported in the first century A.D. to have been under the purview of the governor of Mapharitis, a province in the Himyaritic kingdom of Yemen. The taxing and regulating of the trade along the coast and at Rhapta were farmed out to merchants from the South Arabian port city of Mocha, whose priority in the coastal trade had been established some time previous to the first century. Many of these merchants had married women from the Rhapta area and spoke the local language as well as their own South Arabian tongue.[27] The overall evidence for Kaskazi expansion favors the conclusion that the majority of these local peoples, at least through Rhapta's halcyon days from the first to the fourth centuries, would probably have been of Northeast-Coastal Bantu affiliations in language and culture (see chapters 4 and 6).

Contemporary references to the people who lived in the countryside and on islands near Rhapta in the early first millennium A.D. are few in the available documentation, and not particularly helpful in resolving their ethnic or linguistic connections. In the first-century merchants' guide,[28] *Periplus Maris Erythraei*, the locals are reported to have made sewn boats, an apparent very early reference to the cord-sewn plank boat, the *mtepe*, constructed by the East African coastal boat-builders into much later centuries; to have also used dugout canoes; to have fished using baskets; and to have been "very large-bodied." They are said also to have behaved "each in his own place, just like chiefs."[29] They belonged, in other words, to small, local, independent communities that recognized no higher level of authority, whether indigenous or South Arabian.

The presence of basket fishing (see also chapter 4 and table 22) fits in with the language evidence that Bantu settlers arrived in the region as early as the first century A.D. The rest of the written testimony does not specifically require that conclusion, but does not rule it out either. The description "large-bodied" is particularly impressionistic and ambiguous. Did it mean "sturdily built," as are many eastern Tanzanians today, or did it imply "tall" of stature, as earlier translations of the *Periplus* used to render it? Dugout canoes were anciently a craft of Bantu-speaking societies and thus their use would be consistent with the placing of Northeast-Coastal communities in the environs of Rhapta, although it must also be noted that such vessels were independently invented in more than one part of the tropical world.

Sewn boats raise the most interesting historical issue. They are known to have been made in recent centuries not only by Swahili people at the coast but also by Lakes peoples living far inland along Lake Nyanza. Does the *mtepe* thus represent a technology of the late last millennium B.C., invented by Kaskazi peoples for navigating large bodies of water, a technology then transferred to the coast by the early Northeast-Coastal Bantu settlers? Alternatively, might it reflect a surviving indigenous, pre-Bantu boat-building tradition of the East African coast or else influences arriving via the Indian Ocean commercial connections?

The writer of the *Periplus* intimates that the South Arabian command over the sea trade of the East African coast was already of long standing in the mid-first century A.D. If indeed that trade did extend back into the last two or three centuries B.C., a not unreasonable interpretation of the *Periplus*, then it began at a period just before Kaskazi communities had yet settled there.

If so, who would have been trading then with the South Arabians? Southern Cushites by the last two or three centuries B.C. had long been inhabitants of parts of the eastern side of East Africa, some of them having settled during or before the last millennium B.C. in the immediate hinterland of the Kenya coasts. Before and after their arrival on the scene, Khoisan-speaking fishing and shellfish-collecting communities resided in the coastal areas, while other gathering-hunting bands coexisted with the Cushitic agripastoralists in the hinterland; and these food-collecting peoples often persisted as distinct societies as late as the present millennium.[30]

Perhaps already, then, in the later last millennium B.C., the earliest exporting of East African ivory, rhinoceros horn, and tortoise shell followed a course alike to that known from eastern Kenya in more recent centuries. The gatherer-hunter peoples in this situation collected the product as agents for their dominant agripastoral neighbors, who in turn directly passed the product on to the merchants at the coast. Just such a connection to Rhapta might help to explain the separate early spread of iron to Southern Cushites in eastern Kenya and Tanzania, at a time before the arrival of Bantu settlement (see chapter 4 above). Certainly by the turn of the era, as the documents tell us, the local peoples were importers of iron goods coming from the Middle East, and this pattern no doubt carried on trading habits and expectations already established before then.

So the founding of Rhapta in the last few centuries B.C. brought to Eastern Africa the kind of town, dependent on trade, typical of the Commercial Revolution. But Rhapta apparently long remained an exotic in the Eastern African economic environment, unable apparently to survive the downturn in world commerce of the fifth to seventh centuries A.D. Only in the ninth and tenth centuries A.D., with the rise of the Swahili city-states, long after Rhapta had disappeared from the historical stage, can the commercial town be said to have taken root as a truly indigenous flower.

## Distant Repercussions of Commerce: Interior Africa

Although formal commerce reached only to Rhapta, the movement of goods and people encouraged by the wider Indian Ocean commercial networks had much farther-reaching agricultural consequences for the continent. The key intermediaries in these developments were a group of settlers of Indonesian antecedents, who arrived along the east coast of Africa early in the first millennium A.D. The evidence retained in the language of their modern Malagasy descendants, consisting of early word borrowings from a Kaskazi tongue, shows that they first settled for a time along the Tanzania or Kenya coast. Both the loanwords and glottochronological reckonings place them there at about the first to third centuries A.D., and not before.[31] They most probably arrived by traveling along the then developing sea lanes of the Indian Ocean, first following those connecting Indonesia and India, and then passing from India across to the shores of East Africa. Around about the third or fourth century, having already intermarried to some extent with local East African peoples, they sailed farther south and crossed over the Mozambique Channel to Madagascar, then uninhabited, and laid the basis for the modern-day Malagasy populations of that island.[32]

Although peripheral players in the overall history of the Later Classical Age, the Indonesians had an indirect impact exceeding what

277

their small numbers might be expected to have imparted. They had such an effect for one interconnected pair of reasons—they came from a region with a wet tropical climate similar to that found along the Tanzanian and parts of the Kenya coast; and they brought with them not only food crops well adapted to that climatic regime, but for the most part crops reproduced by planting rather than sowing of seeds, notably Asian yams, taro, bananas, and sugarcane. Moreover, they arrived at a point in time, the second to third centuries A.D., when Northeast-Coastal and other Kaskazi communities, who already practiced a strikingly similar agriculture, had begun to establish themselves in the immediate hinterlands of the Indian Ocean seaboard.

These Bantu-speaking peoples—with their planting agriculture of West African origin, in which indigenous African yams may still have been the preferred staple of the diet—would thus have been able rapidly to add the Asian yams to their crop repertory. Sugarcane, taro, and bananas probably also were adopted relatively early in the first millennium A.D. by the Kaskazi communities of the coastal hinterlands. The consequence for these groups would have been a fairly rapid enrichment in the variety of their diet. Their encounter with influences arriving via the Indian Ocean sea lanes helped them to bring into being an even more productive and successful agricultural technology than had already been created by their Mashariki forebears, whose blending of Sudanese and West African agricultures just a few centuries before, in the later last millennium B.C., had helped set off the Kaskazi and Kusi expansions in the first place.

Because the Asian crops had been domesticated in environments much like those found in many parts of tropical Africa, they spread eventually inland far beyond the areas of direct contact of coastal East Africans with the Commercial Revolution. They had reached the continent in the newer historical fashion, via a long-distance lane of diffusion created by commercial contacts. But within the continent, where the effects of the Commercial Revolution were not strongly to operate until very recent centuries, the new crops diffused the old-fashioned way, from community to neighboring community wherever the climate allowed. For the most part, that wider spread belongs, because its progress was slow and uneven, to a subsequent period of history, from the fourth to the tenth centuries, not dealt with here.

As an example, the banana appears to have spread by two routes during the centuries before 1000. In northern Tanzania and southern Kenya, the the crop moved inland from the coast to become strongly established in the Pare Mountains, around Mount Kilimanjaro, and in the Mount Kenya region only toward the very close of the first millennium A.D. In northern Mozambique, in contrast, the banana may have diffused inland to Malawi several centuries earlier, advancing through the wetter climate zones of that region and then through far western Tanzania all the way to the Great Lakes by probably around a thousand years ago. Over roughly the same centuries, a second arm of this spread passed northward through eastern Congo, then westward through the equatorial rainforest, and eventually into the better-watered parts of West Africa, also by or before 1000 B.C. In the equatorial rainforest, the adoption of the banana has been argued to have revolutionized the productive capacities of the local Bantu agriculture and so allowed new directions of social and political history to emerge.[33] The same kind of case has been made for its consequences in several areas of East Africa, such as around Kilimanjaro[34] and in Buganda and Bukoba in the Nyanza Basin.[35]

One other notable enrichment of the eastern and southern African diet probably owes to the Indonesian influences of the first three or four centuries A.D., and that is the introduction and spread of the chicken, a domesticate of southeast Asian origin. Two solid, block distributions of words for the domestic fowl trace its spread across the eastern side of the continent. One of these, appearing in two shapes *(i)nkúkù and *(i)nkúkú, runs from the Upland and Northeast-Coastal Bantu societies of southeastern Kenya in an almost unbroken distribution south to the Nguni and other Bantu languages of South Africa and southern Mozambique, and westward to the Zambezi flood plain of far southwestern Zambia. West of the Eastern Rift Valley of Kenya and northern Tanzania, a second, nonregularly corresponding form, *(i)nkókò, of the same underlying root appears not only in all the Bantu languages of the Great Lakes region, but in the intervening Southern Nilotic languages of western Kenya and the Rift Southern Cushitic languages of north-central Tanzania. The same basic pronunciation of this word, but lacking in regular sound correspondence, then extends farther westward through the languages of the equatorial rainforest of the Congo Basin as far variously as southeastern Nigeria and the mouth of the Congo River.

These three distributions together demark an undoubted spread of the chicken in several directions, but predominantly westward. The fowl arrived first in the eastern parts of East Africa. It diffused southward from there, following in the train of the expansion of Kusi Bantu groups into southeastern Africa; westward at the same time into the Great Lakes region, where the change of the original vowel *u to *o can be explained by vowel sound–shifts in the early Upland Bantu languages; and finally west across the rainforest, roughly maintaining the pronunciation found in the Great Lakes languages.

From these patterns, it appears probable that the ancient southeast Asian domesticate, the chicken, was first introduced at the East African coast in the first two or three centuries A.D.[36] The spread westward of the chicken toward the Atlantic then proceeded in probably fairly rapid fashion. It would not be surprising if domestic fowl and often their eggs also had become major additions to the diet as far east as southeastern Nigeria well before 1000 A.D.

Across the southern savannas, extending westward to the Atlantic, the further diffusion of the chicken can be discerned in the distributions of two varieties of a different root word for the bird, *-súsúá and *-súsú, the first of these occurring through Angola into Namibia and the second used in languages near and to the west of the stretches of the Congo River that lie north of the Malebo Pool. This particular word appears to derive from two different skewed pronunciations of a term (originally pronounced -chuchu or -shushu) that means "chick" in several of the western East African Bantu languages, such as Nyamwezi; and so they would seem to represent the diffusion of that word by borrowing, and thus the spread of the chicken itself, westward from East Africa.

One other domestic animal may owe its presence in a limited part of Greater Eastern Africa to the Indonesian settlers, and that is the pig. Raised by a number of Kusi communities in the regions surrounding the lower Zambezi, where the name *-kùmbà, of unknown source, is given to the animal, its existence has yet to be established in the early archeology. An alternative introduction, by much later Portuguese intruders in the sixteenth century, is thus still possible; but the great importance of the animal among the Malagasy and among their Indonesian forebears makes its introduction by the ancestors of the Malagasy much the more probable solution for now.

Interestingly, the influences of the ancestors of the Malagasy on developments within Greater Eastern Africa extended into matters musical as well as agricultural. At least one instrument, the xylophone, today widely found in tropical Africa, had its clear historical antecedents in southeast Asia and Indonesia.[37] The language evidence suggests that the initial stage of its spread in the continent passed via the Zambezi region toward Angola and southern Congo.[38] Its establishment in southeastern parts of the continent postdates the invention of the *mbira* (see chapter 8) because, in several instances, older names for the *mbira* were reapplied to the new instrument. Such a history fits best with a conclusion that the xylophone came first into regular use among continental southeastern Africans no earlier than the establishment of Malagasy populations on Madagascar, which lies off the coasts of the lower Zambezi region. Its adoption and spread farther west across the continent thus probably belongs mostly to periods after the third or fourth century A.D.

The xylophone may also separately have been introduced at other points farther north along the East African coast, conceivably during the second to fourth centuries, at the time of the initial Indonesian arrival there. But if so, it did not become important inland from those coasts.

## Broad Themes in Social and Economic Change

The period from the last two or three centuries B.C. up to the fourth century A.D.—the Later Classical Age of Greater Eastern Africa—was, then, a time of great and varied change in social life as well as economy and material culture for almost all the peoples of East and southeastern Africa. Food production in one form or another spread to the farthest corners of southern and eastern Africa. Populations grew both because of their increasing reliance on cultivation or livestock raising and because of the movements into East and southeastern Africa and all across southeastern Africa of large numbers of people new to those regions. For the most part these incoming settlers were of Kaskazi Bantu background in East Africa proper and of Kusi Bantu origin in the areas farther south.

The Kaskazi and Kusi communities brought in with them new ideas of social organization and belief as well as a developed agricultural way of life, and their arrival often precipitated major transformations in both society and economy. Where they introduced agriculture for the first time, their cultural values and practices tended quickly to become the dominant elements in the reconfigurations of society that their arrival set in motion. Where other food-producing traditions were already present, as among Nilo-Saharan and Cushitic peoples in central and northern East Africa and also apparently among the Khoisan of central and western South Africa, the non-Bantu societies often remained the most prominent actors until long after the fourth century, and the contributions of such societies to the values and practices to later Bantu societies were often substantial and salient.

But change and development came not only through the encounter of peoples of different cultural and historical background. The very fact of resettling far away from their earlier areas of habitation altered the internal dynamics of the Kaskazi and Kusi societies, and commonly led to shifts in the distribution of authority and in the kin configurations within those societies. Changes in technology may have had repercussions for the access to power in certain regions, as possibly among the Lakes communities of the second half of the last millennium B.C. And the challenge of coping with new environments especially reshaped culture and economy among those communities that spread into eastern East Africa and south into southeastern Africa.

The Later Classical Age provided the setting also for the wider diffusion of a variety of new technological knowledge and practice westward from the eastern side of the continent. Ironworking in the centuries around the turn of the era spread rapidly across the southern savanna belt from Kusi-speaking communities, along with a complex of new tool types having iron rather than stone blades, notably among them the iron hoe. Over the same rough time period, knowledge of grain and other new seed crops, coming from Mashariki Bantu in eastern Africa, began to be added to the agricultural repertoire of the Central- and Western-Savanna-Bantu societies. Cattle, too, began to gain a scattered presence across the more southerly parts of the western savanna as the early centuries A.D. proceeded.

It is a history the intricacies of which still have barely begun to be revealed.

# Notes

[1] D. Schoenbrun, personal communication, November 1994.

[2] Contra the explanation of Guthrie 1967–72, 3:123.

[3] Ehret 1971, appendices B.2–4, cites a few of these loanwords.

[4] Lewis-Williams 1981, 1982, and elsewhere.

[5] Ehret 1971, appendix B.3.

[6] See evidence in Kubik 1964.

[7] Ehret 1984.

[8] Ehret 1984, 1988.

[9] Ehret 1995/96.

[10] P. Robertshaw, personal communication, July 1994.

[11] Ehret 1988.

[12] Ehret 1995/96.

[13] For a fuller exposition, see Ehret 1995/96.

[14] McMaster 1988.

[15] Ehret 1995/96.

[16] Child 1991.

[17] Ehret 1995/96.
[18] Ehret 1995/96.
[19] Papstein 1978.
[20] Contra Ehret 1973b, this root is of uncertain origin. In recent centuries it has been reapplied in a number of Zambian and southern Zairean languages to maize.
[21] The reconstructed meaning "small seeds" in Guthrie 1967–72 and Ehret 1974a accounts less satisfactorily for its particular meanings in the different Mashariki languages.
[22] See Papstein 1978 for this grouping.
[23] Also see Schoenbrun 1990.
[24] This word consists of the Lamba prefix *iki- added to *-n-, the Bantu 9/10 class prefix of animal nouns, plus the stem, i.e., *iki-n-ka "thing-of-cattle."
[25] Ehret 1982c.
[26] These ideas are taken from Casson 1989, a new and up-to-date translation and annotation of the *Periplus Maris Erythraei*.
[27] Casson 1989.
[28] Casson's 1989 annotated translation of the *Periplus* seems to have settled the matter of the dating of that document. His reassessment, using the most up-to-date evidence for the dating of individuals and events mentioned at various points in the *Periplus*, makes a convincing case that it indeed dates to the mid-first century A.D., and that finding is accepted here.
[29] Casson 1989.
[30] Ehret 1974b.
[31] Ehret, Kreike, et al., in preparation.
[32] Ehret, Kreike, et al., in preparation.
[33] Vansina 1990.
[34] Ehret 1988. An alternative idea, that certain kinds of bananas spread to the Congo Basin via the Ethiopian highlands regions, has been broached in de Langhe, Swennen, and Vuylsteke 1994–95 and elsewhere. But this view seems improbable on the face of it because it requires a long-distance carrying of banana raising 2,000 years ago across several hundred kilometers of lands in which bananas are unknown and where the climate is not suitable for them.
[35] Schoenbrun 1993a.
[36] The language evidence appears to accord with this conclusion. The immediate source of this root word in the Bantu languages was most probably the language of the early Indonesian immigrants. In modern-day Malagasy the word is *akuhu*, from proto-Malagasy *akuku. If this word had been adopted into Malagasy from a Bantu language, its normal outcome, as the evidence of other early Kaskazi loanwords in Malagasy shows, today should have been *ankuhu. In contrast, the early Kaskazi communities, such as the Northeast-Coastal people, would regularly have added their class prefix *(i)n- of animal names to a proto-

283

Malagasy loan form *akuku, converting it into the well-attested shape *(i)nkuku (the original initial vowel *a- would have been dropped as a regular part of this process).

[37] Jones 1971.

[38] Nicolas 1957.

# 9. An Appreciation

## Integrative Themes, 1000 B.C. to A.D. 400

The Classical Age of Greater Eastern Africa encompassed an entire reshaping of the culture and demography of a fifth of Africa. Its economic repercussions spread wider, to perhaps half the continent. Its events entwined with two major developments of contemporary global history, the emergence of the iron age and the spread of the Commercial Revolution; and the cultural foundations laid down in that Classical Age continued to be built upon for the next fifteen hundred years.

Recreating the cultural and economic worlds of the eastern and southeastern Africans between 1000 B.C. and the fourth century A.D. imparts a range of historical lessons, some well understood in theory by the practitioners of Clio's craft but not always applied, and others perhaps a bit more novel. These lessons warn against holding to unilinear expectations of the course of change, against reading modern-day teleologies into the past, and against assuming that the construction of history is coterminous with the availability of written documentation. They point to the importance of environment, both cultural and natural, in channeling the directions people take in playing out their histories. They raise global issues of interpretation and causation in history. And they show that African history moved not along separate, obscure byways, but on paths very like and often integrally linked to the recognized courses of world history. By offering a range of perspectives from which to contemplate cause and effect over the long term, the patterns of change and development that took form in the Eastern and Southern African Classical Age raise important issues for historical practice.

### The Economic Geography of Cultural Expansion

For one thing, the economy and the habits and practices of material culture that people take with them into a new historical situation tend greatly to mold the options that they and their cultural heirs will take up in the future. From the very beginning of the Classical Age,

285

in the African Great Lakes region, the consequences of this tendency were visible.

The seed agricultural economies of the Central Sudanians, Sog, and Rub societies drew them to natural savanna and grassland environments. In such lands their livestock and their crops of sorghum and other tropical African grains could thrive. The Central Sudanians by c. 1000 B.C. had spread their territories southward along and around the Western Rift zone, as far south as the Kivu Basin and possibly the northern end of Lake Tanganyika, attracted there by the natural grasslands of the Rift Valley floors and probably also making use of the forest fringe areas on each side of the Rift. The Sog society, it appears, had expanded south into areas to the immediate east of the Rift, possibly into parts of the savanna zone around the Katonga River. The Rub communities had established themselves in the savannas of northeastern Uganda and, by 1000 B.C., may already have begun to extend their settlements southward along the east side of Lake Nyanza. We do have some weak archeological confirmation in the sites of the Oltome culture for this locating of the Rub people, but finding sites inhabited by the Central Sudanians and the Sog remains an important task for future archeological investigation.

To the east of the Nyanza Basin, their economies driven by an emphasis on cattle raising, the Southern Cushitic peoples even more consistently had chosen open savanna and highland grasslands for their settlements. In the early last millennium B.C., Southern Cushitic communities occupied areas of steppe and dry savanna in what is today lowland eastern Kenya, the lands all along the Eastern Rift Valley of today's central Kenya, and the wide grassy plains of north-central Tanzania. One Cushitic people, the Tale, spread themselves westward during these centuries, across the Mara plains, toward the southern parts of Lake Nyanza, while another society, the Iringa Southern Cushites, soon were to expand southward through the dry, open savannas of central Tanzania and into the southern highlands of that country.

When the Southern Nilotes, another of the early Eastern Sahelian peoples of Eastern Africa, pressed southward from Sudan into Kenya in the first half of the millennium, they too moved into lands more easily converted to their type of economy. As cultivators of grains and major raisers of livestock, they found their niches in western Kenya, at the edges of the montane forests above the Eastern Rift Valley, where they lived as neighbors of the Southern Cushites of the valley floor, and also to the west of the Rift, in the high, cold moorlands above 2,600 meters.

In consequence, the more forested parts of Eastern Africa remained largely untouched by farming settlement until after 1000 B.C. The same was true of the many regions of woodland savanna, especially in Tanzania, where tsetse-flies, the carriers of cattle sleeping-sickness, abounded. Moreover, the population densities of farming peoples and their domestic animals were still relatively low in these eras, and by no means had all the areas naturally well suited to grain agriculture or to cattle raising yet been given over to such pursuits. An economic imperative to clear heavy forest for fields, or to cut back tsetse-harboring woodlands to create more grazing for livestock, did not yet exist. The forests of highland northern East Africa and of the coastal hinterland, and the woodland savannas of western and southern East Africa—and these constituted the majority of the land—remained largely in the possession of very low density gatherer-hunter populations.

For the Mashariki Bantu, entering the Great Lakes region from the west in the early last millennium B.C., this distribution of peoples and economies offered new opportunities for expansion. The large zone of montane forest along both sides of the Western Rift from the Kivu Basin southward, and the warmer tropical forest and woodlands extending from Rwanda to the western shores of Lake Nyanza, lay open to their settlement. Mashariki culture and economy, after all, had taken shape in the savanna–rainforest ecotone areas of the southern Congo Basin. To the Mashariki peoples, the forests of the Great Lakes region were an environment eminently suited to their kinds of productivity. They had the tools, the cultural and customary expectations and expertise, and the crops to make highly effective use of that kind of environment, and they lacked any reliance on cattle keeping that might have made them avoid wooded areas. Above all, they faced no well established, competing farmer societies in those environments, but only much less numerous gatherer-hunters, who in all probability had never felt the need for the kinds of wider cooperation that clan institutions and clan chiefship gave to the Mashariki.

The key point, then, is that new expansions of peoples tend in the first place to go to areas that suit the existing orientations of their material culture. It is an insight reemphasized in the events of the Later Classical Age. When Kaskazi and Kusi communities scattered out across the eastern side of Africa late in the last millennium B.C., they tended to settle initially, even with their changed repertory of agricultural knowledge, in areas of higher rainfall with forested or wooded terrain. Relatively few of the Kaskazi and Kusi settled before the fourth century in the drier arable lands where yams could not be grown.

## The Advantages of Food Production over Food Collection

There is a second interpretive lesson lurking here also, and not a new one—that farmers normally hold a sharp advantage over gathcrer-hunters in the competition for land. But what does this advantage actually consist of?

On one level, it is a productive advantage. Cultivators and herders, once they have a well developed food-producing system, possess a technology that yields a higher volume of food in the same amount of land, and they protect their plants and animals from competitors and predators so as to maximize the growth and reproduction of their food sources.

At the point of contact between farmer and gatherer, this productive advantage translates, however, into one of demographics. Food producers, with their edge in subsistence productivity, can and do support larger local communities than food collectors are able to. Each local gathering and hunting band tends to be sharply smaller in population than the local social and residential unit, the village or collection of homesteads, of its farming or herding neighbors. If and when conflict arises, the advantage in numbers distinctly and recurrently favors the food producers. It was this edge that allowed the Mashariki of the Early Classical Age to establish themselves in forest areas of the western Great Lakes region, where only sparse gatherer-hunter populations had existed before. The same edge allowed the relatively rapid expansion in the Later Classical Age of the Kaskazi across central and southern East Africa and of the Kusi across southeastern Africa.

Despite this kind of advantage, once in a while in history a gatherer-hunter community has adopted animals or crops from nearby food producers quickly enough that they have been able to gain the advantages of food production and themselves begin to expand more widely. The notable case in the history of the Classical Age is that of the Khoikhoi of Southern Africa. The forebears of the Khoikhoi in the early last millennium B.C. had been gatherer-hunters, like all the other speakers of Khoisan languages in that era. Living in the northern or northeastern Kalahari region, they apparently came into contact between 500 and 200 B.C. with a far southern outlier of the Eastern Sahelian populations known farther north at that time in western East Africa. Who exactly these people were and how the contacts came about remain as yet unknown. But the upshot was the adoption by the Khoikhoi of the keeping of sheep and cows, supplemented by the older hunting and gathering pursuits.

Strongly pastoral people, as the Khoikhoi now became, have often to deal with an additional kind of population pressure—from their livestock. Domestic grazing animals have far shorter generation lengths than their keepers, because they reproduce as early as their second year of life. If milking is a more important source of food than the butchering of livestock, as came to be the case among the Khoikhoi, then the herds tend fairly rapidly to grow and, as they grow, require more and more grazing land. As a result, in at least the early stages of a shift to extensive raising of livestock, their human owners embark on relatively rapid expansions into new territories. And this is exactly the kind of history we can see for the early Khoikhoi, who had expanded as far south as the eastern Cape region of modern-day South Africa by the first century A.D. From there they spread westward to the Cape of Good Hope within another two to three centuries. A probably equally rapid spread of livestock raising carried the Kwadi, a related Khoisan people, westward across the northern Kalahari as far the what is today northern Namibia and far southwestern Angola.

After A.D. 400, a longer-term pattern of slower population growth set in among these peoples and their animals. But that is a story that remains to be explored by historians and archeologists and, in any case, belongs to a later time than the tale we tell here.

## Cultural Attitudes and Population Growth

The demographic developments of the Classical Age suggest a third lesson, again not new to historians, but in need of further exploration in its African dimensions—that differences in cultural attitudes have long-term consequences for demographic history. The prevailing trends of ethnic shift from the Later Classical Age onward suggest that Mashariki populations grew not just faster than those of gatherer-hunter groups, but also faster than those of their farming and herding neighbors. The tendency, apparent in the last century or two in many parts of Greater Eastern Africa, for Mashariki peoples to have higher birth rates than Nilotes or Cushites in particular may thus reflect differences in beliefs or cultural practices that extend far back into the past.

One can hardly base any strong explanations on something as yet so vaguely glimpsed. Still, it may be worth mentioning a couple of ideas broached by other commentators. One of these is the proposal that ancestor veneration tends to create a felt need to have descendants who will tend to one's spirit after one has died. Distinctly different from the other religious systems of the Classical Age of Eastern and Southern Africa, Mashariki religion did indeed focus on the ancestors, and the religion of Mashariki peoples continued widely down to the twentieth century to hold to this pattern of belief.

This causative link was proposed, however, as an explanation of male begetting behavior in the generally patrifocal later twentieth century. Whether it makes sense to track it back in time to the matrilineal and often matrifocal Mashariki societies of 2,500 years ago is another matter. As Christine Ahmed, among others, has pointed out, matrilineal societies tend to be especially open to the recruitment of new members and so are often able to expand into a new area and to grow rapidly by incorporating the previous inhabitants.¹ Was such a tendency at work in the early Mashariki expansions? We will leave this vexing issue to others to ponder, and move on to a fourth historical lesson.

## Cultural Encounter as the Mother of Invention

This fourth point of wider import—and it is an idea perhaps not always recognized by historians—is that, more often than not, the heartland areas of new cultural gestalts in history have been regions of cultural *confluence*. Rather than places in which whole suites of key inventions were initiated, they tend to have been regions where different cultural currents flowed together and were reconfigured into a new whole. The flowering of Islamic culture, from the eighth to the eleventh centuries took place, one can propose, principally because Islam brought into being a new cultural synthesis in a part of the world that was home to several strongly held, conflicting worldviews. That part of the globe, moreover, lay at the intersection of all the main routes of long-distance commerce, along which spread new ideas and new things from the distant ends of the Eastern Hemisphere—from as far east as China and as far west and south as the savannas of West Africa. Similarly, the Western Europeans of the fifteenth to eighteenth centuries, it can be argued, moved from prescientific to scientific thinking less because of things indigenous to their part of the earth and much more because of having to grapple with the flood of new information uniquely and rapidly unleashed upon them by their own commercial expansion around the world. Cultural encounter, we might say, is the mother of most invention.

For the African Great Lakes region, the last thousand years B.C. were such a time in history. A multiple confluence of different cultural traditions took place, involving Central Sudanian, Sog, Rub, Southern Cushitic, and the early Mashariki peoples, as well as many gatherer-hunter communities, of whose role we know as yet almost nothing. New developments in tool technology, above all ironworking, spread across the region. New kinds of furnishings were widely adopted. Sharply different ideas about the layout of the household and the village or neighborhood, different kinds of house construction, different religious systems, different social and political institutions, and different repertories of crops and domestic animals characterized the various farming societies. All these ingredients fed the vigorous cultural ferment of the formative centuries of the Classical Age.

The Mashariki Bantu became gradually the focal peoples in this overall reconfiguration of culture. They did contribute some significant new elements of technology of their own into the emerging cultural mix. These included the making of barkcloth, beekeeping, allowed by their invention of a particular kind of beehive, and possibly the making of sewn plank boats. But they also adopted new kinds of wooden wares—deep bowls, stools, and beds—as well as other household items from Rub or Sog peoples and from Southern Cushites; and, most noteworthy of all, they took up ironworking under the conjoined influence of the Central Sudanian and Sog or Rub societies.

Ultimately, however, the growing importance of Mashariki peoples over the course of the last millennium B.C. probably owed little to such developments and nearly everything to their unique historical role as the founders of a new synthesis, combining the planting agriculture of their forebears with the Sudanic seed agriculture of their Great Lakes neighbors. With this new potential for adaptation to different environments in place, the Kaskazi and Kusi descendants of the early Mashariki were able to scatter out across the eastern side of Africa during the Later Classical Age, from the third century B.C. to the fourth century A.D., eventually reshaping culture and livelihood all across that vast sweep of regions.

## The Indigenous Context of Invention

But cultural encounter by itself only spreads information and the possibility of acquiring particular things. The specific cultural and historical circumstances of the encounter shape the uses then made of new ideas and things and determine what is accepted and what ignored. And that brings us to our fifth historical thesis—that although the stimulus for innovation can be external in origin, innovation itself is indigenous. It emerges because the key things or ideas passed from one culture to another resonate in some different way with the felt needs or cultural expressions of the people who adopt them. These people then reformulate the meaning and use of such adoptions in accord with their cultural perceptions and expectations.

Sesame, to cite an example from another time and place, was domesticated before 3000 B.C. in the sudan regions of Africa, probably for its leaves, which were used as cooked greens. When this crop spread outside of Africa, it was viewed in a different light, as a source of grain and of oil made from its grains. The first invention, the domestication of sesame in sub-Saharan Africa enhanced the availability of one's own existing green vegetable. The second invention, outside of Africa, of using sesame as a cooking oil source, came from viewing someone else's innovation in the light of a quite different cultural experience with seeds and oils.

Or we might consider the history of explosives. Explosive powder was first made in China, where its principal use was for fireworks; its functions were celebratory and for show. But when Europeans be-

came acquainted with it, something in their cultural perspective high-
lighted for them its potential as a propellent for the projectiles of war.
Out of that different perspective came the invention of guns and all
the historical consequences that have flowed from that invention.

In the case of the Classical Age of Greater Eastern Africa, the
Mashariki of the middle of the last millennium B.C. incorporated
many things into their culture that originated outside of the Mashariki
tradition. But these things became historically significant because of
the meanings and roles later Mashariki societies gave to them. Grain
crops, for instance, would at first have been something known but
rarely raised by these communities. They were somebody else's invention; they fit a different mode of manipulating nature for food.
But the particular historical experience of the Mashariki over the middle centuries of the last thousand years B.C.—of having gradually
created more open land by clearing forest and of eventually beginning to encroach on drier areas—would have made grain crops a progressively more attractive supplement to the diet. And so by stages
the Mashariki farmers created a new kind of productive adaptability,
not always acted upon in the short run, but crucial in explaining the
longer-term success of the Mashariki expansions.

## The Complexity of Cause in History

This assessment leads us toward a sixth lesson, by now a historian's commonplace—that monocausal explanations always fall short
of making adequate sense of historical change. Because of the great
gaps in our knowledge of early African history, single great causes
have long been tempting to scholars who have studied the periods we
are considering here.

G. P. Murdock almost forty years ago credited "the Bantu Expansion" (more on that inappropriate phrase in a moment) to the
adoption of the banana.[2] But as we have learned, this crop of Southeast Asian origin did not become established anywhere in Africa until
very late in the Classical Age, distinctly after the Kaskazi and Kusi
peoples had begun to scatter across Eastern and southeastern Africa.
The adoption of certain kinds of more intensive banana raising did
indeed have fundamental importance in increasing agricultural productivity and, in some instances, in providing an economic under-
girding for state formation, as David Schoenbrun argues took place in
the last 700–800 years along the northern and western shores of Lake
Nyanza.[3] Jan Vansina has proposed similar consequences for the banana in the social history of the Congo Basin during the second half
of the first millennium A.D. and the early second millennium.[4] But in
these historians' works, banana cultivation is properly understood as
having become an element of key importance not in and of itself, but

292

because of its fit within the overall configuration of other historical factors.

Another monocausal explanation has attributed "the Bantu Expansion" to the mastery by Bantu peoples of ironworking, and this formulation has been far more durable in the scholarly literature than the banana theory.[5] But it equally needs explicit refutation.

The adoption of ironworking did create the part-time occupational specializations of smelter and blacksmith wherever it took place, and that is an important element to consider in reconstructing the early social history of Eastern and southeastern Africa. It appears possible also that in one area, among Lakes Bantu communities living in Bukoba to the immediate southwest of Lake Nyanza, the control of ironworking on a moderately large scale may have contributed to the formation of early, very small states as much as 2,000 years ago. Parenthetically, ironworking in that area apparently led as well, by the fourth or fifth century A.D., to severe environmental degradation, such that Bukoba lost much of its population and did not become as well inhabited again until almost the middle of the second millennium.[6]

On the whole, however, the diffusion of ironworking across Eastern and southeastern Africa was simply an accompanying development of the settlement of Kaskazi and Kusi communities in those regions and not at all a fundamental reshaper of the directions of culture history. This technological spread happens in the Later Classical Age to have been largely, although not entirely, coincident in time with the spread of Bantu-speaking communities. In the Early Classical Age, in contrast, iron metallurgy formed one cultural cross-current in a multicultural mix of influences in the African Great Lakes region. It came into being earliest among non-Bantu communities, who did not thereafter take off on vast cultural expansions of their own. It passed from them to the Kaskazi communities of the early Mashariki Bantu and subsequently diffused from them to their Kusi sister communities, at times that by all appearances were not specifically coincident with the beginnings of expansions by either grouping of people. No more than for the separate Middle Eastern invention of ironworking can the development of iron metallurgy in Eastern Africa be seen to have caused and sustained population movements in and of itself.

## The Event That Never Was

Mention of the short phrase "Bantu Expansion" brings to our attention a seventh lesson of history, specifically African in scope. It has been clear for a long time that the modern-day presence of Bantu languages across most of the southern 40 percent of Africa was not accomplished by anything remotely characterizable as "a single ongoing development."[7] But unfortunately that image continues to color the conceptions of many who write or teach African history.

The preeminence of Bantu languages over so vast a collection of territories arose over a 5,000-year period and reflects the combined outcomes of a great variety of differing regional histories. The earliest speakers of Bantu languages spread at first, in a number of successive stages, gradually and progressively across several parts of the African equatorial rainforest. These initial steps in the demographic growth of Bantu speech communities, dating to the fourth and third millennia B.C., coincided with the southward spread of the West African planting tradition into the western Congo Basin, lands previously inhabited entirely by gatherer-hunters.[8]

Sometime in the second millennium B.C., one group of these early Bantu, by then residing at the southern edge of the rainforest, began a subsequent spread eastward, probably along the route of the Sankuru River. Their farthest eastern outliers at the close of the millennium were the proto-Mashariki communities, whose settlements would by that time have begun to verge on the western edges of the great Western Rift.[9] The subsequent involvement of the cultural heirs of the proto-Mashariki in the events of the Classical Age of Eastern and Southern Africa has formed the warp and sometimes the woof of the story we have woven here. In all this history, the only set of developments that at all resembles the common image of "the Bantu Expansion" was the spreading out of Kaskazi and Kusi communities around the turn of the era across many parts of Eastern and southeastern Africa. Even those events probably took four to five centuries to unfold.

To sum up, there was no single, sudden, vast "Bantu Expansion." There was instead a long and complex history of the spread of agriculture southward and eastward across the continent. A wider and wider establishment of Bantu languages and of many of the cultural traditions of Niger-Congo civilization accompanied this economic history. The Classical Age of Eastern and Southern Africa forms one chapter, although a major one, in that long tale.

## The Way Things Were: A Closing Overview

The key themes of Eastern African history in its Classical Age did not necessarily unfold gradually. Not uncommonly, they surfaced episodically. The most notable examples lie in the sphere of agriculture. Cultivating and herding economies had come by the fourth century A.D. to predominate across most of Greater Eastern Africa; yet developments toward that situation had proceeded by stages irregularly spaced in time and place. First, agriculture had become more varied in the Great Lakes region with the arrival of the Mashariki communities in the early last millennium B.C. But variety did not mean that more complex syntheses of the different cultivating livelihoods began immediately to evolve. Rather, centuries passed before environmental pressures and population growth begat a new major, rapid agricultural changeover and, in the process, triggered off the scattering out of Bantu communities, with a new agriculture synthesis, all across Greater Eastern Africa.

In the meantime, during the middle of the last millennium B.C., new areas were brought much less spectacularly into use for cultivation and pasturage by a different immigrant settlement, that of the Southern Nilotes in the high, cold country of western Kenya. Other similarly less eye-catching episodes of expansion, dating to around mid-millennium—of Tale Southern Cushites westward around the south of Lake Nyanza and, somewhat later, of Iringa Cushites into the Southern Highlands of Tanzania, and also, we believe of Eastern Sahelians into the Corridor Region between Lake Nyasa and Lake Tanganyika—planted the older East African agripastoral traditions in several distinct new regions. The most distant consequence, and the least understood as yet, was the spread of livestock raising alone to Khoisan peoples living south of the middle Zambezi River by perhaps the fourth or third century B.C., with the subsequent farther spread south of that economy to the southernmost part of the continent by the close of the millennium.

The expectation that a society will tend to become more complex as time passes is another piety belied by the experience of Eastern Africans. Southern Cushites, for instance, for untold centuries apparently maintained, with little change, a particular system of clans with hereditary clan heads. Not some kind of inherent conservatism, but the lack of any serious challenge to the workability of this system allowed it to persevere. Southern Cushitic communities, until late in the last millennium B.C., stood, after all, at the forefront of the spread of food-producing economies in central East Africa, with only independent, numerically much smaller gatherer-hunter bands competing for the same land. Even more telling, the Kaskazi and Kusi communities typically decreased the complexity of their kin and authority structures during the very period of their most striking territorial expansion and demographic growth, from the last couple of centuries B.C. up to the third or fourth century A.D. The small size of their settlement groups, the regrouping of people of different clan and lineage backgrounds in new areas, and the distance of their separation from the cultural modalities of their places of origin—all these probably contributed to a social and political downsizing.

An intriguing issue of historical causation raised by this kind of downsizing is the significance of population density in the emergence of social stratification and political complexity. This topic has drawn considerable attention from theorists in the social sciences,[10] but has not greatly engaged the interest of historians. State formations characteristically tended to later emergence in Africa as a whole and in Eastern Africa in particular than in several other parts of the world, and African societies of the Classical Age of Greater Eastern Africa showed, at most, minimal levels of stratification. Only in Egypt and in Nubia did states and strongly marked class formation appear in Africa before the later last millennium B.C.

Why was this so? What distinguished the rest of Africa from Egypt and Nubia and from the ancient Middle East, where early states also arose, and made tropical Africa more like western Europe, where states were similarly late in appearing? The key element, it can be proposed, was that each of the African agricultural traditions initially took hold across an area that comprised just a small portion of the lands readily adaptable to its crops. Enormous areas of the continent lay potentially open to the spread of each kind of agriculture. The uneven decline of the African climatic optimum in the 3,500 years after 6000 B.C. set in motion a retreat of rainforest and an expansion of all kinds of savanna that only further increased the amount of land suitable for the sub–Saharan Africa agricultural traditions. The early African farmers and herders had so much more country into which they could expand their ways of life that thousands of years were to pass in most parts of the continent before their populations would attain densities sufficient to provide material support for states or to engender the scale of competition for scarce resources that could generate social stratification.

Egypt and Nubia encountered these conditions much earlier, in the fourth and third millennia B.C., because of their opposite environmental dilemma during the fading centuries of the climatic optimum. The arable and water-containing soils for their agriculture more and more came to be restricted to the bottomlands along the Nile River, while everywhere else around them lay an increasingly arid desert. Population pressures thus rose rapidly and dramatically, especially in Egypt, even before 3000 B.C. The interspersing of arable lands with desert similarly helped just as early to create areas of notably greater population concentration in the Middle East.

Eastern African history in the centuries around the turn of the era provides a mini-evocation of this causal connection between population density and the direction of social and political developments. As Kaskazi and Kusi peoples scattered out in that era across the immense reaches of East and southeastern Africa, their settlement densities would initially have been very low indeed, much lower than in the western Great Lakes region from which their expansions stemmed. Less complex reckoning of kinship and less complex and often reformulated types of chiefship then appeared among them in most areas where they settled. Not until later centuries, by which time their population densities would have considerably increased, did larger chiefdoms and eventually, in the second millennium A.D., kingdoms evolve in such places. In contrast, as early as the late last millennium B.C. for the areas west of Lake Nyanza, where population densities were probably greater than in any other part of Eastern Africa at that time, there is reason to think that chiefdoms or even tiny protokingdoms may already have begun to develop (see chapter 5).

There is good cause to argue, in other words, that the emergence of more complex social and political structures everywhere in world history has been contingent, in some ill-defined way, on a growth in population density. As population pressure increases, one might propose, the incidence of competition and conflict over the available resources will likely increase as well. Those who hold already culturally recognized roles of authority in society can then use the sanctions and social influence attaching to their positions to establish socially accepted rules for unequal access to resources. In the process, they consolidate new kinds of political and social roles for themselves in a new, layered social order.

Last, but not least, the history of Eastern and southeastern Africans in the last millennium B.C. and first three centuries A.D. bears a lively relevance for the world history of those times. Their agricultural development, different in its particulars, paralleled in its broad outcomes the growth in agricultural complexity and diversity elsewhere in the world. In technology Eastern Africans were major participants in the propagation of ironworking, a development of wide consequence in the Eastern Hemisphere of the last millennium B.C., and the heirs apparently of an independently invented African ironworking tradition. And although peripheral to all but one of the main lanes of commerce, Eastern Africans, some directly and most of them indirectly, nevertheless partook of developments grounded in the Commercial Revolution.

The story our sources allow us to recover is social history truly. Its ecos is the society and the community. Its natural intervals are those of the *longue durée*. The colorful individuals, the movers and shakers, the individual lives illustrative of their times: these do not emerge into view. The story itself is only a first reading of the resources that language and archeology offer on the Classical Age of Greater Eastern Africa, and its plot and its action will surely be greatly revised and reshaped as our knowledge and our critical and methodological skills evolve. But for all that, a beginning has been made, sometimes detailed and complex in its revelations, toward restoring the early Eastern and Southern African past to the domain of history.

# Notes

[1] C. Ahmed 1995.
[2] G. P. Murdock 1959.
[3] D. L. Schoenbrun forthcoming.
[4] J. Vansina 1990.
[5] C. W. Wrigley 1960; R. Oliver 1966, among others. That this explanation is still current among some scholars was brought home to the writer by the responses to a paper he gave at an African archeology conference earlier in this decade.
[4] D. L. Schoenbrun 1990.
[7] C. Ehret 1982b, p. 63.
[8] K. Klieman 1997
[9] See chapter 2 above.
[10] Most notably for Africa, Stevenson 1968.

# Appendix A
## Adjunct Tables of Evidence

### Table 2A.  Natural environment of the early Mashariki society

| | |
|---|---|
| \*-t̪ìt̪ù "forest" | Proto-Bantu (PB) |
| \*-sàká "wild area" | Very early Bantu (< \*-sàk- "to hunt by chasing/driving animals," i.e., area given over to hunting rather than cultivation [secondary forest?]) |
| \*-súbí "flat, grassy area in forest" | Central and eastern rainforest languages; isolated relict retention in Mashariki, specifically in Ganda of the Lakes group; < PB \*-túbí |
| \*-to "gallery forest" (?) | Scattered Savanna and Mashariki (Ndembu *itu* "river jungle"; Luban "thicket"; Kaskazi: NE-Coastal subgroup of Kati: "river") |
| \*-kanga "wilderness (?)" | Savanna and Mashariki (Kongo "wilderness"; Nyiha "steppe"; Yao "thicket"; etc.) |
| \*-ìkà "savanna" | Proto-Mashariki (PM) |
| \*-bándá "flat grassy plain" | PM: Kaskazi (Shambaa "meadow"; Sabaki "plain"; Thagiicu "valley, grassland; plain"; Ruvu "river valley"; Nyiha "plain of Lake Rukwa rift"); Botatwe "plain"); < PB "valley" |
| \*-bila "wild area, uncultivated land" | PM: Kaskazi (Lakes "forest"); Kusi (Tsonga "treeless space") |
| \*-bùgà "sparsely wooded plain" (open savanna) | Kati (Swahili "steppe"; Gogo "large grassy plain"; etc.); Lakes (Jita "plain"; Nyoro "desert") |
| \*-tondo "thicket" | Tumbuka; Shona |
| \*-lala "grassland" or "steppe" | Kusi: Sotho ("plain"); also Nyiha of Kaskazi ("steppe"), spoken adjacent north edge of Kusi regions |

### Table 3A.  Wild animals diagnostic of environment

| | |
|---|---|
| \*-gùlùbè "bushpig" | C.Sav.; W.Sav. (SW-Bantu); Sabi; general Mashariki |
| \*-mbúí "spotted hyena" | Kaskazi: Gogo; Tumbuka *cimbwe* (\*-mbúé); C.Sav.: Luban; W.Sav. |
| \*-pít̪ì "(striped?) hyena" | W.Sav. (SW-Bantu); wide Kaskazi; relict occurrence in Kusi |
| \*-gùè "leopard" | From PB \*-gòyì by vowel assimilation: \*-goi > \*-goe > \*-gwe (represented as \*-gue); pronunciation \*-gòyì reappears isolated in Luyia (Lakes group of Mashariki) and in Rungwe (as \*-gòyè) |

299

| | |
|---|---|
| *-songa "bushbuck (?)" | Scattered, relict occurrence: Kaskazi: Yao "lone bull bushbuck"; W.Sav.: Luvale |
| *-pala "kind of gazelle (?)" | C.Sav.; W.Sav.: Ndembu, Herero, etc.; Sabi; wide Mashariki occurrence |
| *-súbi̧ "serval cat" | W.Sav. (SW-Bantu); Kaskazi (see table 6A.f) |
| *-sékú̧ or *-sè pu̧ "eland" | W.Sav.; C.Sav.; Botatwe; Kaskazi (Yao) |
| *-pókù̧ "eland" | PM: Kaskazi: Kati; Kusi: Shona, SE-Bantu |
| *-pembele "black (?) rhinoceros" | PM: Kaskazi: Takama (Ilamba, Rimi), Rungwe, Matengo "rhinoceros"; Kusi: proto-Nyasa "rhinoceros," Shona, Tsonga "black rhinoceros"; also overlap into Botatwe, Luyana, Lujazi (W.Sav.) "rhinoceros" |
| *-kula, *-ku̧la "white rhinoceros" | PM: Kaskazi: Lakes *-kula "rhinoceros"; Kusi: Shona *-ku̧la "white rhinoceros" |
| *-tù̧gà "giraffe" | PM: general Kaskazi *-tù̧gà; Kusi: Shona *twiza* (< *-tù̧jà < *-tù̧gà) |
| *-gi̧lì "warthog" | PM: general Kaskazi and Kusi; also spread to Luyana of W.Sav. |
| *-si̧umba "lion" | PM: general Kaskazi *-si̧mba; Kusi: Shona *šumba*; also Botatwe *-syumbwa |
| *-pókù̧ "eland" | PM: Kaskazi: Kati; Kusi: Shona, SE-Bantu |
| *-pundu̧(i) "male eland" | PM: Kaskazi: Rufiji-Ruvuma "eland"; areal west-central Tanzania (Gogo, Ilamba, Kimbu, Hehe) "hartebeest"; Kusi: Shona *hundzvi* "bull eland"; also spread to C.Sav.: Kaonde *mpundu* "bull eland" (loan < unidentified source) |
| *-kongoni "sp. large antelope" | PM: Kaskazi: NE-Coastal "hartebeest"; Kusi: Ndau, Venda, Tsonga "wildebeest" |
| *-kulo "waterbuck" | PM: Kaskazi; Kati group; Kusi: Shona; also overlap into Botatwe; also in Lamba (Sabi) |
| *-jóbé "situtunga, marshbuck" | PM: Kaskazi: Lakes "situtunga; marshbuck"; Kati "donkey"; also Botatwe "situtunga" (replaced earlier Bantu root *-bú̧li̧, seen in W.Sav., Kongo, Bobangi, etc.) |
| *-kulungu "bushbuck" | PM: Kaskazi: NE-Coastal subgroup; also outside Mashariki: Sabi (Malungu); C.Sav. (Kaonde) |
| *-bàbàlá "female bushbuck" | PM: Kaskazi: Kati (Swahili, Mijikenda "female bushbuck"; Langi, Ruvu "bushbuck"); general Kusi "bushbuck"; also overlap in Lamba (Sabi) |
| *-palapala "sable antelope" | PM: general Kusi; Kaskazi: Kati group |
| *-gulu(ngu)lu "klipspringer" | PM: Kaskazi: Kati group, Langi *-gulungulu; Kusi: Shona, Sotho, Tsonga *-gululu |
| *-seti̧ "small antelope" (of savanna?) | PM: Kaskazi: Kati group (Giryama *tsesi* "kind of antelope"; Lugulu *sesi* "gazelle"); Kusi (Chopi *tsetsi* "klipspringer") |
| *-sese "duiker sp." | PM: Kaskazi: Shambaa "Silvacapra sp."; outside Mashariki: Botatwe (Tonga) "steinbuck" |

300

| | |
|---|---|
| *-púàlù "rhinoceros" | Relict occurrence (Rundi *kifaru*, Itakho *ɛfúàlǫ̀*, Lugulu *cifwaru*, Swahili *kifaru*, etc.) |
| *-kondį "hartebeest" | PM: Kaskazi: Lakes, Upland, Langi groups, overlap into Sabi, Botatwe groups |
| *-kòlóngò "roan antelope" | Lakes, Kati groups |
| *-tembo "elephant" | Kati, Rufiji-Ruvuma groups |
| *-pélà "rhinoceros" | Kati group, Yao (Rufiji-Ruvuma), Langi; Kati loan in Chaga-Dabida; see also table 7A |
| *-tomondo "hippopotamus" | Kati, Rufiji-Ruvuma groups |
| *-punda "zebra" | Rufiji-Ruvuma group, some Kati |
| *-tandala "greater kudu" | Kati, Rufiji-Ruvuma groups |
| *-jàgí "zebra" | Late Southern-Nyanza areal: Langi; Upland; East-Nyanza |
| *-umbu "wildebeest" | Kati group; with areal spread to Nyanja of Kusi; also Botatwe; overlap into Lamba of Sabi |
| *-bugį "wild dog" | Kati group |
| *-suuji "wild dog" | Luyia, East-Nyanza (see table 33A) |
| *-juui "wild dog" | Upland (see table 33A) |
| *-kųno "red duiker" | Restricted northeastern areal: NE-Coastal, Thagiicu subgroup of Upland group |
| *-bijį "zebra" | General Kusi (Sotho *pitsi* < *-bijį); overlap into Lamba of Sabi group |
| *-pumpi "wild dog" (Lycaon pictus) | Nyasa (Tumbuka); Shona; also Botatwe; overlap into Kaonde (C.Sav.) |
| *-kolo "kind of monkey" | Nyasa; Shona; Makua; overlap into some C.Sav. and Sabi (table 5A) |
| *-pogu(e) "ostrich" | Shona *-pou; SE-Bantu (Sotho, Venda *-pue; Chopi *mɓuu*); also Botatwe *-po(wa) |

## Table 4A. Central Sudanic loanwords in proto-Mashariki

| | |
|---|---|
| *-óngò "bile" (loan to Luba-Kasai?) | CSud: proto–Central Sudanic (PCS) *ɔngɔ "bile" |
| *-gaga "crust, hard covering layer" | CSud: PCS *ga or *ɠa "crust, shell"; *gaga or ɠaɠa "to form crust" |
| *-ŋaaŋa "ibis" | CSud: ECS *ŋa(ŋa) |
| *-tiiti "sp. warbler" | CSud: Lugbara *tritriá* "sp. warbler" (stem *tritri plus CSud *-a diminuative suffix) |
| *-kùmbì "locust" | CSud: Moru-Madi (MM) *(k)ɔmbi (PCS .*mbi) |
| *-pú "sorghum" | CSud: PCS *pu "whole (?) grain" |
| *-pà, *-papa "gruel" | CSud: root *pa- seen in PCS *pai "flour" (*pa- + *-i CSud noun suff. of uncertain meaning) |

301

*-kῠlῠ, *-kῠlu          CSud: PCS *kuru(ku) "kind of calabash" (or alternative
"calabash container"        source: Eastern Sahelian *kʰul "kind of gourd"?)

*-lùmbù "Plectranthus      CSud: MM: Lugbara *lombo* "yam" (< *lòmbò)
esculenta (?)"

*-sᵢabe "edible tuber"    CSud: Yulu *saβa* "wild yam"

*-òndò, *-ùndò            CSud: PCS *(ɔ)ndɔ "to hammer"
"smith's hammer"
(loan diffusion
west to Atlantic)

## Table 5A.  Eastern Sahelian loanwords in proto-Mashariki

*-tòpè "mud"             ESah: Nilotic: Jyang *tiop* "mud" (<*topi; < proto-North
                           Sudanic *t'ɔp' or *tɔp' "to spill, become wet")

*-toolo "bog,            ESah: Nilotic: Bari *tor* "swamp" (also borrowed from Bari
muddy place"               into Madi of Central Sudanic; PNS *ƭ'ɔd or *ƭ'ɔ:d "to
                           flow"; *not* from Rub because PNS *ƭ' > Rub *ts or *c)

*-tòb- "to hit"          ESah: (and PNS) *tʰò:ɓ or *ƭò:ɓ "to strike" (not from Rub: Ik
(also in Sabi)             Ik *tòɓ-* "to (throw) spear")

*-bàk- "to be lit"       ESah (and PNS) *ɓak' "to shine"

*-àyò "sole" (also       ESah *à:'y "palm" (PNS "limb joint")
in C.Sav. group)

*-bèlé "grain sp."       ESah *bel or *ɓel "grain" (Western Nilotic "sorghum")
(> SW-Bantu; also
loan in West Luba)

*-kᵢmà "porridge"        ESah: proto-Nilotic *kim- "porridge" (Southern Nilotic
(also spread across        *kim-; Eastern Nilotic *-kíma "sp. grain": not as yet
western savanna)           known outside Nilotic)

*-púpù "flour (?)"       ESah *p'op'o "flour" (not < Rub because PNS *p' > Rub *ɓ)
Itakho "thin gruel";       PNS *p' > Rub *ɓ)
Sotho "flour")

*-tém- "to cut (vegeta-  ESah (and Sahelian) *ƭem "to cut"
tion)" (also spread to
Sabi, C, Sav., and
Lwena of W.Sav.)

*-tùlì "mortar"          ESah (and Sahelian) *túr "to pound (with tool)" (not Nilo-
                           tic: PNS *t > Nil *d)

*-bágá "livestock        ESah *ba:ɠ "to enclose with a fence" (PNS "to cover, en-
pen"; *-bágò              close") (so far known in ESah from Western Nilotic
"fence"                   *ba:k; but *not* < Western Nilotic because of different
                           sound shift history)

*-teba, *-tiba           ESah *tē:b "to stand, stay, dwell, sit" (PNS "to rise")
"animal pen"              (second-order credibility because it requires noun deriva-
                           tion: "to dwell" > "dwelling place, homestead" > "animal
                           pen": not Nilotic because PNS *t > Nil *d)

# Appendix A: Adjunct Tables

*-bolụ "dewlap" — ESah: Kir *bɔ :l "throat" (Surma: Kwegu bɔ́:lủ "neck"; Nilotic *bɔ :lbɔ :l [Jumjum "neck"; Eastern Nilotic "dewlap"]); not < Nilotic because of distinct morphology; also as ESah loanword in Lugbara (MM) kobolo "dewlap"); for another borrowing of this root see Table 32A

*-golụ "dewlap" — ESah (and Northern Sudanic) *ŋgɔɗ "throat" (possible Rub source because PNS *ŋg > Rub *g /#_VC, C = [-cont]; not < Nilotic or Surma because PNS *ŋg > Surma, Nil *ŋ in all environments)

*-sílè, *-sele, *-seli "fresh milk" — ESah: Kir: Nyimang sil "fresh" (PNS *ṣíl "to be wet")

*-tụba "wooden bowl" — ESah (and Sahelian) *ʈ up or *ʈ ub or *ʈ uɓ "wooden bowl" (> Kir *-tuba)

*-gèlà "iron" (for distribution, see Ehret Ehret 1995/96) — ESah: Rub: Soo kerat , pl. kere "iron" (as with *-gali "porridge," Bantu *g for attested /k/ suggests original Nilo-Saharan tense *k)

*-lìlì "sleeping place" (> "bed" in areal northern Kaskazi; as "bed" spread across southern savanna) — ESah *lil "to become unconscious, fall asleep" (so far known in ESah only from Southern Nilotic; pre-ESah meaning "to not be [present]")

*-solo "unmarried male" (Chaga; Zalamo "large chick"; Xhosa "widower") — ESah: Rub *sore "boy, youth" (Northern Sudanic *ṣò:r "light, slight" [of person]; Rub *-ore# > *-oro#, as in *-Boro, table 33A)

## Table 6A.  Central Sudanic loanwords in Kaskazi

*-inie "liver" (Sabaki *-ini; Lakes: Haya ine , Luyia *-ini, etc.; Nyakyusa inie ; spread to Botatwe as *-ini) — CSud: PCS root *-ɲe "liver" or "spleen"

*-gaala "striped rat" — CSud: extended root *-ngala- seen in Lugbara ongalaka "striped rat" (plus *-ka, Moru-Madi suffix of animal names)

*-kebe, *ki-be "jackal" (2nd shape: *ke- reanalyzed as Bantu class prefix *ki-; spread to Tumbuka of Kusi as "dog") — CSud: MM *gbɛ "jackal" (with CSud 'movable' *k-prefix)

*-(ì)gì , *-ùgì "gruel" — CSud: MM *-ègì "porridge" (< PCS *ǥi "sorghum")

*-(u)nụ́ "mortar" (Guthrie 1967-72 gives *-nụ́; also spread across western savanna) — CSud: root *-nú seen in Mangbetu ne-kúnú "anvil" (CSud *k- prefix plus -V- to maintain syllable structure, plus stem)

303

*-(u)lo "digging stick" CSud: PCS *ɔɗo "to cultivate"
*-kolo "small calabash" CSud: PCS *k-ɔɗɔ "drinking calabash"
(?) *-pio "herd" CSud: PCS *pi "to become much/many" (very weak case: stem plus presumed PCS *-o noun suffix and meaning shift, thus of third-order credibility)
*-èlé "knife" (Rungwe "arrow"); CSud: MM *élé "knife" (< PCS *lé "large blade")
 for western savanna loan
 spread, see Ehret 1995a)
*-òmbò "wooden vessel, CSud: MM *-ɔngbɔ "canoe" (<PCS *ngbɔ "board,
 boat" (also Nyasa group) log")
*-ibo "large basket" (W. CSud: MM *evo "basket"
 Nyanza; Rungwe; also in
 Tumbuka of Nyasa group)
*-ɲa "uncooked gruel" CSud: PCS *aɲa "grain (generic)"
*-titu "black" CSud: Balendru *titi* "black" (< PCS *ti "dark")
*-ba "enclosed yard of house" CSud: PCS *ɓa "homestead"
 (also spread to Botatwe)
*-kapu, *-kapo "basket" CSud: Mangbetu *ne-kokpwo* "basket"
*-àɲàú "large spotted CSud: Lugbara *anyaó* (< PCS *aɲaó "large, danger-
 carnivore; hyena" ous carnivore; the spotted hyena")
*-lu(i), *-lu(e) "lion (?)" CSud: PCS *ɖo "large, dangerous wild animal"
*-kumbi "hoe" CSud: Mangbetu *ne-kombi* "ax" (< PCS *mbi "point")

Langi ǫdo "red sorghum" CSud: Lugbara *ɗö* "finger millet" (see section e
 (*-do) preceding for separate borrowing of same root)
Langi *mbirǫ* "iron ore" (<*-bʉlu) CSud: Beli *ɓolo* "iron"

## Table 7A. Eastern Sahelian loanwords in Kaskazi

*-ŋwali "crested crane" ESah: Nilotic: Maasai ɔ-ŋɔ́ɔ́l "crested crane" (Maasai
 (Yao variant: *-ŋwala) form is itself a loan from unidentified Nilo-Saharan language)
*-saale, *-saale "thorn ESah *sar or *θar "thorn fence" (Rub: Soo *saa* "cattle
 fence" (Ilamba "vil- pen" < *sara; Nubian: Diling *šal* "Gehöft"; SNil
 age; Chaga "a hedge *saRmạ "calf-pen"); see tables 31A, 36A for other
 plant") borrowings of the same root word
*-pìlú "thin straight ESah (and PNS) *pʰil "small stick" (not Nilotic, where it
 stick" (Kamba, Jita names a digging stick)
 "wooden-pointed
 arrow"; Nyamwezi
 "porridge stirrer")
*-tele, *-tili "prepared ESah *ʈér "dough" (Kir: Surma: Murle *tɛlɛ* "porridge";
 grain (W-Ny. "type Temein *ʈɛrɛ* "beer"; also Gaam *tér* "flour paste"

of flour"; Ilamba
"porridge"; Gogo
"stiff porridge")

*-pélà "rhinoceros"
(loan from Kati into
Chaga-Dabida of Up-
land; *p <*b by Dahl's
law)

ESah (Saharo-Sahelian) *obiɗ "rhinoceros"; from language in which *ɗ > *d or *r; not Rub, where *ɗ > *'j;
gbara *óbbíro* is ESah loanword

*-gàlì "porridge" (in
Lakes: only in Ha;
also in some Sabi
dialects)

ESah *kal or *kʰal "cooked grain" (PNS tense *k, but not
*kʰ, would yield *g seen in Bantu shape; see also
*-gèlà root; not Nilotic or Rub because PNS *k > Nilo-
tic and Rub *k, not *g, as seen in Western Nilotic *kal
"finger millet")

*-tapo "iron ore" (also in
Nyanja of Kusi: spread
to some Sabi dialects)

ESah *tʰap' "bare earth" (PNS "dust, dirt, rubbish"): not
< Rub because PNS *p' > Rub *ɓ )

*-kòló "sheep"

ESah: Rub *kol "goat-wether"; earlier Sahelian *kʰ-weḷ
"ram"; here with same prefix as in Rub, but with a different direction of meaning shift, "ram" > "sheep"

*-pelele "(tree?) hyrax"
(Kati loan in Chaga
of Upland; *p > *b by
Dahl's law as in
"rhinoceros" above)

Not attested in available ESah data; appears in CSud:
Moru-Madi (Lugbara *òbìlàkà*) "hyrax": stem *-bila-;
stem structure implies word was borrowed into Moru-
Madi from ESah language (see table 38A for another
borrowing of this root)

*-sakata "monitor
lizard" (Yao)

ESah: Rub: Soo *saɠat* "monitor lizard" (earlier Rub
*sak'at-)

*-belele "sheep" (also
spread through
Malawi across south-
ern Zambia)

ESah *bil "goat" (for *bil > *bel-, *-pel- in this loanword set, see "rhinoceros" and "hyrax" above) (see
also table 39A)

*-pùlà "nose"

Cf. ESah (and PNS) *pʰur "to blow"?

*-tų́mbí "egg" (also in
Thagiicu of Upland)

Source unknown, but has typical Bantu phonological
structure

*-tápik- "to vomit"

From PB *-táp- "to draw water"; replaced PB *-lúk- "to
vomit"

*-tomondo
"hippopotamus"

Cf. ESah (and Northern Sudanic) *t'ɔm "female elephant"?

*-súbì "leopard"

From SavB *-súbì "small wild feline (serval cat?)": progressive vowel assimilation)

*-sábi "witchcraft"

From PB *-sáb- "to be hot" (Schoenbrun 1990)

305

# Appendix A: Adjunct Tables

## Table 8A. Eastern Sahelian and Central Sudanic loanwords in proto-Lakes and its daughter dialects

### a. Eastern Sahelian loanwords in proto-Lakes —

| | |
|---|---|
| *-sela, *-sala "porridge" | ESah: Kir: Daju *seR- "porridge" |
| *-ka "cattle; cow" (Western Lakes; Suguti); "home" (Mara subgroup, Ganda) (spread to Lamba as *ici-n-ka* "cattlepen") | ESah (and Sahelian) *ka: or *ka:h "cattle-camp" (Songay) or "homestead" (Kalen-jin); note that PNS tense *k > k; see also section c below) |
| *-te "cow, head of cattle" | ESah (and Sahelian) *ʈɛ "cow" (not from Central Sudanic because East CSud *ti "cow" would yield Lakes *-ti) |
| *-gono "vessel (wooden?)" (Rundi "pot"; Bukusu "kind of basket") | ESah *kon or *kʰon "(calabash?) container" (Nilotic: Acholi ɔkɔnɔ "edible gourd"; Rub (Nyang'i *kon* "wooden plate") |
| *-tébè "stool" (also spread to contiguous languages of adjacent central savanna) | ESah: *tē:b "to stay, dwell, sit" (see table 5A for the borrowing of a differ ent derivative of this root word) |

### b. Eastern Sahelian loanwords in West-Nyanza —

| | |
|---|---|
| *-gele "foot, sole" | ESah: proto-Kir innovation *k'é:ḷ "foot" (< earlier ESah meaning "extremity, end or edge of anything") |
| (Rutara) *-lip- "to swim" | ESah (and PNS) *lip or *lib or *liɓ "to become wet" |
| (Rutara) *-ho "fog" (< earlier *-po) | ESah (and PNS, but not known in Central Sudanic) *pʰɔ́ "ooze, become liquid" |
| *-sili "cultivated field" | ESah: Rub: Soo *sed* "cultivated field" |
| *-sole "puppy" | ESah: Rub *sore "boy, youth" (see other borrowings of this root in table 5A and following, in section c) |

### c. Eastern Sahelian loanwords in Western-Lakes —

| | |
|---|---|
| (W'n Lakes) *-shuli "young bull" | ESah: Rub *sore "boy, youth" (section b above and table 5A have other borrowings of this root) |

### d. Central Sudanic loanwords in proto-Lakes —

| | |
|---|---|
| *-senyi, *-senyu "sand" | CSud: MM *tsenyi/a "sand" (PCS *tse) |
| *-SuSu(e) "shrew" | CSud: Lugbara dzödzö "shrew" (< *jojo or *dzodzo) |
| *-lo "finger millet" (also in Temi of Upland) | CSud: Lugbara ɗö "finger millet" (<*ɗo) |

306

# Appendix A: Adjunct Tables

*-le "finger millet" (Itakho; also in Ma-lungu, Bemba of Sabi) — CSud: PCS *re "seed" (for parallel semantic derivation in another Central Sudanic loanword, see *-ku "finger millet" in table 48)

## e. Central Sudanic loanwords in West-Nyanza —

*-pu "hide, skin" — CSud: ECS *po "to skin, peel" (PCS *po "to tear off")

*-ambi "arrow" — CSud: PCS *Vmbi "point"

*kameu "hare" (Nyoro akame, Ganda akamyu) — CSud: PCS *komeo "hare" (Moru komo; Bagirmi 'ome)

*-nya "lizard" — CSud: root *-ɲa seen in MM *ma-ɲa "monitor lizard"

*-nju "gruel" — CSud: PCS *nʒu "to ooze" (e.g., Kresh "thick (liquid)"; but of second order credibility and thus a weak case)

## f. Central Sudanic loanwords in Western-Lakes —

(Forest) *-(h)un(y)u "nail, claw" — CSud: PCS *ɔɲɔ "nail, claw"

(Forest) *-shushu, *-shushi "fat" — CSud: ECS *θo "fat" (Balendruθu )

## g. Central Sudanic loanwords in proto-Luyia —

*-ŋeŋe "mosquito" — CSud: Madi nyenye "mosquito" (<*ŋeŋe)

*-jo "large cooking pot" — CSud: PCS *dzo or *jo "pot"

## Table 9A. Southern Cushitic loanwords in proto-Lakes and its daughter dialects

### a. Southern Cushitic loanwords in proto-Lakes —

*-kịa "neck" — SCush: Ma'a kiʔa "chest"

*-gina "stone" (Gungu "egg") — SCush: proto-Southern Cushitic (PSC) *gen- "slope"

*-sagama "blood" — SCush: PSC *sak'- "blood" (plus PSC *m noun suffix; see also table 2B.a)

*-tale "lion" — SCush: PSC *taal- "lion"

*-sama, *-suma "waterbuck" — SCush: Gorowa tsaʔumo "waterbuck" (<proto-Rift (PR) *tsaʔ- "sp. large antelope")

*-punu "bushpig" (< *-bunu by Dahl's law) — SCush: West Rift *bayn- "bushpig" (*ay < PSC *ʌ > Lakes *u /[labial]_

*-kaapụ "cattle; cow" — SCush: PR *kaʔafu "gateway of homestead/cattle pen"

307

# Appendix A: Adjunct Tables

## b. Southern Cushitic loanwords in Western-Lakes —

| | |
|---|---|
| *-masa "bull or cow that has not produced young" | SCush: Kw'adza *mahasiko* "ox" (PSC *mah- "to be sterile" plus PR *-Vs- agent noun suf-fix: *mahas-; *-iko is masculine suffix, added by Kw'adza) |
| *-saato "animal skin" | SCush: root of PR *c'at- "hide tether" |

## c. Southern Cushitic loanwords in West-Nyanza —

| | |
|---|---|
| *-anda "coals" (also in Luyia, presumably as loan to West-Nyanza) | SCush: PSC *ʔant- "to cook" |
| *-baala "flying termite" | SCush: Kw'adza *paʔaliko* "flying termite" (< PSC *p'aara "termite") |
| (Rutara) *-jasi "Colobus monkey" | SCush: PSC *wasi "black and white collored" (Dahalo "Colobus monkey") |
| (Nyoro) *kibaara* "tsetse-fly" | SCush: West Rift *baʔar- "fly" |
| *-tago "skin bag" | SCush: West Rift *tlaqʷ- "skin bag" (< *tlakʷ'-) |

## d. Southern Cushitic loanwords in Western-Lakes —

| | |
|---|---|
| (West Highlands) *-satsi "hair" (*-satị) | SCush: PR *ts'at- "hair" (< PSC *t'at-) |
| (Rundi) *ngerengere* "gazelle" | SCush: Burunge *geraʔi* "Grant's gazelle" |

## Table 10A. Southern Nilotic loanwords common to Luyia, East-Nyanza, and Upland

| | |
|---|---|
| *-tịtịɲo "heel" | SNil: proto–Southern Nilotic (PSN) *titiɲ "heel" |
| *-moolị "calf" | SNil: PSN *mɔ:R "calf" |
| *-keese "sheep" | SNil: PSN *ke:c "sheep" (see commentary in text) |
| *-tịgili, *-tịkili, *-tịgilị "donkey" | SNil: Datoga *dige:da* "donkey" (< PSN *tikeR) |
| *-koolo "black-and-white" (cow) | SNil: Datoga *-qo:l* "black-and-white" (cow) |
| *-samo "gray-apotted" (cow) | SNil: Kalenjin *samɔ "gray-spotted (?)" (uncertain cattle coloration) |
| *mụụma "oath" | SNil: Kalenjin *mu:ma "oath" |

# Appendix A: Adjunct Tables

## Table 16A.  Early Bantu food production terms

### a. Proto-Bantu terms

| | |
|---|---|
| *-kùá "yam" | proto-Bantu (PB; early Niger-Congo word) |
| *-pàmá "yam" | PB (AC zones; C.Sav. [Kanyok, etc.]; Botatwe; relict Mashariki distribution: Kaskazi [Lakes; Yao]; Kusi [Sn Nyasa]) |
| *-kúndè "black-eyed peas (?)" | PB |
| *-bono "castor-bean" | PB |
| *-jùgú "Voandzeia groundnut" | PB |
| *-súpá "bottle gourd" | PB; this meaning does occur in relict Mashariki instances (e.g., in Langi), contra Vansina 1990: 289 |
| *-bílà "oil palm" | PB (early Niger-Congo root word) |
| *-bá "oil palm" | Kongo, some of rainforest languages |
| *-gàlí "oil palm nut" | Savanna Bantu (W.Sav., C.Sav.; relict in Western-Lakes, Mwika groups of Mashariki) |
| *-làgù̀ "palm wine" | PB (Duala, Kongo, and, indirectly, Bobangi and Luba, among others, attest this shape; secondary shape *-lògù̀, is usually viewed as the PB form, but best understood as shift < *-làgù̀ via regressive rounding assimilation; found in Western-Savanna (W.Sav.) languages, Lega, W.Luba and cluster of B zone languages) |
| *-kángà "guineafowl" | PB |
| *-búlì̀ "goat" | PB (early Niger-Congo) |
| *-boko "he-goat" | Bobangi, Mongo, Kongo; Mashariki: Kusi (Nyasa; SE-Bantu [Venda, Sotho "bull"]; loan in Xhosa *bhokwe* "he-goat") |

### b. Savanna-Bantu terms

| | |
|---|---|
| *-lungu "yam" | Central-Savanna (C.Sav.): Luban; W.Sav.: Lunda; Mashariki: Seuta of Kati group |
| *-lèngè "pumpkin" (alternate shape *-lèngi) | Kongo; relict Mashariki distribution: Kaskazi (Upland; Njombe; NE-Coastal group of Kati group: as "bottle gourd"; also spread to Mongo-Kuba fringe of C zone |
| *-lògù̀ "palm wine" (by irregular sound shift < PB *-làgù̀) | (See section a above) |
| *-samba "young female kid" | W.Sav. (Ndembu); relict Mashariki (Langi; Seuta of NE-Coastal) |
| *-jamba "guineafowl cock, he-goat (?)" | W.Sav. (Ndembu "ram"; relict Mashariki distribution (Upland: Thagiicu "cock") |
| *-kómbò "guineafowl cock, he-goat (?)" | W.Sav. "goat" (areal: SW-Bantu, Ovimbundu also spread to Kongo); Botatwe "cock" |

309

*c. Additional terms of the earliest proto-Mashariki period*

*-siabe "edible tuber"   Relict Mashariki distribution (Ganda *ekisebè* ); Botatwe:
                          Tonga *musyaabe* "edible tuber"); see table 4A
*-lagị "kind of yam"     Relict Mashariki distribution: Kaskazi (Sabaki "yam"; also
                          "sweet potato"; Langi "sweet potato"); Kusi (Nyasa "yam")
*-lumbu "Plectranthus    Widely scattered Kaskazi (Ganda "kind of yam"; Takama
   esculentus (?)"         group "sweet potato"; Seuta group of Kati "taro"); Botatwe
                          *-lumbue "medicinal tuber")
*-úngù "gourd plant"     Relict Mashariki distribution: Kaskazi (Lakes, Upland, Rufi-
                          ji-Ruvuma); Kusi (Nyasa); overlap into Luban, Sabi groups,
                          and Luyana
*-sikisi "oil palm"      Relict Mashariki distribution (Kaskazi: Swahili; Kusi: Nyasa
                          subgroup)
*-pòngó "he-goat"        Kusi: Nyasa ("male animal"), SE-Bantu; relict Kaskazi: NE-
                          Coastal, Chaga, Langi "jackass"; Njombe "he-goat";
                          Botatwe; also overlap into Nkoya, Luyana

### Table 19A. Early Mashariki woven goods

*a. proto-Bantu and other pre-proto-Mashariki terms*

*-pìnd- "to plait"       proto-Bantu (PB) and proto-Mashariki (PM)
*-tùngá "basket"         PB and PM
   (of bamboo?)
*-túndù "large, tall     PB; PM: Kaskazi (Seuta, Ruvu of Kati, also Yao); Kusi
   basket"                 (Tumbuka, SE Bantu: Tsonga)
*-tètè "wicker           PB; PM (Nyasa group)
   hamper" (of palm
   or bamboo)
*-titi "small basket     relict distribution: W.Sav. (Southwest-Bantu "wooden
   dish" (of liana         plate"); Mashariki: Kaskazi (Seuta, Sabaki subgroups of
   fiber?)                 Kati; cf. also Upland: Thagiicu *-tịtị "liana-basket": loan
                          from Sabaki subgroup of Kati?)
*-kéká "palm mat"        PB
*-sásá "reed (?)         PB and PM
   mat; open-sided
   shelter" (originally
   with mat roof)

*b. Proto-Mashariki terms*

*-pe "flat basket"       PM: Kaskazi (Gusii, Rungwe); Kusi (Nyanja); spread to sever-
                          al contiguous Sabi languages in northeastern Zambia

*-pìndà "woven bast sack"   PM: Kaskazi (NE-Coastal; Takama; Luyia); Kusi (Nyanja)

*-tumba "woven sack" PM: Kaskazi (Sabaki; Lakes; Takama); Kusi (Nyanja; Makua); also occurs in some Sabi languages

*-làgò "reed mat"   PM: Kaskazi (Lakes, Kati); Kusi (Nguni); some Lakes as "reed (plant)"

## c. Kaskazi terms

*-tándà "reed sleeping mat"   Kaskazi (Kati: Sabaki "bed"; Nyiha "sleeping mat"); spread to Sabi (Malungu "reed sleeping mat." Lamba "sleeping hut")

*-ibo "large, open (?) basket"   Kaskazi (see table 6A)

*-sege/*-seke "basket" (probably palm)   Kaskazi: Kati group (Seuta, Ruvu); Lakes (Rundi); Rungwe group (Nyiha)

*-kapu, *-kapo "small basket"   Kaskazi: Kati group; also in Rundi of Lakes group (see table 6A)

*-ambị "large palm mat"   Kaskazi (Kati group; Yao)

## Table 20A. Early Mashariki containers

### a. Proto-Bantu and other pre-proto-Mashariki terms

*-búmb- "to make pot"   PB and PM

*-bìgá "pot"   PB and PM

*-(j)ùngú "cooking pot"   PB

*-gayenga "potsherd"   PB (Bobangi; Sabi: Lamba, etc.; Mashariki: Shona; Kati group in reduced shape *-gaye)

*-súpá "calabash"   PB and PM

### b. Proto-Mashariki terms

*-tụba "deep wooden bowl" PM (see table 5A)

*-kụlụ/*-kụlu "calabash"   PM (see table 4A)

*-beela "calabash shell or sherd"   PM: Kaskazi (Seuta, Njombe subgroups, Kati); Kusi (Tsonga; Nyanja "cowry shell")

### c. Kaskazi term

*-kolo "small calabash" Kaskazi (see table 6A)

# Appendix A: Adjunct Tables

## Table 21A. Early Mashariki garments

### a. Terms of Savanna-Bantu and Mashariki distribution

*-gùbò "leather garment (worn at the waist?)"  
Relict distribution: W.Sav. (Kwanyama); Mashariki: Kaskazi (Gogo; Temi); Kusi: Nyanja); from proto-Bantu *-gùbò "skin"

*-bàmb- "to peg out (hide)"  
Wide Savanna and Mashariki distribution

*-samba "leaf or grass skirt"  
Relict distribution: W.Sav. (Luvale); Sabi (Lamba); Mashariki: Kaskazi (Sukuma); Kusi (Xhosa) (< early Bantu *-samba "branch, twig, bunch of leaves")

### b. Proto-Mashariki terms

*-sani "barkcloth"  
Relict distribution: Kaskazi (Nyamwezi "barkcloth"); also in Botatwe (as "cloth")

*-beleko "baby-sling"  
Scattered distribution: Kaskazi (Seuta); Kusi (Nyanja, Shona, Xhosa); also spread to Nsenga of Sabi

*-sambi "girl's leaf apron"  
Relict distribution: Kaskazi (Sukuma); Kusi (Xhosa "initiate's palm-leaf apron")

### c. Terms of Kaskazi distribution

*-lolo "(leather?) apron" (girl's?)  
Relict distribution: Upland (Chaga: Mochi: Rufiji-Ruvuma: Yao)

*-limba "man's garment" (leather shawl?)  
Relict distribution: Upland (Gikuyu "elder's cape"); S'n Tanzania (Yao "waistcloth")

## Table 22A. Mashariki hunting and fishing vocabularies

### a. Terms of general Bantu distribution

*-bìng- "to hunt, chase"  
PB

*-sàk- "to hunt" (by driving animals)  
Scattered widely in Bantu (including some north Kaskazi in derived form *-sakat-; < PB *-sàk- "to seek")

*-tég- "to set trap"  
B zone (Guthrie) and general Savanna and Mashariki distribution

*-támbò "snare"  
PB; scattered all across Bantu field

*-tá "bow"  
PB

*-bànjí "arrow; mid- rib of palm"  
PB (A, B, and C zones; scattered alternate shape *-bànjá in A, B, H zones)

*-lób- "to fish with hook and line"  
PB

*-lóbò "fish-hook"  
PB

312

# Appendix A: Adjunct Tables

*-lừb- "to fish with a        C zone (Guthrie); scattered in Savanna and Mashariki; <
   fishbasket"                 PB *-lừb- "to dip"

*b. Terms of Savanna-Bantu and Mashariki distribution*

*-bind- "to hunt"            Scattered Savanna and Mashariki (Luban *kibinda "hunt-
                              er"; Sabaki subgroup of Kati *-bind(i)- "to hunt")
*-líbá "falling trap"        General Savanna and Mashariki
*-gụ́í "arrow"                W.Sav.; wide Mashariki (innovation replacing PB
                              *-bànjí )
*-gomba "kind of arrow"      Relict Savanna and Mashariki
   (barbed?)

*c. Terms of Mashariki provenance*

*-tulo "arrowshaft"          PM (Kaskazi: Nyamwezi *kitulo* "blunt bird arrow"; Zigula
                              *ntulu* "arrowshaft"; Kusi: Xhosa *utulu* "arrow, arrow-
                              shaft"); PB *-túl- "to pierce")
*-pongolo "quiver"           PM (Kusi: Nguni; Kaskazi: Takama)
*-tíngà "tendon              PM (general Kusi; relict Kaskazi distri bution); < PB
   bowstring"                 "vein, tendon"?

*d. Words of Kaskazi distribution*

*-gònò "fish trap"           Wide Kaskazi distribution; also in Botatwe also found in
                              some Luban languages (loanword in Luba-Kasai)
*-ábụ̀ "(hunting) net"        Wide Kaskazi; loanword in Nyasa of Kusi
*-sààlé "arrow"              General Kaskazi; also Makua of Kusi
*-bànò "arrowshaft"          General Kaskazi; also Nyasa of Kusi
*-gayị "tendon bowstring"    Northern Kaskazi
*-lás- "to shoot arrow"      General Kaskazi; also in Nyasa of Kusi
*-pìnd- "to pull bow"        Underlies various Kati, Rujiji-Ruvuma nouns for "bow"
                              (earlier Bantu *-pìnd- "to fold," hence "to bend bow")

*e. Words of Kusi distribution*

*-koka "kind of trap"        Kusi
*-sèbè "arrow"               Kusi (table 38A)

## Table 23A. Beekeeping vocabulary in early Mashariki Bantu

*a. Words of early Bantu provenance*

*-ókì/*-úkì "bee; honey"     PB

| | |
|---|---|
| *-tàná "(natural) beehive" | PB: C zone ("beehive"); W.Sav. (Ndem bu "honeycomb" with larvae"); Mashariki (Gusii "natural beehive") |
| *-saila "honeycomb" | W.Sav.; Mashariki Bantu |
| *-púlá "beeswax" | W.Sav.; C.Sav.; Sabi; Mashariki |

b. *Additional terms in early Mashariki*

| | |
|---|---|
| *-sa "honeycomb" | PM (Kaskazi: Swahili "beeswax"; Kusi: Nyasa group "honeycomb") |
| *-sapa "honeycomb" | PM (Kusi: Venda; Kaskazi: Yao) |
| *-kìndà "cell of honeycomb" | PM |
| *-ánà "bee larva" [sing. *li-ánà, pl.*ma-(li-)ánà] | PM (< PB *mw-ánà "child" but with different singular and plural prefixes) |

c. *Additional term of Kaskazi provenance*

| | |
|---|---|
| *-lìngà "barrel-shaped beehive" | Kaskazi: widespread (Lakes; Kati, Rufiji-Ruvuma, etc.); loanword spread to Nyasa group, also to Shona with shift of meaning to "honeycomb" |

## Table 24A. Developments in proto-Mashariki cultivation

a. *Words of proto-Mashariki distribution not in Ehret 1974a*

| | |
|---|---|
| *-pu, *-pu(e/a) "sorghum" | Relict Kaskazi distribution (Langi "white sorghum"; Suku-ma "maize"); Kusi (Shona *-pua, SE-Bantu *-pue "sweet sorghum"); also in Luyana as "white sorghum" (table 4A) |
| *-selo "winnowing tray" | Kaskazi: Kati relict distribution: Pokomo, Njombe; Kusi: Nyanja, Shona, SE-Bantu; < PM *-sél- "to winnow" |
| *-bùgà "threshing floor" | PEB: widespread Kaskazi; relict Kusi; < PB *-bùgà "open place" |
| *-tàngà "edible cucurbit" | PM: Kaskazi: Kati, Rufiji-Ruvuma "cucumber"; Kusi: Xhosa "cucumber"; also Botatwe "melon"; also spread to west-ern savanna areas (Lamba "melon"; Kwanyama "pump-kin"; etc.) |

b. *Words of Kaskazi distribution*

| | |
|---|---|
| *-pémbá "sorghum" | Widespread Kaskazi |
| *-gimbi "finger millet" (used for beer) | Upland group "finger millet"; Upland loanword in Sabaki subgroup of Kati as "finger millet"; Kati group: Njombe, Ruvu subgroups "beer" |
| *-legì "finger millet" | Southern-Kaskazi areal |
| *-lo "finger millet" | Northern Kaskazi areal: Lakes; Upland: Temi; also Langi |

# Appendix A: Adjunct Tables

|  |  |
|---|---|
|  | *-do (table 6A) |
| *-gàlì "porridge" | General Kaskazi; missing from Lakes |
| *-tele, *-tili "prepared grain" | Relict distribtuion: Lakes: West-Nyanza; Takama: Ilamba (see table 6A) |
| *-pùngò "winnowing tray" | Southern-Nyanza areal: SE-Nyanza group; NE-Coastal; Langi (loan?); from Savanna, Mashariki *-pùng- "to fan" |
| *-taalo "winnowing tray" | Relict northern Kaskazi: Lakes (Nyoro); Upland: Thagiicu: Meru) |
| *-sì- "to grind grain" | General Kaskazi; also Tumbuka of Kusi; source: reconstructed underlying PB *-tì- "to rub against," seen in a variety of extended shapes, with such meanings as "slip," "rub," wipe," etc. (see Guthrie 1967–72) |

### c. Words of Kusi distribution

|  |  |
|---|---|
| *-pila "sorghum" | Sn Nyasa; SE-Bantu (Tsonga, Chopi); also Botatwe; see table 38A |
| *-poko "finger millet" | Sn Nyasa (Tumbuka); Shona; SE-Bantu (Venda, Tsonga); see table 38A |

## Table 25A.  Bantu age-sets and circumcision

### a. Words of certain or probable proto-Bantu (PB) provenance

|  |  |
|---|---|
| *-kúlà "age set" | PB: found in far northwestern languages; W.Sav.: SW-Bantu; Mashariki: Kaskazi: Luyia; SE-Nyanza (Suguti: Kwaya, Jita, etc.) |
| *-tìb- "to circumcise" | Bobangi -tib-; Kaskazi: Langi itibu "circumcision camp"; Kusi: Xhosa ncibi "circumciser" (click by irregular sound shift caused by use of a jargon, called hlonipa, in secret or ritual situations among Xhosa and other Nguni) |

### b. Words of Savanna and Mashariki distribution

|  |  |
|---|---|
| *-alik- "to enter circumcision rites" | W.Sav. (Ndembu); Kaskazi (Mijikenda; Langi) |
| *-alam- "to engage in circumcision observances (of seclusion period)" | W.Sav.: Ndembu -alamish- "to circumcise"; Kaskazi: Shambaa -alam- ; Gogo -alam- "to be circumcised"; Gusii okwarama "seclusion period (after cir cumcision)" |
| *-nkunka "circumcision observances" | W.Sav.: Ndembu nkunka "seclusion hut"; Kaskazi: Gogo muŋhunga "circumcisor" |

315

## c. Words of Mashariki distribution

| | |
|---|---|
| *-lįįka "initiate, boy undergoing circumcision rites" | Kaskazi: Upland "age set"; Upland loanword in Sabaki, Seuta of NE-Coastal; Kusi: Sotho *modika(ni)* "initiate" |
| *-aluk- "to finish circumcision rites and leave seclusion" | Kaskazi: Gusii *-aroki-* "to circumcise"; Kusi: Xhosa *-aluk-* "to be circumcised" (root *-alik- above, with *-u- conversive infix) |

## d. Words of northern areal Kaskazi distribution

| | |
|---|---|
| *-taban- "to perform circumcision rites" (earlier sense "mark by cutting skin": cf. Gusii meaning) | Lakes *-tabani "lad"; Asu *-tavan-*, Tha giicu *-taan- "to circumcise"; Thagiicu, Langi *-tabana "circumcised young man"; Gusii *taban-* "to notch ears (of cattle)" |

## Table 31A. Eastern Sahelian (Rub) loanwords in proto-Upland

| | |
|---|---|
| *-Biu "entire(ly)" | ESah (and Saharo-Sahelian) *p'ì "alone" (PNS *p' > *ɓ in Rub; semantics: one piece, all one; stem plus PNS *-uh adj. suffix) |
| *-Turu- "to pierce" | ESah (and Saharo-Sahelian) *tʰul "to break open" |
| *-ceege "porcupine" (replaced in Chaga-Dabida by *-sasa) | ESah: Rub: Soo *yɛk* "porcupine" |
| *-cuui "wild dog" | ESah: Rub: Ik *tsoi* "wild dog" (< *tsoyi < proto-Rub *coy) |
| *-Boro "cattle pen" (Dabida; also loan in neighboring Saghala from Dabida) | ESah: Rub *ɓóréh "thorn cattle-pen" (proto-Sahelian *ɓórēh; note *-ore# > *-oro# both here and in *-solo, table 5A) |
| *-sara "hedge, thorn fence" (Chaga-Dabida only) | ESah *sar or *θar "thorn fence": Rub: pre-Soo *sara "cattle pen" (see table 35A and table 7A.d, for other other borrowings of this root) |

## Table 32A. Eastern Sahelian loanwords in Langi

| | |
|---|---|
| ntinyi "small black ant" | ESah: Rub: Ik *tinyiny* "black ant"; cf. also Kalenjin: Tuken *tinyi* "small black ant" |
| kęcoci "insect" | Rub *cuc "fly" |
| idoŋa "granary (hut)" (also in Gogo) | ESah: Daju *daŋ- "granary hut" (pre-Daju *doŋ-; < Saharo-Sahelian *doŋ "yard of residence," hence meaning shift in Daju to structure built in yard) |

| | |
|---|---|
| lǫfęre, pl. fęre "porridge stirrer" | ESah (and Sahelian) *pʰír "to spin, especially porridge stirrer or fire drill-stick" (< PNS "to spin") |
| mǫholo, pl. męholo "dewlap" | (See table 5A, "dewlap"; *-polo < original *-bolo by Dahl's law) |
| ǫbǫre "gray cow" | Cf. ESah (and PNS) *pùd "ashes" (PNS *p > Rub *b)? But very weak case. |

## Table 33A. Southern Nilotic and Eastern Sahelian (Rub) loanwords common to Luyia and East-Nyanza

### a. Southern Nilotic loanwords

| | |
|---|---|
| *-tiaaŋi "wild animal" (also isolated in Temi of Upland) | SNil: PSN *tiɔːɲ, pl. *tiɔːŋ "wild animal" |
| *-(h)iili "bull, ox" | SNil: PSN *(y)e:R "male of cattle" (PSN *y > *h here is a Datoga sound shift) |
| *-giluki, *-guluki "bull" | SNil: PSN *kiɾuk "bull" (but could be a W'n Rub loan belonging in table 33A; proto-Rub had *kiruk "bull" also) |
| *-sʉbiinɨ "young ewe or she-goat" | SNil: Kalenjin *supe:n "young ewe or she-goat" (Chaga-Dabida *-supeni is a separate borrowing in a later era) |
| *-suunu "barren animal" (also isolated in Temi of Upland) | SNil: Kalenjin *so:n "barren animal" |

### b. Rub loanwords

| | |
|---|---|
| (?) *-teŋe "elbow" or "back of knee" | ESah: phonology is Nilo-Saharan; but noun is not yet attested in available data |
| *-biiji "bushpig" (also spread to Ganda) | ESah: Nilotic: Ateker *-pege, *-pigi bushpig" (presumed borrowing of an as yet unattested Rub root: West Rub loans are numerous in Ateker) |
| *-suuji "wild dog" | ESah: Rub: Ik tsoi "wild dog" (< *tsoyi) |
| *-tuuju, *-tuuyu "hare" | ESah: *Toːɭo "hare" (> *to:yo, with Nilo-Saharan *ɭ > *y > Bantu *j as in *-suuji preceding; reflexes: Rub: Ik tulu; Nilotic: Lotuko-Maa *-tojo) |
| *-jaalia "tick bird" | ESah: Rub: Ik dzar ʻ "tick bird" (< proto-Rub *jar-) |
| *-bus- "to do second digging of field" | ESah: Rub: Soo bus̩ "to clear field" (proto-Rub *ɓǫs̩ "to clear, make bare") |

## Table 34A.1. Eastern Sahelian (Rub) loanwords in Luyia

### a. General or widely distributed in Luyia (proto-Luyia)

*-topi̧, *-tupi̧ "mud"  ESah: see separate borrowing of this root in table 5A

*-ŋeeni̧ "fish"  ESah (and PNS) *ŋɛyl̞ "to move (intr.) in a drifting, floating manner" (for other PNS *l̞ > *n in Southern Rub loans, see table 36A below)

*-jegeje "porcupine"  ESah: Rub: Soo *yek* "porcupine" (plus probably Nilo-Saharan *'y noun suffix: PNS *'y > Rub *'j; see table 31A for another borrowing of this root unsuffixed)

*-migu "ram"  ESah: Rub: Soo *mek* "ram" (< Sahelian *menk)

### b. North Luyia

*-bofu "big"  ESah (and PNS) *ɓòɓ "big" (Ik "to be deep")

*-gooso "rash"  ESah (and PNS) *Gwa:θ "to scratch" (body)

*-joogi "Goliath heron" (Bukusu [Buk.] *licooki* )  ESah: Rub: Soo *yukan*, pl. *yukut* "crested crane" (root *'yuk; for Soo /y/> Luyia *j, see "porcupine," in section a)

*-lemu "snake" (Buk. *endemu* )  ESah: Rub: Ik *idem* "snake" (< PNS *yid- "to bend" plus Nilo-Saharan *m n. suff.)

*-purupuru "butterfly" (Buk. *sipurupuru* )  ESah: Rub: Soo *purut* "butterfly" (root *pur-, reduplicated in its Luyia form)

*-ŋeeli̧ "big knife" (Buk. *liŋeesi* )  ESah (and PNS) *ŋer "to cut off"

*-jutu "very big calabash" (Buk. *licuru* )  ESah: Rub: Ik *ɗut* "very big calabash" (< Sahelian *ɗut "kind of calabash"; for Rub *ɗ > *j, see table 35A)

*-seeli̧ "half-calabash"  ESah: Rub: Soo *sed* "half-calabash"

### c. Western Luyia

*-bala "big"  ESah (and NSud) *ɓad "large, wide"

### d. South Luyia

*-kubuyu̧ "claw, nail" (< *-gubuyu̧ by Dahl's law)  ESah (and PNS) *gʷapʰ "to claw" plus PNS *'y noun suffix)

*-tija "honey-guide" (Itakho [It.] *intitsa* )  ESah: Rub: Ik *tsetsˮ* "honey-guide" (<earlier *tets- ?)

*-ŋaalo "a large frog" (It. *luŋaalo* )  ESah (and Northern Sudanic) *ŋa:r "to make deep sounds"

*-kole "he-goat"  ESah: Rub *kol "goat-wether"

*-koola "small hoe"   ESah: Rub *okol, seen in Soo *oklat,*, pl. *okol* "hoe"
*-oopo "drinking   ESah: Rub: Ik *k'ɔfɔ* "half-calabash" (*k' > ʔ or Ø)
calabash; calabash
spoon" (It. *xiooho* )

## Table 34A.2. Sample of Southern Cushitic loanwords in early Luyia

*-gòkè "ashes"   SCush: PSC *xȯx- "heat, fire"; not Rift SCush (PSC *xox-
(< *-koke by   > proto-Rift [PR] *xaʔ-); also PSC *xȯx- "to be lit"
Dahl's law)
*-gálí "big"   SCush: PSC *gád- "big"
*-tàlàŋì "lion"   SCush: PSC *tàal- "lioness" (plus SCush *-Vŋ- noun suff.)
*-sàsà(n)gè "spotted   SCush: PR *c'ak'- "spotted carnivore" (redup.)
carnivore"

## Table 35A. Eastern Sahelian (Rub) loanwords in East-Nyanza

*a. Proto-East-Nyanza*

*-salu "cloud"   ESah (and PNS) *ṣal "to rain"
*-gaini "bull"   ESah: Western Rub *ĝaił "ox, steer" (Heine 1976: *gɛł; for PNS
   *ł > *n in Bantu borrowings: table 36A.a)
*-taaŋana "ox"   ESah: Daju *taŋan- "bull" (Kir-Abbaian *tʰaŋ- "large ox")
*-korope "he-goat"   ESah: Rub *kɔrɔb "calf" (proposed semantics: earlier "small
   male domestic animal"?)
*-juuru "ewe-lamb"   ESah: Rub *ɗodo "sheep" (for Rub *ɗ > *j in Bantu borrowings,
   see also table 34A.1.b)

*b. proto-Mara*

*-sense "sand"   ESah (and PNS) *ʈ'ɛ̄:ṣ "sand" (PNS *T' > Rub *c', hence Bantu
   /s/)
*-tʉkia "hair"   ESah: Rub *tuk "feather"
*-tʉrʉrʉ "buttock"   ESah: *ʈu:l "to stoop, bend down (Maasai *ol-tuli* "buttocks") (<
   PNS *ʈu:l "to become low, bend down")
*-boto "cheek"   ESah: Rub: Ik *ob* "cheek" (< pre-proto-Rub *bò plus PNS *tʰ
   noun suffix, < PNS *bo "face")
*-sịrị "rope"   ESah (and PNS) *sî:l "strip"

*c. North Mara (Gusii-Kuria)*

*-ŋera "buffalo"   ESah (and Saharo-Sahelian) *aŋer "buffalo"

## d. Gusii (but not as far as is known in Kuria)

| | |
|---|---|
| *-sinini "small" | ESah (and Saharo-Sahelian) *ʈ,ʼiːn "small" (PNS *T' > *s) |
| ri-uga "bone" | ESah: Rub *ɔk "bone" (< PNS *kɔ́ or *ɔ́k; tense *k > *g, for which see also tables 5A, 7A, and 34A.1) |
| ege-tunwa "mountain" | ESah: Rub: Soo *tulan* , pl. *tuli* "mountain" (influenced by SNil *tulua "hill"); for PNS *ɭ > *n in Southern Rub loans, see other examples here and table 34A.1) |
| ege-sabo "branch, twig" | ESah (and PNS) *nɗa B or *nɗap "pole" (PNS *nɗ > /s/ only in Rub) |
| eke-ene "log" | ESah (and Saharo-Sahelian) *'yan "wood" |
| em-biri "warthog" | ESah: Rub: Soo *pitir*, pl. *pire* "warthog" (contracted shape seen in Soo pl. apparently was borrowed here) |
| ege-cuurɛ "oribi" (Kuria evidence is lacking as yet) | ESah: Rub: Soo *cuuli'* "dikdik" |
| eke-nyinyi, pl. ebi-nyinyi "leech" (Kuria word is lacking) | ESah: Rub *biɲiɲ "leech" (initial *bi- was treated as if it were the Gusii noun plural class prefix *ebi-; also Rub loan in SNil: Kalenjin *piɲiɲ) |
| ɛge-sarate "cattle pen" (Kuria evidence is lacking) | ESah: Rub: Soo *saa* "cattle pen" plust PNS *tʰ noun suffix; < earlier *sara: see table 7A.c) |
| ɛgɛ-tago "hoof" | ESah: Rub *tak'w "foot, leg" |
| obo-sugunya "bushy end of tail" | ESah: Rub *suk' "to scratch" (with semantic shift to "to wipe" and addition of PNS *ɲ suffix; hence, of second-order credibility; semantics: fly-whisk is made from bushy end of tail) |

## e. Suguti

| | |
|---|---|
| *-sirooro "urine" | ESah (and PNS) *ʂíl "to be wet" (plus PNS *r or *l noun suffix; hence, of second-order credibility) |
| (Kwaya) ritajo "hoof" | ESah: Rub *tak'w "foot, leg" (see section d preceding) |

## Table 36A. Southern Cushitic (Central Tale) and Eastern Sahelian loanwords in proto-Takama

### a. Words of proto-Takama provenance

| | |
|---|---|
| *-duulu "zebra" | SCush: Burunge *doro* "zebra" (< PSC *diiri "striped") |
| *-longi "black-tipped mongoose" | SCush: Alagwa *longaʔi* "civet cat" (root *long-) |
| *-gulyati "he-goat" | SCush: PR *gulat- "he-goat" |

320

*-dogootįa "young goat, ewe-lamb"  
SCush: Burunge *daxwadiya* "lamb, kid" (< *daxʷat-)

*-lugu "war" (also in Gogo, Rungwe group)  
SCush: WR *ɬuq- "to strike with weapon" (noun is not known in the extant SCush languages, but occurs as loan in Southern Nilotic lu:k "war"; not adopted into Bantu from Southern Nilotic because lacks SNil long vowel)

*b. Words of West Takama distribution*

*-liimi "sun" (West Takama; also in Fipa of Mwika)  
SCush: Burunge *tlema* "sun" (PR *tlehem-)

n-deelį "tuskless elephant" (Sukuma)  
SCush: PSC *deel- "not yet productive, immature," etc.

n-doi "waterbuck" (Kirurumo)  
SCush: root, probably *dawi, seen in Asa *duoku* "male waterbuck," *duaitu* "female waterbuck"

kalasa "white-tailed mongoose" (Sukuma)  
SCush: Gorowa *qeratlimo* "white-tailed mongoose"(root *qaratl-)

li-kuŋhwani "crane" (Nyamwezi)  
SCush: West Rift *qonq- "crested crane" (plus PSC *-an- noun suffix)

m-beve "cockroach" (Nyamwezi)  
SCush: West Rift babaʕ- "cockroach" (note fronting of *a > [*e] in a pharyngeal environment: not found in extant Southern Cushitic languages)

i-nagu "bee larva" (Nyamwezi)  
SCush: Iraqw *nanagi* "caterpiller"

*c. Eastern Sahelian (Rub?) loanwords in early Takama*

*-bųųbų "dust"  
ESah: Rub *bú "dust" (PNS "earth")

*-pusi "wildebeest"  
ESah: *puθ "blue-gray" (i.e., wildebeest color)

*-laala "Thomson's gazelle" (also in Suguti)  
ESah: *ḻa:ḻ "kind of gazelle" (SNil: Datoga *šɛ:šo:da* " Thomson's gazelle" < PSN *lʸa:lʸ-)

ka-saka "white-necked raven" (West Takama)  
ESah: Rub: Soo *osak* "white-necked raven"

**Table 38A. Eastern Sahelian loanwords in Kusi**

*-bílà "hyrax"  
Not directly attested in available ESah data; see table 7A.b for discussion

*-tàngá "herd; cattle-pen" (also diffused west in southern savanna)  
ESah: Kir-Abbaian *t̪ʰaŋ "ox" (semantics: "oxen" > "cattle, coll.," hence "herd")

| | |
|---|---|
| *-kola "small pen, fold" (variant: Venda *-kolo) | ESah *kʰɔd or *kɔd "enclosed homestead" (Nubian *kor "thorn pen"; Nilotic: Kalenjin *kạr ([kɔr]) "houses" [suppletive pl.]) |
| (?) *-pulu "young cow" (Ndau "suckling calf"; Botatwe "just weaned calf"; Sotho, Venda "ox") | ESah (and PNS) *pʰod "slight, small"; 2nd-order credibility because it requires noun derivation from attested adjective; but shows same semantics as the clear ESah loanwords *-soro, *-sole in tables 5 and 8) |
| (?) *-pila "sorghum" | ESah (and PNS) *pʰil "thin stick"; of third-order credibility, however, and therefore suspect, because requires double semantic shift: "thin stick" > "grainstalk" > "grain plant," hence, "sorghum" |
| *-poko "finger millet" | ESah: root *pʰɔK- (seen in Gaam fəidə "seed" < earlier *fɔk-ita, stem plus ESah *tʰ noun suffix) |
| *-sèbè "arrow" | ESah: Rub: Soo cebat, pl. cib "arrow" |

## Table 39A. Evidence for Eastern Sahelians in the Corridor and northern Malawi regions

*a. Eastern Sahelian loanwords in proto-Nyasa*

| | |
|---|---|
| *nguele "hippopotamus" | ESah (and Saharo-Sahelian) *ŋgwir "class of large herbivores" (of three members: hippotamus, rhinoceros, and elephant); known from Kir-Abbaian but not Rub branch of ESah |
| *-bila "sheep" (Nyanja-Chewa only; also spread to southern Makua dialects) | ESah *bil "goat" (see table 7A for another probable borrowing of this root word, with the same meaning shift, to "sheep") |
| *-kebele "pearl millet" (recent loan spread as word for "maize" to Njombe and Rufiji-Ruvuma groups) | ESah *bel "grain" plus *kʰ- noun-meaning modifying prefix; see table 5A forbor rowing of same word, but without prefix; second-order credibility because it postulates added prefixation |

*b. Eastern Sahelian loanwords in early Rungwe*

| | |
|---|---|
| *-tulu "testicle" (also in Mwika group) | ESah *Tuɗ "male genitals" (Rub: Soo tuɗo' testicle") |
| (?) *-oβe "finger" | ESah (and Sahelian) *wapʰ "to grasp, snatch"; second-order credibility because it requires unattested derivation from atteted verb; but note ESah *pʰ -> *β also in section e |
| *-sepe "hair, fur" (Nyiha subgroup) | ESah (and Sahelian) *θɛyp "to pull out hair" (> Nara sebi "hair") |

322

# Appendix A: Adjunct Tables

*-gola "skin"    ESah *god "skin, hide" (Surma: Zilmamu *gora* "bark")
  (Nyiha-Safwa)
*-gole "sheep"    ESah (and Sahelian) *gor "ewe-lamb"
  (Nyiha, Safwa)

## c. Eastern Sahelian loanwords in Nyakyusa

*-tapatapa "thigh"    ESah *tʰap "upper arm" (redup.)

## d. Eastern Sahelian loanwords in early Mwika

*-tulu "testicle"    ESah *Tudʼ "male genitals" (Rub: Soo *tudʼo'* testicle")
*-fuele "sheep"    ESah *kʰwel̪ "ram" (seen in Rub *kol "goat wether), here
  (< presumed *-kụele;    with meaning shift to "sheep"; table 7A has another bor-
  *kụ > *fu in proto-    rowing of this root with same morphology and meaning
  Mwika)    shift (corrects Ehret 1969 in derivation of this Mwika
      word)
*-aaβo "udder"    ESah (and PNS) *apʰo "front of body" (> breast > udder)
*-kolo "hoe"    ESah: Rub: Soo *okol* "small hoes"; for another borrowing
  (Mambwe-Fipa)    of this root, see table 34A.1

## Table 40A. Eastern Sahelian loanwords in early Khoe dialects

### a. Khoikhoi words with overt Eastern Sahelian parallels

*pere- "grain food (in    ESah *bel "grain (generic)"
  general)" (recent Khoi-
  khoi meaning "bread")
*topo- "porridge"    ESah: Eastern Nilotic *tapa "porridge"
  (only Nama?)
*aro- "ram" (only Nama?)    ESah (and Sahelian) *ado "male ani mal" (Kir-Abbaian:
      Surma: Didinga-Murle *ar- "bull")
*oro- "milk ewe" (only    ESah *Wed "sheep" (> *od; lack of /d/ after a vowel in
  Nama?)    Khoikhoi means it would have changed to the nearest
      similar Khoihkoi sound /r/ in that case
*kuro- "young ram"    ESah: Western Nilotic: stem *kur seen in Ocolo (Shilluk)
  (only Nama?)    *nyikuro* "lamb" (*nyi-* WNil diminuative prefix)

### b. Early Khoikhoi subsistence words of uncertain source

*suro- "broth"    Cf. proto-Kaskazi *-sululu "gruel" (Lakes: Rundi; Njo-
      mbe: Hehe); a non-Bantu source is probable but has
      not yet been identified
*komo- "cow (generic)"    Unknown etymology (contra Ehret 1973)

323

*gu- (proto-Khwe) "sheep" Unknown etymology (contra Ehret 1982b)

## Table 46A. Early Eastern African musical instruments

*a. Proto-Mashariki terms*

| | |
|---|---|
| *-ɣoma "drum" | Proto-Bantu (PB); proto-Mashariki (PM): wide general distribution among Bantu languages |
| *-tumba "large drum" | PM: Kaskazi (Lakes; Takama); Kusi (Shona; Sotho); also in Malungu of Sabi group |

*b. Term of Southern Kaskazi areal distribution*

| | |
|---|---|
| *-pango "lyre" | Ruvu of Northeast Coastal subgroup; Matengo of Rufiji-Ruvuma; Safwa (musical bow) |

*c. Southern Cushitic terms*

| | |
|---|---|
| *pokʷ'an- "lyre" | Pre-proto–West Rift provenance |
| *turer- "flute" | Attested so far only in Burunge of West Rift subgroup; borrowed into Kalenjin (Southern Nilotic) and some Kaskazi |

*d. Nilotic terms*

| | |
|---|---|
| *ture "horn instrument" | S'n Nilotic: Kalenjin (Tuken *turen* "wooden horn"); Eastern Nilotic (Bari *t or e* "kudu or cow horn instrument") |
| *-tar- "horn instrument" | E'n Nilotic: Lotuko-Maa subgroup (Maasai ɛn-táritári ; Lotuko *atar* "horn of palm leaf") |
| *po:ka:n "lyre" | S'n Nilotic: Kalenjin (loanword from Southern Cushitic) |
| *ʈum (Western Nilotic), *tom (Bari, Ateker) "string instrument" | Probable very early areal spread (Bari term shows regular sound correspondence with Western Nilotic shape, but Ateker reflex does not) |
| *ɪkɔːntɪ "kudu horn" | S'n Nilotic: Kalenjin |

*e. Proto-Rub term*

*po'j "flute"

# Appendix B
## Supplementary Tables of Evidence

Table 1B. West Rift Southern Cushitic (Central Tale) loanwords
in the Southern-Nyanza areal cluster of early Kaskazi dialects

*a. Widespread Southern Cushitic loanwords*

| | |
|---|---|
| *-sakame, *-sakami "blood" | SCush: PSC *sak'- "blood" (plus PSC *-Vm- noun suffix) |
| *malenga, *malinga "water" | SCush: Burunge madiŋ "rainy season" (PSC *mad- "rain" plus PSC *-Vŋ- noun suffix) |
| *-lı́1à "umbilical cord" (also Ganda; spread to Botatwe) | SCush: PSC *del- "umbilicus" (Kw'adza dilatiko , stem plus PSC *t noun suffix plus ER masculine marker) |
| *-baso "sun" (Gusii, Upland: Daiso) | SCush: PR *pas- or *pats- "sky, daylight" |
| *-nųųn- "to suck" | SCush: PSC *nunuʔ- or *nuunuʔ- "to suck" |
| *-búlug- "to turn over, stir" (also in Rungwe group) | SCush: PSC *bɨrɨk'- "to turn" (Guthrie attributes the Bantu verb to skewed form of an earlier Bantu verb root) |
| *-lale "soot" (also in Mwika group) | SCush: Ma'a m-laleto "soot" (PSC verb *lal- "to scorch); also ECush: HEC *lal- "soot" |
| *-salu "dung, mud" (also in Nyoro of West-Nyanza) | SCush: PSC *saalo "mud" |
| *-tamu "eland" (also West-Nyanza) | SCush: PR *dam- "eland" (< PSC *ɖooɖaama ) |
| *lu(n)kwiili "kind of mongoose" | SCush: PSC *lukʷeer- "kind of mongoose" |
| *bujulu "gruel" | SCush: PSC *botʸʼolo "gruel" (?) |
| *nyànɨ̀, *-nànɨ̀ "greens" (also in Rungwe) | SCush: PR *nan- "vegetable, greens" |
| *-jagamba "bull" | SCush: Iraqw yaqamba "bull" |
| *-gondɨ, *-gondụ "sheep" (Langi variant: *-gondo; also in Kilombero, Rungwe groups) | SCush: WR *gʷand- "ram" |
| *-tulume "ram" (Luyia,;Thagiicu; Mijikenda of Kati) | SCush: Kw'adza tulungayo "ram" (< root *tud- plus PSC *-Vm- noun suffix, as also in "blood" above) |

# Appendix B: Supplementary Tables

| | |
|---|---|
| *-saata, *-taasa "barren animal" (also in Ganda) | SCush: WR *tsaʔata "barren" |
| *-lịbà "milk" (also in Mwika, Rungwe, Nyasa groups) | SCush: PSC *iliba "milk" |
| *-dogowe "donkey" (also Ganda endo-goyi < *-dogowi; loan to Mwika; recent loans via Takama to Rungwe and W.Lakes groups) | SCush: PR *dakʷ'- "donkey" (plus PSC *-awe noun suffix, i.e., *dakʷ'awe) |
| *-sàl- "to scarify," *-sale "scarification" (in Ganda; also Rungwe group) | SCush: West Rift: Burunge sar- "to scarify" (PSC *sar- "to cut with repeated strokes") |
| *-lam- "to cut, mark, scarify, brand" | SCush: PSC *lam- "mark, cut" |
| *-Saịja "young man" (Lakes "man"; Swahili "bachelor"; also in Nsenga of Sabi for "boy") | SCush: West Rift *sayg- "mature young man" (*g > *j / i_ is a Mashariki sound shift) |
| *-pụngate, *-pụngati "seven" (also Mwika group) | SCush: PR *fanqʷ- "seven" (plus PSC *-ate adjective suffix) |
| *-kasi "beads" (also in Mwika) | SCush: PSC *kʷaɬ- "beads" |

## b. Luyia and East-Nyanza

| | |
|---|---|
| *-sag- "to taste" | SCush: Iraqw tsaq- "to taste" |
| *-sagala "kind of lizard" | SCush: Burunge sangarituʔumo "kind of lizard" (< proto--West Rift *sagar-) |
| *-gaali "shelter in field" | SCush: *gaSar-, root seen in metathesized Iraqw shape garSay "verandah"; a probable parallel word derivation from this root appears in table 4B) |
| *-kooŋa, *-kooŋe "crested crane" | SCush: WR *qonqa "crested crane" (cf. SNil: Kalenjin *ko:ŋoŋ "crested crane,": also a SCush loan) |
| *-agi "granary hut" (also in Ganda) | SCush: PR *Sag- "grain (generic)" (PSC *Saag-) |

### c. Upland and Langi

| | |
|---|---|
| *-sula "cooked whole grain" | SCush: PR *sor- "prepared grain" |

### d. Kati —

| | |
|---|---|
| *-tupa "rhinoceros (bull?)" (also in Kilombero, Mwika groups) | SCush: PR *dof- "rhinoceros" (not from Rub *dob "rhinoceros," which would yield Bantu *-tuba) |

### e. Langi and Kati —

| | |
|---|---|
| *-sale "name" | SCush: PSC *saare "name" |
| *-gµlata "he-goat" | SCush: PR *gurata "he-goat" (PSC (*ʔogur-) |
| *-togota "young she-goat" | SCush: Burunge *daxwadiya* "young she- goat, ewe-lamb" (< *daxʷat-) |

## Table 2B. West Rift Southern Cushitic (Eastern Tale) loanwords in proto-Kati

### a. Broadly distributed loanwords

| | |
|---|---|
| *-lenge "moon(light)" | SCush: WR *ɬeheŋ "moon" (< PSC *ɬeehe plus PSC suffix in *-ŋ-; note *ɬ > Bantu *l here in contrast to *ɬ > *s in table 1B; not ERift group, whose reflexes lack *ŋ suffix) |
| *-dole "finger" | SCush: PSC *dod- "grasp, grip" (this re construction corrects Ehret 1980b: 233) |
| *-dịmµ "wild animal" | SCush: East Rift *dum- "wild animal" |
| *-duma "cheetah" or "leopard" | SCush: PR *duʔuma "leopard" |
| *-goɓe "tortoise" (also Nyiha subgroup of Rungwe) | SCush: PCS *k'ob- "tortoise" |
| *-diim- "to herd" (also Rungwe ) | SCush: West Rift *deʔem- "to herd" (PSC *ɖeʔ-) |
| *-dale "herd" | SCush: no attestations as yet, but root is known from Eastern Cushitic (e.g., Oromo *dala* "cattle pen") |
| *-jeku, *-jiku "ox" | SCush: PSC *yaakʷ- "cattle" |
| *-dama "heifer" (also Mwika, Rungwe) | SCush: PR *dama "heifer, calf" |
| *-kutupa, *-kulupa, *-dupa "cattle-tick" | SCush: PR *xɨdif- "small tick" |

| | |
|---|---|
| *-panko "hoof" | SCush: PR *fok'- "hoof" (< PSC *fonk'- "to trot") |
| *-dali "chest (of animal)" (loan in Chaga from Kati) | SCush: root *dar- seen Iraqw *dararamo* "spleen" and possibly in Kw'adza *daliko* "mane" |
| *-saga "slat bed" | SCush: Burunge *sagay* "sleeping place" (< PR *sag- "to rest") |
| *-sago "head of bed" | SCush: PR *sag- "head" |

*b. Words limited to Northeast-Coastal subgroup*

| | |
|---|---|
| *-sagi̞ "rope bed" | SCush: Burunge *sagay* "sleeping place" (see section a for separate loaning of this word) |
| *-ɡuni "leather garment" | SCush *ɡʌn- "skin" (PSC *ʌ > *u /_n is a Tale sound shift; "bushpig" in table 9A.a) |

*c. Words of Njombe and central Tanzania areal distribution*

| | |
|---|---|
| *-puma "baboon" | SCush: West Rift *poham- "baboon" |
| *-kṳto "mole" | SCush: West Rift *kut- "mole" |
| *-daŋɡi "tree squirrel" (in Gogo as *-danki; Langi "bushbaby") | SCush: Alagwa *daŋɡaʔi* "bush-baby" |

## Table 3B. Southern Nilotic loanwords in proto-Upland (Chaga-Dabida and Thagiicu languages)

| | |
|---|---|
| *-pṳri̞a "rhinoceros" | SNil: Tato *o:puria "rhinoceros" (< Sahelian *obiɗ plus SNil *-ia noun suffix) |
| *-si̞i̞rṳa "eland" | SNil: Kalenjin *si:rua "eland" |
| *-ŋgaaTi̞ "wildebeest" | SNil: PSN *ɪnka:t "wildebeest" |
| *-sṳṳma "piece of hide" | SNil: root *su:m-, seen in Kalenjin *su:mat "piece of hide" |
| *-sṳnya "fatty cut of of meat" | SNil: root *sun-, seen in Kalenjin *sune:t "fatty cut of meat," plus SNil *-ia noun suffix |
| *-To:i̞ "stranger, alien" (Dabida "thief"; Chaga "in-law"; Gikuyu "wild person") | SNil: Kalenjin *tą:y "stranger" (from an earlier borrowing into Southern Nilotic of Rift Southern Cushitic root word *dahay of the same meaning) |
| *-menya "iron ore" (retained today in Chaga as "iron") | SNil: Kalenjin *menya "potting clay" (generalization to any earth from which things are fashioned explains the range of Upland meanings) |

# Appendix B: Supplementary Tables

## Table 4B. Southern Cushitic loanwords in proto-Upland

| | |
|---|---|
| *-raTer- "to follow" | SCush: PSC *rat- "to continue" (plus Bantu *-il- applied extension after borrowing) |
| *-sumbi "peak" | SCush: PSC *sumb- "peak, top" |
| *-sұnị "sp. duiker" | SCush: Ma'a *soni* "blue duiker" |
| *-aga "ostrich" | SCush: root *ʔag-, seen in Burunge *igisiya* "ostrich" (root plus PR *-is- agent noun suffix) |
| *-ŋuaare, *-ŋaarue "scorpion" | SCush: PR *ŋʷar- "scorpion" |
| *-soroko "black-eyed peas" | SCush: PSC *salakʷ'- "black-eyed peas" (Dahalo *solok'o*; Ma'a *salago*) |
| *-jao "bull" | SCush: PSC *yawu/*ʔawu "bull" in 1st shape *yawu (West Rift has *ʔawu) |
| *-tagina "ewe-lamb" | SCush: West Rift *dagina "girl" (earlier pre-West Rift "ewe-lamb": Ehret 1980b: 329) |
| *-siaaka "quiver" | SCush: Ma'a *i-siye* "quiver" (< *siyak-) |
| *-(h)ondo "string bag" (also Langi) | SCush: Ma'a *ki-honto* "string bag" (PSC *honto "calabash [carried in a string bag]") |
| *-jaTa "walking stick" | SCush: root *č'at-, seen in Kw'adza *catayi* "knobkerry" (stem + SC *-ayi noun suff.) |
| *-rịp- "to hammer iron" | SCush: PSC *dịf- "to pound" |
| *-taame, *-taami "strip of hide" | SCush: PSC *taami "strip" |
| *-maịsa "enemy" | SCush: < *maḥisa < PSC *maḥ- "to hit, beat" plus *-is- agent noun suffix |
| *-gaaro "house of circumcized youths" | SCush: *gaʕar-, root seen in metathesized shape in Iraqw *garʕay* "verandah"; for separate borrowing of this root, see table 1B) |

## Table 5B. Early Upland loanwords in Sabaki and Seuta

### a. Upland loanwords in both Seuta and Sabaki

| | |
|---|---|
| *-goma "adult female cow" | Upland *-goma; replaces original NE-Coastal term *-buguma |
| *-mori (Seuta *-moli) "heifer" | See *-moolị, table 2B; reason: regular Setua, Sabaki form would be *-mozi |
| *-rika "age-set" | Upland *-riika (see table 25A.c for this PM root; regularly corresponding NE Coastal shape would be *-zika) |

### b. Upland loanwords in Seuta

| | |
|---|---|
| Shambaa *namu* "eland" | See *-tamu, table 1B.a; borrowing here of shape seen specifically in Upland (Gikuyu) |

| | |
|---|---|
| Zigula *coloha* "oryx" (< *coroa* ) | Gikuyu *cooroa*; reasons: *c* is borrowed Swahili sound in Zigula as is *r* in Swahili (expected proto–NE Coastal *-joloba) |
| *ndolome "ram" | See *-tulume, table 1B.a; reason: regular Seuta reflex would be *ntulume |
| *mwate "ewe-lamb" | Thagiicu *mwate; reason: regular Seuta reflex woould be *mwati |
| Shambaa *suma* "piece of hide" | Upland *-suuma; reason: regular Shambaa reflex would be *šuma* |
| *-galo "circumci-sion ceremony" | See Upland *-gaaro "house of circumcised youths, " table 3B above |
| *-menya "iron ore" | See Upland *menya, table 3B above |

## c. Upland loanwords in early Sabaki

| | |
|---|---|
| *-uele "hair" (Sabaki; *-uili in Pokomo, some S'n Swahili) | Proto-Mashariki *-gụili; reason: *e/*i vowel alternation indicates borrowing from seven-vowel language; also loss of PM initial *g as in *u-imbi (this section) and *aro (section d) |
| *-bulug- "to stir" | See table 7A for this root; regular Sabaki reflex would be *-vulug- |
| *nderi "kind of vulture" | Upland *nderị ; reason: regular Sabaki reflex would be *ndizi |
| *-denge "he-goat" | Thagiicu *nðɛngɛ; reason: regular Sabaki reflex would be *-senge |
| *u-imbi "finger millet" | Upland *-gimbi; reason: regular Sabaki reflex would be *u-gimbi |

## d. Proposed early Upland loanwords in proto-Mijikenda

| | |
|---|---|
| *-jao "bull" | See Upland *-jau, table 4B above; reason: regular Mijikenda reflex would be *-jau |
| *-ɸarika "young she-goat" | Thagiicu *-parika; reason: regular Mijikenda reflex would *-vazika |
| *aro "house of cir-cumcised youths" | See *-galo in section b above; reason: loss of initial *g as in "finger millet" above |

## Table 6B. Proposed Mbuguan (early Ma'a) loanwords in the proto-Northeast-Coastal language

| | |
|---|---|
| *-gome "bark" | SCush: Ma'a *i-gome* "bark" (< PSC *gʌn- "skin") |
| *-gwasi "bushpig" | SCush: Ma'a *gu'a* "bushpig" (pre-Ma'a *guʔas- < PSC *guʕaat'-) |

# Appendix B: Supplementary Tables

*-Bulu "dry dung"   SCush: Ma'a *i-buru* "dry dung"
(borrowed later
from NE-Coastal
into proto-Chaga)

*-bu̧li "short rains"   SCush: Ma'a *bure* "short rains" (< PSC *bohare)

## Table 7B.  Southern Cushitic (East Rift) loanwords in proto-Njombe

*a. Njombe borrowings*

*-jege "bone"   SCush: < PR *ts'igaḥ- "fingers" (proto-Cushitic; not < West
   Rift where root means "four")

*-kanka "egg"   SCush: Kw'adza *kak-eto* "egg" (plus -*eto* East Rift feminine
(also in Gogo)   suffix; < pre-Kw'adza *kank-; < PR *k'anḥ - < PSC
   *k'ok'aanḥ-; not from West Rift, which has *qanḥ-)

*ngwɛhɛ* "warthog"   SCush: PSC *guʕaat'e "bushpig" (not from Ma'a because of
(Kinga; < *gwese)   non-Ma'a vowel fronting shift)

*ngwami* "wild dog"   SCush: root *gʷeḥ-, seen in West Rift "wild dog," plus PSC
(Hehe)   *-am- noun suffix

*-gedenge "tumbili"   SCush: East Rift root *ged-, as in Kw'adza *gedesiko* "tumbi-
(also in Gogo as   li" plus PSC *-Vŋ- noun suff. > Rift *ng /V_)
*ngedengwa* )

*-gwadi "calf"   SCush: Kw'adza *goʔolayo* (<*gʷaroʔ- < East Rift *gʷad-)

*muhomi* "cow's   SCush: Iraqw ʕomi "hump"
hump" (Hehe)

*mbululu* "sheep dung"   SCush: Ma'a *i-buru* "dry dung"
(Kinga)

*balali* "plain" (Hehe)   SCush: *bal- (seen in Kw'adza *balayiko* "bare ground")

*-bilima "thousand"   SCush: Kw'adza *biʔila* "thousand" plus PSC *-Vm noun suffix)

*onkari* "arrowpoison"   SCush: West Rift *qad- "arrow poison"
(Kinga; < *-kari)

*b. Central Tanzania areal borrowings (Njombe, Rimi, Gogo, Ilamba, Langi, and Kimbu)*

*-sengele "zebra"   SCush: Asa *šigiok* "zebra" (root *šig- or *šeg- plus PR *-Vr-
(also in Kimbu)   noun suffix; also appears as loan in Southern Nilotic
   Datoga *singi:ye:da* < pre-Datoga *singiR-)

*-jegumbe "small   SCush: root *kadzag- (plus PSC *-ume noun suffix) seen in
hyena" (also in   Kw'adza *kadzaganko* "hyena": root plus *-aŋ- noun suffix
Gogo; Ilamba   plus *-ko, East Rift masculine suffix (*-VmV# > *-VmbV#
variant, *-jVgumi:   is Kw'adza sound shift); initial *ka- of SCush stem was
separate loan?)   was treated as a noun class prefix and replaced by the nor-

mal 9/10 class prefixes of animal names (*kadzag-ume > *kadzagumbe > borrowed shape *njagumbe, with fronting of 2nd stem vowel)

| | |
|---|---|
| *-sakanka "spotted hyena" (also in Rimi, Ilamba) | SCush: PR *čak'- "spotted carnivore" (here with partial reduplication) |

### *c. Ruvu and Njombe areal distribution*

| | |
|---|---|
| *-kuli "(thick) skin" | SCush: Iraqw *kahari* "skin" (< PSC *xah-; for shift *Vha > *u, see *-puma "baboon" below) |
| *-dunku "red" | SCush: WR *duq- "reddish-brown" (cattle color) |
| *-pa-m-baga "chest" (prefix *pa- locative plus 9/10 class prefix plus stem) | SCush: PSC root *bag- seen in Dahalo *bagama* "belly" |
| *-kwama "cattle-pen" | SCush: PR *kʷ'ama "cattle-pen, herd" |

### *d. Words limited to Hehe of Njombe, Gogo, and Langi*

| | |
|---|---|
| *-sawada "lesser kudu" | SCush: WR *ts'awad- "lesser kudu" (expected ER *ts'od-) |
| *-gera "Grant's gazelle" | SCush: Burunge *geraʔi* "Grant's gazelle" |

## Table 8B. Sample Khoikhoi loanwords in early Shona

| | |
|---|---|
| *-kore "year" | PKK (and proto-Khoisan [PK]) *kuri" year" |
| *-zamu "breast, udder" | PKK *sam-; borrowing in this case may reflect pastoral influences (i.e., borrowing for "udder") rather than borrowing of truly basic vocabulary (as "breast") |

## Table 9B. Sample Khoikhoi loanwords in proto-Southeast-Bantu

| | |
|---|---|
| *-kòmò "cow" | PKK *koma- "cow" (< earlier *komo) |
| *-pi̜ "(sour) milk" | PKK (and proto-Khwe) *pi "milk" |
| *-gǘ "sheep" | PKK (and proto-Khwe) *gu "sheep" |

332

# Bibliography

Ahmed, C. C.
1995.   Before Eve was Eve: 2200 years of gendered history in East Central Africa. Ph.D. diss., University of California at Los Angeles.

Ali, M. N.
1985.   History in the Horn of Africa. Ph.D. diss., University of California at Los Angeles.

Ambrose, Stanley.
1982.   Archaeology and linguistic reconstructions of history in East Africa. In Ehret and Posnansky 1982.
1986.   Stable carbon and nitrogen isotope analysis of human and animal diet in Africa. *Journal of Human Evolution* 15: 707–31.

Armstrong, R. G.
1964.   *The study of West African languages.* Ibadan: Ibadan University Press.

Atkinson, Ronald
1994.   *The roots of ethnicity: The origins of the Acholi of Uganda.* Philadelphia: University of Pennsylvania Press.

Barthelme, J.
1977.   Holocene sites north-east of Lake Turkana: A preliminary report. *Azania* 12: 33–41.

Bastain, Y, A. Coupez, and B. de Halleux.
1983.   Classifications lexicostatistique des langues bantoues (214 relevés). *Bulletin des seances du Academie royale du Sciences d'Outre-mer* 27, 2: 173–99.

Bender, M. L. (ed.)
1989.   *Topics in Nilo-Saharan linguistics.* Hamburg: Hamburg-Buske.

Bennett, P. R.
1967.   Dahl's Law and Thagiicu. *African Language Studies* 8: 127-159.

Blust, R.
1976.   Austronesian culture history: Some linguistic inferences and their relations to the archaeological record. *World Archaeology* 8: 19–43.

Casson, L.
1989.   *The Periplus Maris Erythraei: Text with introduction, translation and commentary.* Princeton: Princeton University Press.

Child, S. T.
1991.   Style, technology, and iron-smelting furnaces in Bantu-speaking Africa. *Journal of Anthropological Archaeology* 10: 332–59.

Clark, J. D.
1974.   *Kalambo Falls prehistoric site, II.* Cambridge: Cambridge University Press.

Close, A. E.
1988.   Current research and recent radiocarbon dates from northern Africa. *Journal of African History* 29: 115–36.

Cohen, M.
1970.   A reassessment of the Stone Bowl cultures of the Rift Valley, Kenya. *Azania* 5: 27–38.

Crazzolara, J. P.
1950–54.   *The Lwoo.* 3 vols. Verona: Instituto Missioni Africane.

Davy, J.I.M., and D. Nurse
1982.   Synchronic versions of Dahl's Law: The multiple applications of a phonological dissimilation rule. *Journal of African Languages and Linguistics* 4: 157–95.

de Langhe, E., R. Swennen, and D. Vuylsteke
1994–95.   Plaintains in the early Bantu world. *Azania* 29/30: 147–60.

de Wet, J.M.J.
1977.   Domestication of African cereals. *African Economic History* 3: 15–32.

de Wolf, J. J.
1983.   Circumcision and initiation in western Kenya and eastern Uganda: Historical reconstructions and ethnographic evidence. *Anthropos* 78, 3/4: 369–410.

Denbow, J. R.
1986.   A new look at the later prehistory of the Kalahari. *Journal of African History* 27: 3–28.

Distefano, J. A.
1985.   The precolonial history of the Kalenjin of Kenya: A methodological comparison of linguistic and oral traditional evidence. Ph.D. diss., University of California at Los Angeles.

Ehret, Christopher.
1964.   A lexicostatistical classification of Bantu, using Guthrie's test languages.
1967.   Cattle keeping and milking in Eastern and Southern African history: The linguistic evidence. *Journal of African History* 8: 1–17.
1968.   Sheep and Central Sudanic Peoples. *Journal of African History* 9: 213–21.
1971.   *Southern Nilotic history: Linguistic approaches to the study of the past.* Evanston: Northwestern University Press.
1973a.   Origins and spread of iron in eastern, southern, and central Africa.
1973b.   Patterns of Bantu and Central Sudanic settlement in central and southern Africa (ca. 1000 B.C.–500 A.D.). *Transafrican Journal of History* 3: 1–71.

# Bibliography

1974a.   Agricultural history in central and southern Africa, c. 1000 B.C. to A.D. 500. *Transafrican Journal of History* 4: 1–25.

1974b.   *Ethiopians and East Africans: The problem of contacts.* Nairobi: East African Publishing House.

1976a.   Aspects of social and economic change in western Kenya. In *Kenya before 1900*, ed. B. A. Ogot . Nairobi: East African Publishing House.

1976b.   Cushitic prehistory. In *The non-Semitic languages of Ethiopia,* ed. M. L. Bender. East Lansing: Michigan State University.

1979.   On the antiquity of agriculture in Ethiopia. *Journal of African History* 20: 161–77.

1980a.   Historical inferences from transformations in culture vocabularies. *Sprache und Geschichte in Afrika* 2: 189–218.

1980b.   *The historical reconstruction of Southern Cushitic phonology and vocabulary.* Berlin: Reimer.

1981a.   The demographic implications of linguistic change and language shift. In *African historical demography II.* Edinburgh: University of Edinburgh.

1981b.   Revising proto-Kuliak. *Afrika und Uebersee* 64: 81–100.

1982a.   The first spread of food production to southern Africa. In Ehret and Posnansky 1982.

1982b.   Linguistic inferences about early Bantu history. In Ehret and Posnansky.

1982c.   Population movement and culture contact in the southern Sudan, c. 3000 B.C. to A.D. 1000. In *Culture history in the Southern Sudan: A preliminary linguistic overview*, ed. J. Mack and P. R. Robertshaw. Nairobi: The British Institute in Eastern Africa.

1983.   Nilotic and the limits of Eastern Sudanic: Classificatory and historical conclusions. In *Proceedings of the International Symposium on Languages and History of the Nilotic Peoples, Cologne, January 4-6, 1982,* ed. R. Vossen and M. Bechhaus-Gerst. Berlin: Reimer.

1984.   Between the coast and Great Lakes. In *Africa from the Twelfth to the Sixteenth Century,* ed. D. T. Niane. Vol. 4 of *General History of Africa.* Paris: UNESCO.

1987.   Proto-Cushitic reconstruction. *Sprache und Geschichte in Afrika* 8: 7–180.

1988.   The East African interior. In *Africa from the seventh to the eleventh century,* ed. M. El Fasi and I. Hrbek. Vol. 3 of *General history of Africa.* Paris: UNESCO.

1992.   Historical reconstruction of the Central Sudanic languages: segmental phonology and vocabulary.

1993.   Nilo-Saharans and the Saharo-Sudanese Neolithic. In T. Shaw et al. 1993.

1995.   *Reconstructing proto-Afroasiatic (proto-Afrasian): Vowels, tone, consonants, and vocabulary.* Berkeley and Los Angeles: University of California Press.

335

1995/96.    The establishment of iron-working in eastern, central, and southern Africa: Linguistic inferences on technological history. *Sprache und Geschichte in Afrika* 19/20 (revision and expansion of Ehret 1973a).

Forthcoming.    Subclassifying Bantu: The evidence of stem morpheme innovations. In Proceedings of Bantu linguistics conference, Lyon, May 1996 (title still to be chosen), ed. L. Hyman and J.-M. Hombert.

In press. *A comparative historical reconstruction of Nilo-Saharan.*

Ehret, C., A. Adedze, E. Kreike, M. Milewski, and D. Schoenbrun.

In preparation.    The settlement of Madagascar.

Ehret, C., M. Bink, T. Ginindza, E. Gtoschall, B. Hall, M. Hlatschwayo, D. Johnson, and R. L. Pouwels.

1972.    Outlining southern Africa history: A reconsideration. *Ufahamu* 3, 1: 9–27.

Ehret, C., T. Coffman, L. Fliegelman, A. Gold, M. Hubbard, D. Johnson, and D. Saxon.

1974b.    Some thoughts on the early history of the Nile-Congo watershed. *Ufahamu* 5, 2: 82–112.

Ehret, C., and M. Kinsman.

1981.    The dialect classification of Shona and its implications for Iron Age history in southern Africa. *International Journal of African Historical Studies* 14, 3: 401–43.

Ehret, C., and D. Nurse.

1981.    The Taita Cushites. *Sprache und Geschichte in Afrika* 3: 125–68.

n.d.    History in the Taita Hills. (accepted for publication by *The Kenya Historical Review*, but journal indefinitely ceased publication)

Ehret, C., G. Okihiro, T. Stamps, B. Turner, and S. Young.

1974.    Lacustrine history and linguistic evidence: Preliminary conclusions.

Ehret, C., and M. Posnansky (ed.).

1982.    *The archaeological and linguistic reconstruction of African history.* Berkeley and Los Angeles: University of California Press.

Garlake, P.

1987.    *The painted caves.* Harare: Modus Publications (PVT).

Gonzales, R.

1995.    The Venda in early southern African history. Seminar paper, University of California at Los Angeles.

Guthrie, M.

1967–72.    *Comparative Bantu.* 4 vols. Farnborough: Gregg International.

Haaland, R.

1995/96.    Dakawa: an early Iron Age site in the Tanzania hinterland. *Azania* 29/30: 238–47.

# Bibliography

Hall, M.

1987.    *The changing past: Farmers, kings and traders in southern Africa, 200–
         1860.* Cape Town and Johannesburg: David Philip.

Hall, M., and J. Vogel

1978.    Enkwazini: Fourth century Iron Age site on the Zululand coast. *South
         African Journal of Science* 74: 70–71.

Hamilton, A. C., D. M. Taylor, and J. C. Vogel

1986.    Early forest clearance and environmental degradation in South-West
         Uganda. *Nature* 320, 6058: 164–67.

Heine, B.

1976.    *Kuliak languages of eastern Uganda.* Nairobi: East African
         Publishing House.

Heine, B, H. Hoff, and R. Vossen.

1977.    Neuere Ergebnisse zur Territorialgeschichte der Bantu. In *Zur
         Sprachgeschichte und Ethnohistorie in Afrika,* ed. Möhlig, F. Rottland, and
         B. Heine. Berlin: Reimer.

Henrici, A.

1973.    Numerical classification of Bantu languages. *African Language Studies* 14:
         82–104.

Hinnebusch, T., D. Nurse, and M. Mould.

1981.    *Studies in the classification of eastern Bantu lLanguages.* Hamburg: Buske.

Huffman, T. N.

1974.    The linguistic affinities of the Iron Age in Rhodesia. *Arnoldia* 7, 7.

1976.    Gokomere pottery from the Tunnel site, Gokomere Mission. *South African
         Archaeological Bulletin* 31: 31–53.

1978.    The origins of Leopard's Kopje: An 11th century Difaqane. *Arnoldia* 8, 23.

1989.    *Iron age migrations.* Johannesburg: Witwatersrand University Press.

Inskeep, R. R.

1978.    *The peopling of southern Africa.* Cape Town: David Phillip.

Inskeep, R. R., and T. M. Maggs.

1975.    Unique art objects in the Iron Age of the Transvaal. *South African
         Archaeological Bulletin* 30: 114–38.

Jones, A. M.

1971.    *Africa and Indonesia: The evidence of the xylophone and other musical and
         cultural factors.* Leiden: J. Brill.

Katenekwa, N. M.

1995.    The Iron Age in Zambia: Some new evidence and interpretations. Paper
         presented at Conference on Agricultural Origins in Eastern Africa,
         Cambridge University, July 1995

337

Klieman, Kairn.

1997.   Peoples of the western equatorial rain forest: A history of society and economy, from ca. 3000 B.C. to 1890. Ph.D. diss., University of California at Los Angeles.

Kubik, G.

1964.   Generic names for the mbira. *African Music* 3, 3.

Laumann, D.

1995.   A critical reevaluation of the historiography of southern Mozambique. Seminar paper, University of California at Los Angeles.

Lewis-Williams, David.

1981.   *Believing and seeing: Symbolic meanings in southern San rock art.* London: Academic Press.

1982.   The economic and social context of southern San rock art. *Current Anthropology* 23: 429–49.

1983.   *The rock art of southern Africa.* Cambridge: Cambridge University Press.

Lienhardt, G.

1961.   *Divinity and experience: The religion of the Dinka.* Oxford: Clarendon Press.

Maggs, T., and M. Michael.

1976.   Ntshekane, an Early Iron Age site in the Tukela Basin. *Annals of the Natal Museum* 22: 705–39

McMaster, Mary A.

1988.   Patterns of interaction: A comparative ethnolinguistic perspective on the Uele region of Zaire ca. 500 B.C. to 1900 A.D. Ph.D. diss., University of California at Los Angeles.

Middleton, J.

1965.   *The Lugbara of Uganda.* New York: Holt, Rinehart and Winston.

1987.   *Lugbara religion: Ritual and authority among an East African people.* Washington, D.C.: Smithsonian Institution Press.

Morris, D.

1991.   Stone bowls in the northern Cape: A new find and its possible context. *South African Archaeological Bulletin* 46: 38–40.

Munson, P.

1977.   Africa's prehistoric past. In *Africa,* ed. P. O'Meara and P. Martin. Bloomington: Indiana University Press.

Murdock, G. P.

1959.   *Africa: Its peoples and their culture history.* New York: McGraw-Hill.

Nicolas, T. J.

1957.   Origine et valeur du vocabulaire désignant les xylophones africains. *Zaire* 11: 69–89.

338

# Bibliography

Nurse, D.

1979.   *Classification of the Chaga dialects: Language and history on Kilimanjaro, the Taita Hills, and the Pare Mountains with 24 tables and 3 maps.* Hamburg: Buske.

1982.   Bantu expansion into East Africa: Linguistic evidence. In Ehret and Posnansky 1982.

1983.   History from linguistics: The case of the Tana River. *History in Africa* 10: 207–38.

1988a.  The diachronic background to the language communities of southwestern Tanzania. *Sprache und Geschichte in Africa* 9: 15–115.

1988b.  Extinct Southern Cushitic communities in East Africa. In *Cushitic-Omotic: Papers from the international symposium on Cushitic and Omotic languages, Cologne, January 6–9, 1986,* ed. M. Bechhaus-Gerst and J. Serzisko. Hamburg: Buske.

Nurse, D., and T. Hinnebusch.

1993.   *Swahili and Sabaki: A linguistic history.* Berkeley and Los Angeles: University of California Press.

Odner, K.

1972.   Excavations at Narosura, a Stone Bowl site in the southern Kenya highlands. *Azania* 7: 25–92.

Oliver, R.

1966.   The problem of the Bantu expansion. *Journal of African History* 7: 361–76.

Ownby, C. P.

1985.   Early Nguni history: The linguistic evidence and its correlation with archaeology and oral tradition. Ph.D. diss., University of California at Los Angeles.

Papstein, R.

1978.   The Upper Zambezi: A history of the Luvale people, 1000–1900. Ph.D. diss., University of California at Los Angeles.

Phillipson, D. W.

1974.   Iron Age history and archaeology in Zambia. *Journal of African History* 15: 321–42.

1976.   *The prehistory of eastern Zambia.* Nairobi: The British Institute in Eastern Africa.

1977.   *The later prehistory of eastern and southern Africa.* London: Heinemann.

1985.   *African prehistory.* Cambridge: Cambridge University Press.

Robertshaw, P.

1991.   Gogo Falls: Excavations at a complex archaeological site east of Lake Victoria. *Azania* 26: 63–195.

1993.    The beginnings of food production in southwestern Kenya. In T. Shaw et al. 1993.

Robertshaw, P., and D. Collett.
1983.    A new framework for the study of early pastoral communities in East Africa. *Journal of African History* 24: 289–301.

Robertson, J.
1991.    Origin and development of the Early Iron Age in south central Africa. Ph.D. diss., University of Cincinnati

Robinson, K. R.
1966.    Bambata ware: Its position in the Rhodesian Iron Age in the light of recent research. *South African Archaeological Bulletin* 21: 81–85.
1973.    *The Iron Age of the Upper and Lower Shire, Malawi.* Malawi Antiquities Department Publication 8.
1976.    A note on the spread of Early Iron Age ceramics in Malawi: Tentative suggestions based on recent evidence. *South African Archaeological Bulletin* 31:166–75.

Robinson, K. R., and B. Sandelowsky
1968.    The Iron Age in northern Malawi: Recent work. Azania 3: 107–46.

Rottland, F.
1982.    *Die suednilotischen Sprachen: Beschriebung, Vegleichung, und Rekonstruction.* Reimer: Berlin.
1989.    Southern Nilotic reconstructions. In Bender 1989, 219–23.

Sassoon, H.
1967.    The Masange bowmen. *Azania* 2: 193-94.

Saxon, D. E.
1980.    Early history of the Chari River Basin. Ph.D. diss., University of California at Los Angeles.

Schmidt, P. R.
1978.    *Historical archaeology: A structural approach in African culture.* Westport: Greenwood Press.

Schoenbrun, D. L.
1990.    Early history in Eastern Africa's Great Lakes region: Linguistic, ecological, and archaeological approaches. Ph.D. diss., University of California at Los Angeles.
1993a.   Cattle herds and banana gardens: The historical geography of the western Great Lakes region, ca. AD 800- 1500. e African Archaeological Review 11.
1993b.   We are what we eat: Ancient agriculture between the Great Lakes. *Journal of African History* 34: 1–32.
Forthcoming.   *A green place, a good place: A social history of the Great Lakes region, earliest times to the 15th century.*

340

Scott, D.C.R.
1957. *Dictionary of the Nyanja language.* London: United Society for Christian Literature.

Shaw, T.
1978/79. Holocene adaptations in West Africa: The Late Stone Age. *Early Man News* 3/4: 51–71.

Shaw, T., P. Sinclair, B. Andah, and A. Okpoko (ed.).
1993. *The archaeology of Africa: Food, metals, and towns.* London and New York: Routledge.

Sinclair, P.J.J., J.M.F. Morais, L. Adamowicz, and R. T. Duarte.
1993. A perspective on archaeological research in Mozambique. In T. Shaw et al. 1993.

Soper, R. C.
1967. Kwale: An Early Iron Age site in southeastern Kenya. *Azania* 2: 1–17.
1982. Bantu expansion into East Africa: Archaeological evidence. In Ehret and Posnansky 1982.

Stevenson, R. F.
1968. *Population and political systems in tropical Africa.* New York and London: Columbia University Press.

Sutton, J.E.G.
1973. *The archaeology of the western highlands of Kenya.* Nairobi: British Institute in Eastern Africa, Memoire 3.
1974. The aquatic civilization of Middle Africa. *Journal of African History* 15: 527–46.
1977. The African aqualithic. *Antiquity* 51: 25–54.

Taylor, D. M.
1990. Late Quaternary pollen records from two Uganda mires: Evidence for environmental change in the Rukiga highlands of southwest Uganda. *Palaeogeography, Palaeo- climatology, Palaeoecology* 80: 283–300.

Van der Merwe, N. J., and R.T.K. Scully.
1971. The Phalaborwa story: Archaeological and ethnographic investigation of a South African Iron Age group. *World Archaeology* 3: 178–96.

Van Grunderbeek, M. C.
1992. Essai de délimitation chronologique de l'Age du Fer Ancien au Burundi, au Rwanda et dans la région des Grands Lacs. *Azania* 28: 53–80.

Van Grunderbeek, M. C., E. Roche, and H. Doutrelepont.
1983. *Le premier age du fer au Rwanda et au Burundi.* Brussels and Butare: Institut National de Recherche Scientifique, Publication No. 23.

341

# Bibliography

Vansina, J.
1984.    Western Bantu expansion. *Journal of African History* 25: 129–45.
1990.    *Paths in the rainforests.* Madison: University of Wisconsin Press.
1995.    New linguistic evidence and 'the Bantu expansion'. *Journal of African History* 36: 173–95.

Vossen, R.
1982.    *The Eastern Nilotes: Linguistic and historical reconstructions.* Berlin: Reimer.

Waite, Gloria, and C. Ehret.
1981.    Linguistic perspectives on the early history of southern Tanzania. *Tanzania Notes and Records* (last issue, never published).

Walker, N. J.
1983.    The significance of an early date for pottery and sheep in Zimbabwe. *South African Archaeological Bulletin* 38: 88–92.

Wasylikowa, K., J. R. Harlan, J. Evans, F. Wendorf, R. Schild, A.E.Close, H.Krolik, and R. A. Housley.
1993.    Examinations of botanical remains from early neolithic houses at Nabta Playa, Western Desert, Egypt, with special reference to sorghum grains. In Shaw et al. 1993.

Wendorf, F., R. Schild, and A. E. Close.
1984.    *Cattle-keepers of the Eastern Sahara: The Neolithic of Bir Kiseiba.* Dallas: Southern Methodist University Press.

Werner, D.
1971.    Some developments in Bemba religious history. *Journal of Religion in Africa* 4: 1–24.
1973.    The coming of the "Iron Age" to the southern Lake Tanganyika region: A discussion of the linguistic evidence. Paper presented at Institute for African Studies, University of Zambia, 12 Jan. 1973.
1979.    Miao spirit shrines in the religious history of the southern Lake Tanganyika region: The case of Kapembwa. In *Guardians of the lands,* ed. J. M. Schoffeleers, 89–130 Gwelo: Mambo Press.

Wilson, Louis Edward.
1980.    The evolution of Krobo society: A history from c. 1400 to 1892. Ph.D. diss., University of California at Los Angeles.

Wrigley, C.
1960.    Speculations on the economic prehistory of Africa. *Journal of African History* 1: 189–203.

# Index

Abbai River, 7
adze, 108-10, 113, 265
Afroasiatic language family, 8, 9
age sets, Bantu, 155-8, 161, 253-5;
    Southern Nilotic, 162-4, 179, 255
agriculture, 1, 2, 4-8, 11-14, 19, 21, 22,
    31, 39, 44-7, 52, 79, 94, 103, 105-
    7, 112, 128, 129, 138-40, 183, 193,
    198, 203, 209, 210, 232, 243, 245,
    247, 263, 268, 269, 272, 277, 278,
    279-82, 286, 287, 291, 292, 294-7
Agumba, 263
Ahmed, C., 71, 243, 289
Aksum, 20
Alagwa, 85, 173
*-àmì (chief), 146, 148, 154, 155, 158,
    165, 248, 250-2
Anatolia, 15, 19
Angola, 45, 132, 133, 151, 213, 237,
    240, 267, 268, 271, 273, 280, 289
*Arabian Nights*, 17
arrow poison, 182
Asu, 36, 187, 192, 249
Atlantic Ocean, 148, 245, 265, 269,
    270, 272, 280,
axes, 108, 109, 267, 275; planting,
    112, 113, 128, 130, 267; polished
    stone, 14, 110, 112; iron, 108, 112,
    267

Bahr-al-Ghazal, 8
Balendru, 76, 78, 88, 144
Bambata ware, 216, 233, 236
bananas, 23, 278, 279, 292, 293
barley, 11
baskets, 57, 79, 80, 119-21, 123,
    124, 176, 180, 200, 275
Batoka Plateau, 216, 237
BaTwa, 92
beds, 51, 118, 119, 139, 176, 180, 189,
    291
beekeeping, 127, 291
beer, 78, 84, 131-3, 174, 175, 180

Bemba, 44, 153, 200, 269, 270, 272
Bena, 36
Benue-Congo, 14
Benue-Kwa, 14
Berber, 9
Bisa, 44, 200
Bisha, 173
black-eyed peas (cowpeas), 7, 13, 104,
    105, 174, 180
boats, 57, 231, 275, 276, 291
Bondei, 36
Bongo-Bagirmi, 88
Boreafrasian, 9
Botatwe (Savanna-Bantu subgroup), 44,
    45, 66, 146, 147, 150, 152, 154,
    200, 212, 234, 235, 237, 238, 265,
    272
Botswana, 212, 215-7, 221, 236, 240
bow and arrows, 109, 123-5, 135, 176,
    182, 230
bowstring, 124, 125, 182
Buans, 43, 44, 47, 265
Buganda, 279
Bukoba, 93, 97, 108, 140, 279, 293
Bunyoro, 61, 77
Burundi, 34, 62, 77, 81, 90, 92-5, 111,
    114, 198
Burunge, 85, 173

calabashes (see *gourds*)
Cameroun, 14, 46, 47, 265
canoe, 80, 109, 275, 276
Cape (region), 1, 213, 217-21, 226,
    240, 259, 289
Capsian culture, 9
Carthage, 17, 18, 21, 275
castor bean, 104-5
catchcloth, leather, 180
cattle, 6-9, 11, 53, 60, 62, 63, 66-8, 70,
    81-7, 89, 90, 103, 104, 107, 117,
    118, 133-6, 138, 140, 166, 167,
    173-5, 178-83, 185, 192, 212, 216,
    217, 219, 221, 224, 225, 229, 235,

# Index

347

# Index